MEF-CECP Study Guide
for Carrier Ethernet Professionals

3rd Edition - October 2015
Updated for MEF-CECP Certification Blueprint C

Fujitsu Network Communications Inc.

https://partners.fnc.fujitsu.com

ISBN 10: 151757398X

ISBN-13: 978-1517573980

This MEF-CECP Study Guide provides a broad range of Carrier Ethernet information useful for those who wish to learn more about MEF-standardized Carrier Ethernet and specifically for those planning to take the MEF Carrier Ethernet Certified Professional exam. Fujitsu has made every effort to ensure the accuracy of the MEF-CECP Study Guide, but editorial errors do occur from time to time.

Fujitsu welcomes your feedback and suggestions for this guide or future Carrier Ethernet educational material. Please use the email address below for all feedback. Finally, Fujitsu does not guarantee, either implicitly or explicitly, that an individual using this MEF-CECP Study Guide will pass the MEF-CECP certification exam.

For comments or questions, contact us at
ReaderFeedback@fnc.fujitsu.com.

All other products or services mentioned in this document are identified by the trademarks, service marks, or product names as designated by the companies that market those products or services or own those marks. Inquiries concerning such products, services, or marks should be made directly to those companies.

This document and its contents are provided by Fujitsu Network Communications Inc. for guidance purposes only. This document is provided "as is" with no warranties or representations whatsoever, either express or implied, without notice, to make including without limitation the implied warranties of merchantability and fitness for purpose. Fujitsu Network Communications Inc. does not warrant or represent that the contents of this document are error free. Furthermore, the contents of this document are subject to update and change at any time without notice by Fujitsu Network Communications Inc., since it reserves the right, changes in equipment design or components as progress in engineering methods may warrant. No part of the contents of this document may be copied, modified, or otherwise reproduced without the express written consent of Fujitsu Network Communications Inc.

Contents

1	Introduction		p. 12
	1.1	Getting Started	p. 14
		1.1.1 About the MEF	p. 14
		1.1.2 About Carrier Ethernet	p. 14
		1.1.3 Explore the MEF Web Site and the MEF Reference Wiki	p. 15
		1.1.4 About MEF-CECP Certification	p. 15
		1.1.5 The MEF-CECP Certification Exam Blueprint	p. 17
		1.1.6 Assumed Knowledge	p. 20
	1.2	Changes To This Update	p. 22
2	Carrier Ethernet Services		p. 23
	2.1	Fundamental Components and Reference Models	p. 24
		2.1.1 Basic Reference Model	p. 24
		2.1.2 UNI Functionality	p. 25
		2.1.3 General Reference Model	p. 27
	2.2	Service Multiplexing	p. 28
	2.3	Service Frames	p. 29
	2.4	Assigning Service Frames to EVCs	p. 30
		2.4.1 CE-VLAN ID	p. 30
		2.4.2 Bundling	p. 31
		2.4.3 Bundling versus Service Multiplexing	p. 31
	2.5	Taxonomy of EVC-Based Services	p. 32
		2.5.1 Port-Based versus VLAN-Based Services	p. 32
		2.5.2 The Three Service Types	p. 33
	2.6	EPL Service	p. 34
	2.7	EVPL Service	p. 35
	2.8	EP-LAN Service	p. 36
	2.9	EVP-LAN Service	p. 37
	2.10	EP-Tree Service	p. 38
	2.11	EVP-Tree Service	p. 39
	2.12	Matrix of Service Distinctions	p. 40
	2.13	Review: Carrier Ethernet Services	p. 41
3	Ethernet Frames and Service Frames		p. 44
	3.1	IEEE Ethernet Frames	p. 45

MEF-CECP Study Guide
3rd Edition - October 2015
Updated for MEF-CECP Certification Blueprint C

	3.1.1	Layer 1 versus Layer 2 Ethernet Frames	p. 45
	3.1.2	Layer 2 Ethernet Frames	p. 46
	3.1.3	C-Tagged Ethernet Frames	p. 47
	3.1.4	S-Tagged Ethernet Frames	p. 50
	3.1.5	I-Tagged Ethernet Frames	p. 51
	3.1.6	Priority-Tagged Ethernet Frames	p. 51
3.2	MEF Service Frames		p. 52
	3.2.1	Ingress and Egress Service Frames	p. 52
	3.2.2	Exclusion of Layer 1 Components	p. 52
	3.2.3	Service Frame Tag Recognition	p. 53
	3.2.4	Data, L2CP, and SOAM Service Frames	p. 55
3.3	Review: Ethernet Frames and Service Frames		p. 56

4	How Carrier Ethernet Services are Defined		p. 58
4.1	Carrier Ethernet Service Attributes		p. 59
	4.1.1	Categories of Service Attributes	p. 59
	4.1.2	Overview of Service Attributes	p. 60
	4.1.3	Logically Related Service Attributes	p. 62
4.2	The MEF Service Agreement Framework (SLA and SLS)		p. 65
4.3	Review: How Carrier Ethernet Services are Defined		p. 66

5	Service Connectivity Attributes		p. 67
5.1	Basic Service Attributes		p. 68
5.2	Maximum Service Frame Size Service Attributes		p. 69
5.3	Service Multiplexing and Bundling Service Attributes		p. 70
5.4	Service Frame Mapping Service Attributes		p. 71
	5.4.1	CE-VLAN ID / EVC Map	p. 72
	5.4.2	CE-VLAN ID for Untagged and Priority Tagged Service Frames	p. 74
5.5	CE-VLAN Tag Preservation Service Attributes		p. 76
	5.5.1	CE-VLAN CoS Preservation	p. 76
	5.5.2	CE-VLAN ID Preservation	p. 77
	5.5.3	CE-VLAN ID Preservation versus Translation	p. 78
	5.5.4	Untagged and Priority Tagged Service Frames with CE-VLAN ID Preservation Disabled	p. 81
5.6	Data Service Frame Delivery Service Attributes		p. 83
5.7	Source MAC Address Limit Service Attribute		p. 85
5.8	Security Considerations for E-Tree Services		p. 86
5.9	L2CP Processing Service Attributes		p. 87
	5.9.1	About Layer 2 Control Protocols	p. 89
	5.9.2	L2CP Behavioral Model	p. 89
	5.9.3	L2CP Frame Processing	p. 91
	5.9.4	Attribute: UNI L2CP Peering	p. 92
	5.9.5	Attribute: UNI L2CP Address Set	p. 92

	5.9.6	Passing L2CP Frames and Tunneling	p. 93
	5.9.7	L2CP Attribute Configuration Requirements	p. 94
	5.9.8	L2CP Requirements for Spanning Tree Protocols	p. 96
	5.9.9	UNI Functionality and L2CP Requirements	p. 97
5.10		Review: Service Connectivity Attributes	p. 98

6	Traffic and Performance Management			p. 103
	6.1		Overview of Traffic and Performance Management	p. 104
		6.1.1	About Performance Objectives	p. 104
		6.1.2	The Multi CoS Framework	p. 104
		6.1.3	Color and EVC Performance Objectives	p. 106
		6.1.4	About Bandwidth Profiles	p. 107
		6.1.5	CoS ID and EEC ID	p. 111
	6.2		CoS ID Service Attributes	p. 114
		6.2.1	Attribute: CoS ID for Data Service Frame	p. 115
		6.2.2	Attribute: CoS ID for L2CP Service Frame	p. 115
		6.2.3	Attribute: CoS ID for SOAM Service Frame	p. 116
		6.2.4	CoS ID Based on CE-VLAN CoS	p. 116
		6.2.5	CoS ID Based on Internet Protocol	p. 117
	6.3		Color ID for Service Frame Attribute	p. 118
	6.4		EEC ID Service Attributes	p. 119
		6.4.1	Attribute: EEC ID for Data Service Frame	p. 120
		6.4.2	Attribute: EEC ID for L2CP Service Frame	p. 120
		6.4.3	Attribute: EEC ID for SOAM Service Frame	p. 121
		6.4.4	EEC ID Based on CE-VLAN CoS	p. 121
		6.4.5	EEC ID Based on Internet Protocol	p. 122
	6.5		Review: Traffic and Performance Management	p. 123

7	Bandwidth Profiles			p. 125
	7.1		Single-Flow Bandwidth Profile	p. 126
		7.1.1	Visualizing the Token Bucket Algorithm	p. 127
		7.1.2	Explaining the Single-Flow Bandwidth Profile Algorithm	p. 128
		7.1.3	Single-Rate versus Dual-Rate Bandwidth Profile Implementations	p. 132
	7.2		Multi-Flow Bandwidth Profiles	p. 133
		7.2.1	Explaining the Multiflow Bandwidth Profile Algorithm	p. 134
		7.2.2	Observations	p. 137
	7.3		More Terminology	p. 138
	7.4		Bandwidth Profile Service Attributes	p. 139
		7.4.1	Attribute: Envelopes	p. 139
		7.4.2	Attribute: Token Share	p. 139
		7.4.3	Attribute: Ingress Bandwidth Profile per-CoS ID	p. 140
		7.4.4	Attribute: Egress Bandwidth Profile per-EEC ID	p. 140
		7.4.5	Bandwidth Profile Attribute Requirements	p. 140

	7.5	Egress Bandwidth Profiles		p. 141
		7.5.1	Egress Bandwidth Profiles for EPL Services	p. 141
		7.5.2	Egress Bandwidth Profiles for EVPL Services	p. 141
		7.5.3	Egress Bandwidth Profiles in E-LAN and E-Tree Type Services	p. 142
	7.6	About Line Rate and CIR		p. 143
	7.7	Review: Bandwidth Profiles		p. 145
8	EVC Performance			p. 147
	8.1	EVC Performance Service Attribute		p. 148
		8.1.1	Performance Metric Caveats and Requirements	p. 149
		8.1.2	Ordered UNI Pair	p. 149
		8.1.3	Frame Delay Performance	p. 150
		8.1.4	Inter-Frame Delay Variation Performance	p. 151
		8.1.5	Frame Loss Ratio Performance	p. 152
		8.1.6	Availability Performance	p. 153
		8.1.7	Resiliency Performance	p. 157
		8.1.8	Group Availability Performance	p. 161
	8.2	Multiple EVC Availability Performance		p. 163
	8.3	Example of EVC Performance Attribute Specification		p. 165
	8.4	Review: EVC Performance Attributes		p. 166
9	UNI Requirements			p. 168
	9.1	Type 2 UNI Requirements		p. 170
		9.1.1	SOAM Requirement for Type 2 UNIs	p. 170
		9.1.2	Enhanced UNI Attributes Requirement for Type 2 UNIs	p. 171
		9.1.3	L2CP Handling Requirement for Type 2 UNIs	p. 171
		9.1.4	LOAM Requirement for Type 2.2 UNIs	p. 171
		9.1.5	E-LMI Requirement for Type 2.2 UNIs	p. 172
		9.1.6	Link Protection Requirement for Type 2.2 UNIs	p. 172
	9.2	UNI Functionality Service Attributes		p. 174
	9.3	Review: UNI Requirements		p. 175
10	Extending MEF Services over Multiple Operator CENs			p. 177
	10.1	Terminology		p. 179
		10.1.1	Service Provider and Operators	p. 179
		10.1.2	ENNI and ENNI-N	p. 180
		10.1.3	External Interface (EI)	p. 180
		10.1.4	OVC	p. 181
		10.1.5	OVC End Point	p. 182
		10.1.6	Ingress and Egress Frames	p. 183
		10.1.7	OVC End Point Role	p. 183
		10.1.8	Hairpin Switch	p. 185
	10.2	Service Handoff at ENNI		p. 187

		10.2.1	Encoding Information in S-Tags	p. 188
		10.2.2	ENNI Tagging Requirements	p. 189
	10.3	Operator Service Model		p. 191
	10.4	Operator Service Attributes		p. 192
		10.4.1	ENNI Service Attributes	p. 192
		10.4.2	OVC Service Attributes	p. 193
		10.4.3	OVC End Point per ENNI Service Attributes	p. 194
		10.4.4	Per UNI Service Attributes (Operator Service)	p. 195
		10.4.5	OVC per UNI Service Attributes	p. 196
	10.5	Highlights of the Operator Service Model		p. 197
		10.5.1	ENNI Frame Format	p. 197
		10.5.2	ENNI and OVC MTU Size	p. 197
		10.5.3	Protection at ENNI	p. 198
		10.5.4	End Point Map	p. 199
		10.5.5	Color-Aware Bandwidth Profiles at ENNI	p. 200
		10.5.6	Color Forwarding	p. 201
		10.5.7	Hairpin Switching	p. 202
		10.5.8	End Point Map Bundling	p. 205
		10.5.9	LOAM Requirement for ENNIs	p. 206
		10.5.10	Service Level Specification (OVC Service Attribute)	p. 206
		10.5.11	Layer 2 Control Protocol Tunneling	p. 207
	10.6	Rooted-Multipoint OVCs		p. 209
		10.6.1	Applications with Root and Leaf OVC End Points Only	p. 209
		10.6.2	Applications with Trunk OVC End Points	p. 211
	10.7	Review: Extending MEF Services over Multiple Operator CENs		p. 217
11	MEF-Standardized Classes of Service			p. 222
	11.1	Definitions and Requirements		p. 223
		11.1.1	CoS Labels and Performance Tiers	p. 223
		11.1.2	Ingress Bandwidth Profile Constraints (per CoS Label)	p. 224
		11.1.3	CoS Label and Color Identification Mechanisms	p. 225
		11.1.4	CoS Label and Color Identification Using PCP Bits, DEI Bit, and/or EVC/OVC End Point	p. 225
		11.1.5	CoS Label and Color Identification Using DSCP Values and/or EVC/OVC End Point	p. 226
		11.1.6	CoS Label Identification for L2CP Frames	p. 227
		11.1.7	Key Observations About CoS Label and Color Identification	p. 227
		11.1.8	Performance Metrics for CoS Labels	p. 227
		11.1.9	CoS Parameter Values (per CoS Label)	p. 228
		11.1.10	CPOs (per CoS Label and Performance Tier)	p. 229
	11.2	Review: MEF-Standardized Classes of Service		p. 230
12	E-Access Services			p. 232

12.1		E-Access Service Applications	p. 233
12.2		Access EPL and Access EVPL	p. 234
12.3		E-Access Service Attributes	p. 235
	12.3.1	ENNI Service Attributes for E-Access	p. 235
	12.3.2	OVC Service Attributes for E-Access	p. 236
	12.3.3	OVC End Point per ENNI Service Attributes for E-Access	p. 237
	12.3.4	Per UNI Service Attributes for E-Access	p. 238
	12.3.5	OVC Per UNI service attributes for E-Access	p. 239
12.4		Highlights of E-Access Service Definitions	p. 240
	12.4.1	Bundling and Multiplexing for E-Access Services	p. 240
	12.4.2	CE-VLAN ID Preservation for E-Access Services	p. 241
	12.4.3	CoS Identification for E-Access Services	p. 241
	12.4.4	CE-VLAN CoS ID Preservation for E-Access Services	p. 242
	12.4.5	Performance Objectives for E-Access Services	p. 242
	12.4.6	Bandwidth Profiles for E-Access Service	p. 242
12.5		E-Access Service Applications	p. 246
	12.5.1	E-Access Services Applied in EVC-Based Services	p. 246
	12.5.2	E-Access Services Applied for IP Network Services	p. 248
	12.5.3	E-Access Compared to E-Line	p. 248
12.6		Review: E-Access Services	p. 249

13	Ethernet OAM		p. 251
13.1		Link OAM	p. 253
13.2		Service OAM Overview	p. 254
	13.2.1	The MEF Service Life Cycle	p. 254
	13.2.2	SOAM Domains	p. 255
	13.2.3	SOAM Frames	p. 256
	13.2.4	SOAM Components	p. 256
	13.2.5	SOAM MEG Levels	p. 260
13.3		SOAM-Related Service Attributes	p. 262
	13.3.1	Attribute: UNI MEG	p. 262
	13.3.2	Attribute: Test MEG	p. 263
	13.3.3	Attribute: Subscriber MEG MIP	p. 263
13.4		SOAM Connectivity Fault Management	p. 264
	13.4.1	Continuity Check Message (CCM)	p. 264
	13.4.2	Remote Defect Indication (RDI)	p. 265
	13.4.3	Alarm Indication Signal (ETH-AIS)	p. 265
	13.4.4	Locked Signal (ETH-LCK)	p. 266
	13.4.5	Test Signal (ETH-Test)	p. 268
	13.4.6	SOAM Loopback	p. 268
	13.4.7	SOAM Link Trace	p. 269
13.5		SOAM Performance Management	p. 270
	13.5.1	SOAM Framework for Measuring Performance Metrics	p. 271

		13.5.2	Synthetic Frames versus Service Frames	p. 273
		13.5.3	Single-Ended versus Dual-Ended PM Functions	p. 274
		13.5.4	Single-Ended Delay	p. 275
		13.5.5	Single-Ended Synthetic Loss	p. 276
		13.5.6	Dual-Ended Delay	p. 277
		13.5.7	Single-Ended Service Loss	p. 278
		13.5.8	The Performance Monitoring Process	p. 279
	13.6	Review: Ethernet OAM		p. 281
14	Access Technologies			p. 285
	14.1	Access versus Transport Technology		p. 288
	14.2	Ethernet over Optical Fiber		p. 289
		14.2.1	Ethernet over Active Fiber	p. 289
		14.2.2	Ethernet over SONET/SDH	p. 290
		14.2.3	Ethernet over PON	p. 290
	14.3	Ethernet over PDH		p. 293
	14.4	Ethernet over Copper		p. 295
		14.4.1	2BASE-TL (G.SHDSL)	p. 295
		14.4.2	10PASS-TS (VDSL)	p. 296
		14.4.3	Bonded Copper Pairs	p. 296
		14.4.4	EoCu versus EoPDH	p. 296
	14.5	Ethernet over Wireless Network		p. 297
	14.6	Ethernet over HFC		p. 299
	14.7	Summary: Access Technologies		p. 301
	14.8	Review: Access Technologies		p. 303
15	Transport Technologies			p. 306
	15.1	Layer 1 Transport Technologies		p. 308
		15.1.1	SONET/SDH (Synchronous Optical Network / Synchronous Digital Hierarchy)	p. 308
		15.1.2	OTN (Optical Transport Network)	p. 310
		15.1.3	WDM (Wavelength Division Multiplexing)	p. 312
	15.2	Layer 2 Transport Technologies		p. 314
		15.2.1	Bridging	p. 315
		15.2.2	PB (Provider Bridging)	p. 317
		15.2.3	PBB (Provider Backbone Bridging)	p. 319
		15.2.4	PBB-TE (Provider Backbone Bridge Traffic Engineering)	p. 324
		15.2.5	ETS (Ethernet Tag Switching)	p. 326
	15.3	Layer 2.5 Technologies (Multiprotocol Label Switching)		p. 327
		15.3.1	MPLS VPWS (MPLS Virtual Private Wire Service)	p. 329
		15.3.2	MPLS VPLS (MPLS Virtual Private LAN Service)	p. 330
		15.3.3	MPLS-TP (MPLS Transport Profile)	p. 331
	15.4	Ethernet Service Protection Technologies		p. 333
		15.4.1	1+1 Linear Protection	p. 333

		15.4.2	1:1 Linear Protection	p. 334
		15.4.3	xSTP-Based Protection	p. 334
		15.4.4	1:1 Ring Protection	p. 335
		15.4.5	Protection Mechanisms and Transport Technologies	p. 336
	15.5	Summary		p. 337
	15.6	Review: Transport Technologies		p. 339
16	Applications			p. 343
	16.1	Target Applications		p. 344
		16.1.1	Wholesale Access Service	p. 344
		16.1.2	Ethernet Access to IP Services	p. 345
		16.1.3	Retail Commercial/Business Services	p. 348
		16.1.4	Mobile Backhaul	p. 350
	16.2	Comparing and Positioning Carrier Ethernet Services with Legacy Services		p. 352
		16.2.1	Support for TDM Private Lines	p. 352
		16.2.2	Replacement of Frame Relay Service	p. 354
		16.2.3	Internet Access	p. 358
		16.2.4	Virtual Private Networks (VPNs)	p. 359
	16.3	Mobile Backhaul Services		p. 362
		16.3.1	Mobile Backhaul Reference Model	p. 363
		16.3.2	Mobile Backhaul Use Cases	p. 364
		16.3.3	Mobile Backhaul for LTE	p. 366
		16.3.4	Mobile Backhaul CoS and Performance Requirements	p. 367
		16.3.5	MEF Service Definitions for Mobile Backhaul	p. 369
		16.3.6	MEG Levels in Mobile Backhaul	p. 371
		16.3.7	Mobile Backhaul Synchronization	p. 371
	16.4	Circuit Emulation Services over Ethernet		p. 374
		16.4.1	CEN Requirements for CESoETH	p. 375
		16.4.2	Inter-Working Function	p. 375
		16.4.3	Synchronization	p. 376
	16.5	Review: Applications		p. 378
17	MEF Certification Program			p. 384
	17.1	Equipment and Services Certification		p. 385
		17.1.1	CE 1.0 Certification	p. 386
		17.1.2	CE 2.0 Certification	p. 386
		17.1.3	Equipment Certification	p. 387
		17.1.4	Service Certification	p. 388
	17.2	Professional Certification		p. 390
	17.3	Review: MEF Certification		p. 391
18	Answers to Review Questions			p. 392
	18.1	Answers: Carrier Ethernet Services		p. 393

18.2	Answers: Ethernet Frames and Service Frames	p. 397
18.3	Answers: How Carrier Ethernet Services are Defined	p. 399
18.4	Answers: Service Connectivity Attributes	p. 400
18.5	Answers: Traffic and Performance Management	p. 406
18.6	Answers: Bandwidth Profiles	p. 408
18.7	Answers: EVC Performance Attributes	p. 411
18.8	Answers: UNI Requirements	p. 414
18.9	Answers: Extending MEF Services over Multiple Operator CENs	p. 416
18.10	Answers: MEF-Standardized Classes of Service	p. 423
18.11	Answers: E-Access Services	p. 426
18.12	Answers: Ethernet OAM	p. 429
18.13	Answers: Access Technologies	p. 433
18.14	Answers: Transport Technologies	p. 436
18.15	Answers: Applications	p. 440
18.16	Answers: MEF Certification	p. 447

Index   p. 449

1 Introduction

In this chapter:

1.1 Getting Started
1.2 Changes To This Update

The MEF awards the Carrier Ethernet Certified Professional (MEF-CECP) certification to individuals who pass the MEF-CECP exam.

This study guide, now in its third edition, is designed to help you prepare for the latest incarnation of the MEF-CECP exam, known as Blueprint C. This edition of the study guide is similar to previous editions in its overall quality, systematic style of presentation, careful explanations, custom color graphics, and numerous practice questions (more than 200). Its content is expanded, restructured, and revised to align with the latest MEF-CECP standards, per MEF-CECP Exam Blueprint C.

Like previous editions, this study guide assumes that you have a basic understanding of Ethernet, but no prior knowledge of Carrier Ethernet.[1] The guide covers all topics that are included in the MEF-CECP exam. Material is presented systematically, beginning with MEF service definitions (the core content that accounts for most exam questions) and building outward. Each lesson ends with a set of multiple-choice review questions, similar to those appearing in the MEF-CECP exam. The guide also includes strategic guidance to help you focus your efforts and efficiently prepare for the exam.

The study guide was created by identifying essential content from MEF specifications, white papers, and reference presentations; reorganizing it into a systematic, logical progression; and adding context as necessary for clarity and continuity. It is intended to be used like a text book. Early lessons introduce fundamental concepts that later lessons build upon.

The guide is complete and comprehensive, but it is not meant to be used in isolation. In places, the guide directs you to visit the MEF Web site and familiarize yourself with its valuable content. It also includes numerous references to MEF specifications that you should consult to verify or enhance your understanding.

Fujitsu welcomes your feedback and suggestions for this guide or future Carrier Ethernet educational material. If you have comments or questions, please contact us at *ReaderFeedback@fnc.fujitsu.com*.

---

1 Fujitsu's book *Introduction to Carrier Ethernet*, available from Amazon.com, provides an entry-level introduction to Carrier Ethernet for people with little or no background in computer networking and/or telecommunications.

About the Authors

Jon Kieffer (MEF-CECP) is a principal technical writer working for Fujitsu Network Communications since 2001. Previous to that, Jon taught software engineering at the University of Hull, U.K., and mechanical engineering at the Australian National University. Jon holds BS, MS, and PhD degrees in mechanical engineering and has authored 12 refereed journal articles and more than 30 conference papers in the fields of mechanical and controls engineering. The MEF recognized Jon as an outstanding contributor for contributions to the MEF-CECP program in 2014 and again in 2015. In 2015, Jon received the MEF Marketing Committee Editors Award for co-editing the MEF white paper Understanding Bandwidth Profiles in MEF 6.2 Service Definitions.

Ralph Santitoro is a MEF founding member, board member and Distinguished Fellow who regularly contributes to projects in all MEF committees. Ralph created the MEF's Carrier Ethernet Professional Certification Program, co-developed the MEF-CECP exams and co-authored the industry's first MEF-CECP exam study guide. Ralph was editor of MEF 6, the industry's first Ethernet Services Definitions specification, and authored the MEF's Ethernet services primer with over 100,000 copies downloaded. Ralph has been a catalyst behind the MEF's Third Network Vision transforming the organization's scope to define multi-layer, multi-domain, Network-as-a-Service (NaaS) automated via lifecycle service orchestration (LSO). Over the past 10 years, Ralph has lectured and conducted seminars at over 70 international events and has published over 30 papers covering Carrier Ethernet, NaaS, Virtual Network Services, Network Virtualization, SDN, LSO, Cloud Computing, QoS, and Cybersecurity. At Fujitsu, Ralph develops solutions using Network Functions Virtualization (NFV) and Software Defined Networking (SDN) that virtualize and orchestrate network functions to deliver on-demand virtual network services.

More MEF-CECP Training Options from Fujitsu

Fujitsu Instructor-Led Training — If you prefer face-to-face training, you can get it from Fujitsu. Fujitsu's MEF-CECP Exam training course uses Fujitsu's study guide and training app and is led by an MEF-CECP certified instructor. Fujitsu's training course is MEF-accredited and culminates with options to take the exam, proctored by the instructor. The course is offered regularly at Fujitsu's Richardson, Texas campus and is available at other locations by request. For more information, email Ed.svcs@fnc.fujitsu.com.

Fujitsu MEF-CECP Exam Trainer App — If you want to practice using questions that are similar to those on the real exam, this mobile app is ideal. The Exam Trainer app offers more than 200 multiple-choice practice questions (from the study guide) in several study modes and provides feedback. The Exam Trainer emphasizes learning over memorization by randomizing the sequence of both questions and answers. Got a question wrong? The app provides a brief explanation or pointer to study guide content. You can even record your scores to see how they improve over time. This app has been updated for MEF-CECP Exam Blueprint C and is available for iPhone, iPad, Android, and Windows 8 devices.

Fujitsu *Introduction to Carrier Ethernet* Book — If you don't have the background to jump right into Carrier Ethernet, this book will get you there. This short book is an entry-level introduction to Carrier Ethernet, intended for anyone new to Carrier Ethernet, including those with little or no background in computer networking and/or telecommunications. It was conceived to be a companion to Fujitsu's MEF-CECP Study Guide (any edition), but can be used alone (as an introduction to Carrier Ethernet) or in combination with other Carrier Ethernet training materials. The book has two aims: to explain networking technology leading up to and motivating Carrier Ethernet, and to explain Carrier Ethernet conceptually within this framework. This book is available in print and Kindle formats from Amazon.com.

1.1 Getting Started

In this section:

1.1.1   About the MEF
1.1.2   About Carrier Ethernet
1.1.3   Explore the MEF Web Site and the MEF Reference Wiki
1.1.4   About MEF-CECP Certification
1.1.5   The MEF-CECP Certification Exam Blueprint
1.1.6   Assumed Knowledge

1.1.1 About the MEF

The MEF[2] is a global industry alliance comprising more than 220 organizations, including telecommunications service providers, cable MSOs, network equipment/software manufacturers, semiconductor vendors, and testing organizations. The MEF's mission is to accelerate the worldwide adoption of Carrier-class Ethernet networks and services. The MEF develops Carrier Ethernet technical specifications and implementation agreements to promote interoperability and deployment of Carrier Ethernet worldwide.

For more information about the MEF, including a complete listing of all current MEF members, visit mef.net.

1.1.2 About Carrier Ethernet

The use of Ethernet for wide area networks (WANs) and services is motivated by the ubiquitous prevalence of Ethernet in local area networks (LANs) and by the pervasive use of Ethernet as the standard interface on most networked devices (PCs, servers, laptops, and so on).

Initially, TDM networks, which support T1/E1 private lines and SONET/SDH, were widely deployed because circuit-based voice traffic accounted for the vast majority of WAN traffic. At that time, data traffic was limited to low-speed, dial-up modem connections over voice circuits and fractional T1/E1 circuits for data transmission.

Today, we experience the opposite scenario where packet-based data traffic is dominant and circuit-based voice traffic accounts for only a tiny percentage of overall network traffic. High-speed, broadband data traffic using the Internet Protocol (IP) is most prevalent and continues to increase as more applications migrate towards IP-based implementations. Interestingly, circuit-based voice traffic, the original driver for TDM networks, is rapidly migrating to Voice over IP (VoIP), which makes voice traffic appear as packet-based data traffic to the network. Video, which originally required a dedicated network, is also migrating to video over IP, thus further driving the need for high-bandwidth packet-based WANs.

Most networked applications are IP-based and run over networking devices that connect to wireline networks over Ethernet. Even applications that run over a wireless network, such as smartphones and tablets, eventually reach a networking device that connects to an Ethernet network. Considering that most applications begin and

---

2   The MEF organization, originally named **Metro Ethernet Forum**, is now the **MEF Forum**.

end on an Ethernet network, the use of Carrier Ethernet as the WAN technology or service enables a common Ethernet technology to be used end-to-end.

Furthermore, compared to legacy, circuit-based TDM networks, Carrier Ethernet, being a packet-based technology, can much more efficiently accommodate the now-dominant packet-based traffic.

The MEF distinguishes Carrier Ethernet from familiar LAN-based Ethernet based on five attributes:
1. Standardized Services
2. Scalability
3. Reliability
4. Quality of Service
5. Service Management

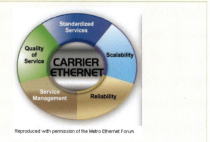

Reproduced with permission of the Metro Ethernet Forum

1.1.3
Explore the MEF Web Site and the MEF Reference Wiki

The MEF Web site is mef.net. Go ahead and explore this Web site now. It is a great way to start preparing for the MEF-CECP exam. In particular, discover how to navigate from the main page to each of the following pages: MEF Technical Specifications, MEF Reference Presentations, MEF White Papers, MEF Certification Programs, and MEF Professional Certification.

The MEF also maintains the *MEF Reference Wiki* at https://wiki.mef.net/display/CESG/MEF+Reference+Wiki. The *MEF Reference Wiki* serves as a tool to make it easier for the general public to access information on Carrier Ethernet as defined by the MEF. Much of its content overlaps with content in these lessons. However, its focus is broader: Carrier Ethernet in general, rather than Carrier Ethernet for the MEF-CECP exam. Also, its content is generated collaboratively and is subject to continuous updating. The general public cannot update its pages directly. However, anyone can write a comment, using the comment dialog at the bottom of each page. Comments are reviewed by MEF authorities and may lead to revision of wiki page content.

1.1.4
About MEF-CECP Certification

MEF-CECP certification targets individuals who perform job roles such as product manager, product planner, product developer, system architect, network engineer, network architect, systems engineer, sales engineer, or technical marketing. MEF-CECP certifies that the individual possesses the knowledge required to define, design, develop, or market Carrier Ethernet products, services, or applications.

Prior to April 2015, there were two MEF-CECP certifications.

Initial MEF-CECP Certification (Offered July 2011 – December of 2013)	MEF-CECP 2.0 Certification (Offered December 2013 – April 2015)
MEF CECP CARRIER ETHERNET Certified Professional	MEF CECP 2.0

In April 2015, these certifications were unified into one certification, called the **MEF-CECP**.

All previous and future certifications are now MEF-CECP certifications, recognized with this logo and distinguished only by date of certification.

The Expiration Policy

In April 2015, the MEF announced the MEF-CECP Certification Expiration Policy, which is explained on the MEF-CECP Certification Expiration Policy Change Notification page on the *MEF Reference Wiki*. The following two paragraphs are copied from that page:

> All MEF-CECP certifications are valid for a period of **3 years** from the "certification date", the date on which the exam was passed and the certification issued. Each MEF-CECP will be able to renew his or her certification at any time by taking and passing the current version of the MEF-CECP examination.

> Individuals that have been issued the MEF-CECP or MEF-CECP 2.0 certification since the launch of the program in July 2011 will continue to be listed in the Ethernet Academy registry regardless of the status of their certification which is now indicated as **Active** or **Inactive**. **Active** means that the certification was issued less than 3 years from the current date and remains valid. **Inactive** indicates that the certification is older than 3 years, is no longer valid, and has not be renewed. *There is a grace period for certifications that were issued prior to January 1, 2013. These will not become Inactive until January 1, 2016.*

The MEF-CECP Exam

To receive MEF-CECP certification or renew your MEF-CECP certification, you must pass the MEF-CECP exam. The MEF-CECP exam is governed by the MEF-CECP Certification Exam Blueprint that is current at the time you take the exam. The MEF publishes past, current, and planned MEF-CECP exam blueprints on the MEF-CECP Exam Blueprints page of the *MEF Reference Wiki*.

The exam is open to anyone and may be taken online from your home or office, at an MEF Approved Testing Center, or from an MEF Accredited Training Provider. Refer to EthernetAcademy.net for more details.

The MEF-CECP exam is a 1-hour 45-minute exam consisting of about 80 multiple-choice questions. About 70 questions are scored and about 10 questions are unscored. The unscored questions are included for statistical purposes (they are considered for use in future exams). To pass the exam, you need to correctly answer about 65% of the scored questions. Exact numbers vary with exam forms as they evolve.

 Caution: *The MEF Web site and MEF standards are continually evolving and may include material that supersedes the material covered by the current MEF-CECP exam. For exam preparation purposes, you should focus on the objectives listed in the current MEF-CECP Certification Exam Blueprint and understand those objects according to the references listed in that blueprint.*

Introduction
Getting Started

The Rewards of Certification

Individuals who pass the MEF-CECP exam are awarded:

- An official MEF-CECP certificate
- A listing, as being MEF-CECP certified, on the online Directory of MEF Certified Professionals posted at the widely visited EthernetAcademy.net Web site
- Qualification to use the MEF-CECP logo (for example, in e-mail signatures, business cards, and resumes) for instant recognition of their status

1.1.5 The MEF-CECP Certification Exam Blueprint

The MEF publishes MEF-CECP exam blueprints (past, current, and planned) on the MEF-CECP Exam Blueprints page[3] of the *MEF Reference Wiki*. These lessons cover MEF-CECP exam material based MEF-CECP Certification Exam Blueprint "C" which is reproduced below for reference. Study it to get a rough sense of the work ahead of you. If you are new to Carrier Ethernet, you should see many unfamiliar topics.

MEF-CECP Certification Exam Blueprint "C"

Objective	Description	Citation / Reference
1	**SERVICES DEFINITIONS** • **1.1** Describe and distinguish between the service attributes of: EPL/EVPL; EP-LAN/EVP-LAN; EP-Tree/EVP-Tree; Access EPL/Access EVPL • **1.2** Describe how EPL, EVPL, EP-LAN, EVP-LAN, EP-Tree, and EVP-Tree are used to meet various subscriber needs.	MEF 6.2 | MEF 45★ | MEF 10.3 | MEF 33
2	**TRANSPORTING CARRIER ETHERNET SERVICES** • **2.1** Describe the connectivity properties of bridging, provider bridging, provider backbone bridging (PBB), provider backbone bridging with traffic engineering extensions (PBB-TE), Ethernet over SONET/SDH, Carrier Ethernet over MPLS VPWS, Carrier Ethernet over MPLS VPLS, Carrier Ethernet over MPLS TP, Carrier Ethernet over OTN, and Carrier Ethernet over WDM • **2.2** Describe the capabilities of the bridging, provider bridging, provider backbone bridging (PBB), provider backbone bridging with traffic engineering extensions (PBB-TE), SONET/SDH, MPLS VPWS, MPLS VPLS, MPLS TP, OTN and WDM with regards to delivery of Carrier Ethernet services • **2.3** (Removed) • **2.4** Describe the advantages of specific Carrier Ethernet transport technologies • **2.5** Describe service protection mechanisms	Carrier Ethernet and Access Technologies | IEEE 802.1Q-2011 | IETF RFC 4448 | IETF RFC 4761 | IETF RFC 5921 | IETF RFC 5960 | ITU-T G.8031 | ITU-T Y.1415 | ITU-T G.8032 | MEF White Paper - Ethernet Services and Access Technologies | Optimizing Mobile Backhaul

---

3 https://wiki.mef.net/display/CESG/MEF-CECP+Exam+Blueprints

Objective	Description	Citation / Reference
3	**CARRIER ETHERNET ACCESS TECHNOLOGIES** • **3.1** Describe the capabilities of Ethernet over PDH, Ethernet over bonded copper, Ethernet over HFC, Ethernet over packet radio, Ethernet over fiber and Ethernet over PON • **3.2** Describe the advantages of specific Carrier Ethernet Access technologies • **3.3** Given a scenario, identify which Carrier Ethernet Access Technology will meet the stated requirements	Carrier Ethernet Access Reference Presentation | IEEE 802.3-2005 | IEEE802.16-2009 | MEF White Paper: Ethernet Services and Access Technologies
4	**BASIC DEFINITIONS** • **4.1** Define Ethernet User-to-Network Interface (UNI), Ethernet External Network-to-Network Interface (ENNI), Ethernet Virtual Connection (EVC), Service Provider, Operator, and Operator Virtual Connection (OVC) • **4.2** Describe the role of Ethernet User-to-Network Interface (UNI), Ethernet External Network-to-Network Interface (ENNI), Ethernet Virtual Connection (EVC), Service Provider, Operator, and Operator Virtual Connection (OVC)	MEF 10.3 | MEF 26.1 | MEF 33
5	**KEY UNI, ENNI, OVC & EVC SERVICE ATTRIBUTES** • **5.1** Define per UNI service attributes (e.g., physical interfaces, Frame format, Ingress/egress Bandwidth Profiles, CE-VLAN ID/EVC Map, UNI protection) • **5.2** Define EVC per UNI service attributes (e.g. ingress/egress Bandwidth Profiles) • **5.3** Define per EVC service attributes (e.g., CE-VLAN ID Preservation, CoS ID Preservation, Relationship between Service Level Agreement and Service Level Specification, Class of Service) • **5.4** Define OVC End Point per UNI and OVC End Point per ENNI service attributes (e.g., ingress/egress bandwidth profiles) • **5.5** Describe bandwidth profiles • **5.6** Given a service scenario, describe relevant service attribute settings/parameters • **5.7** Define and describe the components of a Service Level Specification and the relationship to Service Level Agreement • **5.8** Define and describe ENNI attributes (e.g., physical interfaces, Frame format, Ingress/egress Bandwidth Profiles, End Point Map, ENNI protection) • **5.9** Define and describe OVC attributes (e.g., CE-VLAN ID Preservation, CoS ID Preservation, Relationship between Service Level Agreement and Service Level Specification, Class of Service, hairpin switching) • **5.10** Define and describe the Carrier Ethernet protection mechanisms	MEF 6.2 | MEF 45★ | MEF 10.3 | MEF 20 | MEF 23.1 | MEF 26.1 | MEF 33 | IEEE 802.1AX

Objective	Description	Citation / Reference
6	**CERTIFICATION**	
	• **6.1** Describe the MEF Certification process and requirements for networking equipment	
	• **6.2** Describe the MEF Certification process and requirements for services delivered by a service provider	
	• **6.3** Describe what is covered by CE 2.0 Certifications	
	• **6.4** Describe the deliverables of MEF Certification for equipment vendors, service provider, and Carrier Ethernet certified professionals	
7	**TARGET APPLICATION FOR ETHERNET SERVICES**	MEF 6.2 | MEF 8 | MEF 10.3 | MEF 22.1 | MEF 26.1 | MEF 33 | MEF 45★ | Carrier Ethernet Access Reference Presentation | White Paper Introduction to CESoE | Mobile Backhaul Reference Presentation | Carrier Ethernet Access Reference Presentation
	• **7.1** Describe wholesale access services, retail commercial/business services, mobile backhaul services, Ethernet access to IP services, and supporting legacy services over Ethernet	
	• **7.2** Describe which UNI or ENNI attribute values are selected for a given target application	
	• **7.3** Describe which EVC or OVC attribute values are selected for a given target application	
	• **7.4** Describe how specific service requirements of a target application (e.g., frame relay, Dedicated Internet Access, DSL or Cable Internet access, TDM Private Lines, WDM private network are met using Ethernet services)	
	• **7.5** Given a scenario, determine appropriate Ethernet services.	
8	**COMPARING AND POSITIONING ETHERNET SERVICES**	MEF 6.2 | MEF 8 | MEF 10.3 | MEF 22.1 | MEF 33 |IETF RFC 4448 | White Paper Introduction to CESoE
	• **8.1** Compare and contrast Ethernet services with L2, IP, and TDM private line services	
	• **8.2** Given a scenario, recommend an Ethernet service to meet end user specifications	
9	**CIRCUIT EMULATION OVER ETHERNET**	Carrier Ethernet Access Reference Presentation | MEF 8 | MEF 22.1
	• **9.1** Define the purpose and need for Circuit Emulation over Ethernet applications including identifying critical components	
	• 9.2 (Removed)	
	• **9.3** Define the MEF Service Definitions and EVC service attributes used to deliver emulated circuits	
	• 9.4 (Removed)	
	• **9.5** Define the three techniques and their uses for delivering synchronized clock over emulated circuits (e.g., Adaptive, 1588v2, Synchronous Ethernet, NTP, PTP)	
	• **9.6** Describe how circuit emulation is used in Mobile Backhaul applications	

Objective	Description	Citation / Reference
10	SERVICE OPERATIONS, ADMINISTRATION & MAINTENANCE (SOAM) • **10.1** Describe the various partitioning of responsibilities for Service Operations Administration and Maintenance (SOAM) • **10.2** Describe the basic mechanisms for fault management • **10.3** Describe the basic mechanisms for performance monitoring • **10.4** Describe the basic metrics for performance monitoring • **10.5** Describe the Service Life cycle	MEF 6.2 | MEF 8 |MEF 10.3 | MEF 17 | MEF 30.1 | MEF 30.1.1 | ITU-T Y.1731 |MEF 35 | MEF 35.0.1 | MEF 35.0.2 | Carrier Ethernet Interconnect Reference Presentation

Notes:

- MEF 10.3 supersedes MEF 10.2 and MEF 10.2.1
- MEF 6.2 and MEF 45 supersedes MEF 6.1 and MEF 6.1.1
- 802.1AX replaces 802.3 clause 43
- ★ MEF45 anticipates upcoming changes in OVC services. For exams forms governed by this blueprint, MEF 45 related items should focus on EVC services rather than OVC services.
- MEF 35.0.1, MEF 35.0.2, and MEF 30.1.1 are new

1.1.6
Assumed Knowledge

The following tables list topics of assumed knowledge. Many resources are available for learning this material, including Firewall.cx, Wikipedia.org, and Fujitsu's book *Introduction to Carrier Ethernet: A foundation for MEF-CECP 2.0 training*, by Jon Kieffer and Yongchao Fan, September 2014 (Available from Amazon.com).

7-Layer OSI Reference Model
Focus is on the bottom three layers: • Layer 3 (Network Layer)—Routes IP packets based on network address (IP address) • Layer 2 (Data Link Layer)—Forwards Ethernet frames based on MAC address • Layer 1 (Physical Layer)—Transmits data over a link between two interfaces Each layer provides services to the next-higher layer.
Encapsulation
Refers to the process of putting headers and trailers around some data. A lower layer encapsulates the higher layer's data behind a header.

Protocol Data Unit (PDU)

Generic term for the set of bits that is recognized as a fundamental unit (structured group of bits) at any layer (Layer 2 and above)

A lower-layer PDU is comprised of data (the PDU of the next-higher layer) plus a header, and possibly a trailer.

A Layer 3 PDU is called a **packet** (IP packet, for example).

A Layer 2 PDU is called a **frame** (Ethernet frame, for example).

Ethernet

Ethernet Frame Components:

- MAC destination address—Address of destination interface
- MAC source address—Address of source interface
- Ethertype—Indicates which protocol is encapsulated in the payload
- VLAN tag—Optional component containing VLAN ID and PCP bits
- Frame check sequence (FCS)—Extra checksum characters added to an Ethernet frame for error detection

MAC Destination Addressing: Unicast, Multicast, Broadcast, L2CP (Layer 2 Control Protocol)

Collision Domain—The set of network interface cards (NICs) for which a frame sent by one NIC could result in a collision with a frame sent by any other NIC in the same collision domain

Broadcast Domain—The set of NICs for which a broadcast frame sent by one NIC is received by all other NICs in the same broadcast domain

Bridge—The Layer 2 network device that performs bridging (also commonly called an Ethernet switch or Layer 2 switch).

Bridging—Ethernet frame forwarding based on MAC address, MAC learning, and STP (Spanning Tree Protocol); the process by which bridges learn to forward unicast frames without broadcasting/flooding

Spanning Tree Protocol (STP)—The network protocol that ensures a loop-free topology for a bridged Ethernet LAN

There are several types of STP:
- STP (Spanning Tree Protocol)
- RSTP (Rapid Spanning Tree Protocol)
- MSTP (Multiple Spanning Tree Protocol)

Bridge Protocol Data Unit (BPDU)—Ethernet frames exchanged by bridges to support STP

IEEE 802.1Q (2005)—Basic standard for interconnecting LANs using forwarding based on MAC addresses, STP, and a single VLAN tag (C-Tag)

Router

Layer 3 device that routes packets based on IP address

Also separates broadcast domains

1.2 Changes To This Update

This study guide updates material from Fujitsu's previous MEF-CECP study guide[4] to align with the MEF-CECP Certification Exam Blueprint "C". The following MEF standards are newly recognized Blueprint "C":

- MEF 10.3, Ethernet Service Attributes Phase 3, October 2013

- MEF 45, Multi-CEN L2CP, July 2014

- MEF 6.2, EVC Ethernet Service Definitions Phase 3, August 2014

These changes impact EVC service definitions and refine the system of service attributes that are used to define EPL, EVPL, EP-LAN, EVP-LAN, EP-Tree, and EVP-Tree services.

Highlights include:

- Change in the definition of untagged service frame (Refer to Service Frame Tag Recognition).

- Recognition of DEI bit in CE-VLAN tag (Refer to C-Tagged Ethernet Frames and Color ID for Service Frame Attribute)

- Revisions and additions to EVC service attributes (Refer to Overview of Service Attributes)

- Classification of service frames according to purpose (Refer to Data, L2CP, and SOAM Service Frames).

- Recognition of *CE-VLAN ID / EVC Map* as a Per UNI attribute (Refer to CE-VLAN ID / EVC Map).

- Major revision of L2CP processing service attributes (Refer to L2CP Processing Service Attributes)

- Introduction of multiflow bandwidth profiles (Refer to Multi-Flow Bandwidth Profiles)

- Introduction of CoS ID attributes (Refer to CoS ID Service Attributes)

- Introduction of EEC ID attributes (Refer to EEC ID Service Attributes).

- Introduction of Group Availability Performance Attribute (Refer to Group Availability Performance)

- Introduction of Multiple EVC Performance Attribute (Refer to Multiple EVC Availability Performance)

The study guide is restructured to accommodate these changes. Review questions are updated to align with the revised content.

---

[4] Fujitsu's previous study guide, *MEF-CECP 2.0 Exam Study Guide for Carrier Ethernet 2.0 (CE 2.0) Professionals*, Kieffer and Santitoro, December 2013, aligns with MEF-CECP Certification Exam Blueprint "B".

2
Carrier Ethernet Services

In this chapter:

2.1	Fundamental Components and Reference Models	2.7	EVPL Service
		2.8	EP-LAN Service
2.2	Service Multiplexing	2.9	EVP-LAN Service
2.3	Service Frames	2.10	EP-Tree Service
2.4	Assigning Service Frames to EVCs	2.11	EVP-Tree Service
2.5	Taxonomy of EVC-Based Services	2.12	Matrix of Service Distinctions
2.6	EPL Service	2.13	Review: Carrier Ethernet Services

To date, the MEF has defined eight Carrier Ethernet services. Six of them are retail services (sold to subscribers):

1. EPL (Ethernet Private Line)
2. EP-LAN (Ethernet Private LAN)
3. EP-Tree (Ethernet Private Tree)
4. EVPL (Ethernet Virtual Private Line)
5. EVP-LAN (Ethernet Virtual Private LAN)
6. EVP-Tree (Ethernet Virtual Private Tree)

The other two are E-Access services (sold to service providers for use in supporting retail service to subscribers):

1. Access EPL (Access Ethernet Private Line)
2. Access EVPL (Access Ethernet Virtual Private Line)

This lesson only describes the six retail services. The two E-Access services are described in a later lesson.

Related Links

E-Access Services on p. 232

2.1
Fundamental Components and Reference Models

In this section:

2.1.1   Basic Reference Model
2.1.2   UNI Functionality
2.1.3   General Reference Model

The MEF defines a framework for delivering Ethernet services over carrier grade networks. The business model for this framework involves two principle stakeholders:

- **Subscriber** – The organization purchasing the Carrier Ethernet service

- **Service Provider** – The organization providing the Carrier Ethernet service

In general terms, the service itself is an Ethernet connection between two or more sites. The sites belong to the subscriber. The network connecting the sites belongs to the service provider.

2.1.1
Basic Reference Model

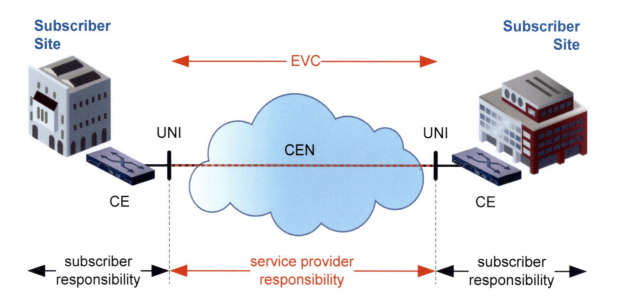

The basic reference model includes two functional components:

- **CEN (Carrier Ethernet Network)** – The service provider network used to transport Carrier Ethernet services.

- **CE (Customer Edge equipment)** – The equipment at the subscriber site that connects to the CEN. The CE can be a router or bridge/switch that is compliant with IEEE 802.1.

Note: In older MEF specifications, the term MEN (Metro Ethernet Network) is used in place of CEN. The terms CEN and MEN mean the same thing. As MEF specifications are updated, the term MEN will be replaced by CEN. Throughout these lessons, the term CEN is used, but the term MEN might still appear in some MEF-CECP exam questions.

The other elements in the preceding figure are:

- **UNI (User-to-Network Interface)** — A physical demarcation point between the subscriber domain and the service provider domain

- **EVC (Ethernet Virtual Connection)** — The logical representation of a service connection between two or more UNIs

Every MEF service has exactly one EVC, but that EVC can connect two or more UNIs. The following figure shows an EVC connecting three UNIs.

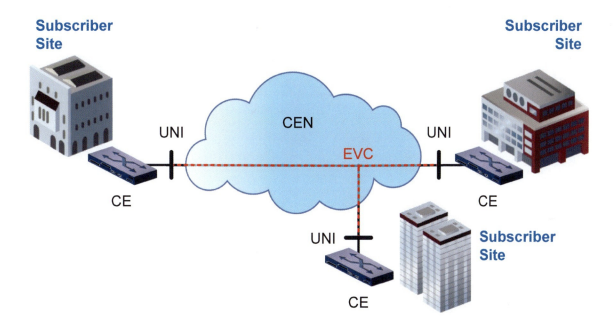

2.1.2
UNI Functionality

The UNI demarcation point is located at a specific place between the CE and the CEN, as agreed by the subscriber and service provider. Typically, it is located at a port on the CE or at a port on the CEN edge device that connects to the CE.

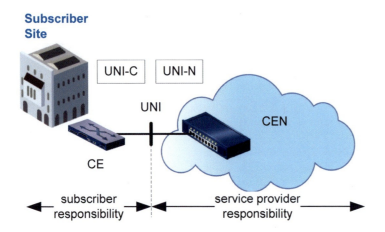

On either side of the UNI demarcation point, the MEF defines two functional elements:

- **UNI-C (UNI Client)** — Represents all of the subscriber-side functions required to connect the CE to the CEN. Individual functions in a UNI-C are entirely in the subscriber domain, but may in some cases be managed by the service provider.

- **UNI-N (UNI Network)** — Represents all of the CEN-side functions required to connect the CEN to the CE. The individual functions in a UNI-N are entirely in the service provider/network operator domain.

Together the UNI-C and UNI-N support a IEEE 802.3 Ethernet PHY/MAC interface, plus additional data, management, and control plane functions defined by the MEF. Details of UNI-C and UNI-N functionality are covered in a later lesson.

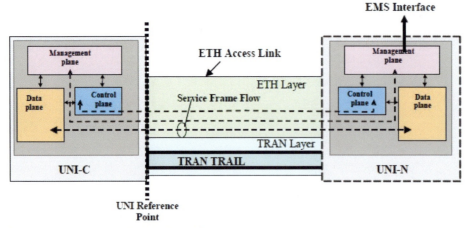

Reproduced with permission of the Metro Ethernet Forum

Related Links

UNI Requirements on p. 168

2.1.3 General Reference Model

MEF 26.1 extends the basic reference model to define MEF services across multiple networks, with each CEN independently owned and operated.

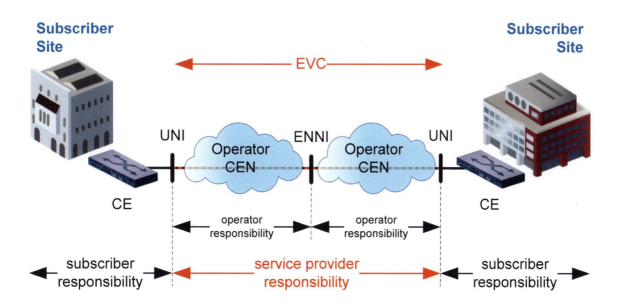

In this model, the independent networks are called **Operator CENs** (not CENs) and an interface between two Operator CENs is called an **ENNI (External Network-to-Network Interface)**.

Note: *MEF 26.1, uses the term Operator MEN (not Operator CEN). As previously noted, older MEF specifications us the term MEN in place of CEN. The terms CEN and MEN mean the same thing.*

This model is covered in detail later in a later lesson. For now, simply recognize that the Carrier Ethernet service is unchanged from the subscriber's perspective:

- There is still only one Carrier Ethernet service provider responsible for the service as a whole.

- The Carrier Ethernet service is still implemented with exactly one EVC connecting two or more UNIs.

- The basic reference model is sufficient to define the service from the subscriber's perspective.

- The general reference model adds details of implementation that are only important to the service provider and subcontracting operators.

Related Links

Extending MEF Services over Multiple Operator CENs on p. 177

2.2 Service Multiplexing

A UNI, in general, can support more than one EVC.

The MEF defines **service multiplexing** as the association of multiple EVCs to a UNI.

In the following figure, services are multiplexed on two of the three UNIs.

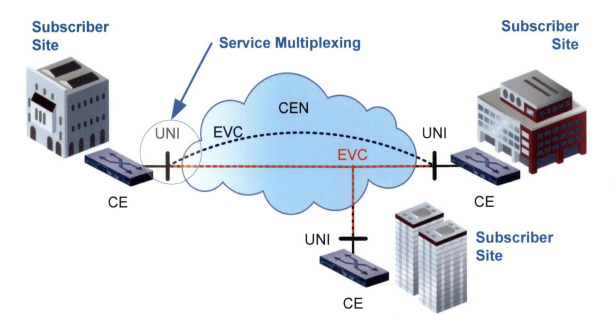

Notice that service multiplexing is a property of a UNI and is not a property of the Carrier Ethernet service or EVC.

The key benefit of service multiplexing is that it allows services to share UNIs, saving ports (physical connections) on subscriber and service provider edge equipment.

Related Links
Service Multiplexing and Bundling Service Attributes on p. 70

2.3 Service Frames

The MEF defines a **service frame** as an Ethernet frame[5] transmitted across the UNI (from the CE toward the CEN, or from the CEN toward the CE). Generally, all service frames are either untagged or include a single customer VLAN tag (C-Tag) in the Ethernet header as shown in the following figure.[6]

MEF standards recognize two types of C-Tagged service frames:

- **VLAN-Tagged Service Frame**: C-Tagged service frame with VID≠0

- **Prority-Tagged Service Frame**: C-Tagged service frame with VID=0. Priority-tagged service frames are not treated like other C-Tagged service frames. They are treated like untagged service frames with extra information (PCP bits) that declares quality of service (QoS) treatment they should receive.

Note: The next lesson explains Ethernet frames and service frames in detail.

Related Links

Ethernet Frames and Service Frames on p. 44

---

[5] Sometimes people use the term **Ethernet packet** in place of **Ethernet frame**. The term **Ethernet frame** is preferred because it complies with terminology defined in the TCP/IP networking reference model: Layer 2 protocol data unit (PDUs) are called **frames**, and Layer 3 PDUs are called **packets**. Because Ethernet PDUs are at Layer 2, they are more properly called frames.

[6] MEF standards were recently updated to recognized all IEEE 802.1Q (2011) Ethernet frames as potential service frames (including S-Tagged and I-Tagged frames which are atypical). The next lesson, devoted to Ethernet frames and service frames, explains how MEF standards accommodate unusual frame formats without disrupting established service definitions (which recognize only untagged and C-Tagged service frames).

2.4
Assigning Service Frames to EVCs

In this section:

2.4.1   CE-VLAN ID
2.4.2   Bundling
2.4.3   Bundling versus Service Multiplexing

Service frames are assigned to EVCs in two basic ways. If the service is port-based, all service frames at each UNI are assigned to a single EVC. If the service is VLAN-based, service frames at each UNI are assigned to EVCs based on CE-VLAN ID. At any UNI, a service frame cannot be assigned to more than one EVC.

2.4.1
CE-VLAN ID

In MEF terminology:

- **CE-VLAN tag** – Refers to the IEEE 801.1Q customer tag in the Ethernet header of a service frame. This tag is also commonly called the C-VLAN tag or C-Tag.

- **CE-VLAN ID** – Generally (<u>but not always</u>) refers to the VLAN identifier (VID) in the CE-VLAN tag.

> MEF 10.3 defines CE-VLAN ID as follows:
>
> **CE-VLAN ID** – The identifier derivable from the content of a service frame that allows the service frame to be associated with an EVC at the UNI.
>
> *Note:* *CE-VLAN ID is defined in this way to accommodate untagged and priority-tagged service frames.*

Every CE-VLAN ID is a value in the range 1...4094. If a service frame is C-Tagged with VID≠0, its CE-VLAN ID is that VID value (the C-Tag VID value). If a service frame is untagged or priority tagged, its CE-VLAN ID can be any value in the range 1...4094, as specified in the service definition (as will be explained in a later lesson).

For now, just think of CE-VLAN ID as the VLAN identifier (VID) in the CE-VLAN tag.

CE-VLAN ID is used to assign service frames to services (to EVCs) as follows:

1. The subscriber encodes the CE-VLAN ID in the service frame (for example, by setting C-Tag VID value) before sending it across the UNI to the service provider.

2. When the service frame arrives at the CEN, the service provider associates it to an EVC based on CE-VLAN ID.

Of course, this requires coordination between the subscriber and the service provider because they must have an agreement about which CE-VLAN IDs are mapped to each EVC (per UNI).

2.4.2 Bundling

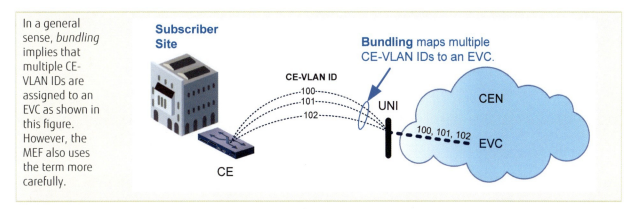

In a general sense, *bundling* implies that multiple CE-VLAN IDs are assigned to an EVC as shown in this figure. However, the MEF also uses the term more carefully.

In MEF service definitions, **bundling** describes a UNI's ability to support *bundling* (the assignment of multiple CE-VLAN IDs to an EVC). MEF service definitions also make a distinction between **bundling** and **all-to-one bundling** as follows:

- **Bundling** — The association of multiple CE-VLAN IDs to an EVC at a UNI
- **All-to-one Bundling** — The association of all service frames to one EVC at the UNI

In MEF service definitions, **bundling** and **all-to-one bundling** are mutually exclusive. A UNI can support bundling or all-to-one bundling, not both.

2.4.3 Bundling versus Service Multiplexing

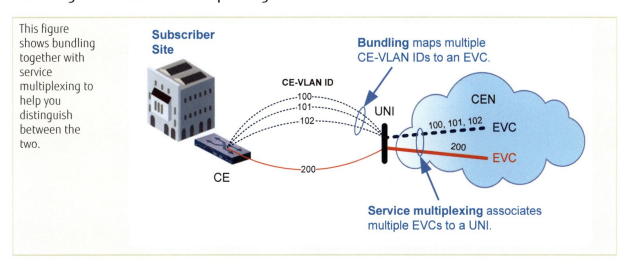

This figure shows bundling together with service multiplexing to help you distinguish between the two.

Test your understanding: *Can a UNI support service multiplexing together with all-to-one bundling? Explain why or why not.* [7]

---

[7] **Answer:** *No. All-to-one bundling implies that all service frames map to one EVC. A service frame cannot map to more than one EVC.*

2.5
Taxonomy of EVC-Based Services

In this section:

2.5.1   Port-Based versus VLAN-Based Services
2.5.2   The Three Service Types

MEF 6.2 defines three Carrier Ethernet service **types**: E-Line, E-LAN, and E-Tree. Then, for each service type, the MEF defines two services: a *port-based* (or *private*) service and a *VLAN-based* (or *virtual private*) service. This results in six Carrier Ethernet services[8], as shown in the following table.

Service Type	Carrier Ethernet Service	
	Port-Based (All-to-One Bundling)	VLAN-Based (Ethernet frames mapped by VLAN ID)
E-Line (point-to-point EVC)	EPL (Ethernet Private Line)	EVPL (Ethernet Virtual Private Line)
E-LAN (multipoint-to-multipoint EVC)	EP-LAN (Ethernet Private LAN)	EVP-LAN (Ethernet Virtual Private LAN)
E-Tree (rooted-multipoint EVC)	EP-Tree (Ethernet Private Tree)	EVP-Tree (Ethernet Virtual Private Tree)

2.5.1
Port-Based versus VLAN-Based Services

In a port-based (or private) service, all UNIs are configured for all-to-one bundling, and all service frames are mapped to the EVC, regardless of VLAN tag and/or CE-VLAN ID. In a VLAN-based (or virtual private) service, CE-VLAN IDs are explicitly mapped to the EVC at each UNI.

The key advantage of a port-based service is that the subscriber and the service provider do not have to coordinate VLAN IDs. The key advantage of a VLAN-based service is that VLAN-based services can share UNIs, saving ports (physical connections) on subscriber and service provider edge equipment. To permit sharing, a UNI must be configured to support service multiplexing. The EVCs that share a UNI must use different CE-VLAN IDs.

Test your understanding: With respect to <u>VLAN-based service</u>, classify each of the following UNI attributes as either mandatory, supported, or not supported: (1) Bundling, (2) All-to-one bundling, and (3) Service multiplexing.[9]

Test your understanding: With respect to <u>port-based service</u>, classify each of the following UNI attributes as either mandatory, supported, or not supported: (1) Bundling, (2) All-to-one bundling, and (3) Service multiplexing.[10]

---

8   In addition to these six services, the MEF has defined two E-Access services (the **Access EPL** and the **Access EVPL**), which are described in a later lesson.
9   **Answers:** (1) supported, (2) not supported, (3) supported.
10 **Answers:** (1) not supported, (2) mandatory, (3) not supported

2.5.2
The Three Service Types

E-Line Service Type

The E-Line service type is for creating a point-to-point service between two UNIs.

Example applications: private line, virtual private line, Internet access

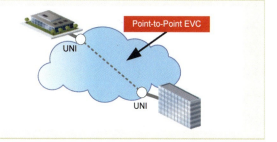

E-LAN Service Type

The E-LAN service type is for creating a multipoint-to-multipoint service that allows any UNI to forward Ethernet frames to any other UNI.

Example applications: Layer 2 virtual private network (VPN), Layer 3 VPN, multicast network

This service type typically forwards frames based on MAC address learning.

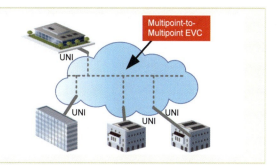

E-Tree Service Type

The E-Tree service type is for creating a rooted-multipoint service that prevents some UNIs from forwarding Ethernet frames to other UNIs. Each UNI is declared to have one of two roles: **Root** or **Leaf**. Roots are allowed to forward Ethernet frames to leaves and roots. A leaf can only forward frames to roots (no leaf-to-leaf forwarding).

Example applications: Internet access, broadcast network, mobile backhaul, residential broadband backhaul

Like the E-LAN service type, this service type typically forwards frames based on MAC address learning. However, unlike the E-LAN service type, frame forwarding is also subject to leaf/root constraints.

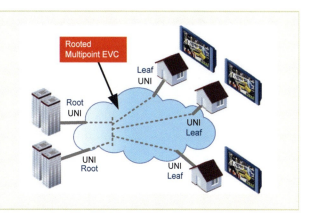

Test your understanding: Why should a type E-Tree service have at least one UNI with role Root? [11]

Test your understanding: Why should a type E-Tree service have at least <u>two</u> UNIs with role Leaf? [12]

---

11 **Answer:** Because no communication is possible if all UNIs have role Leaf.
12 **Answer:** Because otherwise it would behave like a type E-LAN service.

2.6 EPL Service

An Ethernet Private Line (EPL) is a port-based service of type E-Line. It transports all service frames bidirectionally between two UNIs.

In the following figure, the enterprise on the left uses two EPLs: one to connect to a storage service provider and another to connect to the Internet. The two EPLs share no UNIs.

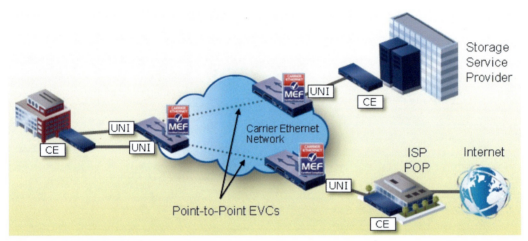

Reproduced with permission of the Metro Ethernet Forum

Distinctions of EPL service include:

- EPL service is the most popular Carrier Ethernet service due to its simplicity.
- EPL service is a replacement for TDM private line service.
- EPL service requires a dedicated physical connection (UNI) to support each EVC end point.
- EPL service requires no VLAN coordination between the subscriber and the service provider.
- EPL service provides a high degree of transparency — It preserves CE-VLAN tags, including VLAN IDs, DEI bit, and PCP bits and it supports tunneling of Layer 2 Control Protocol (L2CP) frames, including Bridge Protocol Data Unit (BPDU) frames to support Spanning Tree Protocol (STP).

Note: Tunneling is the process by which an L2CP service frame is passed through the service provider network without being processed and is delivered unchanged to the proper UNI(s). In other words, a "tunneled" L2CP service frame is treated like a data service frame.

Related Links

Support for TDM Private Lines on p. 352

2.7
EVPL Service

An Ethernet Virtual Private Line (EVPL) is a VLAN-based service of type E-Line.

Two EVPLs are shown in the following figure. Both EVPLs connect to the site on the left through the same UNI.

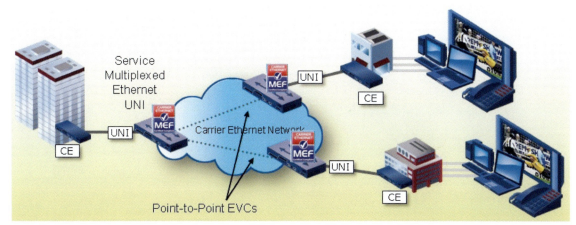

Reproduced with permission of the Metro Ethernet Forum

Distinctions of EVPL service include:

- EVPL service is a replacement for TDM private line service and for Frame Relay or ATM Layer 2 VPN services and also offers higher bandwidth capability.
- EVPL service allows service multiplexing at UNIs (multiple services can be delivered over a single physical connection).
- EVPL service requires VLAN coordination between the subscriber and the service provider.
- EVPL service provides less transparency compared to EPL service because tunneling of certain L2CP service frames, such as Bridge Protocol Data Unit (BPDU) frames to support Spanning Tree Protocol (STP), is not supported.

Note: Tunneling is the process by which an L2CP service frame is passed through the service provider network without being processed and is delivered unchanged to the proper UNI(s). In other words, a "tunneled" L2CP service frame is treated like a data service frame.

Related Links

Support for TDM Private Lines on p. 352
Frame Relay Replacement by EVPLs on p. 355

2.8 EP-LAN Service

An Ethernet Private LAN (EP-LAN) service is a port-based service of type E-LAN. It allows any UNI to forward Ethernet frames to any other UNI.

In the following figure, the EP-LAN service connects three separate locations into one EVC.

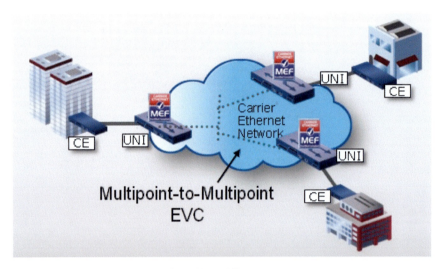

Reproduced with permission of the Metro Ethernet Forum

Distinctions of EP-LAN service include:

- Ethernet frames are typically forwarded based on MAC address learning.
- EP-LAN service requires a dedicated physical connection (UNI) to support each EVC end point.
- EP-LAN service requires no VLAN coordination between the subscriber and the service provider.
- EP-LAN service provides a high degree of transparency:
    - Preserves CE-VLAN tags, including VLAN IDs, DEI bit, and PCP bits
    - Supports tunneling of Layer 2 Control Protocol (L2CP) frames, including Bridge Protocol Data Unit (BPDU) frames to support Spanning Tree Protocol (STP)

Note: *Tunneling is the process by which an L2CP service frame is passed through the service provider network without being processed and is delivered unchanged to the proper UNI(s). In other words, a "tunneled" L2CP service frame is treated like a data service frame.*

2.9
EVP-LAN Service

An Ethernet Virtual Private LAN (EVP-LAN) service is a VLAN-based service of type E-LAN.

In the following figure, an EVP-LAN service shares a UNI with a EVPL service. The same UNI supports both Internet access and access to the corporate LAN.

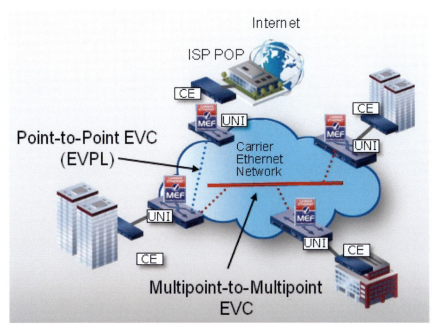

Reproduced with permission of the Metro Ethernet Forum

Distinctions of EVP-LAN service include:

- Ethernet frames are typically forwarded based on MAC address learning.
- EVP-LAN service allows service multiplexing at UNIs (multiple services can be delivered over a single physical connection).
- EVP-LAN service requires VLAN coordination between the subscriber and the service provider.
- EVP-LAN service provides less transparency compared to EP-LAN service because tunneling of certain L2CP service frames, such as Bridge Protocol Data Unit (BPDU) frames to support Spanning Tree Protocol (STP), is not supported.

2.10
EP-Tree Service

An Ethernet Private Tree (EP-Tree) service is a port-based service of type E-Tree.

Recall: *An E-Tree service allows roots to forward Ethernet frames to roots or leaves, but leaves can only forward Ethernet frames to roots.*

In the following figure, the EP-Tree service connects three franchise sites to a common corporate LAN.

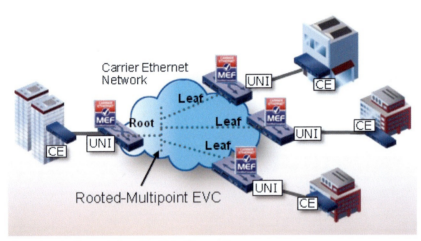

Reproduced with permission of the Metro Ethernet Forum

Distinctions of EP-Tree service include:

- Ethernet frames are typically forwarded based on MAC address learning.
- EP-Tree service enforces security, preventing interaction between leaves.
- EP-Tree service requires a dedicated physical connection (UNI) to support each EVC end point.
- EP-Tree service requires no VLAN coordination between the subscriber and the service provider.
- EP-Tree service provides a high degree of transparency:
    - Preserves CE-VLAN tags, including VLAN IDs, DEI bit, and PCP bits
    - Supports tunneling of Layer 2 Control Protocol (L2CP) frames, including Bridge Protocol Data Unit (BPDU) frames to support Spanning Tree Protocol (STP)

Note: *Tunneling is the process by which an L2CP service frame is passed through the service provider network without being processed and is delivered unchanged to the proper UNI(s). In other words, a "tunneled" L2CP service frame is treated like a data service frame.*

2.11
EVP-Tree Service

An Ethernet Virtual Private Tree (EVP-Tree) service is a VLAN-based service of type E-Tree.

Recall: *An E-Tree service allows roots to forward Ethernet frames to roots or leaves, but leaves can only forward Ethernet frames to roots.*

In the following figure, the EP-Tree service connects a distribution site, at the top, to three leaf sites. Each leaf of the EVP-Tree service shares a UNI with an EVP-LAN service. At each leaf, the same UNI supports the EVP-Tree service and the EVP-LAN service.[13]

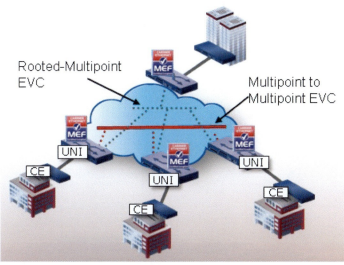

Reproduced with permission of the Metro Ethernet Forum

Distinctions of EVP-Tree service include:

- Ethernet frames are typically forwarded based on MAC address learning.
- EVP-Tree service enforces security, preventing interaction between leaves.
- EVP-Tree service allows service multiplexing at UNIs (multiple services can be delivered over a single physical connection).
- EVP-Tree service requires VLAN coordination between the subscriber and the service provider.
- EVP-Tree service provides less transparency compared to EP-Tree service because tunneling of certain L2CP service frames, such as Bridge Protocol Data Unit (BPDU) frames to support Spanning Tree Protocol (STP), is not supported.

---

13 This example (taken from an MEF power point presentation) is not a typical application because the E-Tree service prevents leaf UNIs from forwarding frames to each other, but the E-LAN service exactly undermines that property. Together the two services offer the same functionality as one type E-LAN service connecting all four sites.

2.12
Matrix of Service Distinctions

The following table lists key distinctions and indicates the Carrier Ethernet services to which each applies.

Distinction	Service					
	Type E-Line		Type E-LAN		Type E-Tree	
	EPL	EVPL	EP-LAN	EVP-LAN	EP-Tree	EVP-Tree
Is the most popular Carrier Ethernet service due to its simplicity	×					
Is a replacement for TDM private line service	×	×				
Is a replacement for Frame Relay or ATM Layer 2 VPN services and offers higher bandwidth capability		×				
Requires a dedicated physical connection (UNI) to support each EVC end point	×		×		×	
Allows service multiplexing at UNIs (multiple services can be delivered over a single physical connection)		×		×		×
Requires VLAN coordination between the subscriber and the service provider		×		×		×
Requires UNIs configured with All-to-One-Bundling	×		×		×	
Allows UNIs configured with Bundling		×		×		×
Provides a high degree of transparency	×		×		×	
Supports tunneling of Bridge Protocol Data Unit (BPDU) frames to support Spanning Tree Protocol (STP)	×		×		×	
Prevents interaction between leaf UNIs					×	×
Typically forwards Ethernet frames based on MAC address learning.			×	×	×	×

2.13
Review: Carrier Ethernet Services

1. The interface between an Operator CEN and the subscriber is called a(an):

   a. ENNI
   b. OVC
   c. UNI
   d. EVC
   e. CE

2. Service multiplexing allows:

   a. Multiple services on one EVC
   b. Multiple EVCs on one UNI
   c. Multiple UNIs on one EVC
   d. Bundling
   e. Multiple CE-VLAN IDs to be mapped to an EVC

3. What is the MEF definition of a UNI?

   a. The logical representation of a service connection between two or more EVCs
   b. The physical demarcation point between the responsibility of the Service Provider and the responsibility of the Subscriber
   c. All functions required to connect the CE to the CEN
   d. The interface between two Operator CENs

4. Equipment on the subscriber side of the UNI that connects to the CEN is called the:

   a. Carrier edge
   b. Subscriber edge
   c. User network interface
   d. Consumer edge
   e. Customer edge
   f. Network edge

5. Which two Carrier Ethernet service combinations can be offered simultaneously at a given UNI?

   a. EP-LAN and EVPL
   b. EVP-Tree and EPL
   c. EVPL and EVP-LAN
   d. EPL and EP-Tree

6. A UNI is configured to support all-to-one bundling. Which statement is NOT true?

   a. Service multiplexing is not supported at the UNI.
   b. Any number of EVCs can be bundled to this UNI.
   c. Bundling is not supported at the UNI.
   d. At this UNI, all CE-VLAN IDs map to the same EVC.

7. Which three service types are defined in MEF 6.2? (Choose three.)

    a. Ethernet Virtual Connection (EVC)
    b. Ethernet Line (E-Line)
    c. Ethernet Tree (E-Tree)
    d. Ethernet Access (E-Access)
    e. Ethernet LAN (E-LAN)
    f. TDM Line (T-Line)

8. An enterprise needs to connect three branch offices with its two payroll processing data centers. The two data centers require interconnectivity for data mirroring (protection). The service should not allow the branch offices to communicate directly with each other. Which two of the following service arrangements supports this application? (Choose two.)

    a. An EP-Tree service with the payroll data center UNIs designated as leaves and the branch office UNIs designated as roots
    b. An EP-Tree service with payroll data center UNIs designated as roots and branch office UNIs designated as leaves
    c. One EP-LAN service connecting all five sites
    d. One EVPL service from each branch office to each payroll data center (six EVPLs in all), plus an EPL between the two payroll centers

9. A UNI is configured without bundling or all-to-one bundling and is also configured to support service multiplexing. How many EVCs can terminate at this UNI?

    a. 0
    b. 0 or 1
    c. Up to 64
    d. Up to 4094

10. Which kind of UNI-to-UNI connectivity is used for the Ethernet Private Line (EPL) service?

    a. Ethernet Private Circuit
    b. Point-to-point Ethernet Private Connection
    c. Point-to-point Ethernet Virtual Connection
    d. Point-to-point Ethernet Virtual Circuit

11. A customer with three locations requests a Carrier Ethernet service that provides the most transparent connectivity for all PDU types between sites. Which service is most suitable?

    a. A single Ethernet Private LAN (EP-LAN)
    b. A single Ethernet Virtual Private LAN (EVP-LAN)
    c. A single Ethernet Private Tree (EP-Tree)
    d. A single Ethernet Virtual Private Tree (EVP-Tree)

Carrier Ethernet Services
Review: Carrier Ethernet Services

12. McBary's, a business enterprise with numerous independently-owned restaurant franchises, wants to connect each franchise to the corporate data center to obtain daily sales information. Which two of the following service arrangements do you recommend for this application? (Choose two.)

    a. A single Ethernet Virtual Private LAN (EVP-LAN) service
    b. One Ethernet Virtual Private Line (EVPL) service between each franchise and the corporate data center
    c. A single Ethernet Private Tree (EP-Tree) service with the corporate data center UNI designated as the root and franchise UNIs designated as leaves
    d. One Ethernet Private Line (EPL) service between each franchise and the corporate data center

13. Which two statements about a VLAN-based (virtual private) service are true? (Choose two.)

    a. All UNIs must be configured to support service multiplexing.
    b. All UNIs must be configured to support bundling.
    c. All UNIs must be configured to support all-to-one bundling.
    d. All UNIs may be configured to support service multiplexing.
    e. All UNIs may be configured to support bundling.
    f. All UNIs may be configured to support all-to-one bundling.

14. A UNI is configured without bundling or all-to-one bundling and is also configured to support service multiplexing. What is the maximum number of CE-VLAN IDs that can be mapped to a given EVC at the UNI?

    a. 0
    b. 1
    c. 256
    d. 4094
    e. 4096

15. Which Carrier Ethernet services typically forward Ethernet frames based on MAC address learning? (Choose all answers that are correct.)

    a. EPL
    b. EVPL
    c. EP-LAN
    d. EVP-LAN
    e. EP-Tree
    f. EVP-Tree

16. The MEF refers to an Ethernet frame transmitted across a UNI towards the subscriber as a (an):

    a. L2CP frame
    b. Subscriber frame
    c. Service frame
    d. UNI frame

Related Links

Answers: Carrier Ethernet Services on p. 393

MEF-CECP Study Guide
3rd Edition - October 2015
Updated for MEF-CECP Certification Blueprint C

3
Ethernet Frames and Service Frames

In this chapter:

3.1 IEEE Ethernet Frames
3.2 MEF Service Frames
3.3 Review: Ethernet Frames and Service Frames

Ethernet computer networking technology was first standardized by the IEEE in 1983 and over time has been refined and expanded through evolving IEEE standards, most notably IEEE 802.3 (defining Layer 1 Ethernet technology) and IEEE 802.1 (defining Layer 2 Ethernet technology).[14]

MEF services are purposefully defined to be independent of networking technology, allowing service providers to implement services across the CEN using any viable technology, including Ethernet technology. However, MEF service definitions require that links between CEs and the CEN be IEEE 802.3-compliant.

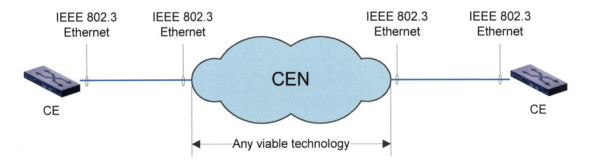

Ethernet frame formats are key to understanding Carrier Ethernet service definitions. This lesson explains Ethernet frame formats from two perspectives: first from the IEEE perspective and then from the MEF perspective.

Related Links

UNI Requirements on p. 168

---

14 Ethernet is both a Layer 1 technology and a Layer 2 technology. It is one of the few networking technologies to be defined over two layers of the OSI reference model.

3.1 IEEE Ethernet Frames

In this section:

3.1.1 Layer 1 versus Layer 2 Ethernet Frames
3.1.2 Layer 2 Ethernet Frames
3.1.3 C-Tagged Ethernet Frames
3.1.4 S-Tagged Ethernet Frames
3.1.5 I-Tagged Ethernet Frames
3.1.6 Priority-Tagged Ethernet Frames

3.1.1 Layer 1 versus Layer 2 Ethernet Frames

In most contexts the term *Ethernet frame* refers to the Layer 2 Ethernet PDU, which starts with the Destination MAC address and ends with the Frame Check Sequence (FCS).

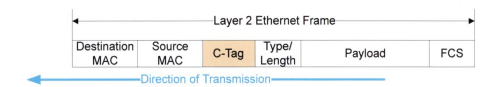

However, in the Layer 1 bit stream this PDU is preceded by two fields sent in the following order:

Interframe GAP — At least 12 bytes of silence (a sequence of at least 96 bits that are either all 1s or all 0s)

Preamble + Start — An 8-byte field containing a *Preamble* (7 bytes, each containing the bit pattern 10101010) followed by a *Start of Frame Delimiter* (1 byte containing byte sequence 10101011, which denotes the start of the frame itself)

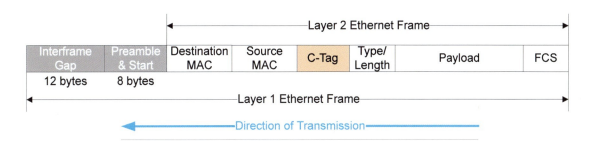

The resulting Layer 1 PDU is sometimes called the Layer 1 Ethernet frame.

Related Links

About Line Rate and CIR on p. 143

3.1.2
Layer 2 Ethernet Frames

At Layer 2, an Ethernet frame includes a header, a trailer, and data between the header and the trailer. The header is sent first, followed by the Layer 2 data (typically a Layer 3 PDU), followed by the trailer.

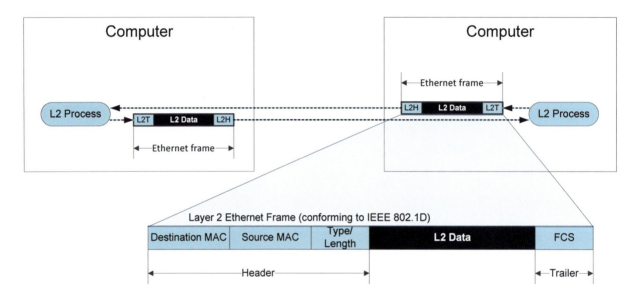

The header includes three fields, sent in the following order:

Destination MAC Address – A 6-byte field containing the address of the target destination(s) of the frame

Source MAC Address – A 6-byte field containing the address of the Ethernet end station that sent the frame

Type/Length – A 2-byte field that defines either the length of the data field or the type of protocol listed inside the frame

The trailer consists of one 4-byte field called the **frame check sequence (FCS)**, which is used for error detection.

Note: At this stage, we consider only IEEE 802.1D–compliant Ethernet frames, the baseline Ethernet frame format that is used in LANs and for MAC Bridging. Frame formats for VLAN Bridging include additional fields for VLAN tagging.

MAC Addresses

Media access control addresses (MAC addresses) come from a 48-bit address space containing nearly 300 trillion MAC addresses. For human recognition, a MAC address is represented by 6 groups of 2 hexadecimal digits:

MAC address = XX:XX:XX:XX:XX:XX

   Where each X represents a hexadecimal digit from the set {0, 1, 2, 3, 4, 5, 6, 7, 8, 9, A, B, C, D, E, F}

Example: 00:0A:95:9D:68:16

Every Ethernet frame contains two MAC addresses: a **destination MAC address** (the target) and a **source MAC address** (the sender).

Layer 2 Ethernet Frame (conforming to IEEE 802.1D)

| Destination MAC | Source MAC | Type/Length | L2 Data | FCS |

← Header → ← Trailer →

The **destination MAC address** does not always target an individual Ethernet interface. If it does, it is called a **unicast** MAC address. Otherwise, it is a **multicast** or **broadcast** MAC address.

Unicast, Multicast, and Broadcast MAC Addresses

Unicast address — Targets a single Ethernet end station

   If the second hexadecimal digit is even (0, 2, 4, 6, 8, A, C, or E), the address is a unicast MAC address.

Example: 0<u>0</u>:0A:95:9D:68:16

Multicast address — Targets a group of interfaces that are provisioned to accept the address

   If the second hexadecimal digit is odd (1, 3, 5, 7, 9, B, D, or F), the address is a multicast or broadcast MAC address.

Example: 0<u>1</u>:0A:95:9D:68:16

Broadcast address — Targets all Ethernet interfaces in the network

Example: FF:FF:FF:FF:FF:FF

The **source MAC address** always corresponds to a unique sender (the Ethernet end station that originated the frame) and consequently conforms to the unicast address space.

3.1.3
C-Tagged Ethernet Frames

Over the years, the IEEE VLAN bridging standard (IEEE 802.1Q) has evolved to include more and more elaborate forms of bridging and Ethernet frame tagging. IEEE 802.1Q (1998) defined the original form of VLAN bridging (now known as customer VLAN bridging) using one VLAN tag that is now known as the customer VLAN tag, or C-Tag. Requirements and terminology have evolved over time with updates to the IEEE 802.1Q standard. Per IEEE 802.1Q (2011), C-Tags are now defined as follows.

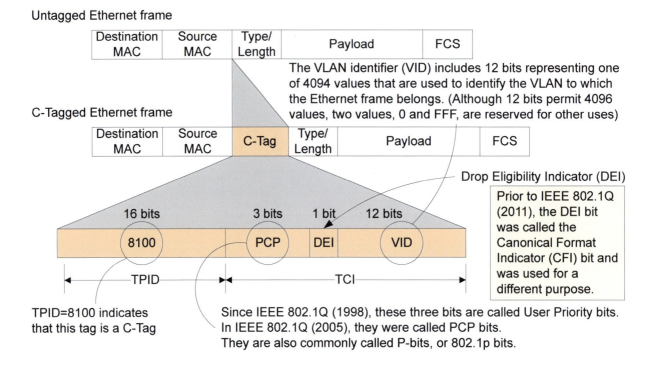

In this figure:

Tag protocol identifier (TPID) – 16 bits with hexadecimal value 8100, which identifies the tag as a C-Tag

Tag control information (TCI) consisting of:

- Priority code point (PCP) – 3 bits representing one of eight priority levels (0–7)

- Drop Eligibility Indicator (DEI) – 1 bit indicating drop eligibility. Normally DEI=0 signifies that the frame is drop-eligible and DEI=1 signifies that the frame is drop eligible.

- VLAN identifier (VID) – 12 bits representing one of 4094 values; identifies the customer VLAN to which the frame belongs

About IEEE 802.1Q Ethernet Frame Terminology: Prior to release of IEEE 802.1Q-2011, the frames depicted in the previous figure were commonly called *IEEE 802.1Q Ethernet frames* because they conform to IEEE 802.1Q-2005. However, with the release of IEEE 802.1Q-2011, several more frame formats were incorporated into the IEEE 802.1Q standard. So, this usage of the term *IEEE 802.1Q Ethernet frame* is no longer valid. In these lessons, we avoid the term *IEEE 802.1Q Ethernet frame*.

About DEI bit in C-Tag: Prior to IEEE 802.1Q-2011, the bit labelled DEI (drop eligibility indicator) in the previous figure was defined differently. It was known as the CFI (canonical format indicator) bit and was used for a different purpose that is now obsolete.

Size of Untagged and C-Tagged Ethernet Frames

An untagged Ethernet frame has 18 more bytes than its payload (for example, IP packet).

Untagged Ethernet frame

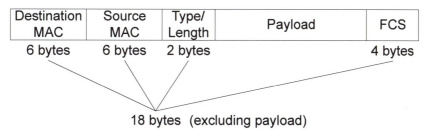

A C-Tagged Ethernet frame requires another 4 bytes (for the C-Tag).

C-Tagged Ethernet frame

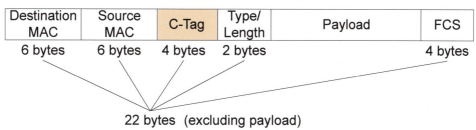

Note: A byte consists of 8 bits.

The payload for a standard IEEE 802.3 Ethernet frame is limited to 1500 bytes, which limits untagged Ethernet frames to 1518 bytes and C-Tagged Ethernet frames to 1522 bytes.

Note: Some implementations of Ethernet allow larger Ethernet frames known as **jumbo frames**.

3.1.4
S-Tagged Ethernet Frames

In 2006, another type of VLAN tag, the service VLAN tag (S-Tag), was introduced to support provider bridging in the IEEE 802.1Q standard.[15] Per IEEE 802.1Q (2011), S-Tags are defined as follows.

Double-Tagged Ethernet frame

| Destination MAC | Source MAC | S-Tag | C-Tag | Type/Length | Payload | FCS |

S-Tag expanded:

88A8	PCP	DEI	VID
16 bits	3 bits	1 bit	12 bits
←—— TPID ——→	←——————— TCI ———————→

TPID=88a8 indicates that this tag is an S-Tag

In IEEE 802.1Q (1998), these three bits are called User Priority bits.
In IEEE 802.1Q (2005), they are called PCP bits.
They are also commonly called P-bits, or 802.1p bits.

The drop eligibility indicator (DEI) bit. Normally DEI=0 signifies that the Ethernet frame is not drop-eligible and DEI=1 signifies that the Ethernet frame is drop-eligible.

The VLAN identifier (VID) includes 12 bits representing one of 4094 values that are used to identify the service VLAN to which the Ethernet frame belongs.

Tag protocol identifier (TPID) — 16 bits with hexadecimal value 8a88, which identifies the tag as an S-Tag

Tag control information (TCI) consisting of:

- **Priority code point (PCP)** — 3 bits representing one of eight priority levels (0–7)
- **Drop Eligibility Indicator (DEI)** — 1 bit indicating drop eligibility. Normally DEI=0 signifies that the frame is drop-eligible and DEI=1 signifies that the frame is drop eligible.
- **VLAN identifier (VID)** — 12 bits representing one of 4094 values; identifies the service VLAN to which the frame belongs

---

Note: *S-Tags are used in Carrier Ethernet to coordinate service handoff at ENNIs (at interfaces between Operator CENs in the general reference model). S-Tags are not generally used at UNIs.*

Related Links

General Reference Model on p. 27

---

15 The S-Tag was introduced in amendment IEEE 802.1ad to IEEE 802.1Q (2005), but has since been rolled into IEEE 802.1Q (2011).

3.1.5
I-Tagged Ethernet Frames

IEEE 802.1Q (2011) defines yet another type of Ethernet tag: the backbone service instance tag (I-Tag), used to support backbone provider bridging. I-Tags are identified by TPID=88e7.

I-Tag details are not included in this lesson because Carrier Ethernet services do not recognize them.

Note: *Carrier Ethernet services can, however, receive and deliver I-Tagged Ethernet frames (by treating them as untagged Ethernet frames as described later in this lesson).*

Related Links

Service Frame Tag Recognition on p. 53

3.1.6
Priority-Tagged Ethernet Frames

A **priority-tagged frame** is a C-Tagged Ethernet frame with customer VLAN identifier (VID) set to 0 (null).[16]

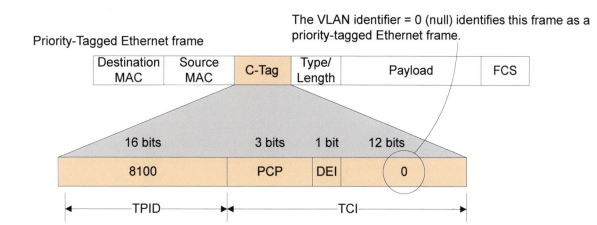

Priority-tagged service frames are not treated like other C-Tagged service frames. They are treated like untagged service frames with extra information (PCP bits) that declares quality of service (QoS) treatment they should receive.

Note: *Priority-tagged service frames are rarely used in practice.*

---

[16] Per IEEE 802.1Q (2011), an S-Tagged Ethernet frame with service VLAN identifier (VID) set to 0 (null) is also a priority-tagged frame. However, S-Tagged priority frames are of little or no interest to Carrier Ethernet and are not considered going forward in these lessons.

3.2 MEF Service Frames

In this section:

3.2.1 Ingress and Egress Service Frames
3.2.2 Exclusion of Layer 1 Components
3.2.3 Service Frame Tag Recognition
3.2.4 Data, L2CP, and SOAM Service Frames

The MEF defines a **service frame** to be the Layer 2 Ethernet frame that is exchanged between the CE and the CEN across the UNI.

3.2.1 Ingress and Egress Service Frames

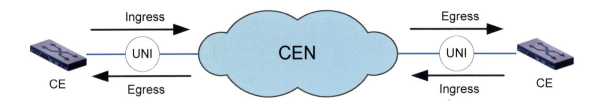

An **ingress service frame** is a service frame sent from the CE to the CEN.

An **egress ENNI frame** is a service frame sent from the CEN to the CE

3.2.2 Exclusion of Layer 1 Components

The service frame includes all fields from Destination MAC Address to FCS, including any Ethernet tags (if present), but it does not include Layer 1 components (Interframe Gap and the Preamble & Start frame delimiters).

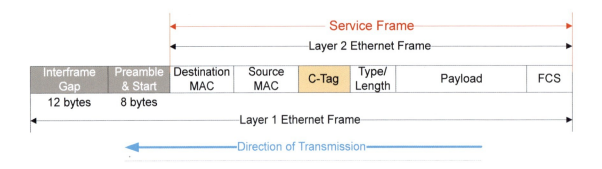

3.2.3
Service Frame Tag Recognition

Prior to MEF 10.3, service frames were required to be untagged or C-Tagged. Three formats were recognized:

- **Untagged Service Frames**: No Ethernet tag
- **VLAN Tagged Service Frames**: C-Tagged (TPID=8100) with VID≠0
- **Priority Tagged Service Frames**: C-Tagged (TPID=8100) with VID=0

Note: *These are the only formats that appear in typical applications.*

However, with MEF 10.3, all IEEE 802.3 (2012) Ethernet frame formats are acceptable (including S-Tagged and I-Tagged Ethernet frames, which are truly atypical).

MEF 10.3 accommodates S-Tagged and I-Tagged frame formats, without disrupting established service definitions, through the following system of service frame definitions:[17]

> **VLAN Tagged Service Frame** — If the field following the service frame's Source Address field encodes TPID=8100 (indicating a C-Tag) and if the corresponding VID≠0, the service frame is a VLAN Tagged Service Frame.
>
> **Priority Tagged Service Frame** — If the field following the service frame's Source Address field encodes TPID=8100 (indicating a C-Tag) and if the corresponding VID≠0, the service frame is a Priority-Tagged Service Frame.
>
> **S-Tagged Service Frame** — If the field following the service frame's Source Address field encodes TPID=88a8 (indicating an S-Tag), the service frame is an S-Tagged Service Frame.
>
> **Untagged Service Frame** — If the two bytes following the service frame's Source Address field do not contain the value 8100 or the value 88a8, the service frame is an Untagged Service Frame.

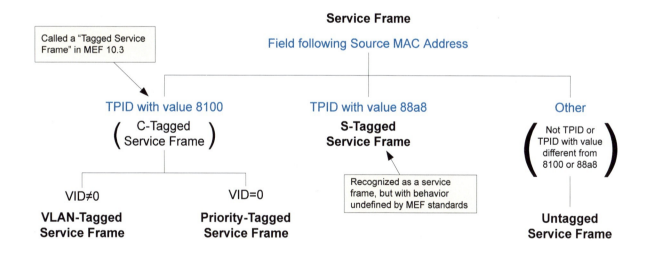

---

17 Refer to page 14 of MEF 10.3.

With these definitions:

- The I-Tagged Ethernet frame (TPID=88e7) is recognized as an untagged service frame, which means it will be treated like a "truly" untagged frame by the service.

- The S-Tagged Ethernet frame (TPID=88a8) is recognized as a service frame (even as a new and distinct type of service frame). However, the S-Tagged frame is only recognized to exclude it from further consideration:

> Excerpt from MEF 10.3
>
> ...the behavior for S-Tagged Service Frames is beyond the scope of this document and the term "S-Tagged Service Frame" does not appear in the remainder of this document. Consequently, the behavior experienced by S-Tagged Service Frames can vary from Service Provider to Service Provider. A Subscriber who wants to use S-Tagged Service Frames is urged to check with his or her Service Provider to determine the behavior for such Service Frames.

Overall, MEF 10.3 has broadened the definition of service frame, but the impact is minimal. There are still only three service frame tag formats of interest:

- **Untagged Service Frames**: not C-Tagged (TPID=8100) AND not S-Tagged (TPID=88a8)

- **VLAN Tagged Service Frames**: C-Tagged (TPID=8100) with VID≠0

- **Priority Tagged Service Frames**: C-Tagged (TPID=8100) with VID=0

The definitions of **VLAN Tagged Service Frame** and **Priority Tagged Service Frame** remain unchanged.

The definition of **Untagged Service Frame** has changed to include certain tagged frames (such as I-Tagged frames), which are not used in typical applications, but are now supported (as untagged frames) if they are used.

The term **Tagged Service Frame** refers to any C-Tagged service frame (any VLAN tagged service frame or any priority tagged service frame).

Test your understanding: Using MEF 10.3 service frame definitions, which two of the following statements are false?[18]

1. A service frame tagged with PVID=88a8 and VID=0 is an S-tagged service frame.
2. A service frame tagged with PVID=8100 and VID=0 is an untagged service frame.
3. A service frame tagged with PVID=8100 and VID=0 is a priority-tagged service frame.
4. A service frame tagged with PVID=88e7 and VID=0 is an untagged service frame.
5. A service frame tagged with PVID=88a8 and VID=0 is priority-tagged service frame.

---

18 **Answer:** Statements **2** and **5** are false.

3.2.4
Data, L2CP, and SOAM Service Frames

MEF 10.3 also classifies service frames according to purpose (independent of tagging):

Data service frame – Supports end user applications

L2CP service frame – Supports one of the many Layer 2 Control Protocols, such as STP/RSTP or Link OAM, which are used for network control purposes

SOAM service frame – Supports Service OAM (Operations, administration, and maintenance) which is used to manage the Carrier Ethernet service (connectivity fault management and performance management)

Per MEF 10.3, service frame type is determined by the following logic:

1. If the service frame's destination MAC address is listed in the following table, it is an **L2CP Service Frame**.

Table 3 in MEF 10.3 or Table 2 in MEF 45	
Destination MAC Addresses	**Description**
01-80-C2-00-00-00 through 01-80-C2-00-00-0F	Bridge Block of protocols
01-80-C2-00-00-20 through 01-80-C2-00-00-2F	MRP (Multiple Registration Protocol) Block of protocols

Note: Per MEF 10.3, a service provider may define additional addresses for identifying L2CP service frames. However, L2CP processing for such frames is beyond the scope of MEF 45.

2. If the service frame is not an L2CP service frame and has Ethertype = 0x8902 (hexadecimal value 8902), it is a **SOAM Service Frame**.

3. If the service frame is not an L2CP service frame or a SOAM service frame, it is a **Data Service Frame**.

3.3 Review: Ethernet Frames and Service Frames

1. MEF service definitions require that physical connectivity between CEs and the CEN at the UNI...

   a. be IEEE 802.3-compliant
   b. be IEEE 802.1-compliant
   c. be IEEE 802.1Q-compliant
   d. be implemented with link aggregation per clause 43 of IEEE 802.3
   e. support Link OAM per clause 57 of IEEE 802.3

2. Per IEEE 802.1Q (2011), which field is NOT in the customer VLAN tag (C-Tag):

   a. Tag protocol identifier (TPID) with value 8100
   b. VLAN identifier (VID)
   c. Drop eligibility indicator (DEI)
   d. Canonical format indicator (CFI)

3. Per MEF 10.3, a priority-tagged service frame must have ... (Choose two.)

   a. Tag protocol identifier (TPID) = 8100
   b. Drop eligibility indicator (DEI) = 0.
   c. VLAN identifier (VID) = 0
   d. Tag protocol identifier (TPID) = 88a8

4. An Ethernet frame is transmitted from the CE to the CEN. Its source MAC address is followed by a TPID field with value 88e7. Per MEF 10.3, that Ethernet frame is:

   a. Untagged
   b. Priority-Tagged
   c. Undefined / Out of scope
   d. S-Tagged
   e. VLAN-Tagged
   f. C-Tagged

5. Egress service frames are transmitted ...

   a. from CE to CEN
   b. from CEN to CE
   c. from UNI to CEN
   d. from CE to UNI

6. A Service frame includes all fields from...

   a. Destination MAC Address to FCS, including any Ethernet tags (if present)
   b. Destination MAC Address to FCS, excluding any Ethernet tags (if present)
   c. Interframe GAP to FCS, including any Ethernet tags (if present)
   d. Interframe GAP to FCS, excluding any Ethernet tags (if present)

7. Three UNIs (UNI A, UNI B and UNI C) are connected by an EP-LAN service. At UNI A, an IEEE 802.3-compliant Ethernet frame is transmitted from the CE to the CEN. Its source MAC address is followed by a TPID field with value 88a8. According to MEF 10.3, how should the EP-LAN service treat this service frame?

   a. It should be discarded.
   b. It should be delivered like any other service frame.
   c. It should be delivered like any other service frame, however performance objectives do not apply to it.
   d. Its delivery is undefined.

8. Using MEF 10.3 service frame definitions, which two of the following statements are false? (Choose two.)

   a. A service frame tagged with PVID=88a8 and VID=0 is an S-tagged service frame.
   b. A service frame tagged with PVID=88e7 and VID=0 is an untagged service frame.
   c. A service frame tagged with PVID=8100 and VID=0 is an untagged service frame.
   d. A service frame tagged with PVID=88a8 and VID=0 is priority-tagged service frame.
   e. A service frame tagged with PVID=8100 and VID=0 is a priority-tagged service frame.

Related Links

Answers: Ethernet Frames and Service Frames on p. 397

4
How Carrier Ethernet Services are Defined

In this chapter:

4.1　Carrier Ethernet Service Attributes
4.2　The MEF Service Agreement Framework (SLA and SLS)
4.3　Review: How Carrier Ethernet Services are Defined

EVC-based Ethernet services[19] are defined in MEF 6.2, EVC Ethernet Services Definitions Phase 3. The following figure, from MEF 6.2, illustrates the framework for specifying an Ethernet service.

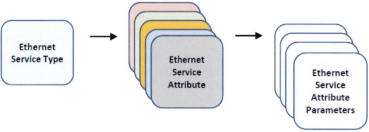

Reproduced with permission of the Metro Ethernet Forum

For each Ethernet service type (E-Line, E-LAN, or E-Tree), the MEF defines a set of *Ethernet service attributes*. Each service attribute represents a service characteristic that can be quite general. Because an Ethernet service attribute can be quite general, it in turn is defined by a set of *Ethernet service attribute parameters*.

To specify a service, you simply choose an *Ethernet service type* and then specify values for a large set of parameters. Some Ethernet service attributes are defined by only one parameter that can be set to only a few possible values. Other Ethernet service attributes are specified by assigning values to a large set of well-defined parameters. In a few cases, the MEF intentionally avoids parametrizing the Ethernet service attribute, leaving it up to the service provider and subscriber.

Going forward in these lessons, the focus will be on *Ethernet service attributes*, and you will not see the term *Ethernet service attribute parameter* again. However, you should understand that an Ethernet service attribute is a general object that may require many parameters to define.

19　This lesson relates to EVC-based services only (EPL, EVPL, EP-LAN, EVP-LAN, EP-Tree, and EVP-Tree services). OVC-based E-Access services (Access EPL and Access EVPL services) are defined in a later lesson.

4.1
Carrier Ethernet Service Attributes

In this section:

4.1.1   Categories of Service Attributes
4.1.2   Overview of Service Attributes
4.1.3   Logically Related Service Attributes

4.1.1
Categories of Service Attributes

MEF 6.2 associates every Carrier Ethernet service attribute to one of three categories: **Per UNI** service attributes, **EVC per UNI** service attributes, and **Per EVC** service attributes. To understand why, consider the following figure.

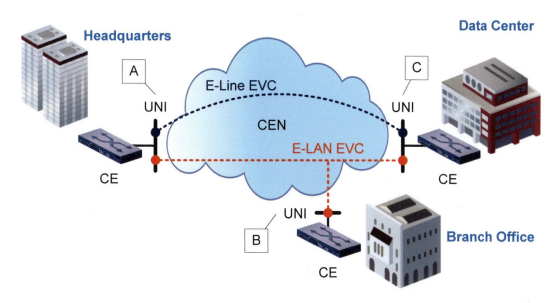

A **Per UNI service attribute** is an attribute that applies to a particular UNI (A, B, or C in the figure). To support the two services shown, UNIs A and C must be configured to support service multiplexing. *Service multiplexing* is one example of a Per UNI service attribute.

An **Per EVC service attribute** is an attribute that applies to an EVC as a whole. *CE-VLAN ID Preservation* is an example.

An **EVC per UNI service attribute** is an attribute that applies to a particular EVC at a particular UNI. You can think of it as an attribute that applies to an EVC at the point where the EVC and UNI meet. In the figure, the E-LAN service has three UNIs: A, B, and C. An EVC per UNI service attribute, such as *Class of Service Identifier for Data Service Frame* is independently specified at each UNI for each EVC.

Test your understanding: Bundling = Enabled/Disabled is another example of a Per UNI service attribute. Suppose UNI A in the figure is configured with Bundling = Disabled and UNI C is configured with Bundling = Enabled. How many CE-VLAN IDs can the E-Line service support at UNI C? [20]

Test your understanding: You are configuring the E-Line and E-LAN services shown in the previous figure. The Data Center houses three business critical servers on separate VLANs: VLAN 15, VLAN 16 and VLAN 22. The headquarters is permitted access to all three servers, but the branch office is only allowed to access the servers on VLAN 15 and VLAN 16. Configure Bundling and Service Multiplexing attributes at each UNI to support these two services. [21]

4.1.2
Overview of Service Attributes

The following tables list all of the Carrier Ethernet service attributes for overview purposes. For now, just look these tables over to get a rough idea about what can be involved in defining a Carrier Ethernet service. Each attribute is explained later in later lessons.

Note: Attributes in the following tables are collectively defined by three standards: MEF 6.2, EVC Ethernet Services Definitions Phase 3, MEF 10.3, Ethernet Services Attributes Phase 3, and MEF 45, Multi-CEN L2CP. MEF 10.3 provides baseline definitions for most of the attributes. MEF 45 defines L2CP-related attributes. MEF 6.2, the defining standard for EVC-based Carrier Ethernet services, references attribute definitions from MEF 10.3 and MEF 45 and augments some of those definitions with additional requirements. MEF 6.2 also defines two service attributes (Token Share and Envelopes) on its own.

Per UNI Service Attributes

Per UNI Service Attribute	Requirement					
	Port-Based Service			VLAN-Based Service		
	EPL	EP-LAN	EP-Tree	EVPL	EVP-LAN	EVP-Tree
UNI ID	String					
Physical Layer	List of physical layers					
Synchronous Mode	List of Enabled / Disabled for each link in the UNI					
Number of Links	Number of Links					
UNI Resiliency	None / 2-Link Aggregation / Other					
Service Frame Format	IEEE Standard 802.3 (2012)					
UNI Maximum Service Frame Size	At least 1522 bytes					
Service Multiplexing	Disabled			Enabled / Disabled		

---

20 **Answer:** Only one because the E-Line service supports only one CE-VLAN ID at UNI A.
21 **Answer:** For correct VLAN connectivity, the E-LAN service needs to support VLANs 15 and 16 and the E-Line service needs to support VLAN 22. To support the E-LAN service (which includes two VLANs) all three UNIs must be configured with Bundling = Enabled. UNIs A and C must be configured with Service Multiplexing = Enabled because they both support more than one EVC. UNI B can be configured with Service Multiplexing = Enabled or Service Multiplexing = Disabled.

Per UNI Service Attribute	Requirement					
	Port-Based Service			VLAN-Based Service		
	EPL	EP-LAN	EP-Tree	EVPL	EVP-LAN	EVP-Tree
CE-VLAN ID for Untagged and Priority Service Frames	Not applicable			A value in the range 1 to 4094		
CE-VLAN ID / EVC Map	All CE-VLAN IDs map to the EVC.			A map containing a least 1 CE-VLAN ID for each EVC		
Maximum number of EVCs	1			At least 1		
Bundling	Disabled			Enabled / Disabled		
All to One Bundling	Enabled			Disabled		
Token Share	Enabled / Disabled					
Envelopes	List of <Envelope ID, CF^0, n>					
Link OAM	Enabled / Disabled					
UNI MEG	Enabled / Disabled					
E-LMI	Enabled / Disabled					
UNI L2CP Address Set	CTB / CTB-2	CTB		CTA		
UNI L2CP Peering	None or list of {Destination Address, Protocol Identifier} or list of {Destination Address, Protocol Identifier, Link Identifier} to be peered					

EVC per UNI Service Attributes

EVC per UNI Service Attribute	Requirement					
	Port-Based Service			VLAN-Based Service		
	EPL	EP-LAN	EP-Tree	EVPL	EVP-LAN	EVP-Tree
UNI EVC ID	String formed by the concatenation of the UNI ID and the EVC ID					
CoS ID for Data Service Frame	EVC or CE-VLAN CoS or IP value(s) and corresponding CoS Name					
CoS ID for L2CP Service Frame	"All" or list of each L2CP in the EVC and corresponding CoS Name					
CoS ID for SOAM Service Frame	Basis same as for Data Service Frames					
Color ID for Service Frame	None or EVC or CE-VLAN CoS or CE-VLAN Tag DEI or IP					
EEC ID for Data Service Frame	EVC or CE-VLAN CoS or IP value(s) and corresponding EEC					
EEC ID for L2CP Service Frame	"All" or list of each L2CP in the EVC and corresponding EEC					
EEC ID for SOAM Service Frame	Basis same as for Data Service Frames					
Ingress Bandwidth Profile Per CoS ID	No / Parameters (as required)					
Egress Bandwidth Profile Per EEC ID	No	Parameters (as required)				

EVC per UNI Service Attribute	Requirement					
	Port-Based Service			VLAN-Based Service		
	EPL	EP-LAN	EP-Tree	EVPL	EVP-LAN	EVP-Tree
Source MAC Address Limit	Disabled	Enabled / Disabled		Disabled	Enabled / Disabled	
Test MEG	Enabled / Disabled					
Subscriber MEG MIP	Enabled / Disabled					

Per EVC Service Attributes

Per EVC Service Attribute	Requirement					
	Port-Based Service			VLAN-Based Service		
	EPL	EP-LAN	EP-Tree	EVPL	EVP-LAN	EVP-Tree
EVC Type	Point-to-Point	Multipoint-to-Multipoint	Rooted-Multipoint	Point-to-Point	Multipoint-to-Multipoint	Rooted-Multipoint
EVC ID	String					
UNI List	List of <UNI ID, UNI Role> pairs					
Maximum Number of UNIs	2	At least 3		2	At least 3	
Unicast Service Frame Delivery	Discard / Deliver Unconditionally / Deliver Conditionally					
Multicast Service Frame Delivery	Discard / Deliver Unconditionally / Deliver Conditionally					
Broadcast Service Frame Delivery	Discard / Deliver Unconditionally / Deliver Conditionally					
CE-VLAN ID Preservation	Enabled			Enabled / Disabled		
CE-VLAN CoS Preservation	Enabled			Enabled / Disabled		
EVC Performance	A list of performance metrics and associated parameters and performance objectives					
EVC Maximum Service Frame Size	(≥ 1522 bytes) AND (≤ minimum UNI Maximum Service Frame Size for all UNIs in the EVC)					

4.1.3
Logically Related Service Attributes

There are almost 50 Carrier Ethernet service attributes. To explain them systematically in these lessons, they are organized into groups as shown in the following tables.

Note: *You do not need to know these groups for the MEF-CECP exam. However, you should know the three categories of service attributes:* **Per UNI** *service attributes,* **EVC per UNI** *service attributes, and* **Per EVC** *service attributes.*

UNI Functionality Attributes

These attributes are explained in Lesson UNI Requirements.

Sub Group	Category	Service Attributes
UNI Functionality Service Attributes	Per UNI	Physical Layer Synchronous Mode Number of Links UNI Resiliency Service Frame Format Link OAM E-LMI

Service Connectivity Attributes

These attributes are explained in Lesson Service Connectivity Attributes.

Sub Group	Category	Service Attributes
Basic Service Attributes	Per UNI	UNI ID Maximum number of EVCs
	EVC per UNI	UNI EVC ID
	Per EVC	EVC Type EVC ID UNI List Maximum Number of UNIs
Maximum Service Frame Size Service Attributes	Per UNI	UNI Maximum Service Frame Size
	Per EVC	EVC Maximum Service Frame Size
Service Multiplexing and Bundling Service Attributes	Per UNI	Service Multiplexing Bundling All to One Bundling
Service Frame Mapping Service Attributes	Per UNI	CE-VLAN ID for Untagged and Priority Service Frames CE-VLAN ID / EVC Map
CE-VLAN Tag Preservation Service Attributes	Per EVC	CE-VLAN ID Preservation CE-VLAN CoS Preservation
Data Service Frame Delivery Service Attributes	Per EVC	Unicast Service Frame Delivery Multicast Service Frame Delivery Broadcast Service Frame Delivery
Source MAC Address Limit Service Attribute	EVC per UNI	Source MAC Address Limit
L2CP Processing Service Attributes	Per UNI	UNI L2CP Address Set UNI L2CP Peering

Traffic Management Attributes

These attributes are explained in three Lessons: Traffic and Performance Management, Bandwidth Profiles, and EVC Performance.

Sub Group	Category	Service Attributes
CoS ID Service Attributes	EVC per UNI	CoS ID for Data Service Frame CoS ID for L2CP Service Frame CoS ID for SOAM Service Frame
Color ID for Service Frame Attribute	EVC per UNI	Color ID for Service Frame
EEC ID Service Attributes	EVC per UNI	EEC ID for Data Service Frame EEC ID for L2CP Service Frame EEC ID for SOAM Service Frame
Bandwidth Profile Service Attributes	Per UNI	Token Share Envelopes
	EVC per UNI	Ingress Bandwidth Profile Per CoS ID Egress Bandwidth Profile Per EEC ID
EVC Performance Service Attribute	Per EVC	EVC Performance

Service OAM Attributes

These attributes are explained in Lesson Ethernet OAM.

Sub Group	Category	Service Attributes
SOAM-Related Service Attributes	Per UNI	UNI MEG
	EVC per UNI	Test MEG Subscriber MEG MIP

4.2
The MEF Service Agreement Framework (SLA and SLS)

The MEF framework for service agreements includes two components, defined in MEF 10.3 as follows:

Service Level Agreement (SLA) — The contract between the subscriber and service provider specifying the agreed to service-level commitments and related business agreements

Service Level Specification (SLS) — The technical specification of the service level being offered by the service provider to the subscriber.

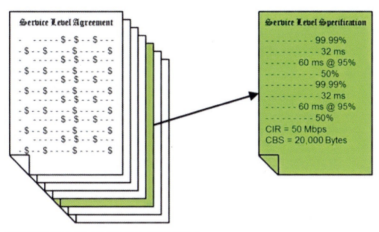

Reproduced with permission of the Metro Ethernet Forum

The SLA defines everything related to the service, both from the technical perspective (for example, service connectivity, behavior, and performance) and from the business perspective (for example, cost of the service and any refunds due if performance levels are not met).

The SLS is that part of the SLA that lays out performance commitments for the service:

- The SLS usually states commitments in engineering terms.

- The SLS usually includes the generic specification of one or more service levels offered by the service provider, not customized to the particular subscriber.

- The SLS defines service performance objectives, such as frame delay, inter-frame delay variation, frame loss ratio, and availability.

Note: *Service Level Specification* is also the name of an OVC service attribute (to be described in a later lesson).

Related Links
Service Level Specification (OVC Service Attribute) on p. 206

4.3 Review: How Carrier Ethernet Services are Defined

1. Which one of the following service attributes is an *EVC per UNI* attribute?

   a. Maximum number of EVCs
   b. Ingress Bandwidth Profile per CoS Identifier
   c. CE VLAN ID Preservation
   d. CE-VLAN ID / EVC Map
   e. Bundling

2. Which one of the following statements is false?

   a. The SLS is considered part of the SLA.
   b. The SLS contains technical details in engineering terms.
   c. The SLA includes all business agreements related to the service.
   d. The SLA is considered part of the SLS.

3. A Service Level Agreement (SLA) is which one of the following?

   a. A contract between the subscriber and service provider specifying a business agreement
   b. An agreement stating service-level commitments in engineering terms
   c. A technical specification for the service
   d. A specification of service levels offered by the service provider
   e. An agreement about service performance attributes, including frame delay, inter-frame delay variation, frame loss ratio, and availability

Related Links

Answers: How Carrier Ethernet Services are Defined on p. 399

5
Service Connectivity Attributes

In this chapter:

- 5.1 Basic Service Attributes
- 5.2 Maximum Service Frame Size Service Attributes
- 5.3 Service Multiplexing and Bundling Service Attributes
- 5.4 Service Frame Mapping Service Attributes
- 5.5 CE-VLAN Tag Preservation Service Attributes
- 5.6 Data Service Frame Delivery Service Attributes
- 5.7 Source MAC Address Limit Service Attribute
- 5.8 Security Considerations for E-Tree Services
- 5.9 L2CP Processing Service Attributes
- 5.10 Review: Service Connectivity Attributes

Note: *This lesson relates to EVC-based services only (EPL, EVPL, EP-LAN, EVP-LAN, EP-Tree, and EVP-Tree services). OVC-based E-Access services (Access EPL and Access EVPL services) are defined in a later lesson.*

Related Links

E-Access Services on p. 232

5.1
Basic Service Attributes

Service Attribute		Requirement					
		Port-Based Service			VLAN-Based Service		
Cat.	Name	EPL	EP-LAN	EP-Tree	EVPL	EVP-LAN	EVP-Tree
Per UNI	UNI ID	String					
	Max. number of EVCs	1			At least 1		
EVC per UNI	UNI EVC ID	String formed by the concatenation of the UNI ID and the EVC ID					
Per EVC	EVC Type	Point-to-Point	Multipoint-to-Multipoint	Rooted-Multipoint	Point-to-Point	Multipoint-to-Multipoint	Rooted-Multipoint
	EVC ID	String					
	UNI List	List of <UNI ID, UNI Role> pairs					
	Max. Number of UNIs	2	At least 3		2	At least 3	

Three attributes declare identifiers:

- **UNI ID** – An arbitrary string[22] administered by the service provider that is used to identify a UNI within the CEN

- **EVC ID** – An arbitrary string administered by the service provider that is used to identify an EVC within the CEN

- **UNI EVC ID** – A string formed by the concatenation of the UNI ID and the EVC ID that is used to identify an EVC at the UNI

The **EVC Type** attribute is set to one of three values: *Point-to-Point* (for E-Line service), *Multipoint-to-Multipoint* (for E-LAN service), or *Rooted-Multipoint* (for E-Tree service).

The **UNI List** attribute is a list of <UNI ID, UNI Role> pairs for each UNI associated by the EVC. Each UNI in an E-Line or E-LAN service has *UNI Role=Root*. Each UNI in an E-Tree service can have *UNI Role=Root* or *UNI Role=Leaf*.

Two attributes declare support limitations:[23]

- **Maximum Number of EVCs** – Declares how many EVCs the UNI can support. If the UNI is configured for *All-to-one Bundling*, it can support only one EVC. Otherwise, a number ≥1 is declared.

- **Maximum Number of UNIs** – Declares how many UNIs the EVC can support. For type E-Line services, the EVC supports two UNIs. Otherwise, a number ≥3 is declared.

---

22 Of course the string is not completely arbitrary. Refer to MEF 10.3 for details.
23 These attributes do not declare the number of EVCs/UNIs that are actually supported. They declare limits on how many might be supported. The purpose is to capture future potential complexity and to limit it. For example, if the subscriber is certain that there will never be more than 4 UNIs associated with the EVC, it may help the service provider lower cost.

5.2
Maximum Service Frame Size Service Attributes

Service Attribute		Requirement					
		Port-Based Service			VLAN-Based Service		
Cat.	Name	EPL	EP-LAN	EP-Tree	EVPL	EVP-LAN	EVP-Tree
Per UNI	UNI Maximum Service Frame Size	≥ 1522 bytes					
Per EVC	EVC Maximum Service Frame Size	(≥ 1522 bytes) AND (≤ minimum *UNI Maximum Service Frame Size* for all UNIs in the EVC)					

The *UNI Maximum Service Frame Size* (for any UNI) must be at least 1522 bytes.

The *EVC Maximum Service Frame Size* (for a given EVC) must meet two requirements: it must be at least 1522 bytes and it must be no larger than the smallest value of *UNI Maximum Service Frame Size* across all UNIs associated to the EVC.

Note: *The value 1522 is related to IEEE 802.3 Ethernet frame size standards. The payload for a standard 802.3 Ethernet frame is limited to 1500 bytes, which limits untagged Ethernet frames to 1518 bytes and C-Tagged Ethernet frames to 1522 bytes.*

MEF standards also include the following recommendations (which are not mandatory):

MEF 6.2	[D2] *UNI Maximum Service Frame Size* should be ≥ 1600 bytes
	[D15] *EVC Maximum Service Frame Size* should be ≥ 1600 bytes
MEF 10.3	[D1] An ingress tagged service frame that is mapped to the EVC and whose length exceeds the *EVC Maximum Service Frame Size* should be discarded.
	[D2] An ingress untagged service frame that is mapped to the EVC and whose length exceeds the *EVC Maximum Service Frame Size* minus 4 should be discarded. (Minus 4 anticipates for possible tag addition prior to egress UNI)
	Note: *An ingress service frame that is discarded per [D1] or [D2] does not consume tokens in a bandwidth profile.*

An ingress service frame with length that is less than 64 bytes must be discarded.[24]

Note: *In multi-network applications (the subject of another lesson), ENNIs and OVCs are required to support at least 1526 bytes (four more bytes than UNIs and EVCs).*

Related Links

Size of Untagged and C-Tagged Ethernet Frames on p. 49
ENNI and OVC MTU Size on p. 197

---

24 Per [R70] of MEF 10.3, which enforces Clause 4.2.4.2.2 of IEEE Std 802.3 – 2012.

5.3
Service Multiplexing and Bundling Service Attributes

Service Attribute		Requirement					
		Port-Based Service			VLAN-Based Service		
Cat.	Name	EPL	EP-LAN	EP-Tree	EVPL	EVP-LAN	EVP-Tree
Per UNI	Service Multiplexing		Disabled			Enabled / Disabled	
	Bundling		Disabled			Enabled / Disabled	
	All to One Bundling		Enabled			Disabled	

The concepts of *Service Multiplexing*, *Bundling*, and *All to One Bundling* were introduced in a previous lesson. MEF 10.3 captures these concepts in three Per UNI service attributes:

Service Multiplexing	If Enabled, the UNI can support multiple VLAN-based services and no port-based services.
Bundling	If Enabled, the UNI can support the association of multiple CE-VLAN IDs to an EVC.
All to One Bundling	If Enabled, the UNI can support one port-based service and no VLAN-based services.

The following table (Table 12 from MEF 10.3) shows valid combinations of these attributes. Observe that *All-to-One Bundling* precludes both *Bundling* and *Service Multiplexing*.

Attribute	Combination 1	Combination 2	Combination 3	Combination 4	Combination 5
Service Multiplexing	Disabled	Enabled	Enabled	Disabled	Disabled
Bundling	Disabled	Disabled	Enabled	Enabled	Disabled
All to One Bundling	Disabled	Disabled	Disabled	Disabled	Enabled

Test your understanding: For each of the five valid combinations shown in the preceding table, describe the support that the UNI provides for services. [25]

Related Links

Service Multiplexing on p. 28
Bundling on p. 31

---

[25] **Combination 1** supports one VLAN-based service with one CE-VLAN ID mapped to the service. **Combination 2** supports multiple VLAN-based services with only one CE-VLAN ID mapped to each service. **Combination 3** supports multiple VLAN-based services with one or many CE-VLAN IDs mapped to each service. **Combination 4** supports one VLAN-based service with one or many CE-VLAN IDs mapped to it. **Combination 5** supports one port-based service with all service frames mapped to the service.

5.4 Service Frame Mapping Service Attributes

In this section:

5.4.1 CE-VLAN ID / EVC Map
5.4.2 CE-VLAN ID for Untagged and Priority Tagged Service Frames

Service Attribute		Requirement					
		Port-Based Service			VLAN-Based Service		
Cat.	Name	EPL	EP-LAN	EP-Tree	EVPL	EVP-LAN	EVP-Tree
Per UNI	CE-VLAN ID / EVC Map	Not applicable (All CE-VLAN IDs map to the EVC)			A map containing a least one CE-VLAN ID for each EVC		
	CE-VLAN ID for Untagged and Priority Tagged Service Frames	Not applicable			A value in the range 1 to 4094		

These two attributes apply to VLAN-based services only. They declare how service frames map to EVCs at a given UNI. Neither attribute applies to port-based services because service frame mapping is already understood for them.[26] Before explaining in more detail, let us review service frame tagging.

Review of Service Frame Tag Recognition

Recall that a *CE-VLAN tag* refers to the customer VLAN tag (C-Tag) in the Ethernet header of a service frame.

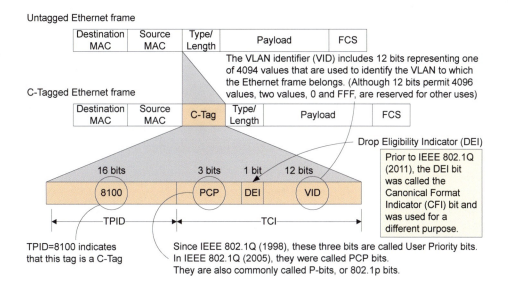

---

26 For a port-based service, all service frames, regardless of tagging or absence of tagging, map to the same EVC (the only EVC that is supported at the UNI). However, VLAN-based services allow several EVCs to share a UNI, which leads to the question: Which service frames map to which EVC? These two attributes resolve this question.

Also recall that MEF 10.3 classifies service frames into four formats (VLAN Tagged, Priority Tagged, S-Tagged, and Untagged) based on outer VLAN tag, if present.

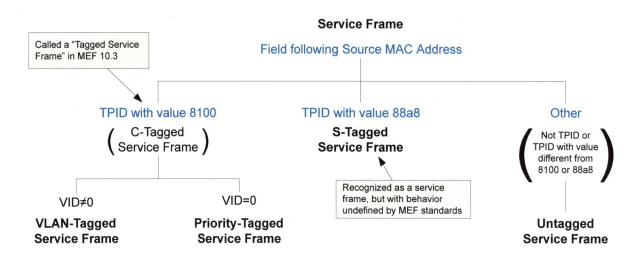

Finally recall that, because MEF standards do not define behavior for S-Tagged service frames, service definitions are only concerned with three of the four service frame formats:

- **Untagged Service Frames**: No tag or tag that is not a C-Tag or an S-Tag

- **VLAN Tagged Service Frames**: C-Tagged (TPID=8100) with VID≠0

- **Priority Tagged Service Frames**: C-Tagged (TPID=8100) with VID=0

Related Links

Service Frame Tag Recognition on p. 53

5.4.1 CE-VLAN ID / EVC Map

Note: Prior to MEF 10.3, this attribute was classified as an **EVC per UNI** attribute. It is now a **Per UNI** attribute.

Note: This attribute applies to VLAN-based services only.

At a given UNI, the *CE-VLAN ID / EVC Map* attribute lists the EVCs that are supported at the UNI and the CE-VLAN IDs (from the set 1...4094) that map to each EVC. The following figure shows an example.

Service Connectivity Attributes
Service Frame Mapping Service Attributes

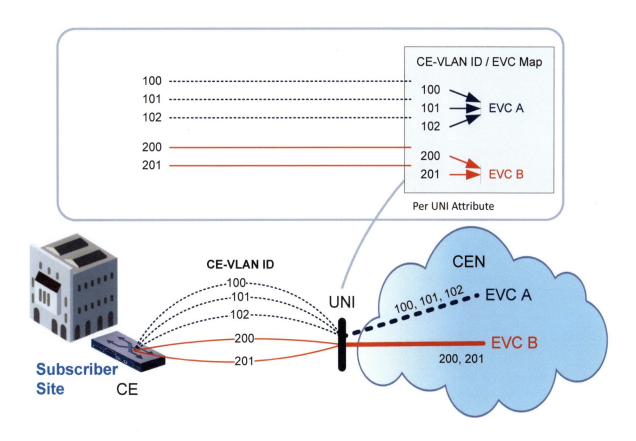

Each CE-VLAN ID (from the set 1...4094) can map to no more than one EVC at a given UNI.[27]

If more than one CE-VLAN ID maps to an EVC at a UNI, the list of CE-VLAN IDs mapping to the EVC must match at each UNI of the EVC.[28] This is illustrated for both EVCs in the following figure.

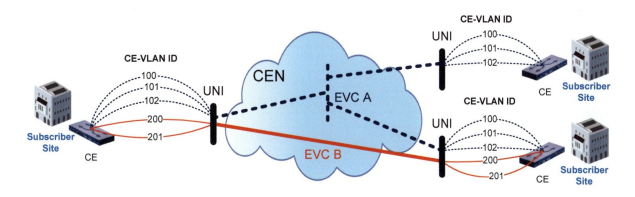

---

27 Per [R76] in MEF 10.3.
28 [R81] in MEF 10.3 states: An EVC with more than one CE-VLAN ID mapping to it must have the same list of CE-VLAN IDs mapping to the EVC at each UNI in the EVC.

If only one CE-VLAN ID maps to an EVC at each UNI, the values of CE-VLAN ID do not have to match. They may match, but they are not required to match.[29] The following example, illustrates a case for which the values of CE-VLAN ID do not match.

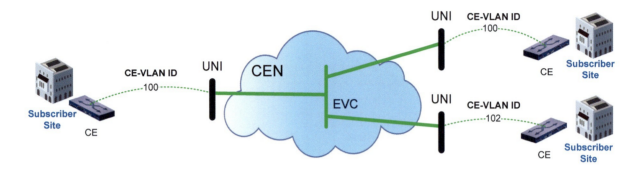

In this case, the service must translate service frame content (typically C-Tag VID) to align with egress UNI requirements, as follows.

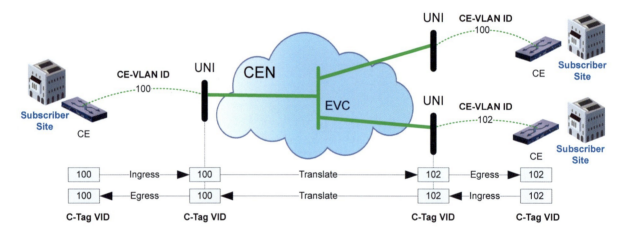

This explains how attribute *CE-VLAN ID / EVC Map* maps VLAN tagged service frames to EVCs at a given UNI. But what about untagged and priority tagged service frames?

Related Links

CE-VLAN ID Preservation on p. 77

5.4.2
CE-VLAN ID for Untagged and Priority Tagged Service Frames

Note: *This attribute applies to VLAN-based services only.*

---

[29] If CE-VLAN IDs do not match, another service attribute (explained later in this lesson) is also involved: Per EVC attribute *CE-VLAN ID Preservation* must be set to *Disabled*.

Service Connectivity Attributes
Service Frame Mapping Service Attributes

At a given UNI, attribute *CE-VLAN ID for Untagged and Priority Tagged Service Frames* declares one value of CE-VLAN ID (from the set 1...4094) to which untagged and priority tagged service frames are associated. Untagged and priority tagged service frames map to an EVC through two attributes (*CE-VLAN ID for Untagged and Priority Tagged Service Frames* and *CE-VLAN ID / EVC Map*). The following figure shows an example.

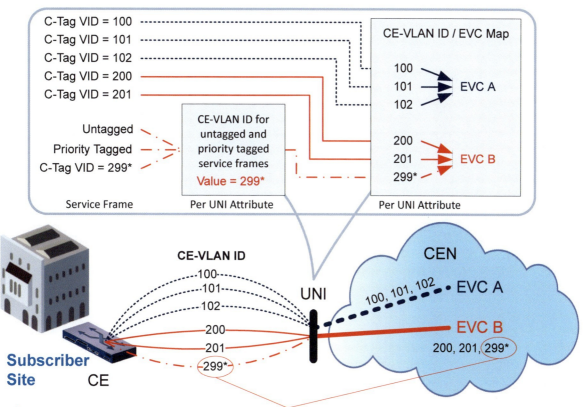

* CE-VLAN ID value 299 identifies untagged, priority tagged, and VID=299 service frames with EVC B.

In this example, attribute *CE-VLAN ID for Untagged and Priority Tagged Service Frames* is set to 299 and attribute *CE-VLAN ID / EVC Map* maps CE-VLAN ID 299 to EVC B. The two attributes work together to map untagged and priority tagged service frames to EVC B.

Notice that C-Tagged service frames with VID = *CE-VLAN ID for Untagged and Priority Tagged Service Frames* (299 in this example) also map to EVC B through the same value of CE-VLAN ID. So, three types of service frames map to EVC B through the same value of CE-VLAN ID: untagged service frames, priority tagged service frames, and C-Tagged service frames with VID = 299 (in this example). This is significant because special rules govern the egress of service frames under such conditions (as explained later in this lesson).

Related Links

CE-VLAN ID Preservation on p. 77
Untagged and Priority Tagged Service Frames with CE-VLAN ID Preservation Disabled on p. 81

5.5
CE-VLAN Tag Preservation Service Attributes

In this section:

5.5.1 CE-VLAN CoS Preservation
5.5.2 CE-VLAN ID Preservation
5.5.3 CE-VLAN ID Preservation versus Translation
5.5.4 Untagged and Priority Tagged Service Frames with CE-VLAN ID Preservation Disabled

Service Attribute		Requirement					
		Port-Based Service			VLAN-Based Service		
Cat.	Name	EPL	EP-LAN	EP-Tree	EVPL	EVP-LAN	EVP-Tree
Per EVC	CE-VLAN CoS Preservation		Enabled			Enabled / Disabled	
	CE-VLAN ID Preservation		Enabled			Enabled / Disabled	

These two attributes are concerned with preserving specific CE-VLAN Tag content within service frames (ensuring that values at ingress match values at egress).

5.5.1
CE-VLAN CoS Preservation

If service attribute *CE-VLAN CoS Preservation = Enabled*, the EVC must preserve the values of PCP bits (User Priority Bits) in the CE-VLAN tag of service frames (PCP bit values at ingress and egress must match).

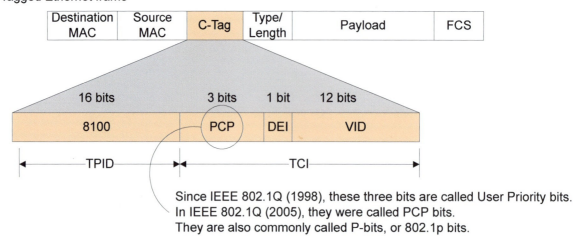

Note: *The attribute name, CE-VLAN CoS Preservation, is somewhat confusing because the attribute is only concerned with preserving PCP bit values, which may or may not be used to identify class of service (CoS).*[30]

This attribute accommodates service providers who may want to use service frame PCP bits for their own purposes. If the subscriber is using PCP bits for internal purposes and does not want the service to change them, *CE-VLAN CoS Preservation* should be set to *Enabled*. However, if the subscriber does not care about this, setting *CE-VLAN CoS Preservation* to *Disabled* may help some service providers by allowing them to modify PCP bit values in service frames for their own purposes.

MEF 10.3 requires that EVCs for port-based services be configured with *CE-VLAN CoS Preservation = Enabled*. EVCs for VLAN-based services can be configured with *CE-VLAN CoS Preservation = Enabled* or *Disabled*.

5.5.2 CE-VLAN ID Preservation

MEF 10.3 defines *CE-VLAN ID Preservation* in two ways: as a *behavior* and as an *attribute*.

A service frame exhibits CE-VLAN ID preservation behavior if its ingress format relates to its egress format as described in the following table (Table 4 in MEF 10.3):

Ingress Service Frame Format	Egress Service Frame(s) Format
Untagged	Untagged
Tagged (VLAN Tagged or Priority Tagged)	Tagged with VLAN ID = VLAN ID of ingress service frame

In other words, to exhibit CE-VLAN ID preservation behavior:

- If a service frame is *untagged*[31] at ingress, it must be untagged at egress.

- If a service frame is C-Tagged at ingress, it must be C-Tagged at egress and have the same VID value.

CE-VLAN ID Preservation Attribute

The *CE-VLAN ID Preservation* attribute regulates *CE-VLAN ID preservation* behavior. If attribute *CE-VLAN ID Preservation = Enabled*, all service frames associated with the EVC must exhibit CE-VLAN ID Preservation behavior (as defined in the preceding table), with one exception[32]:

> If the service is VLAN-based (not port-based) and if the value of attribute *CE-VLAN ID for Untagged and Priority Tagged Service Frames* maps to the EVC, then service frames that map to the EVC through attribute *CE-VLAN ID for Untagged and Priority Tagged Service Frames* are not required to exhibit CE-VLAN ID preservation behavior.

This exempts three types of service frames (untagged, priority tagged, and C-Tagged service frames with VID = *CE-VLAN ID for Untagged and Priority Tagged Service Frames*) from CE-VLAN ID preservation (as defined in the previous table), but only under the previously-stated conditions. For example, suppose attribute *CE-VLAN ID Preservation = Enabled* for both EVCs in the following figure.

---

30 As explained in a later lesson, class of service (CoS) is an indicator that is used to differentiate service frames with respect to quality of service (QoS) treatment in the CEN. CoS can be encoded in service frames in several ways, including using PCP bits or using DSCP bits.

31 Recall that MEF 10.3 only recognizes C-Tags and S-Tags. So service frames that are tagged with something other than a C-Tag or an S-Tag are considered to be *untagged*.

32 This exception, introduced in MEF 10.3, relaxes CE-VLAN ID preservation requirements, giving service providers a little more flexibility for handling service frames that map to the EVC through attribute *CE-VLAN ID for Untagged and Priority Tagged Service Frames*.

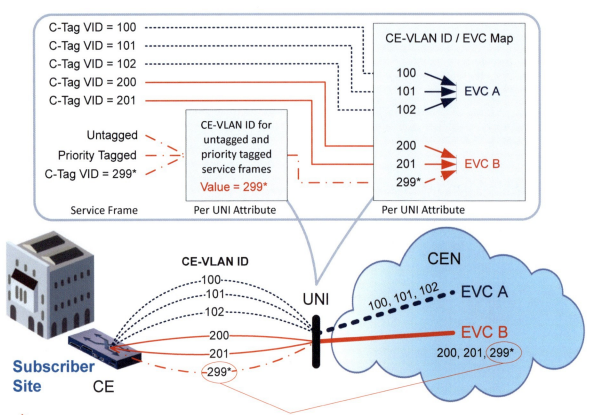

* CE-VLAN ID value 299 identifies untagged, priority tagged, and VID=299 service frames with EVC B.

Because both EVCs are configured with *CE-VLAN ID Preservation = Enabled*, service frames with CE-VLAN IDs 100, 101, 102, 200 and 201 must exhibit CE-VLAN ID preservation behavior as previously defined.

However, untagged, priority tagged, and *VID=299*–tagged service frames are not required to exhibit CE-VLAN ID preservation behavior. For these service frames, the service provider may choose to preserve CE-VLAN ID (as previously defined) or do something else. For example, the service provider might reconcile these three ingress service frame formats to a common format (by changing tagging and VID as required) such that they conform to one format (say untagged, or tagged with VID=299) at egress. Excluding this exception, if *CE-VLAN ID Preservation = Enabled*, the EVC will preserve CE-VLAN ID as previously defined.

Related Links

CE-VLAN ID / EVC Map on p. 72

5.5.3
CE-VLAN ID Preservation versus Translation

The key benefit of CE-VLAN ID preservation is enhanced operational simplicity. If *CE-VLAN ID Preservation = Disabled*, the service may be required to translate service frame content (typically, C-Tag VID value), adding

Service Connectivity Attributes
CE-VLAN Tag Preservation Service Attributes

complexity to the service implementation and requiring greater coordination between the service provider and the subscriber.

On the other hand, allowing translation (*CE-VLAN ID Preservation = Disabled*) can be useful, for example, if a subscriber needs to interconnect a VLAN on multiple campuses and each campus currently uses a different customer VLAN ID value. Instead of renumbering the campus VLANs to a common VLAN ID (required if *CE-VLAN ID Preservation = Enabled*), the service could be configured with *CE-VLAN ID Preservation = Disabled* and then implemented to perform VLAN ID translations, as required.

MEF 10.3 permits *CE-VLAN ID Preservation = Disabled* (which allows CE-VLAN ID translation) under two conditions:[33]

> 1. The service is VLAN-based (attribute *All to One Bundling = Disabled* at each UNI), and
> 2. Attribute *CE-VLAN ID / EVC Map* at each UNI maps only one CE-VLAN ID to the EVC.

Note: Prior to MEF 6.2, MEF standards required CE-VLAN ID Preservation = Enabled for any EVC that connects to a UNI configured with Bundling = Enabled.[34] However, this is no longer a requirement.[35]

If follows that, CE-VLAN ID translation is only allowed for VLAN-based services that map one CE-VLAN ID at each UNI, and then only if attribute *CE-VLAN ID Preservation* for the EVC is set to *Disabled*. In this case, the service must translate service frame content (typically C-Tag VID) to align with requirements at the egress UNI, as shown in the following example.

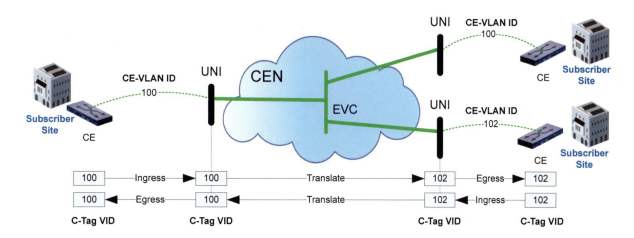

If more than one CE-VLAN ID maps to an EVC at a UNI, then *CE-VLAN ID Preservation* must be *Enabled*, which means CE-VLAN ID translation is not permitted.[36] This applies to both EVCs in the following example.

---

33 Per [R25] MEF 10.3
34 Entries for Bundling in Tables 14, 21, and 27 of MEF 6.1 state: "If [Bundling =] Yes, then CE-VLAN ID Preservation MUST be Yes."
35 EVCs configured with CE-VLAN ID Preservation = Disabled can connect to UNIs configured with Bundling = Enabled, but the CE-VLAN ID / EVC Map at such UNIs can only map one CE-VLAN ID to such EVCs.
36 This requirement aligns with [R81] in MEF 10.3: An EVC with more than one CE-VLAN ID mapping to it must have the same list of CE-VLAN IDs mapping to the EVC at each UNI in the EVC.

Service Connectivity Attributes
CE-VLAN Tag Preservation Service Attributes

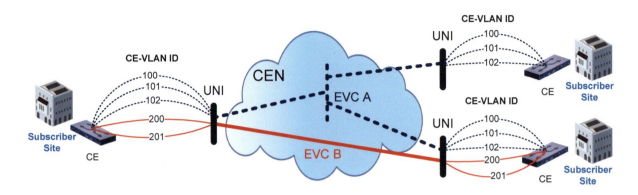

Test your understanding: A subscriber wants to interconnect three VLANs that are on three separate campuses. Currently these VLANs use different VLAN IDs (101, 230, and 44), and the subscriber does not want to renumber them. Answer the following questions: [37]

1. How should the UNIs be configured with respect to Bundling?
2. How should the UNIs be configured with respect to Service Multiplexing?
3. How should the EVC be configured with respect to CE-VLAN ID Preservation?
4. Can the service be expanded later to connect more VLANs between campuses?

Test your understanding: Which combinations of Per UNI attributes **Service Multiplexing**, **Bundling**, and **All to One Bundling** shown in the following table (Table 12 from MEF 10.3) support CE-VLAN ID translation? [38]

Attribute	Combination 1	Combination 2	Combination 3	Combination 4	Combination 5
Service Multiplexing	Disabled	Enabled	Enabled	Disabled	Disabled
Bundling	Disabled	Disabled	Enabled	Enabled	Disabled
All to One Bundling	Disabled	Disabled	Disabled	Disabled	Enabled

Test your understanding: For each of the following MEF services, list the components (CE-VLAN ID, PCP bits, CE-VLAN ID and PCP bits, or none) that the service is required to preserve: [39]

1. For a EP-LAN service
2. For an EVP-LAN service between UNIs configured with Bundling=Enabled
3. For a EVPL service with EVC configured with CE-VLAN CoS Preservation = Enabled
4. For a EVP-LAN service with two CE-VLAN IDs mapped to the EVC at each UNI

---

[37] **Answers: 1.** Bundling can be Enabled or Disabled; **2.** Service Multiplexing can be Enabled or Disabled; **3.** CE-VLAN ID Preservation must be Disabled; **4.** No, because CE-VLAN ID Preservation is set to Disabled (to allow CE-VLAN ID translation), additional CE-VLAN IDs cannot be mapped to the EVC.

[38] **Answer:** Valid combinations 1, 2, 3, and 4. Each of these UNI configurations can support at least one EVC configured with CE-VLAN ID Preservation = Disabled.

[39] **Answers: 1.** CE-VLAN ID and PCP bits (Any port-based service must preserve both CE-VLAN ID and PCP bits in service frames.); **2.** None (CE-VLAN ID translation is allowed if only one CE-VLAN ID maps to the EVC at each UNI and if the EVC is configured with CE-VLAN ID Preservation = Disabled. CE-VLAN CoS preservation is optional for VLAN-based services.); **3.** PCP bits (CE-VLAN CoS Preservation = Enabled requires PCP bits to be preserved. CE-VLAN ID preservation is not required for VLAN-based services.); **4.** CE-VLAN ID (If multiple CE-VLAN IDs map the EVC, CE-VLAN ID Preservation must be Enabled. CE-VLAN CoS preservation is optional for VLAN-based services.)

5.5.4
Untagged and Priority Tagged Service Frames with CE-VLAN ID Preservation Disabled

As previously explained, when CE-VLAN ID Preservation is Disabled:

- Attribute *CE-VLAN ID / EVC Map* at each UNI maps only one value of CE-VLAN ID to the EVC, and

- A different value of CE-VLAN ID can be mapped to the EVC at each UNI (this allows translation).

Now let's consider a special case: when a UNI of this EVC is configured to map untagged and priority-tagged service frame to the EVC, as shown in the following example.

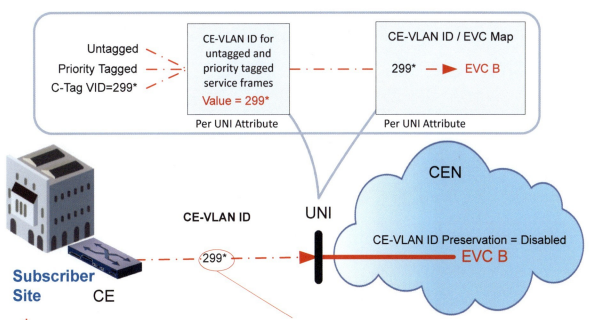

* CE-VLAN ID value 299 identifies untagged, priority tagged, and VID=299 service frames with EVC B.

In this example, the value of attribute *CE-VLAN ID for Untagged and Priority Tagged Service Frames* is set to 299 and the value 299 is mapped to EVC B. As previously explained, this maps three types of service frames to EVC B: untagged service frames, priority tagged service frames, and C-Tagged service frames with VID = 299. These service frames, if transmitted from CE to CEN at this UNI, will be associated to EVC B upon ingress. But how should service frames egress from EVC B at this UNI? Per MEF 10.3:

> [R75] When CE-VLAN ID Preservation is Disabled for an EVC to which the CE-VLAN ID for Untagged and Priority Tagged Service Frames is mapped, egress Service Frames mapped to this EVC at the given UNI MUST be Untagged Service Frames.

As shown in the following figure, all frames must egress the UNI untagged. The service translates service frame content, as required, to make this happen.

Service Connectivity Attributes
CE-VLAN Tag Preservation Service Attributes

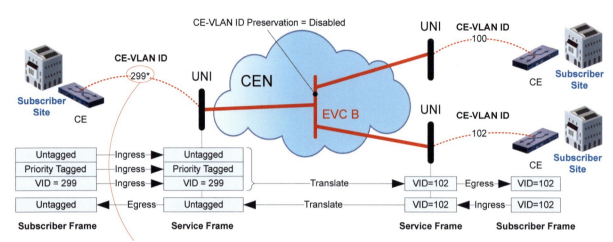

* In this example, CE-VLAN ID value 299 identifies untagged, priority tagged, and C-Tag VID=299 service frames with EVC B at this UNI.

Related Links

CE-VLAN ID for Untagged and Priority Tagged Service Frames on p. 74

5.6
Data Service Frame Delivery Service Attributes

Service Attribute		Requirement					
		Port-Based Service			VLAN-Based Service		
Cat.	Name	EPL	EP-LAN	EP-Tree	EVPL	EVP-LAN	EVP-Tree
Per EVC	Unicast Service Frame Delivery	Discard / Deliver Unconditionally / Deliver Conditionally					
	Multicast Service Frame Delivery	Discard / Deliver Unconditionally / Deliver Conditionally					
	Broadcast Service Frame Delivery	Discard / Deliver Unconditionally / Deliver Conditionally					

These three attributes apply to Data service frames. They do not apply to L2CP or SOAM service frames.[40] Like every service frame, every *data* service frame is subject to many MEF 10.3 requirements at ingress that can result in its discard.[41] If a data service frame not discarded at ingress, its delivery becomes governed by one of three attributes:

Unicast Service Frame Delivery governs data service frames with **unicast** destination MAC address.
Multicast Service Frame Delivery governs data service frames with **multicast** destination MAC address.
Broadcast Service Frame Delivery governs data service frames with **broadcast** destination MAC address.

Each attribute can be configured to one of three *data service frame dispositions*:

Discard – The EVC discards the data service frames.
Deliver Unconditionally – The EVC delivers the data service frames to all other UNIs (excluding the ingress UNI) unconditionally, in effect broadcasting them like and Ethernet Hub. Of course, this excludes delivery from leaf-UNI to leaf-UNI, if service is type E-Tree.
Deliver Conditionally – The EVC delivers the data service frames to other UNIs (excluding the ingress UNI) conditionally, per any set of conditions specified in the SLA.

The following table summarizes requirements and recommendations from MEF 6.2:

Service	Unicast Service Frame Delivery	Multicast Service Frame Delivery	Broadcast Service Frame Delivery
EPL		**Must Deliver Unconditionally**	
EVPL		Should Deliver Unconditionally	

---

40 Recall that MEF 10.3 classifies service frames into three categories according to purpose: Data service frames, L2CP service frames, and SOAM service frames.
41 Per MEF 10.3, a service frame can/must be discarded at ingress for many reasons, including: if it is invalid per Clause 3.4 of IEEE Std 802.3 – 2012; if it is smaller than 64 bytes; if it maps to a CoS ID that is mapped to discard, if the *Source MAC Address Limit* is exceeded, if it is declared Red by an ingress or egress bandwidth profile, and if its length exceeds the *EVC Maximum Service Frame Size*.

Service	Unicast Service Frame Delivery	Multicast Service Frame Delivery	Broadcast Service Frame Delivery
EP-LAN	Should Deliver Conditionally	Discard / Deliver Unconditionally / Deliver Conditionally	Should Deliver Unconditionally
EP-Tree			
EVP-LAN			
EVP-Tree			

EPL services must deliver all data service frames (unicast, multicast, and broadcast data service frames) unconditionally. MEF 6.2 recommends that EVPL service do the same, but do not make it a requirement.

Multipoint EVCs are normally configured with *Unicast Service Frame Delivery = Deliver Conditionally* and with conditions defined to produce bridging behavior (MAC address-based learning and frame forwarding behavior) in the EVC, in order to reduce network traffic.

Multicast and broadcast frames are normally delivered unconditionally. However conditional delivery might be useful in some cases. For example, conditions might be defined to throttle multicast/broadcast service frames at ingress[42] in order to limit multicast/broadcast traffic.

 Important: *Regardless of the data service frame's disposition, its delivery is still subject to bandwidth limitations as defined by bandwidth profiles and enforced by policing. Bandwidth profiles and policing are covered in the next lesson.*

Data Service Frame Transparency Requirements

Excluding changes to the CE-VLAN tag, MEF 10.3 requires that all fields of a data service frame remain unchanged by the service. A data service frame's content at egress must match its content at ingress.

If the CE-VLAN tag is modified (for example, if CE-VLAN ID and/or PCP bits are changed as is permitted if Per EVC service attributes *CE-VLAN ID Preservation* and *CE-VLAN CoS Preservation* are set to No), added, or removed, the frame check sequence (FCS) at egress must be recalculated.

Test your understanding: *The service provider's implementation of an EP-LAN service includes MAC address-based learning and frame forwarding behavior. For this service, attribute* **Unicast Service Frame Delivery** *should be set to which value:* **Deliver Unconditionally** *or* **Deliver Conditionally**? [43]

Related Links

Data, L2CP, and SOAM Service Frames on p. 55
Unicast, Multicast, and Broadcast MAC Addresses on p. 47
Single-Flow Bandwidth Profile on p. 126

---

42 To discard multicast and/or broadcast data service frames above a set threshold
43 **Answer:** *Deliver Conditionally (with conditions defined to produce MAC address-based learning and frame forwarding behavior)*

5.7
Source MAC Address Limit Service Attribute

Service Attribute		Requirement					
		Port-Based Service			VLAN-Based Service		
Cat.	Name	EPL	EP-LAN	EP-Tree	EVPL	EVP-LAN	EVP-Tree
EVC per UNI	Source MAC Address Limit	Disabled	Enabled / Disabled				

This attribute is used with multipoint EVCs that forward service frames based on MAC address learning.

Its purpose is to prevent learning tables in the CEN from overloading and thereby contain problems that can result from misprovisioning[44] and/or denial of service attacks[45].

For EPL services, MEF 6.2 requires *Source MAC Address Limit = Disabled*.

For EVPL services, MEF 6.2 requires *Source MAC Address Limit = Disabled* if all three data service frame delivery attributes (*Unicast Service Frame Delivery*, *Multicast Service Frame Delivery*, and *Broadcast Service Frame Delivery*) are set to *Deliver Unconditionally*.

If *Source MAC Address Limit = Enabled*, two parameters define a process that discards ingress service frames after the limit is reached:

N	A positive integer (the maximum number of unique source MAC addresses accepted in time interval tau)
tau	A time interval

The process maintains a list of unique source MAC addresses sent into the EVC at the UNI. The list can include no more than N MAC addresses. If a particular MAC address is not seen during time interval tau, it is aged-out (removed from the list). If an ingress service frame arrives with a new source MAC address when the list is full, that service frame is discarded.

---

[44] For example, if the subscriber accidentally connects an Ethernet switch to service that is configured to support a router.
[45] A denial of service attack attempts to bring down a service by bombarding it with numerous Ethernet frames and MAC addresses in an effort to overload MAC learning tables.

5.8
Security Considerations for E-Tree Services

Because E-Tree services prohibit direct Leaf-to-Leaf communication, communication between each Leaf UNI and the set of Root UNIs is commonly assumed to be secure. However, E-Tree services can, in some cases, deliver unknown unicast service frames, meant for one Leaf UNI, to other Leaf UNIs. This is of no concern in many applications because the peer networks (at Leaf UNIs) can be trusted. However, in other applications, the peer networks (at Leaf UNIs) may belong to different organizations.

Leaf-to-Root communication is inherently secure.[46] However, in the other direction (Root-to-Leaf), special issues should be considered. The security issue involves the delivery of unicast service frames from a Root UNI to a Leaf UNI. For E-Tree services, EVC attribute *Unicast Service Frame Delivery* is typically configured to *Deliver Conditionally*[47] with conditions defined to produce bridging behavior (MAC address-based learning and frame forwarding behavior). In this case, any <u>unknown unicast</u> service frame that ingresses at a Root UNI will be delivered to all Leaf UNIs, as shown in the following example (Fig. 3 from MEF 10.3).

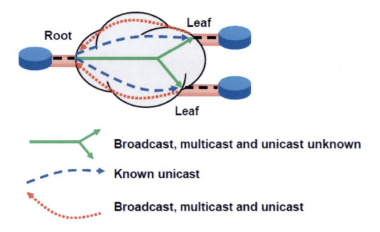

Reproduced with permission of the Metro Ethernet Forum

If the unicast service frame's Destination MAC Address is in the service's current MAC address table, there is no problem: the E-Tree service will deliver the service frame (as a known unicast service frame) only to the correct Leaf UNI. However, if the Destination MAC address is not in the current MAC table (the address may have been "aged-out", for example), the E-Tree service will deliver the service frame (as a unknown unicast service frame) to all UNIs of the EVC (including other Leaf UNIs). This may be of concern in some applications.

This issue can be mitigated by using routers (as CEs) at Leaf UNIs. This mitigates the issue because a router exposes only a single MAC destination address to the E-Tree service (MAC addresses for hosts beyond the UNI are not exposed). This makes the potential security issue more manageable because only one MAC address per Leaf UNI is involved.

---

46 A service frame that ingresses at a Leaf UNI cannot egress at another Leaf UNI, it can only egress at Root UNIs.
47 If attribute *Unicast Service Frame Delivery* is configured to *Deliver Unconditionally*, <u>every unicast service frame</u> that ingresses at a Root UNI will be delivered to all Leaf UNIs .

5.9
L2CP Processing Service Attributes

In this section:

- 5.9.1 About Layer 2 Control Protocols
- 5.9.2 L2CP Behavioral Model
- 5.9.3 L2CP Frame Processing
- 5.9.4 Attribute: UNI L2CP Peering
- 5.9.5 Attribute: UNI L2CP Address Set
- 5.9.6 Passing L2CP Frames and Tunneling
- 5.9.7 L2CP Attribute Configuration Requirements
- 5.9.8 L2CP Requirements for Spanning Tree Protocols
- 5.9.9 UNI Functionality and L2CP Requirements

Service Attribute		Requirement					
		Port-Based Service			VLAN-Based Service		
Cat.	Name	EPL	EP-LAN	EP-Tree	EVPL	EVP-LAN	EVP-Tree
Per UNI	UNI L2CP Address Set	CTB / CTB-2	CTB	CTB	CTA	CTA	CTA
	UNI L2CP Peering	None or list of {Destination Address, Protocol Identifier} or list of {Destination Address, Protocol Identifier, Link Identifier} to be peered					

MEF 45 Compared to MEF 6.1.1

MEF 45 supersedes MEF 6.1.1, redefining L2CP processing attributes and requirements (previously defined in MEF 6.1.1) to extend L2CP processing to services delivered across multiple CENs. In doing so, MEF 45 maintains as much consistency with the requirements in MEF 6.1.1 as possible given the expanded scope of covering multiple CENs. However, requirements are expressed differently, using new attributes, concepts, and terminology. The concept of *tunneling*, in particular, is depreciated because it represents behavior across the CEN as a whole. MEF 45 instead focuses on L2CP processing at external interfaces (UNIs and ENNIs). Tunneling behavior can emerge, but the MEF 45 behavioral model and attributes do not address tunneling directly.

L2CP Service Frame

As explained in a previous lesson, a service frame is recognized as an *L2CP Service Frame* if its destination MAC address is listed in the following table (Table 3 in MEF 10.3 or Table 2 in MEF 45).[48, 49, 50]

L2CP Destination MAC Addresses	Description
01-80-C2-00-00-00 through 01-80-C2-00-00-0F	Bridge Block of protocols
01-80-C2-00-00-20 through 01-80-C2-00-00-2F	MRP (Multiple Registration Protocol) Block of protocols

---

48 These 32 addresses are reserved for Layer 2 control protocols by IEEE 802.1Q-2011.
49 Per MEF 10.3, a service provider may define additional addresses for identifying L2CP service frames (in addition to those shown in the table). However, L2CP processing for such frames is beyond the scope of MEF 45.
50 The destination address does not identify the protocol, but is sufficient to identify the service frame as an L2CP service frame. The Protocol Identifier (Ethertype or LLC Address) in the L2CP frame identifies the protocol.

The following table lists L2CP protocols supported by the Bridge and MRP address blocks.

L2CP Addresses and Protocols

Block	Destination MAC Address	Protocol Type (Standard)	Ethertype/subtype
Bridge Block	01-80-C2-00-00-00	STP/RSTP (IEEE 802.1D), MSTP (IEEE 802.1Q)	N/A
	01-80-C2-00-00-01	PAUSE (IEEE 802.3)	0x8808
	01-80-C2-00-00-02	LACP (IEEE 802.3)	0x8809/01
		LAMP (IEEE 802.3)	0x8809/02
		Link OAM (IEEE 802.3)	0x8809/03
		ESMC (ITU-T G.8264-2008)	0x8809/0A
	01-80-C2-00-00-03	Port Authentication (IEEE 802.1X)	0x888E
	01-80-C2-00-00-04	—	N/A
	01-80-C2-00-00-05	—	N/A
	01-80-C2-00-00-06	—	N/A
	01-80-C2-00-00-07	E-LMI (MEF 16)	0x88EE
	01-80-C2-00-00-08	—	N/A
	01-80-C2-00-00-09	—	N/A
	01-80-C2-00-00-0A	—	N/A
	01-80-C2-00-00-0B	—	N/A
	01-80-C2-00-00-0C	—	N/A
	01-80-C2-00-00-0D	—	N/A
	01-80-C2-00-00-0E	LLDP (IEEE 802.1AB)	0x88CC
		PTP Peer Delay (IEEE 1588-2008)	0x88F7
	01-80-C2-00-00-0F	—	N/A
MRP Block	01-80-C2-00-00-20 through 01-80-C2-00-00-2F	GARP (IEEE 802.1Q), MRP (IEEE 802.1ak)	N/A

Related Links

Data, L2CP, and SOAM Service Frames on p. 55

5.9.1
About Layer 2 Control Protocols

There are many Layer 2 control protocols serving various network control functions. Each instance of a Layer 2 control protocol involves two or more L2CP protocol entities. An L2CP protocol entity is a network function located in a Layer 2 network that communicates with peer entities located elsewhere in the network using L2CP frames and a particular Layer 2 control protocol.

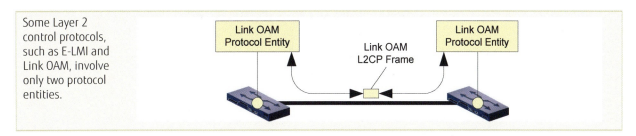

Some Layer 2 control protocols, such as E-LMI and Link OAM, involve only two protocol entities.

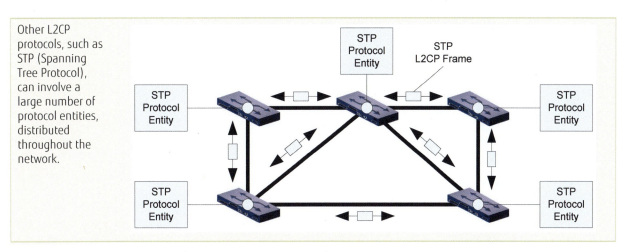

Other L2CP protocols, such as STP (Spanning Tree Protocol), can involve a large number of protocol entities, distributed throughout the network.

Most Layer 2 control protocols have been defined to operate according to rules defined in IEEE 802.1Q-2011. MEF 45 defines L2CP processing for Carrier Ethernet services based largely on IEEE 802.1Q-2011. This helps ensure that customer equipment using Layer 2 control protocols will interoperate with the CEN.

5.9.2
L2CP Behavioral Model

The *L2CP Behavioral Model* defined in MEF 45 explains how individual L2CP frames are handled. This model includes *L2CP Decision Points* located in the CEN between the UNI and the EVC as shown in the following figure.[51]

---

[51] In the multi-CEN context, L2CP Decision Points are also located in Operator CENs between the ENNI and the OVC endpoint.

L2CP protocol entities are understood to be located at L2CP Decision Points (as needed).

In this example only one EVC is shown at the UNIs, although other EVCs might be present if the UNIs are configured for service multiplexing.

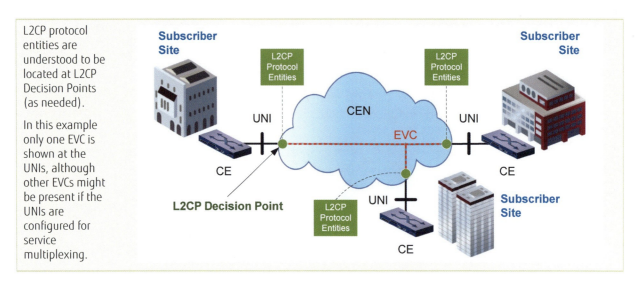

An individual L2CP service frame (like every service frame) maps to one EVC at most, regardless of how many EVCs are at the UNI.[52]

The following figure (based on Figure 2 in MEF 45) illustrates L2CP service frame processing at the L2CP Decision Point.

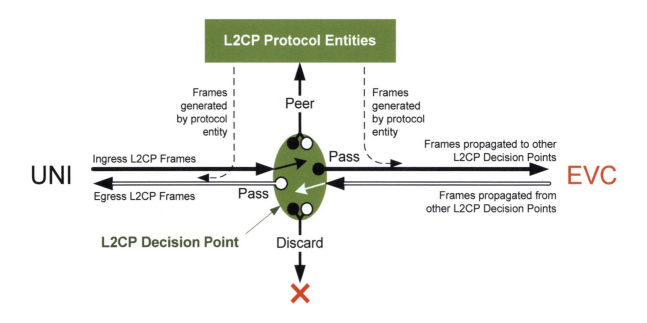

---

52 If the UNI is configured with All-to-One Bundling, all service frames map to the EVC. Otherwise, service frames map to at most one EVC through service frame mapping attributes (*CE-VLAN ID / EVC Map* and *CE-VLAN ID for Untagged and Priority Tagged Service Frames*).

At the L2CP Decision Point, one of three actions is assigned to the L2CP frame:

- **Discard** — The L2CP service frame is discarded (not propagated or delivered to a protocol entity).

- **Peer** — The L2CP service frame is delivered to the appropriate protocol entity for processing. Processing may trigger the protocol entity to generate new L2CP frames in one or both directions (toward the UNI and/or toward the EVC).

- **Pass** — The L2CP frame is forwarded in the same manner as a data service frame with multicast destination MAC address (If the EVC is multipoint, a passed ingress L2CP frame will be forwarded to multiple UNIs).

Note: *The term **tunnel**, used to describe L2CP frame processing behavior prior to MEF 45, is not used in this model. However, if all L2CP decision points associated by a service pass an L2CP frame, then the end-to-end service behavior is the same as tunnel.*

5.9.3
L2CP Frame Processing

The action (Peer, Discard, or Pass) taken for a given L2CP service frame at a given L2CP Decision Point depends upon the Destination Address and the Protocol Identifier within the frame, and upon the configured values of the L2CP Service Attributes (*UNI L2CP Peering* and *UNI L2CP Address Set*), as illustrated in the following flowchart (equivalent to Figure 6 in MEF 45).

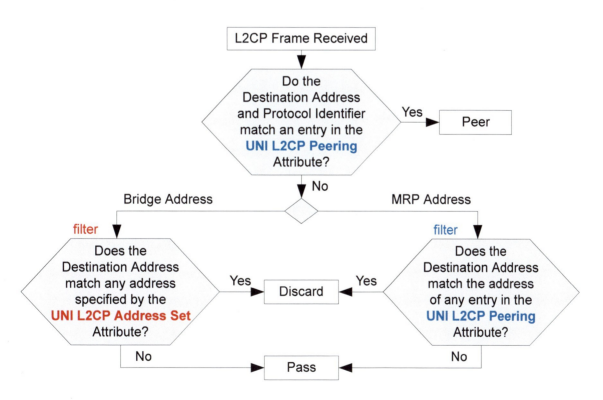

When the L2CP frame is received at the L2CP Decision Point, it is tested for peering against the entries in the *UNI L2CP Peering* attribute. If the L2CP frame's Destination Address and Protocol Identifier match an entry in the *UNI*

L2CP Peering attribute, the L2CP frame is peered. Otherwise (if the L2CP frame is not peered), the L2CP frame becomes subject to one of two filtering operations:

1. **Bridge Address** filter – If the L2CP frame's Destination Address is from the Bridge block of reserved addresses, that address is tested against the set of addresses specified by the *UNI L2CP Address Set* attribute. If there is a match, the L2CP frame is discarded. Otherwise, the L2CP frame is passed.

2. **MRP Address** filter – If the L2CP frame's Destination Address if from the MRP block of reserved addresses, that address is tested against the set of addresses specified by the *UNI L2CP Peering* attribute. If there is a match, the L2CP frame is discarded. Otherwise, the L2CP frame is passed.

5.9.4
Attribute: UNI L2CP Peering

Attribute *UNI L2CP Peering* lists all L2CP protocols that peer at the UNI. In most cases, two values {Destination MAC Address, Protocol Identifier} are sufficient to identify a protocol. In some cases three values {Destination MAC Address, Protocol Identifier, Link Identifier} are required.[53]

Each protocol that peers at the UNI is individually listed. Protocols from both address blocks (Bridge Reserved and MRP) can be included. The following table (Table 6 in MEF 45) shows an example specification of the *UNI L2CP Peering* attribute.

Protocol to be Peered	Protocol Identifier	L2CP Destination Address
Link Aggregation (LACP)	Ethertype: 0x8809 Subtypes: 01,02	01-80-C2-00-00-02
Link OAM	Ethertype: 0x8809 Subtype: 03	01-80-C2-00-00-02
E-LMI	Ethertype: 0x88EE	01-80-C2-00-00-07
Spanning Tree (RSTP/MSTP)	LLC Address: 0x82	01-80-C2-00-00-00

5.9.5
Attribute: UNI L2CP Address Set

Attribute *UNI L2CP Address Set* specifies the subset of Bridge Reserved Addresses that are filtered (discarded, if not peered). Rather than listing addresses individually, this attribute is set to one of three values:

Value of attribute *UNI L2CP Address Set*		Application
CTA	C-VLAN Tag Aware	VLAN-based services
CTB	C-VLAN Tag Blind	Port-based services
CTB-2	C-VLAN Tag Blind Option 2	EPL services that support the EPL Option 2 L2CP processing

---

[53] If the UNI is implemented with multiple physical links, certain protocols (for example, LLDP and ESMC) can operate over individual physical links. In this case the UNI L2CP Peering entry can require three values, {Destination Address, Protocol Identifier, and Link Identifier}.

The following table (Based on Table 5, MEF 45) shows the L2CP Destination MAC Addresses that are filtered (discarded, if not peered) for each attribute value (CTA, CTB, and CTB-2). Symbol **X** indicates filtering.

L2CP Destination Address	802.1Q Assignment	Corresponding Protocols (Ethertype/subtype)	Filtered By:		
			CTA	CTB	CTB-2
01-80-C2-00-00-00	Nearest Customer Bridge	STP/RSTP, MSTP	X	—	—
01-80-C2-00-00-01	IEEE MAC Specific Control Protocols	PAUSE (0x8808)	X	X	X
01-80-C2-00-00-02	IEEE 802 Slow Protocols	LACP (0x8809/01) LAMP (0x8809/02) Link OAM (0x8809/03) ESMC (0x8809/0A)	X	X	—
01-80-C2-00-00-03	Nearest non-TPMR Bridge	Port Authentication (0x888E)	X	X	—
01-80-C2-00-00-04	IEEE MAC Specific Control Protocols	—	X	X	—
01-80-C2-00-00-05	Reserved for Future Standardization	—	X	X	—
01-80-C2-00-00-06	Reserved for Future Standardization	—	X	X	—
01-80-C2-00-00-07	ELMI	E-LMI (0x88EE)	X	X	—
01-80-C2-00-00-08	Provider Bridge Group	—	X	X	—
01-80-C2-00-00-09	Reserved for Future Standardization	—	X	X	—
01-80-C2-00-00-0A	Reserved for Future Standardization	—	X	X	—
01-80-C2-00-00-0B	Reserved for Future Standardization	—	X	—	—
01-80-C2-00-00-0C	Reserved for Future Standardization	—	X	—	—
01-80-C2-00-00-0D	Provider Bridge MVRP	—	X	—	—
01-80-C2-00-00-0E	Nearest Bridge, Individual LAN Scope	LLDP (0x88CC) PTP Peer Delay (0x88F7)	X	X	—
01-80-C2-00-00-0F	Reserved for Future Standardization	—	X	—	—

To say that an L2CP frame is filtered (discarded, if not peered), is to say that it cannot pass at the UNI. Attribute *UNI L2CP Address Set* specifies addresses that cannot pass at the UNI. It says nothing about peering or discard.

Notice that PAUSE protocol frames are filtered (cannot be passed) by any UNI, regardless of *UNI L2CP Address Set* value.

UNIs configured with *UNI L2CP Address Set* = *CTA* filter all bridge-address frames (cannot pass any of them).

5.9.6
Passing L2CP Frames and Tunneling

Tunneling behavior occurs when an ingress L2CP service frame passes through the CEN without being processed and is delivered unchanged to the proper egress UNI(s) associated by the EVC.

Although MEF 45 attributes do not address tunneling directly, tunneling behavior results if the L2CP frame is passed (not peered or discarded) at each L2CP decision point.

> A Bridge-block L2CP service frame is passed if two conditions are met:
> 1. Its {Destination Address, Protocol Identifier} pair does not match any entry in the *UNI L2CP Peering List*, and
> 2. Its Destination Address does not match any address specified in the *UNI L2CP Address Set*.

> An MRP-block L2CP service frame is passed if its Destination Address does not match the destination address of any entry in the *UNI L2CP Peering List*.

If an L2CP service frame meets these conditions at all UNIs of the EVC, it is tunnelled.

5.9.7
L2CP Attribute Configuration Requirements

Requirements [R2], [R3], and [R4] in MEF 45 require that *UNI L2CP Address Set* be configured as follows:

Service Attribute		Requirement					
		Port-Based Service			VLAN-Based Service		
Cat.	Name	EPL	EP-LAN	EP-Tree	EVPL	EVP-LAN	EVP-Tree
Per UNI	UNI L2CP Address Set	CTB / CTB-2	CTB		CTA		

UNIs for EVPL, EVP-LAN, and EVP-Tree services must be configured with **CTA** (C-VLAN Tag Aware). UNIs for EP-LAN and EP-Tree services must be configured with **CTB** (C-VLAN Tag Blind). UNIs for EPL services can be configured with **CTB** (C-VLAN Tag Blind) or **CTB-2** (C-VLAN Tag Blind Option 2).

As previously explained, each attribute value (CTA, CTB, and CTB-2) defines a set of Bridge Block MAC Addresses that are filtered (discarded, if not peered) and must not be passed.

Requirement [R11] in MEF 45 states: "**When the UNI L2CP Address Set service attribute is CTB, any entry in the UNI Peering Service Attribute MUST NOT have a [bridge-block destination address that is] not in the CTB subset of [bridge-block destination addresses]**". It follows that such frames must be passed (as they are not peered or discarded).

Requirement [D1] in MEF 45 recommends: "**When the UNI L2CP Address Set service attribute is CTB-2, the UNI L2CP Peering Service Attribute SHOULD be an empty list**". If follows that all frames with L2CP Destination Address not in the *UNI L2CP Address Set* should be passed (as they should not be peered and are not discarded).

The following table summarizes the impact of all L2CP requirements on passing.

Impact of L2CP Requirements on Passing

Block	L2CP Destination Address	Corresponding Protocols (Ethertype/subtype)	EVPL, EVP-LAN, EVP-Tree (CTA)	EPL, EP-LAN, EP-Tree (CTB)	EPL (CTB-2)
Bridge block	01-80-C2-00-00-00	STP/RSTP, MSTP	must not pass	must pass [R11]	should pass [D1]
	01-80-C2-00-00-01	PAUSE (0x8808)		must not pass	must not pass
	01-80-C2-00-00-02	LACP (0x8809/01) LAMP (0x8809/02) Link OAM (0x8809/03) ESMC (0x8809/0A)		must not pass	should pass [D1]
	01-80-C2-00-00-03	Port Authen. (0x888E)			
	01-80-C2-00-00-04	—			
	01-80-C2-00-00-05	—			
	01-80-C2-00-00-06	—			
	01-80-C2-00-00-07	E-LMI (0x88EE)			
	01-80-C2-00-00-08	—			
	01-80-C2-00-00-09	—			
	01-80-C2-00-00-0A	—			
	01-80-C2-00-00-0B	—			
	01-80-C2-00-00-0C	—		must pass [R11]	
	01-80-C2-00-00-0D	—			
	01-80-C2-00-00-0E	LLDP (0x88CC) PTP Peer Delay (0x88F7)		must not pass	
	01-80-C2-00-00-0F	—		must pass [R11]	
MRP block	01-80-C2-00-00-20 through 01-80-C2-00-00-2F	GARP, MRP	no requirement	no requirement	should pass [D1]

You do not have to memorize all of these requirements for the MEF-CECP exam, but you should probably understand those related to bridge protocol data units (BPDUs) used in spanning tree protocols (STP/RSTP, MSTP).

5.9.8
L2CP Requirements for Spanning Tree Protocols

L2CP processing capability is especially important for subscribers who choose to deploy IEEE 802.1Q customer bridges (as opposed to routers) as CEs. The following figure shows LANs at three customer sites that are already interconnected by some means (external to the CEN). The customer want to interconnect all three LANs through the CEN for redundancy. The CEs are 802.1Q customer bridges.

In this example, the customer wants to run spanning tree protocol (STP) across the aggregation of connected LANs so the service must support bridge protocol data units (BPDUs) in some fashion. To the CEN, BPDUs are recognized as L2CP service frames with destination MAC address 01-80-C2-00-00-00.

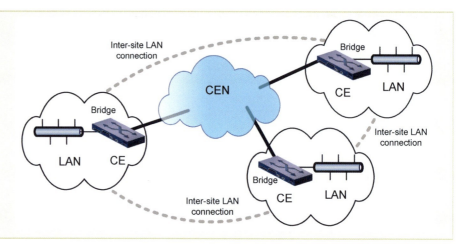

If the service is port-based, the three UNIs must be configured with UNI L2CP Address Set = CTB. Furthermore, [R11] in MEF 45 stipulates that BPDUs must be passed (not peered). So the service must "tunnel" BPDUs: that is, pass them through the CEN and deliver them unchanged to the proper (egress) UNI(s).

If the service is VLAN-based, the three UNIs must be configured with UNI L2CP Address Set = CTA, which means BPDUs must either peer at each UNI or be discarded. To run STP across the aggregation of connected LANs, the service must peer BPDUs at each UNI.

The following table summarizes L2CP processing requirements from MEF 45 for bridging protocols (L2CP service frames with destination MAC address 01-80-C2-00-00-00).

Service	L2CP Requirement
Port-based (EPL, EP-LAN, EP-Tree)	Must pass BPDUs at all UNIs **Note:** EPL services configured with CTB-2 <u>should</u> (not must) pass BPDUs at all UNIs per [D1] in MEF 45.
VLAN-based (EVPL, EVP-LAN, EVP-Tree)	Must peer or discard BPDUs at all UNIs

Key observations:

- BPDU "tunneling" is required for port-based services (all UNIs must, or should, be configured to pass BPDUs).
- BPDU "tunneling" is not allowed for VLAN-based services (all UNIs must be configured to peer or discard BPDUs).

5.9.9
UNI Functionality and L2CP Requirements

Several Per UNI service attributes (Synchronous Mode, UNI Resiliency, Link OAM, and E-LMI, which are explained in a latter lesson) declare UNI functionalities that rely on Layer 2 control protocols to operate.

MEF 45 associates L2CP peering requirements with certain values of these attributes, as follows:

Per UNI Attribute		Protocol(s) that must peer at the UNI		MEF 45 Requirement
Name	Value	L2CP Destination Address	Corresponding Protocol(s) (Ethertype/subtype)	
Synchronous Mode	Enabled	1-80-C2-00-00-02	ESMC (0x8809/0A)	[R17], [R18]
UNI Resiliency	2-Link Aggregation	1-80-C2-00-00-02	LACP (0x8809/01) LAMP (0x8809/02)	[R13]
Link OAM	Enabled	1-80-C2-00-00-02	Link OAM (0x8809/03)	[R15]
E-LMI	Enabled	01-80-C2-00-00-07	E-LMI (0x88EE)	[R16]

If a UNI is configured with an attribute value shown in the table, the associated protocol(s) shown in the table must peer at the UNI (must be listed in the *UNI L2CP Peering* service attribute). For example, if a UNI is configured with *Link OAM = Enabled*, the pair <01-80-C2-00-00-02, 0x8809/03> must be listed in the *UNI L2CP Peering service attribute*.

Related Links
UNI Functionality Service Attributes on p. 174

5.10
Review: Service Connectivity Attributes

1. An EVC is configured with EVC Maximum Service Frame Size set to 1526 bytes. A service frame containing 1530 bytes is transmitted to the UNI from the CE. Which statement is correct?

   a. The frame should be discarded.
   b. The frame should be marked yellow (drop-eligible) and forwarded.
   c. The service level specification (SLS) applies to the frame.
   d. The frame should be truncated to 1526 bytes and forwarded.

2. A broadcast service frame is transmitted from the subscriber to a UNI that is provisioned to support service multiplexing. Where will the service frame be delivered, assuming that it is not discarded?

   a. To all UNIs of each EVC multiplexed at the UNI
   b. To all UNIs in the EVC
   c. To all EVCs multiplexed at the UNI
   d. To all UNIs in the EVC, except the ingress UNI
   e. To all UNIs in the EVC, except the egress UNI

3. Which two services cannot tunnel L2CP service frames containing Bridge Protocol Data Units (BPDUs) to support Spanning Tree Protocol (STP)? (Choose two.)

   a. EVP-LAN
   b. EP-LAN
   c. EVPL
   d. EPL

   Note: Tunneling is the process by which an L2CP service frame is passed through the service provider network without being processed and is delivered unchanged to the proper UNI(s).

4. A EVPL service has to support an application that uses IP packets of length up to 800 bytes. What is the smallest value of attribute *EVC Maximum Service Frame Size* that can be specified for this service?

   a. 800 bytes
   b. 818 bytes
   c. 822 bytes
   d. 1500 bytes
   e. 1518 bytes
   f. 1522 bytes

5. Which statement is true for a UNI that is configured with bundling?

   a. All CE-VLAN IDs are mapped to a single EVC.
   b. The UNI must be configured to support service multiplexing.
   c. Only VLAN-based services can be provisioned on it.
   d. More than one EVC must terminate at the UNI.

6. A UNI is configured without bundling or all-to-one bundling and is also configured to support service multiplexing. What is the maximum number of CE-VLAN IDs that can be mapped to a given EVC at the UNI?

   a. 4095
   b. 4094
   c. 64
   d. 1

7. A UNI is configured with service multiplexing. Which statement is not true?

   a. The UNI can support up to 4094 EVCs.
   b. Bundling is optional at the UNI.
   c. At the UNI, at least one CE-VLAN ID must be mapped to each EVC.
   d. At the UNI, all-to-one bundling is permitted.

8. Which statement is not true for a UNI configured with all-to-one bundling?

   a. Service multiplexing is Disabled.
   b. Bundling is Disabled.
   c. CE-VLAN ID preservation is Enabled.
   d. CoS Preservation is Enabled.
   e. The UNI can support up to 4094 EVCs.

9. An EPL service has to support jumbo frames with payload of up to 3000 bytes. What is the smallest value of attribute *EVC Maximum Service Frame Size* that can be specified for this service?

   a. 3000 bytes
   b. 3018 bytes
   c. 3022 bytes
   d. 3026 bytes
   e. 3030 bytes

10. The *CE-VLAN ID for Untagged and Priority Tagged Service Frames* service attribute applies to which three of the following services? (Choose three.)

    a. EPL services
    b. EVPL services
    c. EP-LAN services
    d. EVP-LAN services
    e. EP-Tree services
    f. EVP-Tree services

11. The smallest value allowed for the *EVC Maximum Service Frame Size* attribute is:

    a. 1518 bytes
    b. 64 bytes
    c. 1526 bytes
    d. 1522 bytes

12. An EVP-LAN service is implemented between three UNIs. One of the UNIs is configured with *Bundling = Enabled* and *UNI Maximum Service Frame Size = 1550 bytes*. The other two UNIs are configured with *Bundling = Enabled* and *UNI Maximum Service Frame Size = 1600 bytes*. Which one of the following attribute configurations is allowed for this service?

    a. EVC Maximum Service Frame Size = 1650 bytes, CE-VLAN ID Preservation = Disabled.
    b. EVC Maximum Service Frame Size = 1600 bytes, CE-VLAN ID Preservation = Enabled.
    c. EVC Maximum Service Frame Size = 1550 bytes, CE-VLAN ID Preservation = Disabled.
    d. EVC Maximum Service Frame Size = 1500 bytes, CE-VLAN ID Preservation = Enabled.

13. An EVP-LAN service is implemented between three UNIs: UNI A, UNI B, and UNI C. At UNI A four values of CE-VLAN ID map to the EVC. How many values of CE-VLAN ID map to the EVC at UNI C?

    a. Up to 4
    b. Exactly 4
    c. Up to 4094
    d. Up to 1522

14. According to MEF 45, what options are available for handling an ingress L2CP service frame?

    a. Peer, Discard, Pass to EVC, Peer and Pass to EVC
    b. Peer, Discard, Tunnel
    c. Peer, Discard, Pass
    d. Peer, Discard, Peer and Tunnel

15. The subscriber needs an EVP-Tree service that includes Link OAM and Link Aggregation (LACP) at all UNIs. To what value must attribute *UNI L2CP Address Set* be configured?

    a. CTA
    b. CTB
    c. CTA-2
    d. CTB-2

16. The subscriber wants an EP-LAN service that tunnels BPDUs to support spanning tree protocol (STP). How should attributes *UNI L2CP Peering* and *UNI L2CP Address Set* be configured at the UNIs?

    a. Set *UNI L2CP Address Set = CTB* and include STP in the *UNI L2CP Peering* list.
    b. Set *UNI L2CP Address Set = CTB* and omit STP from the *UNI L2CP Peering* list.
    c. Set *UNI L2CP Address Set = CTA* and include STP in the *UNI L2CP Peering* list.
    d. Set *UNI L2CP Address Set = CTA* and omit STP from the *UNI L2CP Peering* list.

17. An E-Tree service is configured with attribute *Unicast Service Frame Delivery* set to *Deliver Unconditionally*. A unicast service frame ingresses through a Leaf UNI. That service frame...

    a. Is delivered to all other UNIs in the EVC
    b. Is delivered to all other UNIs in the EVC, excluding other Leaf UNIs
    c. Is delivered to all other UNIs in the EVC, excluding Root UNIs
    d. Is delivered only to the correct destination UNI (after that UNI becomes known through MAC address learning)

18. An EVP-Tree service connects three UNIs (A, B and C). Three values of CE-VLAN ID map to the EVC at UNI A which is configured as a Root UNI. If UNI B is configured as a Leaf UNI, the value of *Bundling* at UNI B ...

   a. Must be Enabled
   b. Must be Disabled
   c. Can be Enabled or Disabled

19. To reduce network traffic the subscriber wants an EP-LAN services that produces MAC address learning and forwarding behavior over the CEN. Attribute *Unicast Service Frame Delivery* should be set to which value?

   a. Deliver Unconditionally
   b. Deliver Conditionally
   c. Deliver with Bridging
   d. Deliver per IEEE 802.1Q

20. An E-Tree service has 3 Leaf UNIs and 2 Root UNIs. Attribute *Unicast Service Frame Delivery* is set to *Deliver Unconditionally*. A unicast service frame is sent from CE to CEN through a Leaf UNI. To how many UNIs will it be delivered?

   a. 1
   b. 2
   c. 3
   d. 4
   e. 5
   f. 6

21. EVC-1 connects UNI A, UNI B and UNI C. At UNI A, CE-VLAN IDs 101 and 102 map to EVC-1. What is the value of *Bundling* at UNI B and the value of *CE-VLAN ID Preservation* for EVC-1?

   a. Bundling = Disabled, CE-VLAN ID Preservation = Disabled
   b. Bundling = Disabled, CE-VLAN ID Preservation = Enabled
   c. Bundling = Enabled, CE-VLAN ID Preservation = Disabled
   d. Bundling = Enabled, CE-VLAN ID Preservation = Enabled

22. An EVP-Tree service connects four leaf UNIs and one root UNI. Its EVC is configured with *CE-VLAN ID Preservation = Disabled*. The root UNI is configured with attribute *CE-VLAN ID for Untagged and Priority Tagged Service Frames* set to 321 and that value (321) is mapped to the EVC at the root UNI. How many CE-VLAN IDs can be mapped to the EVC at the Root UNI?

   a. 1
   b. 2
   c. 3
   d. 4
   e. 321
   f. 4094

23. An E-LAN service connects three UNIs. Two of the UNIs are configured with *UNI Maximum Service Frame Size* = 1800 bytes. The EVC is configured with *EVC Maximum Service Frame Size* = 1600 bytes. From the following options, pick the smallest value that is acceptable for *UNI Maximum Service Frame Size* at the third UNI.

    a. 1518 bytes
    b. 1522 bytes
    c. 1526 bytes
    d. 1600 bytes
    e. 1800 bytes

24. UNI-A is configured with *Bundling=Disabled, All to One Bundling = Disabled*, and *CE VLAN ID for Untagged and Priority Tagged Service Frames = 33*. CE-VLAN ID 33 maps to EVC-B at UNI-A. EVC-B is configured with *CE VLAN ID Preservation = Disabled*. At UNI-A, all service frames transmitted to the subscriber from EVC-B must be in which format(s)?

    a. untagged
    b. untagged or priority tagged
    c. untagged, priority tagged, or C-Tagged with VID=33
    d. untagged, priority tagged, or C-Tagged with any VID value in the range 1...4094

Related Links

Answers: Service Connectivity Attributes on p. 400

6
Traffic and Performance Management

In this chapter:

- 6.1 Overview of Traffic and Performance Management
- 6.2 CoS ID Service Attributes
- 6.3 Color ID for Service Frame Attribute
- 6.4 EEC ID Service Attributes
- 6.5 Review: Traffic and Performance Management

Note: *This lesson relates to EVC-based services only (EPL, EVPL, EP-LAN, EVP-LAN, EP-Tree, and EVP-Tree services). OVC-based E-Access services (Access EPL and Access EVPL services) are defined in a later lesson.*

> **Quality of service (QoS)** refers to service frame delivery performance as defined in the SLS using EVC performance service attributes, such as availability, resiliency, frame loss ratio, frame delay, and inter-frame delay variation.

> **Traffic management** is the set of mechanisms, tools, and policies used by the service provider to achieve QoS.

> **Class of service (CoS)** is an indicator used to differentiate service frames with respect to QoS, allowing different traffic management treatment. Without class of service, all frames receive the same traffic management treatment.

Traffic and performance management involves the following interrelated elements: **class of service (CoS)**, **color**, **egress equivalence class (EEC)**, **bandwidth profiles**, and **EVC performance**. This lesson starts with a conceptual overview of these elements in relation to each other and traffic and performance management. It then describes service attributes related to CoS, color, and EEC identification. Details about bandwidth profiles and EVC performance are deferred to later lessons.

Related Links

The MEF Service Agreement Framework (SLA and SLS) on p. 65
Bandwidth Profiles on p. 125
EVC Performance on p. 147
E-Access Services on p. 232

6.1 Overview of Traffic and Performance Management

In this section:

6.1.1   About Performance Objectives
6.1.2   The Multi CoS Framework
6.1.3   Color and EVC Performance Objectives
6.1.4   About Bandwidth Profiles
6.1.5   CoS ID and EEC ID

6.1.1 About Performance Objectives

QoS is defined, per CoS, in the SLS through the specification of **EVC performance** service attributes. As explained in a later lesson, EVC performance service attributes specify two things:

1. **How performance is measured** – using **performance metrics** (such as availability, resiliency, frame loss, frame delay, and inter-frame delay variation) and associated parameters

2. **Expected levels of performance** – by specifying **performance objectives** (values for performance metrics that characterize performance level)

Most service providers offer a small number of CoS in their network and define performance objectives, per CoS, in the SLS.

Related Links

The MEF Service Agreement Framework (SLA and SLS) on p. 65
EVC Performance Service Attribute on p. 148

6.1.2 The Multi CoS Framework

Recognizing that different types of traffic have different QoS requirements, the MEF defines a framework that allows service providers to offer more than one CoS.

Traffic and Performance Management
Overview of Traffic and Performance Management

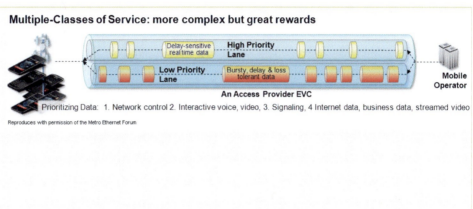

This figure shows a mobile backhaul service with only one CoS.

With only one CoS, all traffic must be treated the same. Delay and loss-tolerant data, such as Internet traffic, must be treated the same as delay-sensitive real-time data, such as voice traffic. For the service provider, this is inefficient and costly.

This figure shows the same application implemented in a network that supports multiple CoS. This network allows the mobile backhaul operator to use their network resources more efficiently. More revenue can be generated for the same cost by providing QoS only as required and charging for it.

In this multi-CoS framework:

- The service provider defines QoS for a small number of CoS to be offered in their network (normally eight or fewer).
- The subscriber purchases a service with bandwidth quantified per-CoS.
- The subscriber ensures that service frames are marked prior to CEN ingress to reflect CoS as agreed in the SLA.
- The service provider may police service frames at CEN ingress (and possibly CEN egress) to monitor conformance to bandwidth agreements and to classify service frames with respect to drop-eligibility for traffic management purposes.
- The service provider delivers the service, ensuring QoS per CoS as specified by EVC performance objectives.

This framework serves both business parties (the subscriber and the service provider) by establishing a clear understanding about delivery commitments and QoS.

Note: The MEF has also defined 12 standardized classes of service, which are the subject of a later lesson.

Related Links

MEF-Standardized Classes of Service on p. 222

6.1.3
Color and EVC Performance Objectives

QoS is specified, per CoS, by defining EVC performance objectives in the SLS. However, not all service frames are subject to EVC performance objectives.

> **Color** indicates a service frame's status with respect to performance objectives.

Frames are assigned one of two colors:

- **Green** indicates that performance objectives can[54] apply to the frame.

- **Yellow** indicates that performance objectives do not apply to the frame.

MEF standards do not associate any performance objectives with yellow service frames.[55] Yellow service frames are commonly characterized as being **drop eligible**.

It is important to understand that color only indicates the frame's <u>current status</u> with respect to performance objectives. This status (color) can change due to bandwidth profile processing at ingress and egress.

Encoding Color in Service Frames

If the service requires it, the color status of individual service frames can be communicated across the ingress UNI and/or egress UNI(s) via an encoding scheme specified by service attribute *Color ID for Service Frame* (as described later in this lesson). This mechanism enables the subscriber to convey color information to the service provider at CEN ingress (if needed) and/or the service provider to convey color information to the subscriber at CEN egress (if needed). However, this mechanism is not commonly used.

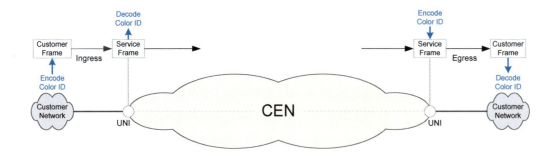

Color at Ingress

Each service frame is assigned an initial color (Green or Yellow) at the ingress UNI. If service attribute *Color ID for Service Frame* is specified, initial color is decoded from the service frame as specified by that attribute. Otherwise (more common), every service frame is initially colored Green by default.[56]

---

54 Subject to various conditions, including that the frame has a valid Frame Check Sequence (FCS) and that the frame is not discarded or recolored yellow by future processing within the CEN, such as ingress bandwidth profile processing (if applicable) and egress bandwidth profile processing (if applicable).
55 The service provider is free to define performance objectives for yellow service frames in the SLA, but is not required to do so.
56 Per [R103] in MEF 10.3.

If the service frame is subject to an ingress bandwidth profile (common), the initial color is only provisional because the frame may be discarded or recolored by ingress bandwidth profile processing .

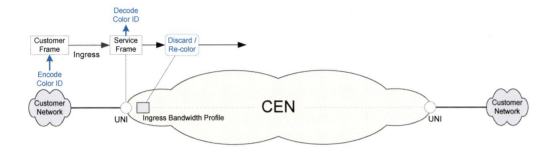

After ingress bandwidth profile processing (if applicable), the frame's color is no longer provisional. Green indicates that performance objectives will likely[57] apply, so the frame should be treated accordingly.

Color at Egress

At egress the service frame may be subject to egress bandwidth profile processing (not common), which like ingress bandwidth profile processing can result in the frame being discarded or recolored.

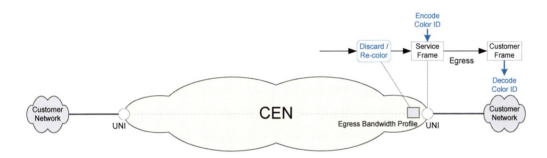

If service attribute *Color ID for Service Frame* is specified, the frame's final color at egress (after egress bandwidth profile processing, if applicable) can be encoded[58] in the service frame, before the frame is sent across the egress UNI to the subscriber. However, this is not commonly done because most services do not require it.

Related Links

Color ID for Service Frame Attribute on p. 118

6.1.4
About Bandwidth Profiles

Bandwidth profiles are used to bound the amount of traffic that a Carrier Ethernet service supports.

---

57 Unless the frame is recolored at egress, by egress bandwidth profile processing (if applicable)
58 Using the encoding scheme specified by the *Color ID for Service Frame* service attribute

At every UNI, traffic is already bounded by UNI speed[59] however, that bound is not especially useful because UNI speed can be oversized to accommodate traffic bursts and because multiple services and/or CoS flows may share a UNI. The bandwidth profile provides a practical mechanism for bounding traffic within an individual flow of service frames (or set of flows); a mechanism that is more flexible than a simple rate limit.

> Bandwidth profiles limit traffic (on average) to predefined rate limits, but also permit traffic to burst for short periods of time up to predefined limits.

The **bandwidth profile algorithm**, explained in a later lesson, includes a variety of parameters that are set to meet application requirements. This parameter set is called the **bandwidth profile**. Bandwidth profiles can be applied at ingress and/or at egress. Bandwidth profiles act as a gatekeepers, forwarding frames (up to a limit) and discarding frames (exceeding that limit). Bandwidth profiles also color forwarded frames, Green or Yellow (as previously explained), to indicate whether performance objectives can apply to the frame.

Note: *Prior to MEF 10.3, the bandwidth profile algorithm supported only a single flow of service frames. However, MEF 10.3 has generalized the bandwidth profile algorithm to support <u>one or more</u> flows (as explained later in this lesson).*

Ingress Bandwidth Profile

In the following conceptual example, the bandwidth profile algorithm is visualized as a user-configurable machine that processes frames within a specified flow of ingress service frames. This machine operates according to the MEF-defined bandwidth profile algorithm and is configured by setting various control dials (CIR, CBS, EIR, and EBS) and switches (CM, CF) to specific values. These control settings (the bandwidth profile), in effect, define a gate keeping policy that admits frames (up to limits) and discards frames (exceeding those limits).

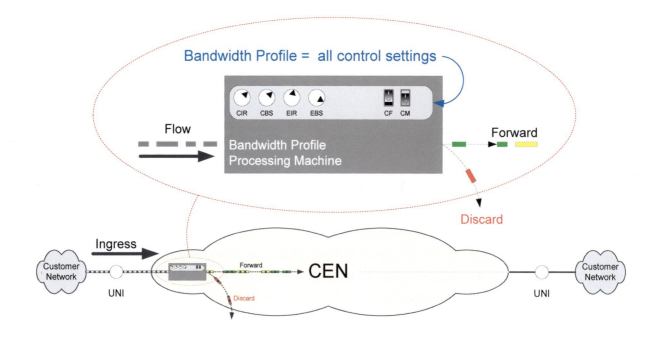

---

59 Defined by the UNI's physical layer speed (for example, 10Mb/s, 100 Mb/s, 1Gb/s, or 10 Gb/s).

The bandwidth profile algorithm (machine) declares each frame to be conformant or non-conformant relative to the bandwidth profile (machine control settings). The level of conformance is expressed as one of three colors:

- **Green** (CIR-conformant) — Service frames are in-profile with respect to service performance objectives and are forwarded.

- **Yellow** (EIR-conformant) — Service frames are out-of-profile with respect to service performance objectives, but are still forwarded (with discard-eligible status)

- **Red** (Non-conformant) — Service frames are out-of-profile and immediately discarded

Green and Yellow service frames are forwarded. Red frames are discarded.

At ingress, bandwidth profiles protect the CEN from excess traffic, while ensuring that traffic, up to the contracted bandwidth, is allowed into the CEN. Service frames allowed into the CEN are colored, Green or Yellow, to indicate their status with respect to performance objectives.

Policing

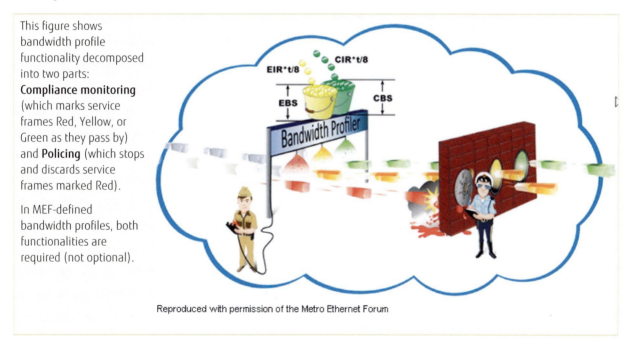

This figure shows bandwidth profile functionality decomposed into two parts: **Compliance monitoring** (which marks service frames Red, Yellow, or Green as they pass by) and **Policing** (which stops and discards service frames marked Red).

In MEF-defined bandwidth profiles, both functionalities are required (not optional).

Egress Bandwidth Profile

Bandwidth profiles are used less commonly at egress, but work in the same way. The bandwidth profile algorithm processes frames identically, assigning color (Green, Yellow, or Red) to each frame, discarding Red frames, and forwarding Green and Yellow frames. However, the use case for egress bandwidth profiles is a little less obvious.

When bandwidth profiles are used at egress, they modify traffic support limitations beyond what would be expected based on ingress bandwidth profiles alone. In the following example, traffic from two branch offices aggregate to the same UNI at company headquarters.[60]

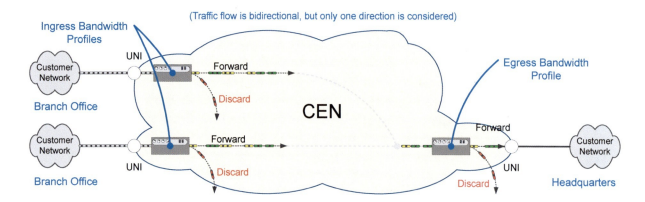

The egress bandwidth profile would be unnecessary if it were practical to support worst-case traffic aggregating from both branch offices (which is already limited by the ingress bandwidth profiles applied at the branch offices). However, the worst-case aggregate total may be more than the headquarters UNI can support or may cost more than the subscriber wishes to pay. For these reasons, an egress bandwidth profile is applied at the headquarters UNI.

About Discarding Red Frames at Egress

Discarding Red frames at <u>ingress</u> makes sense intuitively because the service provider is highly motivated to support no more traffic than is required by contract. However, discarding Red frames at egress is harder to understand because the service provider has already done the work (born the cost) of transporting these frames across the CEN. Why not forward them to the subscriber, if possible?

> MEF specifications require Red frames to be discarded (even at egress).

One way to make sense of this requirement is to consider its effect on the subscriber. If red frames were delivered (not discarded) at egress, the subscriber would not experience service performance limitations that, if experienced, may motivate them to either (1) upgrade their service or (2) modify traffic management policies within their own networks to use their current service more efficiently.

Multiflow Bandwidth Profiles

In MEF 10.3 the single flow bandwidth profile algorithm (previously defined in MEF 10.2) is generalized to support multiple flows.

---

60 This can occur in a variety of ways. For example, if all three UNIs are connected by a multipoint service, or if the headquarters UNI connects to each branch office UNI through an EVPL service.

The multiflow bandwidth profile algorithm can be visualized as a user-configurable machine formed by a stack of user-configurable modules.

This architecture allows a set of flows to share a common pool of bandwidth in a prioritized (hierarchically structured) fashion. Bandwidth that is not used by one flow is made available for potential use by other flows.

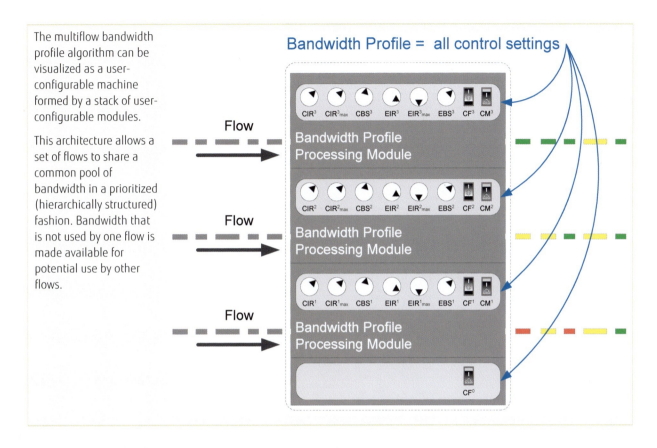

Bandwidth Profile Flows

Prior to MEF 6.2, EVC service definitions allowed bandwidth profiles at three levels of flow granularity: per UNI, per EVC, or per CoS. However, with MEF 6.2, per UNI and per EVC bandwidth profiles are no longer used.[61]

Per UNI and per EVC bandwidth profiles are no longer needed because all CoS flows that are present at the UNI (or EVC) can now be assigned to a single multiflow per CoS bandwidth profile. The result is equivalent because all service frames at the UNI (or EVC) are processed by one bandwidth profile.

MEF 10.3 also introduced another change: at egress, per-CoS bandwidth profiles are replaced by per-EEC bandwidth profiles.[62]

6.1.5
CoS ID and EEC ID

CoS ID and EEC ID are indicators that are used to differentiate service frames. However, they serve different purposes.

---

61 Requirements [R6] and [R8] in MEF 6.2 explicitly disallows per-UNI and per-EVC bandwidth profile attributes (even though both are defined in MEF 10.3).

62 Here, EEC refers to **egress equivalence class**, a new mechanism for service frame classification (similar to CoS).

CoS ID

Every service frame is assigned a CoS ID at ingress. If ingress bandwidth profiles apply, CoS ID assigns the frame to a particular per-CoS ID ingress bandwidth profile flow. CoS ID also determines the frame's QoS treatment in the CEN (assuming the frame's color status after ingress processing is Green).

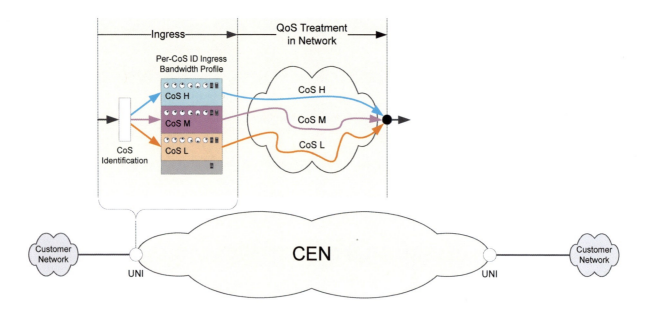

EEC ID

Service frames that are subject to egress bandwidth profile processing are assigned an EEC ID <u>at egress</u>. EEC ID, in turn, assigns the frame to a particular per-EEC ID egress bandwidth profile flow.

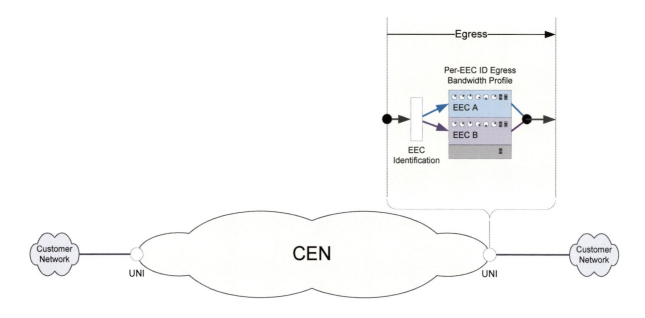

Traffic and Performance Management
Overview of Traffic and Performance Management

Page 113

CoS ID and EEC ID are independent systems of service frame classification. In MEF service definitions, three EVC per UNI service attributes specify CoS ID[63] and three more EVC per UNI service attributes specify EEC ID.[64]

Assignment at Ingress versus Egress

Both CoS ID and EEC ID can be specified several ways, including based on PCP bits or DSCP values. However, regardless of the scheme used, it is important to understand that CoS ID is assigned at CEN ingress and EEC ID is assigned at CEN egress. Consider the following example.

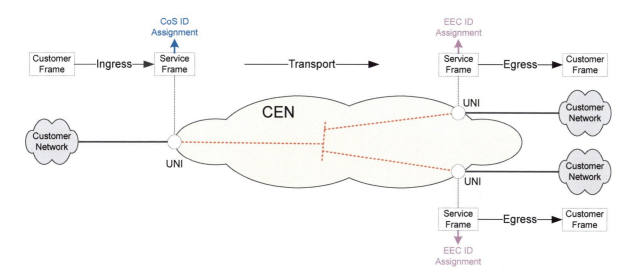

Assignment may be different for different UNIs. Both CoS IC and EEC ID can be assigned per-EVC (at the UNI) or based on service frame content (PCP or DSCP values) at the UNI. CoS ID assignment is independent of EEC ID assignment.

Related Links

CoS ID Service Attributes on p. 114
EEC ID Service Attributes on p. 119

---

63 CoS ID is specified with attributes **CoS ID for Data Service Frame**, **CoS ID for L2CP Service Frame**, and **CoS ID for SOAM Service Frame**.
64 EEC ID is specified with attributes **EEC ID for Data Service Frame**, **EEC ID for L2CP Service Frame**, and **EEC ID for SOAM Service Frame**.

MEF-CECP Study Guide
3rd Edition - October 2015
Updated for MEF-CECP Certification Blueprint C

6.2
CoS ID Service Attributes

In this section:

6.2.1 Attribute: CoS ID for Data Service Frame
6.2.2 Attribute: CoS ID for L2CP Service Frame
6.2.3 Attribute: CoS ID for SOAM Service Frame
6.2.4 CoS ID Based on CE-VLAN CoS
6.2.5 CoS ID Based on Internet Protocol

Note: *Prior to MEF 10.3, there were no service attributes dedicated to CoS identification. MEF 10.2 defined mechanisms and requirements for identifying CoS, but left it up to the service provider and the subscriber to specify details in the SLA. MEF 10.3, which supersedes and replaces MEF 10.2, formalizes CoS identification using three EVC per UNI service attributes.*

Service Attribute		Requirement					
		Port-Based Service			VLAN-Based Service		
Cat.	Name	EPL	EP-LAN	EP-Tree	EVPL	EVP-LAN	EVP-Tree
EVC per UNI	CoS ID for Data Service Frame	EVC or CE-VLAN CoS or IP value(s) and corresponding CoS Name					
	CoS ID for L2CP Service Frame	"All" or list of each L2CP in the EVC and corresponding CoS Name					
	CoS ID for SOAM Service Frame	Basis same as for Data Service Frames					

These service attributes specify how CoS is encoded in ingress service frames. A service provider might, for example, offer three CoS options named *gold*, *silver*, and *bronze*, with performance objectives for each option defined in the SLS. With guidance from the service provider, the subscriber chooses appropriate CoS options for their application and chooses CoS ID attributes to specify how CoS will be encoded in ingress service frames.

Each ingress service frame maps to a single **CoS Name**, such as *gold*, *silver*, or *bronze*. The CoS Name identifies QoS treatment in the CEN (as defined in the SLS), or calls for discard. If a CoS Name calls for discard, ingress service frames that map to that CoS Name must be discarded.[65]

MEF 10.3 defines three CoS ID attributes to assign CoS separately to Data, L2CP, and SOAM ingress service frames. CoS assignment is not necessarily the same for each EVC at a given UNI, or for each UNI of a given EVC.

Related Links

Data, L2CP, and SOAM Service Frames on p. 55
EEC ID Service Attributes on p. 119
CoS ID and EEC ID on p. 111

---

65 Per [R89] in MEF 10.3

6.2.1
Attribute: CoS ID for Data Service Frame

This attribute is specified using one of three methods:

1. **Based on EVC** — A single CoS Name is specified. That CoS Name is assigned to all ingress data service frames that map to the EVC at the UNI.

2. **Based on CE-VLAN CoS** — A CoS Name is specified for each possible value of **priority code point (PCP) bits** in a CE-VLAN tag. CE-VLAN tagged ingress data service frames are assigned CoS Name accordingly.

   Untagged ingress data service frames are mapped to a CoS Name as agreed by the subscriber and the service provider. However, MEF 10.3 recommends that untagged frames map to the same CoS Name as frames with CE-VLAN CoS = 0 (PCP bits value = 0).

   Note: Per MEF 10.3, the term **CE-VLAN CoS** is defined as the value or PCP bits in a CE-VLAN tag.

3. **Based on Internet Protocol** — A CoS Name is specified for each possible **differentiated services code point (DSCP) value** within an IPv4 or IPv6 packet (CoS Names for Pv4 packets are independent of CoS Names for IPv6 packets). Ingress data service frames that carry IPv4 or IPv5 packets are assigned CoS Name accordingly.

   Frames that do not contain either an IPv4 or IPv6 packet are assigned CoS Name as agreed by the subscriber and the service provider.

Related Links
CoS ID Based on CE-VLAN CoS on p. 116
CoS ID Based on Internet Protocol on p. 117

6.2.2
Attribute: CoS ID for L2CP Service Frame

If this attribute is set to "All", a single CoS Name is specified and that CoS Name is assigned to all ingress L2CP service frames that map to the EVC at the UNI.

Otherwise, Layer 2 protocols are listed individually and a CoS Name is assigned to each protocol. If an ingress L2CP service frame is received for a Layer 2 protocol that is not listed in the *CoS ID for L2CP Service Frame* attribute, that frame's CoS Name is determined as if it were a data service frame.[66]

---

66 Per [R99] in MEF 10.3.

6.2.3
Attribute: CoS ID for SOAM Service Frame

MEF 10.3 requires that CoS Name be assigned to ingress SOAM service frames in the same way that CoS Name is assigned to ingress Data service frames (using the same method and the same details).[67] So, at present, the specification of *CoS ID for SOAM Service Frame* must match the specification of *CoS ID for Data Service Frame*.

Related Links
Attribute: CoS ID for Data Service Frame on p. 115

6.2.4
CoS ID Based on CE-VLAN CoS

If CoS ID is based on CE-VLAN CoS (an option for Data and SOAM service frames), each possible PCP bit value must map to exactly one CoS Name. The following table provides examples of valid and invalid specifications.

CE-VLAN CoS Values (PCP bit Values)			Notes
Gold	Silver	Bronze	
0, 1	2, 3	4, 5, 6, 7	Valid
7, 5, 3, 1	6, 4, 2, 0	—	Valid
7	6	5	Not valid because PCP values 0 through 4 are not mapped to a CoS Name.
1, 2, 3, 4	4, 5, 6	7, 0	Not valid because PCP value 4 is mapped to two CoS Names.

CoS identification can be different for different EVCs at the same UNI. The following table shows a valid example of CoS ID specification for two EVCs at the same UNI.

EVC	CE-VLAN CoS Values (PCP bit Values)				
	Platinum	Gold	Silver	Bronze	Discard
EVC A	—	4, 5, 6, 7	0, 3	—	1, 2
EVC B	7	0, 1, 2, 3, 4, 5, 6	—	—	—

Note: When the *CoS ID* is based on CE-VLAN CoS, attribute **Color ID for Service Frame** (if used) must be based on either CE-VLAN CoS or CE-VLAN Tag DEI. (Per [R111] in MEF 10.3)

---

67 Per [R100] and [R101] of MEF 10.3.

Related Links

Attribute: CoS ID for Data Service Frame on p. 115
Attribute: CoS ID for SOAM Service Frame on p. 116
Color ID for Service Frame Attribute on p. 118

6.2.5
CoS ID Based on Internet Protocol

If CoS ID is based on Internet Protocol (an option for Data and SOAM service frames), each possible DSCP value (for both IPv4 and IPv6 packets) must map to exactly one CoS Name. The following table shows a valid example of CoS ID specification for three EVCs at the same UNI.

EVC		CoS Name:			
		Platinum	Diamond	Ruby	Discard
EVC A	IPv4 DSCP Values:	11, 37, 45	8, 10, 12	—	All other values
	IPv6 DSCP Values:	11, 37, 45	—	38, 213	All other values
EVC B	IPv4 DSCP Values:	11, 37, 45	8, 10, 12	—	All other values
	IPv6 DSCP Values:	—	—	—	All other values
EVC C	IPv4 DSCP Values:	—	—	—	All other values
	IPv6 DSCP Values:	11, 37, 45	8, 10, 12	—	All other values

The mapping of IPv4 DSCP value to CoS Name is independent of the mapping of IPv6 DSCP value to CoS Name. Both mappings must be specified, regardless of whether the EVC supports both IPv4 and IPv6 (as does EVC A), only IPv4 (as does EVC B), or only IPv6 (as does EVC C).

Note: When the CoS ID is based on Internet Protocol, attribute **Color ID for Service Frame** (if used) must be based on Internet Protocol. (Per [R112] in MEF 10.3)

Related Links

Attribute: CoS ID for Data Service Frame on p. 115
Attribute: CoS ID for SOAM Service Frame on p. 116
Color ID for Service Frame Attribute on p. 118

6.3
Color ID for Service Frame Attribute

Note: *Prior to MEF 10.3, there was no service attribute dedicated to Color identification.*[68]

Service Attribute		Requirement					
		Port-Based Service			VLAN-Based Service		
Cat.	Name	EPL	EP-LAN	EP-Tree	EVPL	EVP-LAN	EVP-Tree
EVC per UNI	Color ID for Service Frame	None or EVC or CE-VLAN CoS or CE-VLAN Tag DEI or IP					

This attribute (if used) specifies how color is encoded in service frames at ingress and egress. There are five mutually-exclusive options. Two options map all service frames (for the EVC at the UNI) to one color:

> **None** – All service frames are assigned color Green by default.
>
> **EVC** – One color (Green or Yellow) is assigned to all service frames.

The other three options define schemes for encoding color within the frames themselves:[69]

> **CE-VLAN CoS** – Green or Yellow is specified for each possible value of **priority code point (PCP) bits** in the CE-VLAN tag of a tagged service frames. Untagged ingress data service frames are assigned color Green.
>
> **CE-VLAN Tag DEI** – Tagged ingress service frames are assigned Green if DEI = 0 and Yellow if DEI =1. Untagged ingress data service frames are assigned color Green.
>
> **Internet Protocol** – Green or Yellow is specified for each possible **differentiated services code point (DSCP) value** within an IPv4 or IPv6 packet (independent specifications are made for Pv4 packets and IPv6 packets). Frames that do not contain either an IPv4 or IPv6 packet are assigned color Green.

It is important to understand that color only indicates the frame's current status with respect to performance objectives. This status (color) can change due to bandwidth profile processing at ingress and egress.

When the CoS ID is based on CE-VLAN CoS, attribute *Color ID for Service Frame* (if used) must be based on either CE-VLAN CoS or CE-VLAN Tag DEI (per [R111] in MEF 10.3). When the CoS ID is based on Internet Protocol, attribute *Color ID for Service Frame* (if used) must be based on Internet Protocol (per [R112] in MEF 10.3).

Related Links

Color and EVC Performance Objectives on p. 106
Color Mode on p. 129
CoS ID Based on CE-VLAN CoS on p. 116
CoS ID Based on Internet Protocol on p. 117

---

68 MEF 10.2 defined requirements for identifying Color, but left it to up to the service provider and subscriber to specify details in the SLA.
69 These encoding options allow the subscriber to convey color information to the service provider at CEN ingress (if needed) and/or the service provider to convey color information to the subscriber at CEN egress (if needed).

6.4 EEC ID Service Attributes

In this section:

6.4.1 Attribute: EEC ID for Data Service Frame
6.4.2 Attribute: EEC ID for L2CP Service Frame
6.4.3 Attribute: EEC ID for SOAM Service Frame
6.4.4 EEC ID Based on CE-VLAN CoS
6.4.5 EEC ID Based on Internet Protocol

Note: *Egress equivalency class (EEC) did not exist in MEF specifications prior to MEF 10.3.*

Service Attribute		Requirement					
		Port-Based Service			VLAN-Based Service		
Cat.	Name	EPL	EP-LAN	EP-Tree	EVPL	EVP-LAN	EVP-Tree
EVC per UNI	EEC ID for Data Service Frame	CE-VLAN CoS or IP value(s) and corresponding EEC					
	EEC ID for L2CP Service Frame	"All" or list of each L2CP in the EVC and corresponding EEC					
	EEC ID for SOAM Service Frame	Basis same as for Data Service Frames					

These service attributes only apply to EVCs that are subject to one or more egress bandwidth profiles. For such EVCs, these attributes only apply at UNIs where the EVC is subject to at least one egress bandwidth profile. At such UNIs, each egress service frame (in the EVC) maps to a single EEC, such as *First*, *Business*, or *Economy*.[70] The EEC associates the egress service frame to a particular egress bandwidth profile flow which, in turn, determines its egress bandwidth profile processing.

EEC ID service attributes specify how EEC is determined from inspection of the content of the egress service frame.

> **Observations:**
> - Unlike CoS Name which is assigned to service frames at ingress, EEC is assigned at egress.
> - Unlike CoS Name which is assigned to <u>every</u> ingress service frame, EEC is only assigned as needed (to support egress bandwidth profile processing, if applicable) at egress.
> - Unlike CoS Name which may be assigned per EVC (regardless of service frame content, in addition to other ways), EEC must be determined from inspection of the content of the egress service frame.
> - Unlike CoS Name which serves two purposes (determines QoS treatment in the CEN and assigns the ingress service frame to a particular ingress bandwidth profile flow, if applicable), EEC serves only one purpose (assigns the egress service frame to a particular egress bandwidth profile flow, if applicable).

If per-EEC egress bandwidth profiles apply to a service, EEC ID service attributes specify how EEC is encoded in egress service frames.

---

70 EEC values are defined as required (similar to CoS Names).

MEF 10.3 defines three EEC ID attributes to assigned EEC separately to Data, L2CP, and SOAM egress service frames. EEC assignment is not necessarily the same for each EVC at a given UNI, or for each UNI of a given EVC.

Related Links
Data, L2CP, and SOAM Service Frames on p. 55
CoS ID Service Attributes on p. 114
CoS ID and EEC ID on p. 111

6.4.1
Attribute: EEC ID for Data Service Frame

This attribute is specified using one of two methods:

1. **Based on CE-VLAN CoS** — EEC is specified for each possible value of **priority code point (PCP) bits** in a CE-VLAN tag. CE-VLAN tagged egress data service frames are assigned EEC accordingly.

   Untagged egress data service frames are mapped to EEC as agreed by the subscriber and the service provider. However, MEF 10.3 recommends that untagged frames map to the same EEC as frames with CE-VLAN CoS = 0 (PCP bits value = 0).

   Note: Per MEF 10.3, the term **CE-VLAN CoS** is defined as the value or PCP bits in a CE-VLAN tag.

2. **Based on Internet Protocol** — EEC is specified for each possible **differentiated services code point (DSCP) value** within an IPv4 or IPv6 packet (EEC for Pv4 packets are independent of EEC for IPv6 packets). Egress data service frames that carry IPv4 or IPv5 packets are assigned EEC accordingly.

   Frames that do not contain either an IPv4 or IPv6 packet are assigned EEC as agreed by the subscriber and the service provider.

Related Links
EEC ID Based on CE-VLAN CoS on p. 121
EEC ID Based on Internet Protocol on p. 122

6.4.2
Attribute: EEC ID for L2CP Service Frame

If this attribute is set to "All", a single EEC is specified and that EEC is assigned to all egress L2CP service frames that map to the EVC at the UNI.

Otherwise, Layer 2 protocols are listed individually and an EEC is assigned to each protocol. If an egress L2CP service frame is received for a Layer 2 protocol that is not listed in the *EEC ID for L2CP Service Frame* attribute, that frame's EEC is determined as if it were a data service frame.[71]

---

71 Per [R121] in MEF 10.3.

6.4.3
Attribute: EEC ID for SOAM Service Frame

MEF 10.3 requires that EEC be assigned to egress SOAM service frames in the same way that EEC is assigned to egress Data service frames (using the same method and the same details).[72] So, at present, the specification of *EEC ID for SOAM Service Frame* must match the specification of *EEC ID for Data Service Frame*.

Related Links
Attribute: EEC ID for Data Service Frame on p. 120

6.4.4
EEC ID Based on CE-VLAN CoS

If EEC ID is based on CE-VLAN CoS (an option for Data and SOAM service frames), each possible PCP bit value must map to exactly one EEC. The following table provides examples of valid and invalid specifications.

CE-VLAN CoS Values (PCP bit Values)			Notes
First	Business	Economy	
0, 1	2, 3	4, 5, 6, 7	Valid
7, 5, 3, 1	6, 4, 2, 0	—	Valid
7	6	5	Not valid because PCP values 0 through 4 are not mapped to an EEC.
1, 2, 3, 4	4, 5, 6	7, 0	Not valid because PCP value 4 is mapped to two EECs.

EEC identification can be different for different EVCs at the same UNI. The following table shows a valid example of EEC ID specification for two EVCs at the same UNI.

EVC	CE-VLAN CoS Values (PCP bit Values)			
	First	Business	Economy	Baggage
EVC A	—	4, 5, 6, 7	0, 3	1, 2
EVC B	7	0, 1, 2, 3, 4, 5, 6	—	—

Related Links
Attribute: EEC ID for Data Service Frame on p. 120
Attribute: EEC ID for SOAM Service Frame on p. 121

---

72 Per [R122] and [R123] of MEF 10.3.

6.4.5 EEC ID Based on Internet Protocol

If EEC ID is based on Internet Protocol (an option for Data and SOAM service frames), each possible DSCP value (for both IPv4 and IPv6 packets) must map to exactly one EEC. The following table shows a valid example of EEC ID specification for three EVCs at the same UNI.

EVC		EEC:			
		First	Business	Economy	Baggage
EVC A	IPv4 DSCP Values:	11, 37, 45	8, 10, 12	—	All other values
	IPv6 DSCP Values:	11, 37, 45	—	38, 213	All other values
EVC B	IPv4 DSCP Values:	11, 37, 45	8, 10, 12	—	All other values
	IPv6 DSCP Values:	—	—	—	All other values
EVC C	IPv4 DSCP Values:	—	—	—	All other values
	IPv6 DSCP Values:	11, 37, 45	8, 10, 12	—	All other values

The mapping of IPv4 DSCP value to EEC is independent of the mapping of IPv6 DSCP value to EEC. Both mappings must be specified, regardless of whether the EVC supports both IPv4 and IPv6 (as does EVC A), only IPv4 (as does EVC B), or only IPv6 (as does EVC C).

Related Links

Attribute: EEC ID for Data Service Frame on p. 120
Attribute: EEC ID for SOAM Service Frame on p. 121

6.5 Review: Traffic and Performance Management

1. At UNIs, which three of the following are MEF-permissible CoS identifiers for data service frames? (Choose three.)

    a. Ethernet DEI bit
    b. Differentiated services code point (DSCP) in the IP header
    c. PCP bits in IEEE 802.1Q customer VLAN tag (CE-VLAN tag)
    d. Ethernet CFI bit
    e. EVC identifier

2. A Subscriber requires an EVC that supports three Classes of Service: *Silver*, *Gold*, and *Diamond*. Which one of the following schemes is acceptable for identifying CoS at UNIs using PCP bit values (0-7)?

    a. Silver (5); Gold (6); Diamond (7)
    b. Silver (7, 6); Gold (5, 4); Diamond (3, 2, 1, 0)
    c. Silver (6); Gold (4); Diamond (2)
    d. Silver (0,1, 2); Gold (5); Diamond (6)
    e. Silver (4); Gold (5); Diamond (4)

3. EVC services defined by MEF 6.2 can include which two bandwidth profiles? (Choose two.)

    a. Ingress Bandwidth Profile Per CoS ID
    b. Ingress Bandwidth Profile Per EEC ID
    c. Ingress Bandwidth Profile Per EVC
    d. Egress Bandwidth Profile Per CoS ID
    e. Egress Bandwidth Profile Per EEC ID
    f. Egress Bandwidth Profile Per EVC

4. Which service frame field <u>cannot</u> be used to convey color information across the UNI?

    a. DEI in CE-VLAN tag
    b. DSCP in the IP header
    c. PCP in CE-VLAN tag
    d. TPID in CE-VLAN tag

5. A service frame colored green at ingress ...

    a. Must be delivered (must not be discarded)
    b. Must not be recolored yellow or red
    c. Is in-profile with respect to service performance objectives
    d. Will be delivered with the highest CoS defined for the service

6. A service frame that is declared red by egress bandwidth profile processing ...

    a. Becomes eligible for discard
    b. Must be discarded
    c. May be delivered, but is not subject to service performance objectives
    d. May be delivered, but only after green and yellow frames are delivered

7. For a particular EVC and UNI, attribute *EEC ID for Data Service Frame* is specified based on *Internet Protocol*. Which one of the following statements is NOT a requirement for this specification?

    a. It must match the specification of attribute *EEC ID for SOAM Service Frame* (for the same EVC and UNI).
    b. It must map each possible DSCP value for IPv4 to exactly one EEC.
    c. It must map each possible DSCP value for IPv6 to exactly one EEC.
    d. It must match the specification of attribute *EEC ID for Data Service Frame* at other UNIs of the EVC.

Related Links

Answers: Traffic and Performance Management on p. 406

7
Bandwidth Profiles

In this chapter:

7.1 Single-Flow Bandwidth Profile
7.2 Multi-Flow Bandwidth Profiles
7.3 More Terminology
7.4 Bandwidth Profile Service Attributes
7.5 Egress Bandwidth Profiles
7.6 About Line Rate and CIR
7.7 Review: Bandwidth Profiles

This lesson explains bandwidth profiles, the bandwidth profile algorithm, and bandwidth profile service attributes. Before studying it, please review the conceptual description of bandwidth profiles in the overview of traffic and performance management that was provided in the previous lesson.

Note: Bandwidth profiles used in MEF 6.2 EVC service definitions have significantly changed compared to those used in MEF 6.1. The MEF white paper Understanding Bandwidth Profiles in MEF 6.2 Service Definitions describes and explains the changes.[73]

Related Links

Overview of Traffic and Performance Management on p. 104
About Bandwidth Profiles on p. 107

---

73 Available from the MEF White Papers area of the MEF web site: mef.net.

7.1 Single-Flow Bandwidth Profile

In this section:

7.1.1 Visualizing the Token Bucket Algorithm
7.1.2 Explaining the Single-Flow Bandwidth Profile Algorithm
7.1.3 Single-Rate versus Dual-Rate Bandwidth Profile Implementations

Recall that the single-flow bandwidth profile algorithm can be visualized as a user-configurable machine that processes service frames within a single flow of service frames, assigning color (Green, Yellow, or Red) to each service frame, discarding Red frames, and forwarding Green and Yellow service frames.

This conceptual machine is configured using four control dials (CIR, CBS, EIR, EBS) and two switches (CF, CM), which are **parameters** of the bandwidth profile algorithm, defined as follows:

Parameter		Units of Measure or Values
CIR	Committed Information Rate	Bits per second
CBS	Committed Burst Size	Bytes
EIR	Excess Information Rate	Bits per second
EBS	Excess Burst Size	Bytes
CF	Coupling Flag	N or Y
CM	Color Mode	color-blind or color-aware

These six parameters constitute a single-flow **bandwidth profile**.

The single-flow **bandwidth profile algorithm** defines how service frames are processed. To understand this algorithm it is helpful to first understand the well-known **token bucket algorithm**.[74]

---

[74] **Token bucket** and **leaky bucket** are two well-known algorithms that can be used to explain the bandwidth profile algorithm. In this lesson, we use the token bucket algorithm.

7.1.1
Visualizing the Token Bucket Algorithm

This visualization of the token bucket algorithm includes a token bucket and a traffic stream.

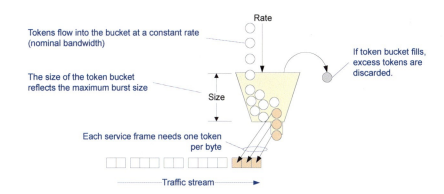

The token bucket is characterized by two parameters:

- **Rate**—Tokens flow into the token bucket at a constant rate, which is specified by a value called Rate.

- **Size**—The token bucket can hold only a limited number of tokens, which is specified by a value called Size.

Tokens can be removed from the bucket by the traffic stream (as will soon be explained). If the token bucket fills, overflowing tokens are discarded.

Service frames stream past the token bucket. As each service frame passes the token bucket, it is classified as **compliant** or **noncompliant** as follows:

1. If the token bucket contains one token for each byte in the current service frame, two actions are taken:

    a. The service frame is classified as compliant.

    b. Tokens, equal to the number of bytes in the current service frame, are drained from the token bucket.

2. Otherwise, the service frame is classified as noncompliant.

Test your understanding: An 8-byte service frame arrives when the token bucket contains 13 tokens. **(a)** Is the service frame classified as compliant or noncompliant? **(b)** How many tokens are in the token bucket after the service frame is classified? [75]

Test your understanding: An 8-byte service frame arrives when the token bucket contains 7 tokens. **(a)** Is the service frame classified as compliant or noncompliant? **(b)** How many tokens are in the token bucket after the service frame is classified? [76]

---

[75] **Answers: (a)** Compliant. **(b)** Five (13 - 8 = 5).
[76] **Answers: (a)** Noncompliant. **(b)** Seven.

Test your understanding: A token bucket has Rate = 60 (tokens per second) and Size = 15 (tokens). **(a)** How many bytes might a compliant service frame contain? **(b)** How many bytes might a noncompliant service frame contain? **(c)** If the token bucket is empty, how long does it take to fill the token bucket, assuming no service frames arrive? [77]

7.1.2
Explaining the Single-Flow Bandwidth Profile Algorithm

Single-Flow Bandwidth Profile Parameter		Units of Measure or Values
CIR	Committed Information Rate	Bits per second
CBS	Committed Burst Size	Bytes
EIR	Excess Information Rate	Bits per second
EBS	Excess Burst Size	Bytes
CF	Coupling Flag	N or Y
CM	Color Mode	color-blind or color-aware

Green and Yellow Token Buckets

The single-flow bandwidth profile algorithm is explained using two token buckets:

- A green token bucket with fill rate of CIR/8 and size CBS

- A yellow token bucket with fill rate of EIR/8 and size EBS

Note: CIR and EIR are divided by 8 to determine fill rates because CIR and EIR are specified in bits per second and each token represents 1 byte (or 8 bits).

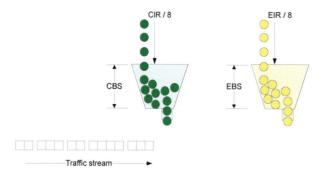

Incoming service frames stream past the two token buckets, which are used to determine compliance with respect to the bandwidth profile.

---

[77] **Answers: (a)** Up to 15 bytes but no more than that because the token bucket can only hold up to 15 tokens (bytes). **(b)** Any number. If a service frame contains more than 15 bytes, it will definitely be classified as noncompliant. If it has 15 bytes or less, classification depends how many tokens are in the token bucket when the service frame arrives. If the number of tokens is less than the number of bytes, it will be classified as noncompliant. **(c)** 0.25 seconds (60 tokens/second x 0.25 seconds = 15 tokens).

Coupling Flag

If the coupling flag (CF) is set to Y, tokens that overflow the green token bucket go into the yellow token bucket. Normally, CF is set to N, and such tokens are discarded.

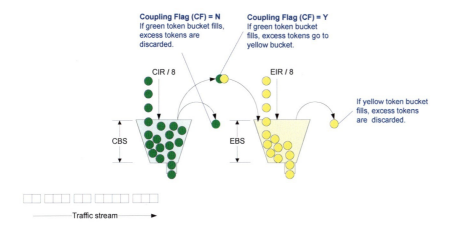

The coupling flag increases the rate of token flow into the yellow token bucket when the green token bucket is full. If CF=Y and the green token bucket is full, tokens flow into the yellow token bucket at a rate of EIR/8+CIR/8. Tokens that overflow the yellow token bucket are always discarded.

Color Mode

Color mode (CM) can be set to two values:

- **Color-blind**—The bandwidth profile algorithm disregards any prior coloring information (if present).
- **Color-aware**—The bandwidth profile algorithm uses prior coloring information (if present).

Here, *prior coloring information* refers to any green/yellow color status that is already be assigned to the service frame. For example, if *CM = color-aware*, the ingress bandwidth profile will make use of prior color information encoded in ingress service frames per the *Color ID for Service Frame* attribute. MEF 10.3 includes the following requirement:

[R154] A UNI MUST be able to support color-blind mode for Bandwidth Profiles.

Note: *CM=color-aware is mandatory at ENNI (as is explained in another lesson). At ENNI, coloring can be encoded in the DEI bit of the S-Tag or in the PCP bits of the S-Tag.*

Related Links

Color and EVC Performance Objectives on p. 106
Color ID for Service Frame Attribute on p. 118
Color-Aware Bandwidth Profiles at ENNI on p. 200

Color-Blind Bandwidth Profile Operation

If CM=color-blind, the bandwidth profile algorithm disregards any prior coloring information (if present) and works as follows:

1. If the green (CIR/CBS) token bucket contains one token for each byte in the current service frame, three actions are taken:

    - The service frame is classified as green (drop-ineligible).
    - The service frame is forwarded.
    - Tokens, equal to the number of bytes in the service frame, are drained from the green token bucket.

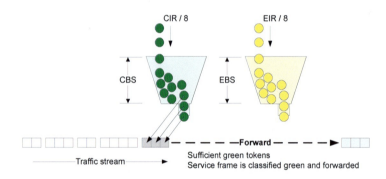

2. Otherwise, the green token bucket lacks enough tokens to process the current service frame, and processing continues as follows:

    a. If the yellow (EIR/EBS) token bucket contains one token for each byte in the current service frame, three actions are taken:

        - The service frame is classified as yellow (drop-eligible).
        - The service frame is forwarded.
        - Tokens, equal to the number of bytes in the service frame, are drained from the yellow token bucket.

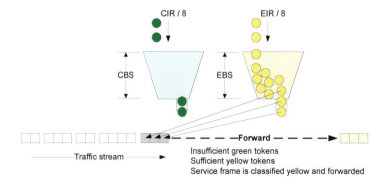

    b. Otherwise, both token buckets lack sufficient tokens to process the current service frame, and the current service frame is dropped (not forwarded).

Bandwidth Profiles
Single-Flow Bandwidth Profile

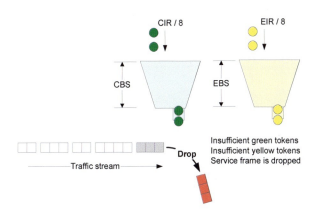

Color-Aware Bandwidth Profile Operation

If CM=color-aware, bandwidth profile operation is influenced by prior coloring that is already encoded in service frames.

If the current service frame has been classified as drop-eligible (yellow), the bandwidth profile algorithm processes the service frame as described in this section. Otherwise, the service frame is processed as described previously (Color-Blind Bandwidth Profile Operation).

If the current service frame is drop-eligible (yellow), the bandwidth profile algorithm works as follows:

1. The state of the green token bucket is disregarded.

2. If the yellow token bucket contains one token for each byte in the current service frame, three actions are taken:

   - The service frame is classified as yellow (drop-eligible).
   - The service frame is forwarded.
   - Tokens, equal to the number of bytes in the service frame, are drained from the yellow token bucket.

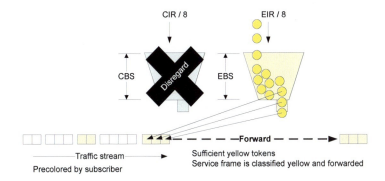

3. Otherwise, the yellow token bucket lacks enough tokens to process the current service frame, and the service frame is dropped (not forwarded).

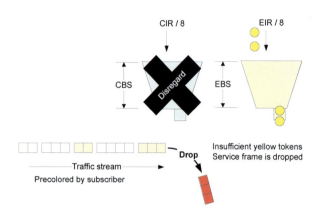

7.1.3
Single-Rate versus Dual-Rate Bandwidth Profile Implementations

Some applications do not require both components (green and yellow token buckets) in the previously described **dual-rate** bandwidth profile algorithm. To accommodate single-rate applications, some components of the bandwidth profile are set to zero:

- In real-time applications (such as voice or video conferencing) or mission critical applications it is not appropriate to mark any service frames yellow (drop-eligible). However, bandwidth profiles are still needed for rate-enforcement purposes. For such applications, a single-rate bandwidth profile is defined using CIR and CBS components only (EIR and EBS are set to zero).

- In best-effort applications, including Internet traffic, all service frames may be marked yellow (drop-eligible). For such applications, a single-rate best-effort bandwidth profile is defined using EIR and EBS components only (CIR and CBS are set to zero).

Test your understanding: Consider the following bandwidth profile. How many seconds are needed to fill the green token bucket if it is empty? [78] If a service frame contains 183 bytes, can it be marked green? Yellow? Red? [79]

Parameter		Value
CIR	Committed Information Rate	200 bits per second
CBS	Committed Burst Size	100 bytes
EIR	Excess Information Rate	800 bits per second
EBS	Excess Burst Size	300 bytes
CF	Coupling Flag	N
CM	Color Mode	color-blind

---

78 **Answer:** The green token bucket holds 800 bits (CBS * 8 bits/byte). So, with a fill rate of 200 bits per second (CIR), <u>it takes 4 seconds to fill</u>.

79 **Answer:** The service frame cannot be marked green because the green bucket can only hold 100 bytes (CBS). It might be marked yellow because the yellow bucket can hold up to 300 bytes (EBS). However it might also be marked red because the yellow bucket might not contain 183 bytes when the service frame arrives.

7.2
Multi-Flow Bandwidth Profiles

In this section:

7.2.1 Explaining the Multiflow Bandwidth Profile Algorithm
7.2.2 Observations

Conceptually, the multi-flow bandwidth profile algorithm can be viewed modularly (as a linked system of single-flow algorithms). Each module processes frames quasi-independently, using two token buckets as previously described. However, the overall algorithm includes new mechanisms that allow unused tokens to pass between modules (token sharing), so frame processing by each module is not truly independent.

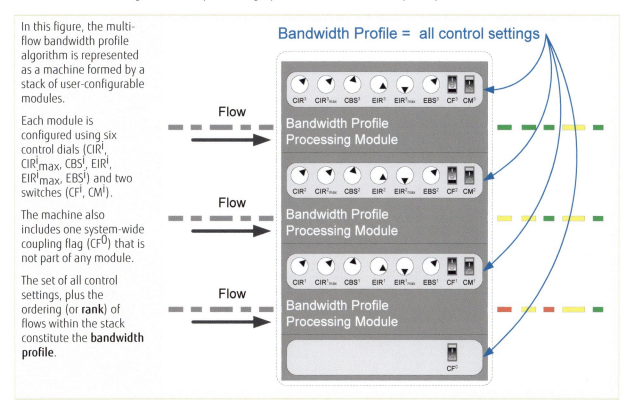

In this figure, the multi-flow bandwidth profile algorithm is represented as a machine formed by a stack of user-configurable modules.

Each module is configured using six control dials (CIR^i, CIR^i_{max}, CBS^i, EIR^i, EIR^i_{max}, EBS^i) and two switches (CF^i, CM^i).

The machine also includes one system-wide coupling flag (CF^0) that is not part of any module.

The set of all control settings, plus the ordering (or **rank**) of flows within the stack constitute the **bandwidth profile**.

Note: Bandwidth profile parameters are <u>indexed</u> with superscripts. Do not confuse indexing with power notation. For example, CIR^3 denotes CIR for the third bandwidth profile flow, not CIR cubed.

Note: All flows processed by a bandwidth profile must all be of the same type. A bandwidth profile can be assigned to process multiple per-CoS ingress flows or multiple per-EEC egress flows, but not a combination of per-CoS ingress flows and per-EEC egress flows.

Bandwidth Profile Parameters

Per Flow Parameters		Units of Measure or Values
CIR^i	Committed Information Rate	Bits per second
CIR^i_{max}	Rate limit for adding tokens to the green token bucket	Bits per second
CBS^i	Committed Burst Size	Bytes
EIR^i	Excess Information Rate	Bits per second
EIR^i_{max}	Rate limit for adding tokens to the yellow token bucket	Bits per second
EBS^i	Excess Burst Size	Bytes
CF^i	Coupling Flag	N or Y
CM^i	Color Mode	color-blind or color-aware
System-Wide Parameter		**Units of Measure or Values**
CF^0	Coupling Flag	N or Y

7.2.1
Explaining the Multiflow Bandwidth Profile Algorithm

As a starting point, assume that each module processes frames independently, per the single-flow bandwidth profile algorithm. No tokens are shared between modules.

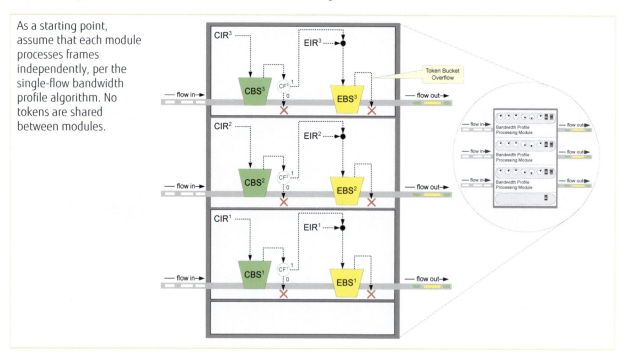

Bandwidth Profiles
Multi-Flow Bandwidth Profiles

Now add pathways to allow tokens (previously lost due to bucket overflow) to flow downward. Yellow bucket overflow goes to the next yellow bucket. Green bucket overflow when $CF^i=0$ goes to the next green bucket.

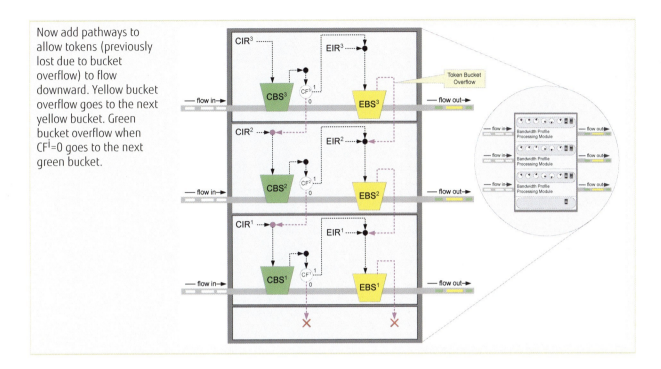

Rate Limiters

Now add a new rate limiting mechanism (shown graphically as a funnel) above each token bucket.

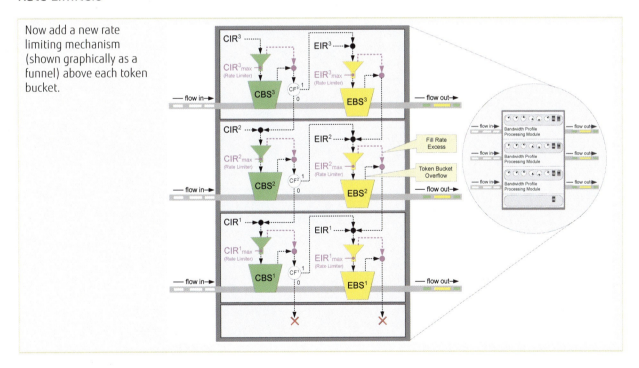

Each of these mechanisms has one control setting, CIR^i_{max} (green bucket) or EIR^i_{max} (yellow bucket), which limits the rate of token flow into the token bucket.

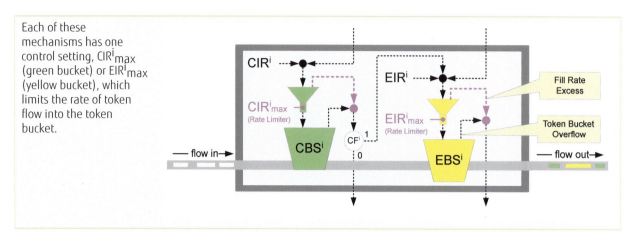

The rate limiting mechanism does not store or discard tokens. It functions like a gatekeeper that admits all tokens to the token bucket unless tokens arrive at a rate greater than the limit set (CIR^i_{max}/EIR^i_{max}). When tokens arrive faster than the limit (CIR^i_{max}/EIR^i_{max}), the rate limiter fills the token bucket at the limiting rate (CIR^i_{max}/EIR^i_{max}) and passes remaining tokens onward, to be combined with tokens from token bucket overflow.

Notice that all modules, except the bottom one, preserve unused tokens (representing available bandwidth) by passing them downward for possible use by lower ranking flows.

System-Wide Coupling Flag

If $CF^0=0$, the algorithm operates as so-far described.

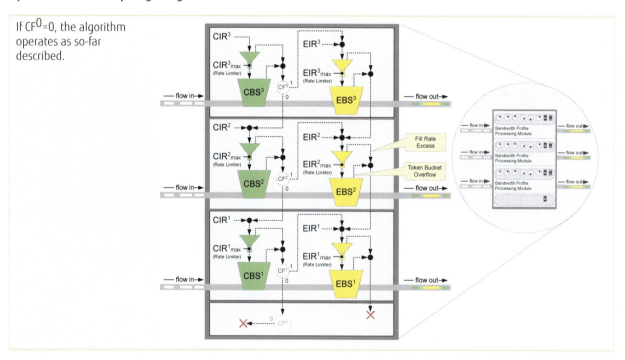

Otherwise (if $CF^0=1$), there are two changes: (1) tokens overflowing from the bottom green bucket flow upward to the top yellow bucket and (2) all of the other coupling flags are set to zero (per [R150] in MEF 10.3).

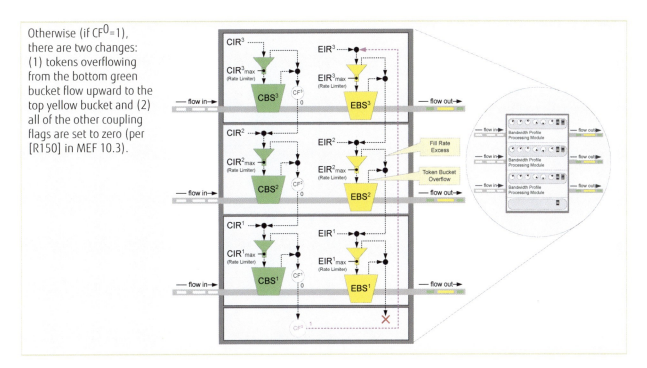

Notice that $CF^0=1$ forces all the other coupling flags to have the value 0, defining the path for token sharing. Unused tokens pass through the chain of green buckets (top to bottom), then through the chain of yellow buckets (top to bottom).

7.2.2
Observations

The key feature differentiating the multiflow bandwidth profile algorithm from the single-flow bandwidth profile algorithm is the ability to govern more than one flow with bandwidth shared among flows in a flexible and explicitly-defined manner. The system for sharing bandwidth is flexible, but is not without structure:

- A green bucket cannot overflow to higher ranking green bucket.

- A yellow bucket cannot overflow to higher ranking yellow bucket.

- A yellow bucket cannot overflow to green bucket.

Unused bandwidth is only shared downwardly (from higher-ranking flows to lower-ranking flows) or with color demotion (from green to yellow). This implies that flows should be ordered (ranked) such that unused bandwidth is downwardly shareable. For example, high-performance flows are typically ranked higher than low-performance flows because unused bandwidth from a high-performance flow can usually be reallocated to a low-performance flow without increasing service commitment.

7.3 More Terminology

Note: *Prior to MEF 6.2, EVC service definitions allowed bandwidth profiles at three levels of flow granularity: per UNI, per EVC, or per CoS. However, with MEF 6.2, per UNI and per EVC bandwidth profiles are no longer used.*

Bandwidth profile flow — The flow of service frames processed by one "module" of the bandwidth profile algorithm.

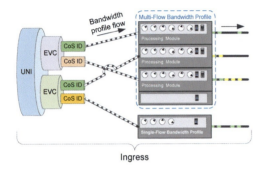
Ingress

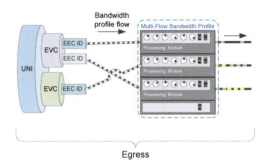
Egress

At ingress, each bandwidth profile flow contains service frames for a particular CoS within a particular EVC. Service frames from different EVCs cannot be in the same bandwidth profile flow, even if they have same CoS.

At egress, each bandwidth profile flow contains service frames for a particular EEC within a particular EVC. Service frames from different EVCs cannot be in the same bandwidth profile flow, even if they have same EEC.

Note: *CoS flows (or EEC flows) within an EVC can be left unassigned to any bandwidth profile. Service frames that are not assigned to a bandwidth profile are not subject to bandwidth profile processing.*

Envelope — The collection of bandwidth profile flows processed by a particular bandwidth profile is called an envelope.

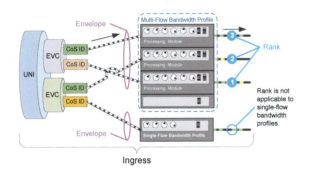
Ingress

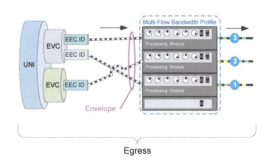
Egress

Rank — Within an envelope, each bandwidth profile flow is assigned a unique rank between 1 (lowest) and n (highest) that determines the "module" that it is processed by. The flow assigned rank 1 is processed by the bottom "module".

Note: *Unused bandwidth is only shared downwardly (from higher-ranking flows to lower-ranking flows) or with color demotion (from green to yellow).*

7.4
Bandwidth Profile Service Attributes

In this section:

7.4.1   Attribute: Envelopes
7.4.2   Attribute: Token Share
7.4.3   Attribute: Ingress Bandwidth Profile per-CoS ID
7.4.4   Attribute: Egress Bandwidth Profile per-EEC ID
7.4.5   Bandwidth Profile Attribute Requirements

Service Attribute		Requirement					
		Port-Based Service			VLAN-Based Service		
Cat.	Name	EPL	EP-LAN	EP-Tree	EVPL	EVP-LAN	EVP-Tree
Per UNI	Token Share	Enabled / Disabled					
	Envelopes	List of <Envelope ID, CF^0, n>					
EVC per UNI	Ingress Bandwidth Profile Per CoS ID	No / Parameters (as required)					
	Egress Bandwidth Profile Per EEC ID	No			No / Parameters (as required)		

7.4.1
Attribute: Envelopes

Attribute *Envelopes* specifies three values for each envelope that includes <u>two or more</u>[80] bandwidth profile flows:

> **Envelope ID** (the string used to identify the envelope)
> CF^0 (the value of the envelope-wide coupling flag, N or Y)
> **n** (the number of bandwidth profile flows in the envelope)

7.4.2
Attribute: Token Share

Attribute *Token Share* indicates whether or not the UNI can support multiflow bandwidth profiles (is capable of sharing tokens across bandwidth profile flows):

> If *Token Share = Enabled*, the UNI must be able to support two or more bandwidth profile flows in at least one envelope, per [R2] in MEF 6.2.
>
> If *Token Share = Disabled*, the UNI must have exactly one bandwidth profile flow per envelope (per [R3] in MEF 6.2) and the *Envelopes* per UNI attribute will be an empty list.

---

80 Per [R5] in MEF 6.2, envelopes that include only one bandwidth profile flow are not included in the *Envelopes* service attribute. Single-flow bandwidth profiles are defined without Envelope ID, with n=1, and, per [R142] in MEF 10.3, with $CF^0=0$.

7.4.3
Attribute: Ingress Bandwidth Profile per-CoS ID

This EVC per UNI service attribute applies to all CoS flows <u>within a given EVC</u> at the UNI:

> If the CoS Name is not assigned to a bandwidth profile, no parameters are specified.
>
> If the CoS Name is assigned to a single-flow bandwidth profile, seven parameters are specified: CoS Name, CIR, CBS, EIR, EBS, CF, and CM.
>
> If the CoS Name is assigned to a multi-flow bandwidth profile, eleven parameters are specified: CoS Name (for flow^i), CIR^i, CIR$^i_{max}$, CBS^i, EIR^i, EIR$^i_{max}$, EBS^i, CF^i, CM^i, and ER^i, where ER^i = <Envelope ID, rank>.

7.4.4
Attribute: Egress Bandwidth Profile per-EEC ID

This EVC per UNI service attribute applies to all EEC flows <u>within a given EVC</u> at the UNI:

> If the EEC Name is not assigned to a bandwidth profile, no parameters are specified.
>
> If the EEC Name is assigned to a single-flow bandwidth profile, seven parameters are specified: CoS Name, CIR, CBS, EIR, EBS, CF, and CM.
>
> If the EEC Name is assigned to a multi-flow bandwidth profile, eleven parameters are specified: CoS Name (for flow^i), CIR^i, CIR$^i_{max}$, CBS^i, EIR^i, EIR$^i_{max}$, EBS^i, CF^i, CM^i, and ER^i, where ER^i = <Envelope ID, rank>.

7.4.5
Bandwidth Profile Attribute Requirements

Requirement Category	Requirement	
	Single Flow Bandwidth Profile	Multiflow Bandwidth Profile
Rate	CIR ≥ 0 and EIR ≥ 0	CIR^i ≥ 0, CIR$^i_{max}$ ≥ 0, EIR^i ≥ 0 and EIR$^i_{max}$ ≥ 0
Burst size	If CIR > 0, then CBS ≥ largest *EVC Maximum Service Frame Size* for the EVC to which the bandwidth profile applies.	If CIR^i > 0, then CBS^i ≥ largest *EVC Maximum Service Frame Size* over all EVCs to which the bandwidth profile applies.
Coupling flag	No requirement. CF can be set to 1 or 0.	If CF^0 = 1, then CF^i = 0 for all flows that map to the envelope.
Rank	Not applicable.	Rank ≤ n, where n is the number of flows assigned to the envelope. Also, the rank for each flow assigned to the envelope must be unique.

Test your understanding: Explain why CBS must be ≥ largest EVC Maximum Service Frame Size if CIR>0. [81]

---

[81] **Answer:** Because, otherwise, a service frame of largest EVC Maximum Service Frame Size would have no chance of being marked green. Also note that if CIR=0, the MEF places no restriction on CBS because it is irrelevant.

7.5
Egress Bandwidth Profiles

In this section:

7.5.1 Egress Bandwidth Profiles for EPL Services
7.5.2 Egress Bandwidth Profiles for EVPL Services
7.5.3 Egress Bandwidth Profiles in E-LAN and E-Tree Type Services

7.5.1
Egress Bandwidth Profiles for EPL Services

The MEF does not allow egress bandwidth profiles for EPL services. As explained in the following footnote taken from MEF 6.2, there is no use case for them:

> For EPL Services, it is expected that an Ingress Bandwidth Profile will be applied at the ingress UNI such that traffic on the EVC is already controlled; therefore, there is no need to apply [a bandwidth profile] at the egress UNI.

7.5.2
Egress Bandwidth Profiles for EVPL Services

Egress bandwidth profiles can be used with EVPL services, for example as follows.

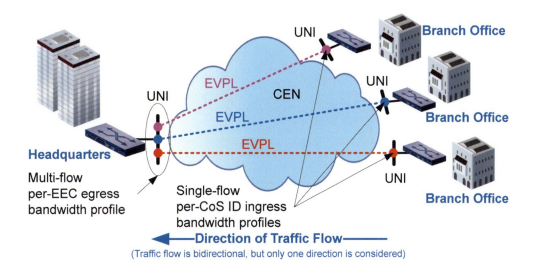

In this use case, EVPLs from three branch offices are service multiplexed at headquarters to one UNI. Ingress bandwidth profiles applied at the branch offices already limit egress traffic aggregating to headquarters. However, the worst-case aggregate total may be more than the headquarters UNI can support (or may cost more than the subscriber wishes to pay for). So an egress bandwidth profile is applied at the headquarters UNI to clarify service commitments.

7.5.3
Egress Bandwidth Profiles in E-LAN and E-Tree Type Services

Egress bandwidth profiles are used in E-LAN and E-Tree type services to reign in delivery commitments for worst-case scenarios.

For example, in this EP-LAN service:

- All ingress service frames map to one CoS
- Each UNI supports 10 Mb/s.
- At each UNI, an ingress bandwidth profile is applied with CIR=8 Mb/s.
- Any three UNIs can potentially simultaneously direct 8 Mb/s of CIR (green) traffic to the fourth UNI.

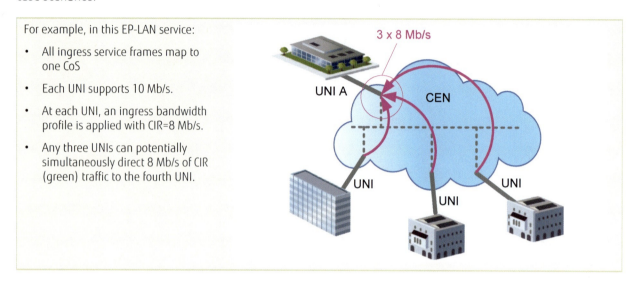

Without an egress bandwidth profile at each UNI, the service provider is formally committed to delivering traffic at the rate of 3✕8=24 Mb/s through UNIs that can only support rates up to 10 Mb/s. For example, as shown in the figure, three UNIs might simultaneously forward 8 Mb/s of traffic to UNI A, resulting in 24 Mb/s of aggregated traffic at UNI A. However, UNI A can only support rates up to 10 Mb/s. Similarly, the same scenario applies to the other three UNIs.

One possible solution is to apply an egress bandwidth profile (for example, with CIR=9 Mb/s) at each UNI. The application of such egress bandwidth profiles makes it clear that the service is not expected to deliver green service frames in all circumstances.

The Bottom Line: *When egress bandwidth profiles are used, service frames marked green at ingress can be dropped at egress due to egress traffic exceeding the agreed egress bandwidth profiles.*

7.6 About Line Rate and CIR

 Important: *This topic is not included in the MEF-CECP exam, but practicing Carrier Ethernet professionals need to understand it.*

Note: *This material is adapted from Appendix A of MEF 33.*

The relationship between CIR and physical layer bandwidth (line rate) is commonly misunderstood. For example, a UNI with physical speed 100 Mb/s is commonly expected to support CIR values up to 100 Mb/s. However, the physical layer cannot support CIR values up to the line rate because the MEF bandwidth profile algorithm only counts service frame bits, not the bits used to separate frames in the physical layer (interframe gap and preamble bits).

As shown in the following figure, an Ethernet frame in the physical layer (Layer 1) includes 20 bytes (160 bits) which are not part of the MEF service frame and therefore are not counted by the MEF bandwidth profile algorithm.

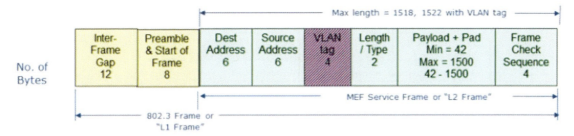

Reproduced with permission of the Metro Ethernet Forum

These interframe bits consume physical layer bandwidth, but the MEF bandwidth profile algorithm does not account for them.

So, how close can CIR be set to the physical layer bit rate (line rate, UNI speed)?

The answer depends on the size of MEF service frames, as shown in the following graph for an example 100 Mb/s physical interface.

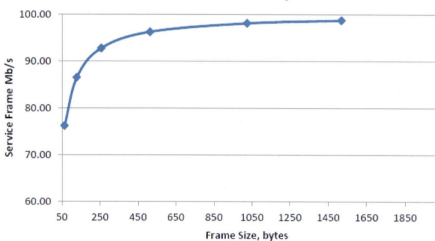

Reproduced with permission of the Metro Ethernet Forum

Observations:

- As frame size decreases, an increasing fraction of the line rate is consumed by interframe overhead.

- If the size of service frames (on average) is greater than 200 bytes, the physical layer can support CIR values up to about 90% of the line rate.

- If CIR < 76% of the line rate, the physical layer should support MEF services without issue, regardless of service frame size.[82]

This issue (line rate versus CIR) commonly surfaces during testing. For example, a subscriber might test a CIR=90 Mb/s EPL service implemented over 100 Mb/s UNIs using a test set configured to produce a 90 Mb/s stream of service frames. If the test is performed with 500-byte service frames, the physical layer traffic rate is 520/500*90 = 93.6 Mb/s, which is well below the line rate (100 Mb/s) and the service performs as expected (meeting CIR expectations). However, if the test is performed with 64-byte service frames, the calculated physical layer traffic rate is 84/64*90 = 118 Mb/s, which exceeds the physical UNI speed (100 Mb/s) and the excess above 100 Mb/s cannot be delivered. In this case the tester may falsely conclude that the service is at fault.

Related Links

Layer 1 versus Layer 2 Ethernet Frames on p. 45

---

[82] This observation can be justified as follows. Service frames can be no smaller than 64 bytes (the minimum frame size permitted by IEEE 802.3). If all service frames are 64 bytes and there is 20 bytes of physical layer overhead (interframe gap and preamble bits) between frames, then CIR will account for 64/(64+20), or 76%, of the line rate.

7.7 Review: Bandwidth Profiles

1. A Carrier Ethernet service for a bank needs to deliver critical data that cannot be dropped. Bandwidth profiles should be set with:

   a. CIR>0, CBS=0, EIR=0, EBS=0
   b. CIR>0, CBS>0, EIR=0, EBS=0
   c. CIR>0, CBS>0, EIR>0, EBS>0
   d. CIR=0, CBS>0, EIR=0, EBS=0
   e. CIR=0, CBS=0, EIR>0, EBS>0

2. Given a continuous stream of service frames with rate greater than EIR + CIR bits per second, approximately how many bytes of service frames will the single-flow bandwidth profile algorithm declare to be Yellow over a time interval of T seconds.

   a. EIR * T bytes
   b. EIR/8 * T bytes
   c. CIR/8 * T bytes
   d. (CIR+EIR) * T bytes
   e. (EIR-CIR)/8 * T bytes

3. What happens to an Ethernet service frame that is marked Green by the bandwidth profile algorithm?

   a. It is discarded.
   b. It is placed in a higher class of service.
   c. It becomes drop-eligible.
   d. It is forwarded.
   e. It is buffered.

4. If the ingress bandwidth profile marks a service frame Yellow, which one of the following statements is true?

   a. The subscriber is exceeding CIR/CBS, but not EIR/EBS.
   b. The subscriber is exceeding CIR/CBS and EIR/EBS.
   c. The subscriber is exceeding EIR/EBS, but not CIR/CBS.
   d. The subscriber is not exceeding EIR/EBS or CIR/CBS.

5. Per EEC ID egress bandwidth profiles are NOT allowed for which service?

   a. EPL
   b. EVPL
   c. EP-LAN
   d. EVP-LAN
   e. EP-Tree
   f. EVP-Tree

6. Three EVCs are service multiplexed at a UNI that is configured with attribute *Token Share = Enabled*. Each EVC supports two classes of service: CoS Argon and CoS Krypton. How many bandwidth profile flows can a single ingress bandwidth profile process at this UNI?

   a. Exactly 1
   b. Up to 2
   c. Up to 3
   d. Up to 6

7. A two-flow bandwidth profile is to be configured to limit egress traffic at a UNI. Color mode parameters CM^1 and CM^2 are both set to 1. Coupling flag CF^0 is set to 1. How can parameters CF^1 and CF^2 be configured?

   a. Both can be set independently, to either 0 or 1.
   b. Both must be set to the same value, either 0 or 1.
   c. Both must be set to 0.
   d. Both must be set to 1.

8. A particular two-flow bandwidth profile includes the following settings. **For flow² (assigned Rank=2)**: CIR^2=10 Mb/s, CIR^2_{max}=10 Mb/s, and CF^2=1. **For flow¹ (assigned Rank=1)**: CIR^1=10 Mb/s, CIR^1_{max}=20 Mb/s, and CF^1=0. If there is no traffic in flow², what is the maximum continuous rate of green traffic in flow¹ (that is permitted by this bandwidth profile)?

   a. 10 Mb/s
   b. 20 Mb/s
   c. 30 Mb/s

9. Which one of the following cannot impact the disposition (green, yellow, or red) of a service frame processed by a bandwidth profile?

   a. Number of tokens in the green token bucket at the time when the service frame arrives.
   b. Destination MAC address of the service frame
   c. Number of tokens in the yellow token bucket at the time when the service frame arrives.
   d. Size of the service frame

10. A bandwidth profile at a UNI must be able to support which one of the following?

    a. CM=color-aware
    b. CF=Y
    c. CM=color-blind
    d. CF=N

Related Links

Answers: Bandwidth Profiles on p. 408

8
EVC Performance

In this chapter:

8.1 EVC Performance Service Attribute
8.2 Multiple EVC Availability Performance
8.3 Example of EVC Performance Attribute Specification
8.4 Review: EVC Performance Attributes

EVC performance is defined per CoS in the SLS using one or more performance metrics, along with related parameters, and performance objectives, as defined in MEF 10.3.

Performance metric — a measure of service frame delivery performance as experienced by the subscriber.

Performance parameter — a value that is needed to fully define a performance metric

Performance objective — the value of the performance metric that is deemed acceptable (characterizing the level of performance with respect to the metric)

The performance metrics, parameters, and objectives that apply to a particular EVC constitute the *EVC Performance* service attribute.

The problem of <u>measuring</u> EVC performance is addressed in a later lesson (SOAM Performance Management). This lesson is focused on <u>defining</u> EVC performance.

Related Links

SOAM Performance Management on p. 270

8.1 EVC Performance Service Attribute

In this section:

- 8.1.1 Performance Metric Caveats and Requirements
- 8.1.2 Ordered UNI Pair
- 8.1.3 Frame Delay Performance
- 8.1.4 Inter-Frame Delay Variation Performance
- 8.1.5 Frame Loss Ratio Performance
- 8.1.6 Availability Performance
- 8.1.7 Resiliency Performance
- 8.1.8 Group Availability Performance

Service Attribute		Requirement					
		Port-Based Service			VLAN-Based Service		
Cat.	Name	EPL	EP-LAN	EP-Tree	EVPL	EVP-LAN	EVP-Tree
Per EVC	EVC Performance	A list of performance metrics and associated parameters and performance objectives					

The *EVC performance* service attribute lists one or more **performance metrics** along with associated **parameter values** and **performance objectives**, as required.

MEF 10.3 defines nine performance metrics in five performance areas.

Performance Area	Performance Metrics
Frame Delay	One-way **Frame Delay (FD)** Performance
	One-way **Frame Delay Range (FDR)** Performance
	One-way **Mean Frame Delay (MFD)** Performance
Inter-Frame Delay Variation	One-way **Inter-Frame Delay Variation (IFDV)** Performance
Frame Loss Ratio	One-way **Frame Loss Ratio (FLR)** Performance
Availability	One-way **Availability** Performance
Resiliency	One-way Resiliency Performance expressed as **High Loss Intervals (HLIs)**
	One-way Resiliency Performance expressed as **Consecutive High Loss Intervals (CHLIs)**
Group Availability	One-way **Group Availability** Performance

The *EVC Performance* service attribute for a given service does not need to include performance objectives for all performance metrics. However, per [D13] in MEF 6.2, it should include at least one performance objective.

Each performance metric name begins with **one-way** to emphasize that only one-way performance measurements are needed to evaluate the metric.[83]

---

[83] The problem of measuring EVC performance is addressed in a later lesson (SOAM Performance Management). This lesson is focused on defining EVC performance.

8.1.1
Performance Metric Caveats and Requirements

Four key caveats apply to all performance metrics:

- Performance metrics apply to **Green service frames only**. MEF-defined performance metrics say nothing about delivery of Yellow service frames.

- Performance metrics are measured over an agreed subset of **ordered UNI pairs**.

- When measurement is over multiple ordered UNI pairs, the **worst case** (lowest performing) **UNI pair** defines the measurement.

- **Maintenance intervals**[84] **are excluded** from performance measurements.

Additionally, all performance metrics, <u>excluding Availability</u>, are measured only when the service is judged to be "Available" (per criteria that will be explained).

Within an SLS, the following parameters (each common to more than one performance metric) must be set to the same value in each performance metric that uses the parameter.[85]

T	The time interval over which the SLS applies. Applicable to all performance metrics.
Δt	A time interval much smaller than T. Applicable to *Availability*, *Group Availability*, *Resiliency* and *Inter-Frame Delay Variation (IFDV)* performance metrics.
C	Unavailability frame loss ratio threshold. Applicable to *Availability*, , *Group Availability* and *Resiliency* performance metrics.
n	Number of consecutive small time intervals, Δt, for assessing availability. Applicable to *Availability* , *Group Availability* and *Resiliency* performance metrics.

8.1.2
Ordered UNI Pair

Every service frame travels one way between two UNIs: a source UNI and a destination UNI. The term **ordered UNI pair** refers to a unique combination (source UNI and destination UNI) in an EVC.

A point-to-point EVC between UNI A and UNI B has two ordered UNI pairs:	(UNI A, UNI B),	(UNI B, UNI A)
A multipoint-to-multipoint EVC with three UNIs has six ordered UNI pairs:	(UNI A, UNI B), (UNI A, UNI C), (UNI B, UNI C),	(UNI B, UNI A). (UNI C, UNI A), (UNI C, UNI B).
A multipoint-to-multipoint EVC with n UNIs has **n*(n-1)** ordered UNI pairs.		

An ordered UNI pair can be visualized as a directed line segment (arrow) between two UNIs.

---

[84] Maintenance intervals are periods of time when the service is not expected to perform well (or at all) per agreement between the service provider and subscriber. A maintenance interval might be used, for example, to upgrade network equipment, to isolate a fault, or to change service features.

[85] Per [R28], [R29], [R30], and [R32] in MEF 10.3.

Test your understanding: *The following figure shows an EP-LAN service involving five UNIs and two CoS. The subscriber has nominated important paths for each CoS as shown.* ***(a)*** *List the ordered UNI pairs that are important for CoS 1.* ***(b)*** *How many ordered UNI pairs are important for CoS 2?* ***(c)*** *What is the total number of ordered UNI pairs, considering all UNIs and all possible paths between them?* [86]

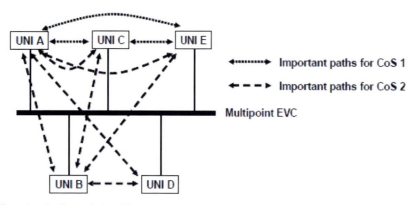

8.1.3
Frame Delay Performance

In general terms, frame delay quantifies the time a green service frame spends in transit between CEs. MEF 10.3 uses the following figure to explain how one-way frame delay is measured for a single service frame.

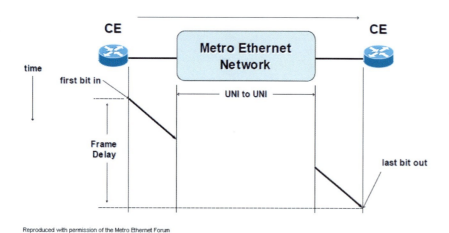

One-way frame delay is a measurement of elapsed time:

- The timer starts when the first bit of the service frame leaves the source CE.
- The timer stops when the last bit of the service frame arrives at the destination CE.

---

86 **Answers: (a)** *(UNI A, UNI C), (UNI C, UNI A); (UNI A, UNI E), (UNI E, UNI A); (UNI C, UNI E), (UNI E, UNI C).* **(b)** *Fourteen. 7 bidirectional paths x 2 ordered UNI pairs per path = 14 ordered UNI pairs.* **(c)** *Twenty. Using the formula n*(n-1) with n=5, you get 5*(5-1)=20.*

Frame delay performance metrics are defined with the following parameters.

Parameter	Description	Example Value
T	The time interval over which the SLS applies	30 days
S	Non-empty subset of ordered UNI pairs	All
CoS Name	The Class of Service name	Gold
P_d	Percentile defining nominal frame delay performance	99.5%
P_r	Percentile defining frame delay range performance	99.99%

Percentiles P_d and P_r allow performance metrics to ignore service frames that perform poorly compared to <u>most</u> service frames, where <u>most</u> is defined by the declared percentile. For example, if P_d=99.5%, then 99.5 % of qualified green service frames must meet the Frame Delay (FD) performance objective for the performance objective to be satisfied.

MEF 10.3 defines three frame delay performance metrics:

Performance Metric	Example Objective
Mean Frame Delay (MFD) is the average value of one-way frame delay over time interval T.	200 ms
Frame Delay (FD) is the maximum one-way frame delay experienced by percentile P_d of service frames over time interval T.	230 ms
Frame Delay Range (FDR) quantifies one-way frame delay with respect to the minimum value of one-way frame delay experienced over time interval T. It is the maximum difference (from the minimum) experienced by percentile P_r of service frames over time interval T.	40 ms

Note: *Per [D14] in MEF 6.2, when frame delay performance objectives are specified in an SLS, EVC performance* should *include one of {FD, FDR} or {FD, IFDV} or {MFD, FDR} or {MFD, IFDV}.*

Note: *More than one performance objective can be specified (per CoS Name) for the same performance metric if different parameter values are used for each performance objective. For example an SLS can include two Frame Delay (FD) performance objectives, one defined for P_d = 90 and another defined for P_d=99.9.*

Related Links
Performance Metric Caveats and Requirements on p. 149

8.1.4
Inter-Frame Delay Variation Performance

Inter-Frame Delay Variation (IFDV) for two consecutive green service frames is defined as the difference between their one-way frame delays. The IFDV performance metric is defined with the following parameters.

Parameter	Description	Example Value
T	The time interval over which the SLS applies	30 days
S	Non-empty subset of ordered UNI pairs	All
CoS Name	The Class of Service name	Gold
P_V	Percentile defining IFDV performance	99.5%
Δt	The separation between frame pairs for which IFDV is defined	1 sec

Performance Metric	Example Objective Value
Inter-Frame Delay Variation (IFDV) is the maximum IFDV experienced by percentile P_V of service frames over time interval T.	32 ms

Note: Multiple IFDV performance objectives can be specified (per CoS Name) if different values of P_v are specified for each IFDV performance objective.

Related Links

Performance Metric Caveats and Requirements on p. 149

8.1.5
Frame Loss Ratio Performance

The *Frame Loss Ratio (FLR)* performance metric is defined with the following parameters.

Parameter	Description	Example Value
T	The time interval over which the SLS applies	30 days
S	Non-empty subset of ordered UNI pairs	All
CoS Name	The Class of Service name	Gold

Performance Metric	Example Objective
Frame Loss Ratio (FLR) measures frames lost as a percentage of frames sent	0.1% (1 in 1000)

Related Links

Performance Metric Caveats and Requirements on p. 149

8.1.6 Availability Performance

Availability performance is based on the concept that a service <u>at any instant of time</u> is in one of two states: Available (working satisfactorily) or Unavailable (not working satisfactorily). With this concept, availability performance is easily defined:

> **Availability Performance**—The percentage of time within a specified time interval (T) during which the service is available

However, this definition side steps the difficult part of defining availability: determining which state (available or unavailable) the service is in at each instant of time.

Note: *Defining availability state is critical to defining all service performance attributes (not just Availability performance). FD, IFDV, FLR, and Resiliency performance are each measured during "available" periods only.*

Availability Specification

The *Availability* performance metric is defined with the following parameters.

Parameter	Description	Example Value
T	The time interval over which the SLS applies	30 days
S	Non-empty subset of ordered UNI pairs	All
CoS Name	The Class of Service name	Gold
Δt	A time interval much smaller than T	1 second
C	Unavailability frame loss ratio threshold	0.1
n	Number of consecutive small time intervals, Δt, for assessing availability	10

Performance Metric	Example Objective
Availability performance expressed as a percentage.	99.9%

Availability performance is measured over a time interval T (for example, 30 days) that is divided into much smaller time intervals Δt (for example, 1 second), as specified in the SLS.

How Availability is Determined

For each Δ*t*, the one-way service between an ordered pair of UNIs is declared to be either *unavailable* or *available*, based on frame loss ratio measurements and the following process.[87]

1. Each Δ*t* is assigned a color, white or grey, as follows:

    If frame loss ratio (*flr*) during time interval Δ*t* exceeds threshold C, Δ*t* is assigned color grey. Otherwise, Δ*t* is assigned color white.

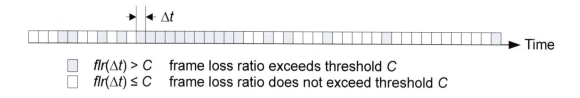

flr(Δt)— The number of service frames lost as a fraction of the number of service frames sent over time interval Δ*t*

Note: The color, white or grey, <u>does not</u> represent availability during interval Δ*t*. Availability is assigned in the next step.

2. The availability state of each time interval Δ*t* is determined by a process (algorithm) that involves two things:

    - A sliding window of *n* time intervals Δ*t* that is imagined to advance through time (from left to right)

    - A binary window state, white or grey, that is initialized to value *white* to start the process

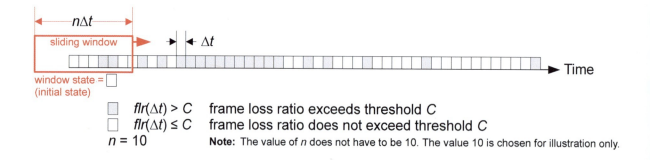

---

[87] Refer to MEF 10.3 for a formal precise description of the process. This informal description of the process is meant to be easier to understand.

Each time the left side of the sliding window reaches a new time interval Δt, availability for that time interval is determined by a two-step process:

a. If the color (white or grey) of all Δt's in the sliding window is opposite to the window state, then change the window state to match the color of all Δt's within the window.

b. Set availability value for the left-most Δt to:

- 1 (available), if the window state is white
- 0 (not available), if the window state is grey

Assignment of availability, for this example, progresses as follows.

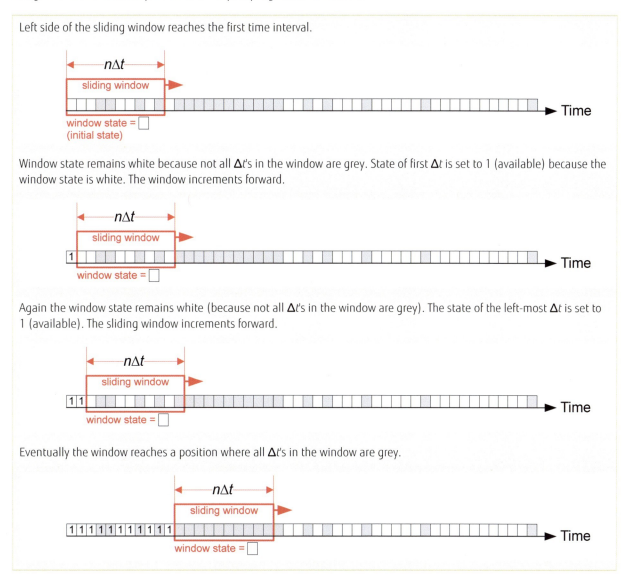

Left side of the sliding window reaches the first time interval.

Window state remains white because not all Δt's in the window are grey. State of first Δt is set to 1 (available) because the window state is white. The window increments forward.

Again the window state remains white (because not all Δt's in the window are grey). The state of the left-most Δt is set to 1 (available). The sliding window increments forward.

Eventually the window reaches a position where all Δt's in the window are grey.

The window state is now changed from white to grey. The state of the left-most Δt is set to 0 (unavailable) because the window state is grey. The window increments forward.

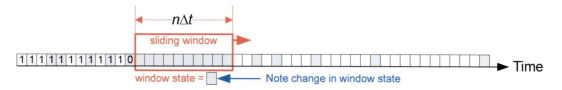

Now many subsequent Δt's are set to 0 (unavailable) as the window advances because the window state is grey and the Δt's within the window are not all white (opposite color to the window state).

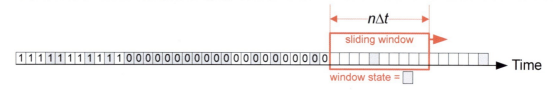

Eventually, the sliding window reaches a position where all Δt's in the window are white.

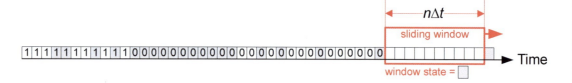

The window state is now changed from grey to white. The state of the left-most Δt is set to 1 (available) because the window state is white. The window increments forward.

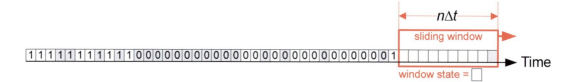

The process eventually completes, resulting in the assignment of availability to each Δt.

Summary

Availability performance is measured over a time interval *T* that is divided into small time intervals Δ*t* that are much smaller than *T*.

For each Δ*t*, the service is declared to be unavailable or available, based on frame loss ratio measurements and using an algorithm specified in MEF 10.3, which depends on performance parameters specified in the SLS. The algorithm involves a sliding window and is not easily explained, but the result is just the assignment of an availability state to each Δ*t*.

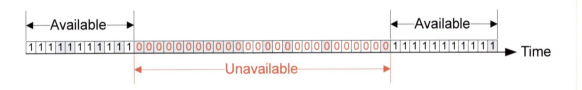

Once availability has been assigned to each Δ*t*, availability performance is computed as the percentage of available Δ*t*'s, compared to all Δ*t*'s over the interval T. The availability performance objective specified in the SLS declares the level of availability performance that the service is expected to deliver.

Performance Metric	Example Objective
Availability performance expressed as a percentage.	99.9%

Related Links

Performance Metric Caveats and Requirements on p. 149

8.1.7
Resiliency Performance

Resiliency performance is defined using the same framework that was used to define Availability performance. Performance metrics are defined with the following parameters.

Parameter	Description	Example Value
T	The time interval over which the SLS applies	30 days
S	Non-empty subset of ordered UNI pairs	All
CoS Name	The Class of Service name	Gold
Δ*t*	A time interval much smaller than T	1 second

Parameter	Description	Example Value
C	Unavailability frame loss ratio threshold	0.1
p	The number of consecutive small time intervals for assessing CHLI, where $p < n$	3

The first five parameters (T, S, $CoS\ Name$, Δt, and C) are the same ones used to define Availability performance. They are defined in the same way and are required to have the same values within an SLS. Parameter n is not used to define Resiliency. Instead, parameter p is used (which serves a similar role).

MEF 10.3 defines two resiliency performance metrics:

Performance Metric	Example Objective
High Loss Interval (HLI) performance expressed as an integer.	100
Consecutive High Loss Interval (CHLI) performance expressed as an integer.	20

MEF 10.3 does not provide concise definitions for HLI or CHLI. Instead, it provides equations and algorithms to define how HLIs and CHLIs are counted. However, the following definitions are consistent with those equations and algorithms:

- **HLI** — High Loss Interval. A small time interval Δt over which service has been declared *Available* even though its frame loss ratio $flr(\Delta t)$ exceeds C (the unavailability frame loss ratio threshold).

- **CHLI** — Consecutive High Loss Interval. A sequence of p or more HLIs.

Note: *As stated in MEF 10.3, Resiliency attributes HLI and CHLI are similar to the definitions of Severely Errored Seconds (SES) and Consecutive SES in ITU-T standard Y.1563.*

For better clarity, let's unpack these definitions. Recall that Availability classifies service during each small time interval, Δt, as *Available* or *Unavailable*.

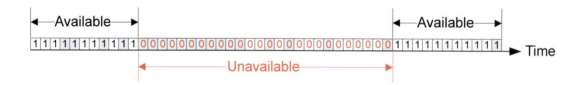

Also recall that prior to classification of Δt's as *Available/Unavailable*, each Δt is assigned a color, white or grey.

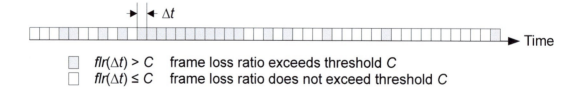

A High Loss Interval (HLI) is a Δt that is both *grey* and *Available*. This example contains five HLIs.

A Consecutive High Loss Interval (CHLI) is a sequence of *p* or more HLIs. If *p*=2, this example contains one CHLI.

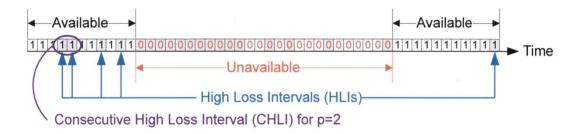

For *p*>2, this example contains no CHLIs. The following example contains two CHLIs for *p*=2 or *p*=3.

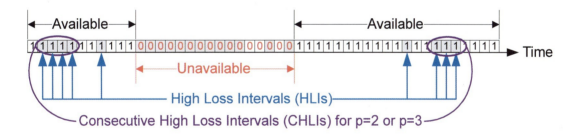

For *p*=4, this example contains one CHLI. For *p*>4, it contains no CHLIs.

Hierarchy of Service Time Classification

The following figure from MEF 10.3 illustrates how service time is classified in relation to Availability and Resiliency.

Time within the big time interval *T* (over which Availability and Resiliency are defined) consists of three types of time: *Unavailable* time, *Available* time, and *Maintenance Interval* time.

Available time is further classified into two types: *HLI* time and *Non-HLI* time.

HLI time is further classified into two types: *CHLI* time and *Non-CHLI* time.

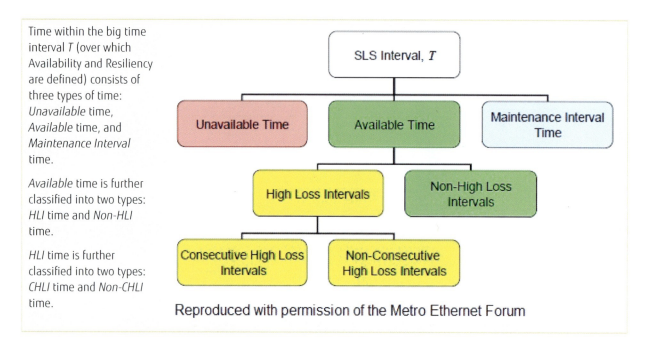

Reproduced with permission of the Metro Ethernet Forum

Summary

Resiliency performance metrics are defined by **six parameters** specified in the SLS: five parameters (T, S, CoS $Name$, Δt, and C) used for Availability performance measurement, plus a new integer parameter p (where $p < n$).

Resiliency performance metrics are defined as the number of HLIs and the number of CHLIs in T, where:

- **HLI** — High Loss Interval. A small time interval Δt over which service has been declared *Available* even though its frame loss ratio $flr(\Delta t)$ exceeds C (the unavailability frame loss ratio threshold).

- **CHLI** — Consecutive High Loss Interval. A sequence of p or more HLIs.

Performance Metric	Example Objective
High Loss Interval (HLI) performance expressed as an integer.	100
Consecutive High Loss Interval (CHLI) performance expressed as an integer.	20

Note: MEF 22.1, Mobile Backhaul Implementation Agreement – Phase 2, uses resiliency performance metrics HLI and CHLI to quantify "short term disruptions" in mobile backhaul services.

Related Links

Performance Metric Caveats and Requirements on p. 149
Availability Performance on p. 153
Mobile Backhaul CoS and Performance Requirements on p. 367

8.1.8
Group Availability Performance

Group Availability performance (newly introduced in MEF 10.3) is used to characterize availability in applications where groups of UNI pairs back up one another. For example, in a mobile backhaul application, it may be important to connect a cell site[88] to two controllers[89] (a primary controller and a backup controller) for the purpose of redundancy. This can be accomplished using three UNIs and a multipoint EVC as shown in the following figure.

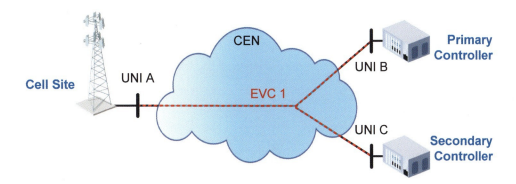

In this application, Group Availability provides a metric for measuring the percentage of time that the cell site can reach at least one of the controllers.

The *Group Availability* performance metric is defined with the following parameters.

Parameter	Description	Example Value
T	The time interval over which the SLS applies	30 days
$S_1, S_2, ..., S_m$	Two or more non-empty subsets of ordered UNI pairs in the EVC	S1={(A,B), (B,A)}, S2={(A,C), (C,A)}
CoS Name	The Class of Service name	Gold
Δt	A time interval much smaller than T	1 second
C	Unavailability frame loss ratio threshold	0.1
K	Minimum number of S's that are to be available	1
n	Number of consecutive small time intervals, Δt, for assessing availability	10

Parameters *T*, *CoS Name*, Δt, *C*, and *n* are the same ones used to define Availability performance. They are defined in the same way and are required to have the same values within an SLS.

Performance Metric	Example Objective
Group Availability performance expressed as a percentage.	99.99%

---

88 Here **cell site** refers to the Radio Access Network (RAN) base station which provides wireless connection to mobile devices.
89 RAN network controllers

To understand Group Availability, imagine that the availability algorithm is applied independently to each subset of ordered UNI pairs, $S_1, S_2, ..., S_m$. For each subset, the algorithm declares each Δt to be *available* or *unavailable*.

For the mobile backhaul example, there are two subsets of ordered UNI pairs, $S_1=\{(A,B), (B,A)\}$ and $S_2=\{(A,C), (C,A)\}$, so the availability algorithm is applied twice and the result might look as follows.

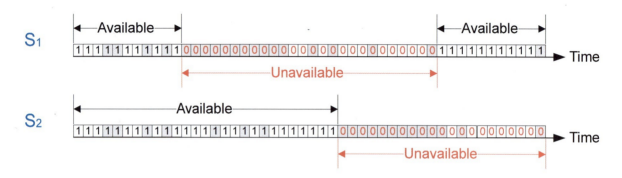

Group Availability — If a given Δt is available with respect to K or more subsets of ordered UNI pairs, that Δt is declared to be *group available*. Otherwise, that Δt is declared to be *group unavailable*.

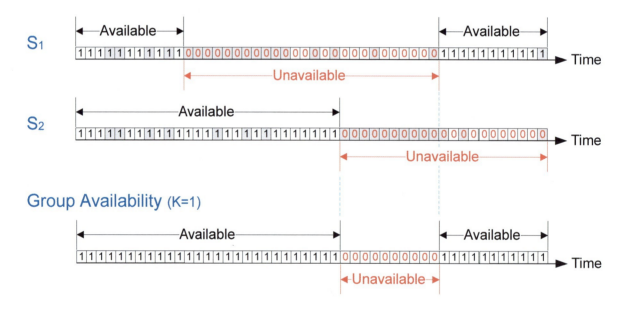

Once group availability has been assigned to each Δt, Group Availability performance is computed as the percentage of available Δt's, compared to all Δt's over the interval T.

Related Links
Availability Performance on p. 153

8.2 Multiple EVC Availability Performance

Multiple EVC Availability performance (newly introduced in MEF 10.3) is nearly identical to Group Availability performance. However, it is for applications involving more than one EVC; applications in which multiple EVCs (not just groups of UNI pairs) back up one another.

For example, consider the previously-described mobile backhaul application, but let the cell site connect to controllers through separate EVCs as shown in the following figure.

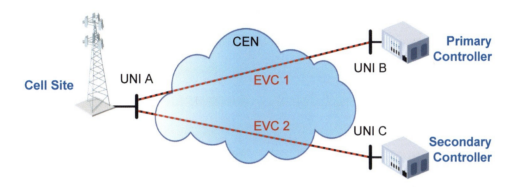

In this application, Multiple EVC Availability provides a metric for measuring the percentage of time that the cell site can reach at least one of the controllers.

The *Multiple EVC Availability* performance metric is defined with the following parameters.

Parameter	Description	Example Value
T	The time interval over which the SLS applies	30 days
$S_1, S_2, ..., S_m$	Two or more non-empty subsets of ordered UNI pairs <u>in two or more EVCs</u>	$S1=\{(A,B), (B,A)\}$, $S2=\{(A,C), (C,A)\}$
CoS Name	The Class of Service name	Gold
Δt	A time interval much smaller than T	1 second
C	Unavailability frame loss ratio threshold	0.1
K	Minimum number of S's that are to be available	1
n	Number of consecutive small time intervals, Δt, for assessing availability	10

Notice that these parameters are identical to those used to define Group Availability performance, except that the subsets of ordered UNI pairs now come from <u>two or more EVCs</u>. Again, parameters *T*, *CoS Name*, Δt, *C*, and *n* are the same ones used to define Availability performance. They are defined in the same way and are required to have the same values within an SLS.

Performance Metric	Example Objective
Multiple EVC Availability performance expressed as a percentage.	99.99%

Multiple EVC Availability performance is calculated in the same way that Group Availability is calculated:

1. The availability algorithm is applied independently to each subset of ordered UNI pairs, $S_1, S_2, ..., S_m$ and, for each subset, the algorithm declares each Δt to be *available* or *unavailable*.

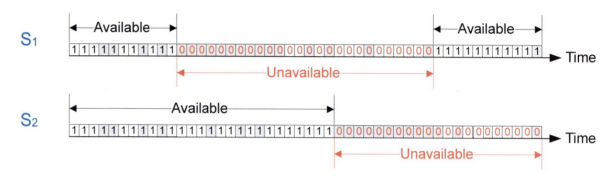

2. If a given Δt is available with respect to K or more subsets of ordered UNI pairs, that Δt is declared to be *multiple EVC available*. Otherwise, that Δt is declared to be *multiple EVC unavailable*.

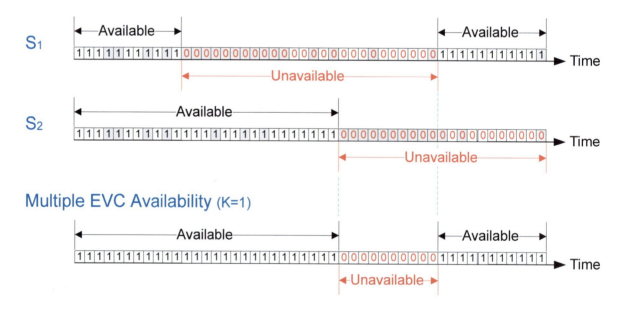

3. Once *multiple EVC availability* status has been assigned to each Δt, Multiple EVC Availability performance is computed as the percentage of available Δt's, compared to all Δt's over the interval T.

Related Links
Availability Performance on p. 153

8.3 Example of EVC Performance Attribute Specification

The following table (based on Table 25 in MEF 6.2) shows an example of how the EVC performance service attribute might be specified for a service involving three CoS.

EVC Performance Attribute	Parameter/Objective	Class of Service Offering		
		Krypton	Argon	Neon
CoS ID	Priority Code Point value	PCP=5	PCP=3	PCP=1
Frame Delay (FD)	Subset of ordered UNI pairs (S)	All	All	All
	FD Objective	X ms	Y ms (Y>X)	Z ms (Z>Y)
	Percentile (P_d)	99.9%	99%	95%
	Time Interval (T)	1 month	1 month	1 month
Frame Delay Range (FDR)	Not Specified (N/S)			
Mean Frame Delay (MFD)	Not Specified (N/S)			
Inter-Frame Delay Variation (IFDV)	Subset of ordered UNI pairs (S)	All	All	All
	IFDV Objective	Q ms	N/S	N/S
	Percentile (P_v)	99%	N/S	N/S
	Time Interval (T)	1 month	N/S	N/S
	Pair Interval (Δt)	1 second	N/S	N/S
Frame Loss Ratio (FLR)	Subset of ordered UNI pairs (S)	All	All	All
	FLR Objective	A %	B% (B>A)	C% (C>B)
	Time Interval (T)	1 month	1 month	1 month
Availability	Subset of ordered UNI pairs (S)	All	All	All
	Availability Objective	α%	β% ($\beta<\alpha$)	γ% ($\gamma<\beta$)
	Time Interval (T)	1 month	1 month	1 month
	Number of consecutive small time intervals (n)	10	10	10
	Small time interval (Δt)	1 second	1 second	1 second
	Unavailability frame loss ratio threshold (C)	50%	75%	100%
Resiliency (HLI)	Not Specified (N/S)			
Resiliency (CHLI)	Not Specified (N/S)			
Group Availability	Not Specified (N/S)			
Multiple EVC Availability	Not Specified (N/S)			

8.4
Review: EVC Performance Attributes

1. Performance metrics estimate frame delivery performance for:

   a. All service frames admitted to the EVC
   b. Yellow service frames
   c. All service frames, except L2CP service frames
   d. Green service frames, per CoS
   e. Green and Yellow service frames

2. Which three performance objectives are defined using a sliding window? (Choose three.)

   a. Availability
   b. Frame Delay (FD)
   c. Mean Frame Delay (MFD)
   d. Inter-Frame Delay Variation (IFDV)
   e. High Loss Intervals (HLI)
   f. Consecutive High Loss Intervals (CHLI)

3. What is the maximum number of ordered UNI pairs in an EP-Tree service that has four leaf UNIs and two root UNIs?

   a. 6
   b. 8
   c. 9
   d. 10
   e. 18

4. The Mean Frame Delay (MFD) performance objective for an EP-LAN service is specified as 80 ms. Which statement best describes the meaning of this performance objective?

   a. During an agreed time period, green service frames on average should spend no more than 80 ms in transit between CEs.
   b. For each ordered UNI pair in the pre-agreed subset of UNI pairs, the average time a green service frame spends in transit between CEs should not exceed 80 ms.
   c. No service frame should spend more than 80 ms in transit between CEs.
   d. For each ordered UNI pair in the set of all ordered UNI pairs, the average time a green service frame spends in transit between CEs should not exceed 80 ms.
   e. No green service frame should spend more than 80 ms in transit between CEs.

5. FLR (Frame Loss Ratio) performance is determined by:

   a. [1 + (green service frames delivered)/(green service frames sent)] ✕ 100
   b. [1 + (total service frames delivered)/(total service frames sent)] ✕ 100
   c. [1 − (total service frames delivered)/(total service frames sent)] ✕ 100
   d. [1 − (green service frames delivered)/(green service frames sent)] /100
   e. [1 − (green service frames delivered)/(green service frames sent)] ✕ 100

6. When a performance attribute is measured over an agreed subset of UNI pairs (more than one UNI pair), how is the final value of the performance attribute calculated?

   a. By taking the best case (highest performing) UNI pair measurement
   b. By averaging the UNI pair measurements
   c. By taking the worst-case (lowest performing) UNI pair measurement
   d. By determining the median value within the set of UNI pair measurements

7. Availability for a particular one-way service between two UNIs is defined with a sliding window of $n=13$ small time intervals Δt. Which condition ensures that the first Δt in the sliding window is declared to be **available**? (No Δt is part of a maintenance interval.)

   a. The frame loss ratio (*flr*) for at least 7 Δt's in the sliding window is greater than threshold *C*.
   b. The frame loss ratio (*flr*) for at least 7 Δt's in the sliding window is less than threshold *C*.
   c. The frame loss ratio (*flr*) for all Δt's in the sliding window is less than threshold *C*.
   d. The frame loss ratio (*flr*) for all Δt's in the sliding window is greater than threshold *C*.

8. Which two performance metrics are defined as a percentage?

   a. *Availability* and *Frame Loss Ratio (FLR)*
   b. *High Loss Interval (HLI)* and *Consecutive High Loss Interval (CHLI)*
   c. *Inter-Frame Delay Variation (IFDV)* and *Mean Frame Delay (MFD)*
   d. *Frame Delay (FD)* and *Mean Frame Delay (MFD)*

9. What is the maximum number of ordered UNI pairs in a EP-LAN service that includes four UNIs?

   a. 4
   b. 6
   c. 8
   d. 12
   e. 16

10. Which two performance objectives are defined using two or more non-empty subsets of ordered UNI pairs? (Choose two.)

    a. Availability
    b. High Loss Intervals (HLI)
    c. Consecutive High Loss Intervals (CHLI)
    d. Group Availability
    e. Multiple EVC Availability

Related Links

Answers: EVC Performance Attributes on p. 411

9
UNI Requirements

In this chapter:

9.1 Type 2 UNI Requirements
9.2 UNI Functionality Service Attributes
9.3 Review: UNI Requirements

The user-to-network interface (UNI) serves both as a boundary between the subscriber and the service provider (point of demarcation) and as a point of connection between the subscriber and the service provider. On either side of the UNI demarcation point, the MEF defines two functional elements:

UNI-C (UNI Client)—Represents all of the subscriber-side functions required to connect the CE to the CEN. Individual functions in a UNI-C are entirely in the subscriber domain but may in some cases be managed by the service provider.

UNI-N (UNI Network)—Represents all of the CEN-side functions required to connect the CEN to the CE. The individual functions in a UNI-N are entirely in the service provider/network operator domain.

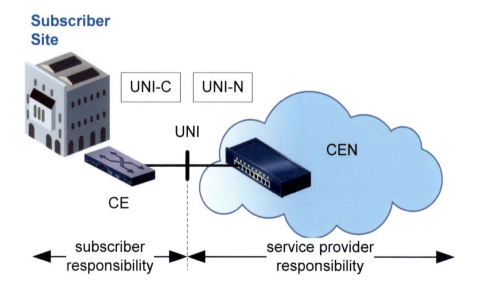

UNI Requirements

Together the UNI-C and UNI-N provide all linking functionality, including IEEE 802.3 Ethernet PHY/MAC interface support and additional data, management, and control plane functions defined by the MEF.

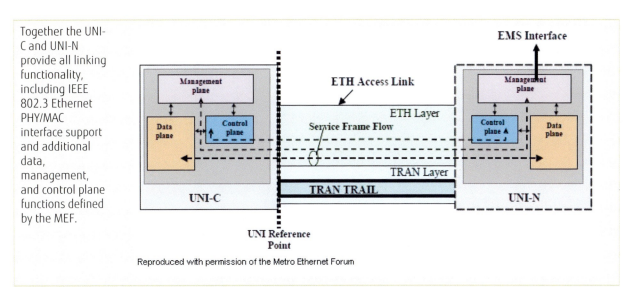

Reproduced with permission of the Metro Ethernet Forum

The MEF defines UNI functionality to promote interoperability between equipment suppliers. The UNI-C and UNI-N equipment may come from different manufacturers, but must still work together.

Various MEF specifications are devoted to UNI functionality. Of these, MEF 20 is the most important for the MEF-CECP exam.

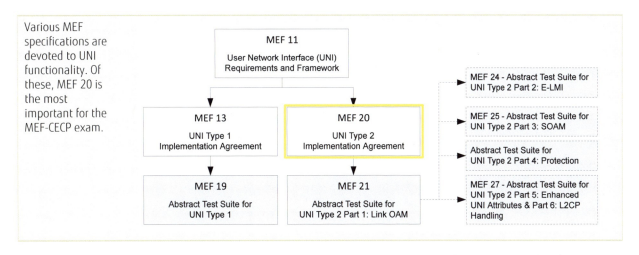

Currently, the MEF defines two types of UNIs:

UNI Type 1 – (Defined in MEF 13) Provides basic functionality and is only manually configurable

UNI Type 2 – (Defined in MEF 20) Adds the following functionalities: SOAM, Enhanced UNI attributes, L2CP handling, E-LMI (optional), LOAM (optional), and Protection (optional)

UNI Type 2 is backward compatible with UNI Type 1. If a Type 2 UNI includes all of the *optional* functionalities, it is classified as Type 2.2. Otherwise, it is classified at Type 2.1.

Related Links

UNI Functionality on p. 25

9.1 Type 2 UNI Requirements

In this section:

- 9.1.1 SOAM Requirement for Type 2 UNIs
- 9.1.2 Enhanced UNI Attributes Requirement for Type 2 UNIs
- 9.1.3 L2CP Handling Requirement for Type 2 UNIs
- 9.1.4 LOAM Requirement for Type 2.2 UNIs
- 9.1.5 E-LMI Requirement for Type 2.2 UNIs
- 9.1.6 Link Protection Requirement for Type 2.2 UNIs

The following list summarizes requirements for Type 2 UNIs.

SOAM, Service operations, administration, and management (OAM) — allows the subscriber and the service provider to monitor and diagnose end-to-end connectivity and performance.
Enhanced UNI Attributes — adds support for the newer UNI attributes, as defined in MEF 10.2 and MEF 6.1.
L2CP Handling — governs the passing, processing, or filtering of Layer 2 control protocols to the EVC.
E-LMI (optional), Ethernet Local Management Interface — allows UNI-C to retrieve EVC status and service attributes from UNI-N as specified in MEF 16
LOAM (optional), Link OAM — allows the subscriber and the service provider to monitor and diagnose link-level connectivity issues between UNI-C and UNI-N per clause 57 of IEEE 802.3
Link Protection (optional) — supports link aggregation per clause 43 of IEEE 802.3 to protect the UNI against port failure

Note: Type 2 UNIs support all Type 1 UNI requirements and are backward compatible with Type 1 UNIs.

9.1.1 SOAM Requirement for Type 2 UNIs

Note: This requirement is mandatory for UNI Type 2.1 and 2.2.

A Type 2 UNI is required to support Service OAM (operations, administration, and management) as defined by the MEF based on ITU-T Y.1731 and IEEE 802.1Q standards. SOAM includes mechanisms for end-to-end connectivity fault detection and performance management.

SOAM functionality is covered later in a later lesson (in a larger context that includes more than just UNI functionality). For now, just note that SOAM support is an important requirement for Type 2 UNIs.

Related Links

Service OAM Overview on p. 254

9.1.2
Enhanced UNI Attributes Requirement for Type 2 UNIs

Note: *This requirement is mandatory for UNI Type 2.1 and 2.2.*

Type 2 UNIs must support the newer UNI attributes, including *bandwidth profile per egress UNI* and *MTU size*, as defined in MEF 10.2 and MEF 6.1. Basically, this requirement adds functionality needed to support enhancements to the MEF service definitions (MEF 6.1 and MEF 10.2) that occurred after Type 1 UNI requirements were defined.

Note: *These requirements may not align with MEF 6.2/10.3 which have superseded and replaced MEF 6.1/10.2.*

Related Links
Maximum Service Frame Size Service Attributes on p. 69
Bandwidth Profile Service Attributes on p. 139

9.1.3
L2CP Handling Requirement for Type 2 UNIs

Note: *This requirement is mandatory for UNI Type 2.1 and 2.2.*

Type 2 UNIs must support the L2CP processing as defined in MEF 10.2 and MEF 6.1.

Note: *These requirements may not align with MEF 6.2/10.3 which have superseded and replaced MEF 6.1/10.2.*

Related Links
L2CP Processing Service Attributes on p. 87

9.1.4
LOAM Requirement for Type 2.2 UNIs

Note: *This requirement is optional for UNI Type 2.1 and is mandatory for UNI Type 2.2.*

Type 2.2 UNIs are required to support Link operations, administration, and management (OAM) as defined in MEF 20, based on clause 57 of IEEE 802.3. LOAM allows the subscriber and the service provider to monitor and diagnose link-level connectivity issues between UNI-C and UNI-N.

LOAM functionality is covered later in a later lesson, within a larger context that includes all types of links (not just UNI-C to UNI-N links). For now, just note that LOAM support is an important requirement for Type 2.2 UNIs.

Related Links
Link OAM on p. 253

9.1.5
E-LMI Requirement for Type 2.2 UNIs

Note: *This requirement is optional for UNI Type 2.1 and is mandatory for UNI Type 2.2.*

The Ethernet Local Management Interface (E-LMI) protocol allows UNI-C to acquire configuration information from UNI-N so that it can automatically configure itself.[90]

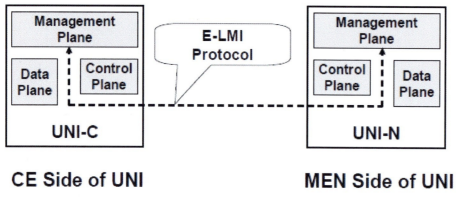

The E-LMI protocol also notifies the UNI-C of changes to EVC status, including notification of the addition/deletion of an EVC, notification of a change in EVC state (Active, Not Active, or Partially Active), and the communication of UNI and EVC attribute values. Technical requirements for E-LMI are specified in MEF 16.

9.1.6
Link Protection Requirement for Type 2.2 UNIs

Note: *This requirement is optional for UNI Type 2.1 and is mandatory for UNI Type 2.2.*

To be Type 2.2, UNI equipment (UNI-C or UNI-N) must be capable of protecting against port failure, using link aggregation as currently defined in IEEE 802.1AX – 2008.

Link aggregation associates two or more links (port-cable-port connections) between two neighboring NEs to form a link aggregation group (LAG) that functions like a single link.

There are two types of LAGs:

---

[90] The E-LMI protocol is based on ITU-T Q.933, X.36 and other relevant recommendations as well as Frame Relay Local Management Interface (FR-LMI) Implementation Agreement document defined by the Frame Relay Forum and related ITU-T recommendations.

UNI Requirements
Type 2 UNI Requirements

1:1 Lag associates two links, one active and one standby, for 1:1 protection.

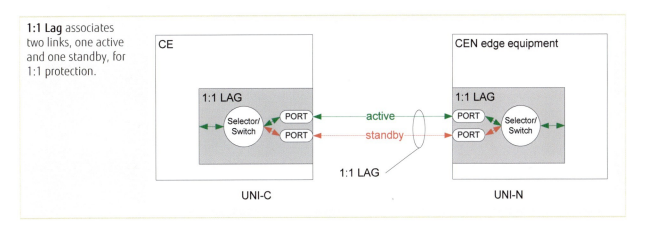

0:N Lag associates N links to form a pseudo link with greater bandwidth. This mechanism is primarily intended to support link bandwidth scalability but also provides limited protection (if one link fails, traffic is distributed over the remaining links).

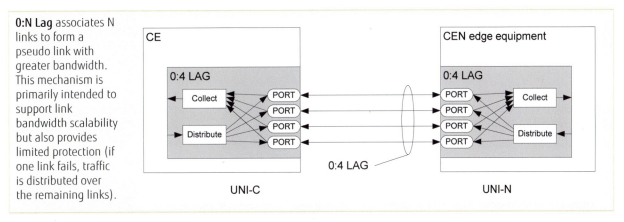

Link bandwidth scalability refers to the problem of supporting links in a graduation of sizes (1, 2, 3, ..., 10 Gb/s) using ports that are available in only a few sizes (1 Gb/s, 10 Gb/s). For example, 0:3 LAG of three 1 Gb/s ports provides a link with a bandwidth of 3 Gb/s.

0:N LAG includes hashing algorithms to distribute traffic evenly between ports and to avoid reordering packets within an information stream.

9.2
UNI Functionality Service Attributes

Service Attribute		Requirement					
Cat.	Name	EPL	EP-LAN	EP-Tree	EVPL	EVP-LAN	EVP-Tree
Per UNI	Physical Layer	List of physical layers (one for each link in the UNI)					
	Synchronous Mode	List of Enabled / Disabled for each link in the UNI					
	Number of Links	Number of Links (integer ≥ 1)					
	UNI Resiliency	None / 2-Link Aggregation / Other					
	Service Frame Format	IEEE Standard 802.3 (2012)					
	Link OAM	Enabled / Disabled					
	E-LMI	Enabled / Disabled					

Attribute **Service Frame Format** (not configurable) specifies that service frames conform to IEEE 802.3 – 2012.[91]

Attribute **Number of Links** specifies the number of physical links used to implement the UNI. The value must be at least 1. *Number of Links*, in turn, determines the value of attribute **UNI Resiliency** as follows:[92]

Number of Links	UNI Resiliency	Meaning
1	None	No protection
2	2-Link Aggregation	UNI-C and UNI-N must support 1:1 LAG as defined in IEEE 802.1AX – 2008.
3	Other	Allows an unspecified protection mechanism to be used by agreement.

Attribute **Physical Layer** declares the physical layer (PHY) for each physical link used to implement the UNI. Per MEF 10.3 [R60], each physical link must be one of the PHYs listed in IEEE 802.3– 2012, but excluding 1000BASE-PX-D and 1000BASE-PX-U. Per MEF 10.3 [R61], the physical layer for each physical link must operate in full duplex mode.

Attribute **Synchronous Mode** is set to *Enabled/Disabled* for each physical link of the UNI. The value *Enabled* declares that the physical link can be used by the CE as a bit clock reference. If *Synchronous Mode = Enabled*, the service provider must specify the quality of the clock reference that is provided.

Attribute **Link OAM** is set to *Enabled/Disabled*. If *Link OAM = Enabled*, the CEN must support Link OAM (active DTE mode capabilities as specified in clause 57.2.9 of IEEE 802.3– 2012) on each physical link of the UNI.

Attribute **E-LMI** is set to *Enabled/Disabled*. If *E-LMI = Enabled*, the CEN must meet mandatory E-LMI requirements as specified in MEF 16 (applicable to the UNI-N) .

---

91   Service frame format must conform to Clause 3 of IEEE 802.3 – 2012, per MEF 10.3 [R68]. Any ingress service frame that is invalid per Clause 3.4 of IEEE 802.3 – 2012 must be discarded, per MEF 10.3 [R69]. Any ingress service frame that is less than 64 bytes in length must be discarded as per Clause 4.2.4.2.2 of IEEE 802.3 – 2012, per MEF 10.3 [R70].
92   Per requirements [R64], [R65], and [R66] in MEF 10.3.

9.3 Review: UNI Requirements

1. A MEF Type 2.2 UNI is required to support which type of protection?

   a. Layer 2 Control Protocol (L2CP)
   b. Link OAM per clause 57 of IEEE 802.3
   c. G.8031 Ethernet Linear Protection Switching
   d. Link aggregation per clause 43 of IEEE 802.3
   e. G.8032 Ethernet Ring Protection Switching

2. Which of the following provides port protection?

   a. L2CP
   b. Link aggregation
   c. E-LMI
   d. Link OAM
   e. Type 1 UNI

3. Which two of the following statements about the Ethernet Local Management Interface (E-LMI) are true? (Choose two.)

   a. E-LMI protects against port failure using link aggregation.
   b. E-LMI is required for Type 2.1 UNIs.
   c. E-LMI notifies the UNI-C of changes to EVC status.
   d. E-LMI allows the subscriber and the service provider to monitor and diagnose link-level connectivity issues between UNI-C and UNI-N.
   e. E-LMI allows UNI-C to acquire configuration information from UNI-N so that it can automatically configure itself.

4. Which three of the following requirements are mandatory for Type 2.2 UNIs, but optional for Type 2.1 UNIs? (Choose three.)

   a. Link aggregation support
   b. Service OAM support
   c. Link OAM support
   d. Support of multiplexed UNI for services such as EVPL
   e. Backward compatibility with UNI Type 1
   f. E-LMI support

5. Which one of the following statements about Type 2 UNIs is *not* true?

   a. Type 2 UNIs support Service OAM.
   b. MEF 20 describes two types of Type 2 UNIs.
   c. Type 2 UNI requirements apply only to the UNI-N (they are not applicable to the UNI-C).
   d. Type 2 UNIs are backward compatible with Type 1 UNIs.
   e. Type 2 UNIs support L2CP handling as defined in MEF 6.1 and MEF 10.2.

6. UNI Type 2.2 required protection mechanisms protect against which three types of failure? (Choose three.)

   a. Port failure on UNI-N
   b. Loss of timing
   c. Loss of "green" service frames due to bandwidth oversubscription
   d. E-LMI denial of service (DOS) attack
   e. Port failure on UNI-C
   f. Disconnection or failure of a cable connecting the CE and CEN

7. Per MEF 10.3, which three values are recognized for the *UNI Resiliency* per UNI service attribute? (Choose three.)

   a. LACP
   b. None
   c. 2-Link Aggregation
   d. E-LMI
   e. Other

Related Links

Answers: UNI Requirements on p. 414

10

Extending MEF Services over Multiple Operator CENs

In this chapter:

10.1 Terminology
10.2 Service Handoff at ENNI
10.3 Operator Service Model
10.4 Operator Service Attributes
10.5 Highlights of the Operator Service Model
10.6 Rooted-Multipoint OVCs
10.7 Review: Extending MEF Services over Multiple Operator CENs

So far we have focused on defining MEF services in a simple business context involving two stakeholders:

- **Subscriber**—The organization purchasing the Carrier Ethernet service

- **Service Provider**—The organization providing the Carrier Ethernet service

However, in some cases, the service provider network may not be able to reach (or connect to) all of the subscriber sites, so collaboration is required. For this reason, MEF 26.1 extends the basic reference model to include additional participants called operators.

- **Operator**—The administrative organization responsible for a particular network in a multi-network Carrier Ethernet service implementation

The following figure shows a service implemented across three independent networks.

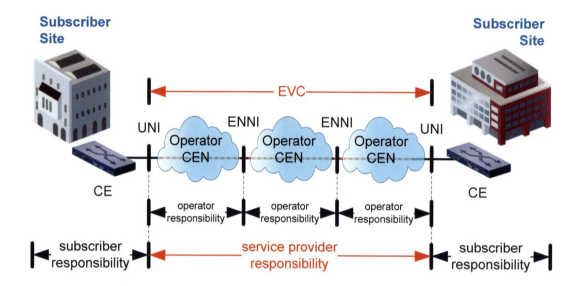

The introduction of operators enhances the service implementation framework, but it does not change the Carrier Ethernet service from the subscriber's perspective:

- There is still only one Carrier Ethernet service provider responsible for the service as a whole.

- The Carrier Ethernet service is still implemented with exactly one EVC connecting two or more UNIs.

- The basic reference model is sufficient to define the service from the subscriber's perspective.

- The general reference model adds details of implementation that are only important to the service provider and subcontracting operators.

Although nothing changes from the subscriber's perspective, the service provider now has a new relationship with one or more operators. If an operator is internal to the service provider's business organization, the relationship can be informal. Otherwise, a formal business relationship is generally required. For this purpose the operator's contribution to the overall service is elevated to the status of an Ethernet service:

- **Operator Service** – An Ethernet service deployed by an operator and sold to a service provider

This lesson describes how the MEF defines operator services in general. The next lesson describes two standardized operator services (the **Access EPL** and the **Access EVPL**) that the MEF has defined for Ethernet access applications.

Related Links

Operator Service Model on p. 191
E-Access Services on p. 232
General Reference Model on p. 27

10.1
Terminology

In this section:

10.1.1	Service Provider and Operators	10.1.5	OVC End Point
10.1.2	ENNI and ENNI-N	10.1.6	Ingress and Egress Frames
10.1.3	External Interface (EI)	10.1.7	OVC End Point Role
10.1.4	OVC	10.1.8	Hairpin Switch

10.1.1
Service Provider and Operators

In MEF 26.1, an independent network that participates in providing a service is called an **Operator CEN** (not a CEN). In these lessons, we follow the same convention:

CEN—A carrier Ethernet network comprising a single administrative domain
Operator CEN— An independent network that participates in providing the service

Other MEF specifications (and reference presentations) are sometimes less careful with terminology. For example, the following figure shows two service providers participating in a service.

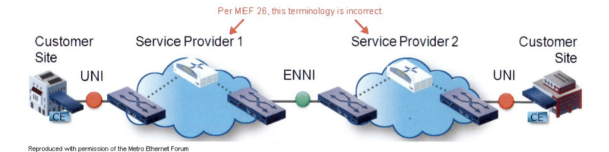

Terminology in the preceding figure is incorrect because a MEF service can have only one service provider (responsible to the subscriber for the end-to-end service as a whole). Knowing this, it is clear that the "service providers" shown in the preceding figure should be interpreted as operators. The following figure shows an example of correct terminology.

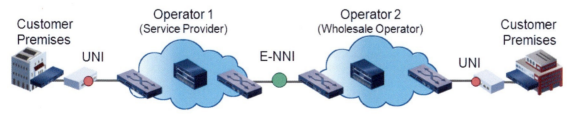

The collaborating networks are associated to operators (not service providers). The network labeled *Operator 1* also belongs to the service provider (responsible for the end-to-end service), but the other network does not. Normally, the service provider owns and operates one or more of the Operator CENs involved in the service. However, this is not a requirement. The service provider might not operate any of the Operator CENs, but only coordinate operators and take responsibility for the overall service.

10.1.2
ENNI and ENNI-N

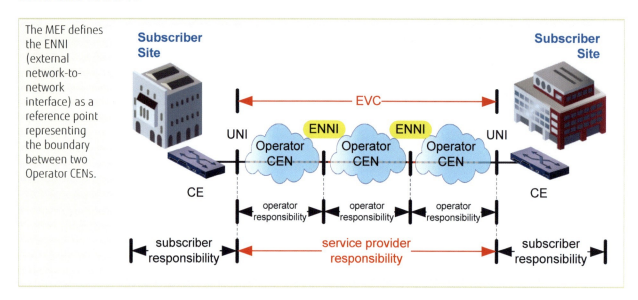

The MEF defines the ENNI (external network-to-network interface) as a reference point representing the boundary between two Operator CENs.

Similar to the UNI, the ENNI serves two roles: (1) as a boundary between two Operator CENs (point of demarcation), and (2) as a point of connection between two Operator CENs. The ENNI demarcation point is located at a specific place between two Operator CENs. Typically, it is a port on one of the Operator CEN edge devices.

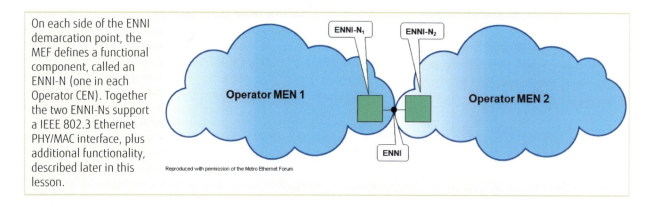

On each side of the ENNI demarcation point, the MEF defines a functional component, called an ENNI-N (one in each Operator CEN). Together the two ENNI-Ns support a IEEE 802.3 Ethernet PHY/MAC interface, plus additional functionality, described later in this lesson.

10.1.3
External Interface (EI)

Per MEF 4, an **External Interface (EI)** is defined as either a UNI or an ENNI.

10.1.4
OVC

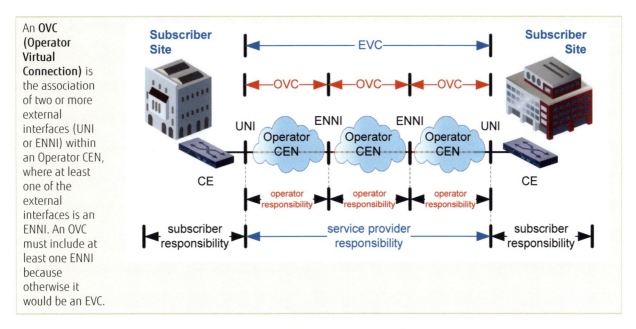

An **OVC (Operator Virtual Connection)** is the association of two or more external interfaces (UNI or ENNI) within an Operator CEN, where at least one of the external interfaces is an ENNI. An OVC must include at least one ENNI because otherwise it would be an EVC.

OVCs can be type point-to-point, multipoint-to-multipoint, or rooted-multipoint.

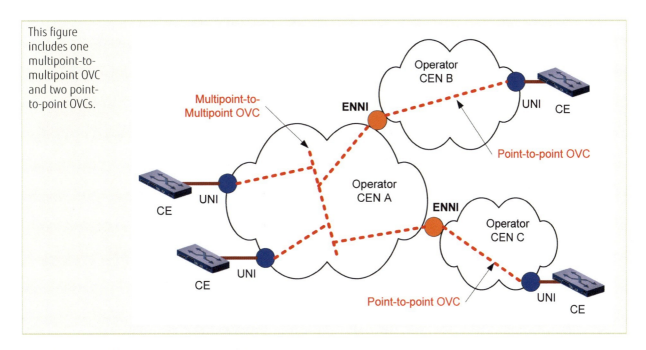

This figure includes one multipoint-to-multipoint OVC and two point-to-point OVCs.

An EVC is formed by the concatenation of OVCs.

The EVC for the previous example looks as follows:

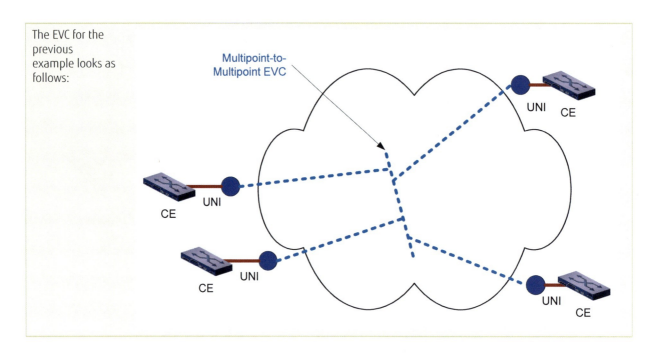

10.1.5
OVC End Point

An **OVC End Point** associates an OVC with a specific external interface (UNI or ENNI).

The OVC end point is not the UNI or ENNI. UNIs and ENNIs are not OVC end points.

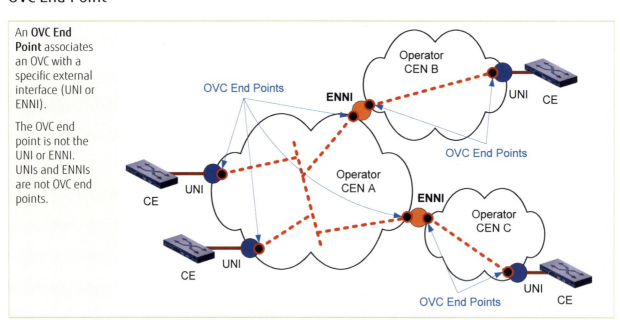

10.1.6
Ingress and Egress Frames

Ingress ENNI frame—An ENNI frame received by an Operator CEN is called an ingress ENNI frame (from the perspective of the receiving Operator CEN).

Egress ENNI frame—An ENNI frame transmitted by an Operator CEN is called an egress ENNI frame (from the perspective of the transmitting Operator CEN).

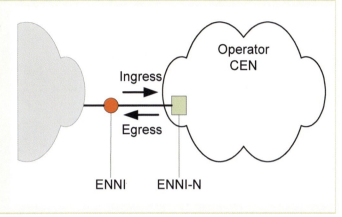

At an OVC end point:

- An **Ingress frame** is a frame **received by the OVC** through the external interface (UNI or ENNI)
- An **Egress frame** is a frame **sent from the OVC** through the external interface (UNI or ENNI)

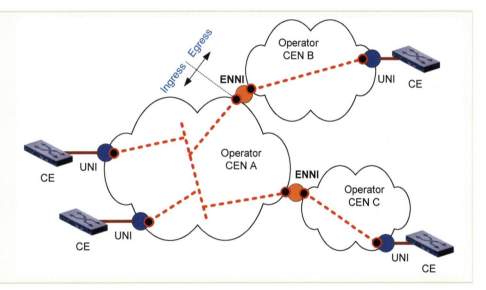

10.1.7
OVC End Point Role

Per MEF 26.1, every OVC end point is assigned an OVC end point role (Root, Leaf, and Trunk), but only the rooted-multipoint OVC supports more than one OVC end point role:[93]

OVC Type	Supported OVC End Point Roles
Point-to-point	Root
Multipoint-to-multipoint	Root
Rooted-multipoint	Root, Leaf, and Trunk

[93] For point-to-point and multipoint-to-multipoint OVCs, OVC end point role assignment is trivial. It is done for consistency only.

Rooted-multipoint OVCs support three OVC end point roles (Root, Leaf, and Trunk) for the same reason that rooted-multipoint EVCs support two UNI designations (Root and Leaf). In both cases, the purpose is to identify E-Tree-service-related frame forwarding constraints. The following example illustrates the use of OVC end point roles Root and Leaf, which are easy to explain compared to OVC end point role Trunk.

OVC end point role **Root** — Indicates that all frames ingressing to the OVC end point originated at a Root UNI and can be forwarded to any OVC end point (Root, Leaf, or Trunk)

OVC end point role **Leaf**— Indicates that all frames ingressing to the OVC end point originated at a Leaf UNI and must not be forwarded to a Leaf OVC end point.

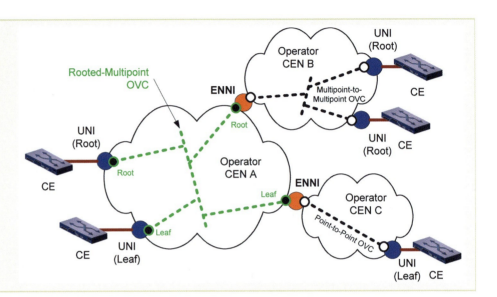

As shown in this example, OVC end point role **Trunk** is used when ingress frames have mixed origin (some originating at a Root UNI and others originating at a Leaf UNI).

OVC end point roles are explained in more detail later in this lesson.

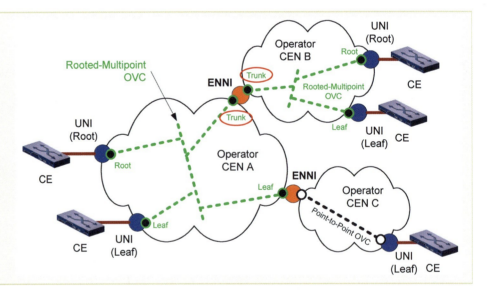

Related Links

Rooted-Multipoint OVCs on p. 209
OVC Service Attributes on p. 193

10.1.8 Hairpin Switch

The following figure illustrates a hairpin switch:

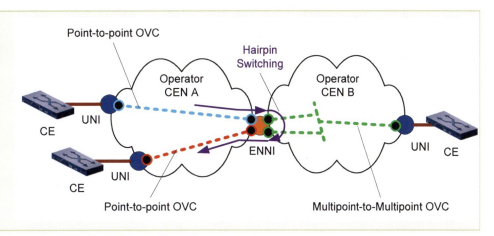

Operator CEN B receives an ingress ENNI frame from Operator CEN A and then returns the frame with changes (defined later in this lesson) that cause the frame to be associated to a different OVC upon return to Operator CEN A.

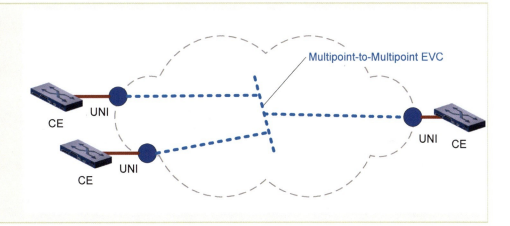

Hairpin switching is needed because subscriber requires the following EVP-LAN service.

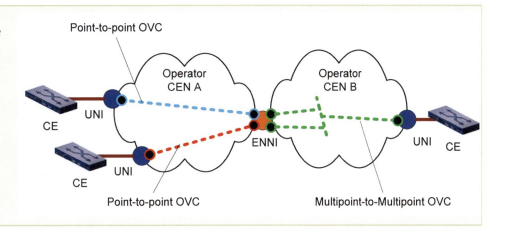

However, the service is implemented with three OVCs in two Operator CENs as follows.

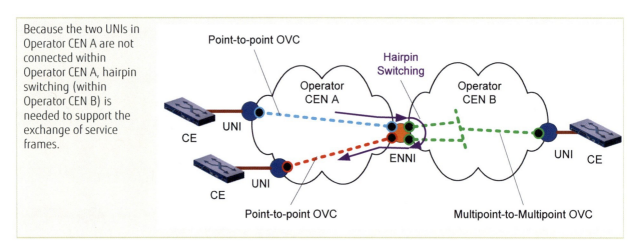

Because the two UNIs in Operator CEN A are not connected within Operator CEN A, hairpin switching (within Operator CEN B) is needed to support the exchange of service frames.

Additional details are presented later in this lesson.

Related Links

Hairpin Switching on p. 202

10.2
Service Handoff at ENNI

In this section:

10.2.1 Encoding Information in S-Tags
10.2.2 ENNI Tagging Requirements

Service handoff at ENNIs is key to defining services across Operator CENs. ENNIs are defined to be high bandwidth (1 Gb/s or 10 Gb/s or more) and to support multiple services. The following figure shows two EPL services implemented across two Operator CENs. The ENNI must support both services (and, potentially, many others).

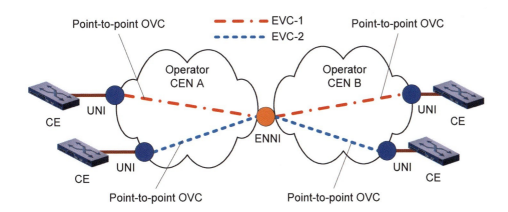

At the ENNI, principle concerns include:

- Distinguishing which ENNI frames belong to which OVC end point

- Propagating CoS (class of service) from one Operator CEN to the next

- Propagating Color (green/yellow drop-eligibility) from one Operator CEN to the next

Recall that service frames are assigned CoS and Color at UNIs per the SLA (service-level agreement) between the subscriber and the service provider. After CoS and Color are established at the ingress UNI, they typically remain fixed for the duration of the service frame's travel, UNI to UNI, through any number of Operator CENs.

MEF 26.1 requires ENNIs to support S-Tags[94] for the purpose of propagating CoS, Color, and OVC end point mapping information between Operator CENs.

Related Links

S-Tagged Ethernet Frames on p. 50

---

94 The service VLAN tag (S-Tag) was introduced in amendment IEEE 802.1ad to IEEE 802.1Q (2005), but has since been rolled into IEEE 802.1Q (2011).

10.2.1
Encoding Information in S-Tags

Double-Tagged Ethernet frame

```
| Destination MAC | Source MAC | S-Tag | C-Tag | Type/Length | Payload | FCS |
```

S-Tag fields: 88A8 (16 bits), PCP (3 bits), DEI (1 bit), VID (12 bits). TPID = 88A8 (16 bits); TCI = PCP + DEI + VID.

TPID=88a8 indicates that this tag is an S-Tag

In IEEE 802.1Q (1998), these three bits are called User Priority bits. In IEEE 802.1Q (2005), they are called PCP bits. They are also commonly called P-bits, or 802.1p bits.

The drop eligibility indicator (DEI) bit. Normally DEI=0 signifies that the Ethernet frame is not drop-eligible and DEI=1 signifies that the Ethernet frame is drop-eligible.

The VLAN identifier (VID) includes 12 bits representing one of 4094 values that are used to identify the service VLAN to which the Ethernet frame belongs.

Note: *The 12-bit VID field allows 4096 values, but only 4094 values can be used for VLAN identification because VID values 0 and FFF are reserved for other uses.*

Per MEF 26.1, the following information is encoded in the S-Tag at ENNIs:

- **OVC End Point Identification** — Ingress ENNI frames are mapped to OVC end points based on S-VLAN ID value.

- **CoS identification** — Ingress ENNI frames are mapped to CoS based on S-Tag PCP value.[95]

- **Color identification**—Color (green/yellow drop-eligibility) can be assigned to an ingress ENNI frame in either one of two ways: based on S-Tag DEI bit value, or based on S-Tag PCP value.

The information contained in the ENNI frame S-Tag pertains to the Operator CEN receiving the frame, not the Operator CEN sending the frame. Thus, it is the responsibility of the transmitting Operator CEN to set S-Tag values appropriately for the receiving Operator CEN.

Related Links

S-Tagged Ethernet Frames on p. 50

---

[95] Per MEF 26.1, for each OVC end point, each S-Tag PCP value (0–7) must be explicitly mapped to exactly one CoS. To explicitly discard frames, one CoS can be equated to discard.

10.2.2
ENNI Tagging Requirements

Per MEF 26.1, all ENNI frames must be in one of three formats:

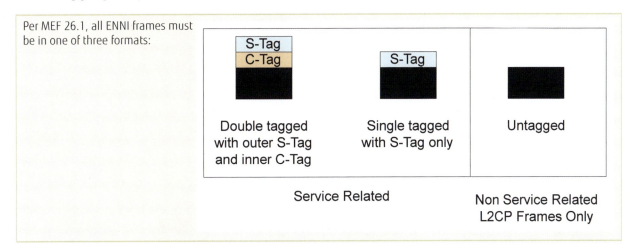

Untagged frames are allowed at the ENNI only to support L2CPs, such as Link Aggregation Control Protocol (LACP), **which are not service specific**. All frames associated with a service require an outer S-Tag. This includes service-associated L2CP frames, such as Spanning Tree Protocol (STP) bridge protocol data units (BPDUs).

The following figure shows tagging operations for two service frames as they progress through two Operator CENs. For clarity, only one direction of bidirectional traffic flow is shown.

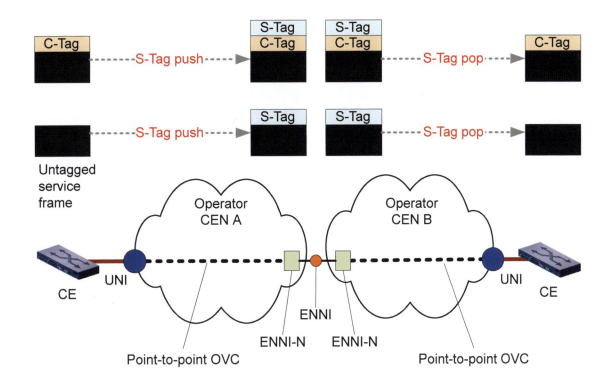

Two operations are required:

- Operator CEN A pushes an S-Tag onto the service frame before transmitting it to Operator CEN B.

- Operator CEN B pops the S-Tag from the service frame before transmitting it to the CE.

The S-Tag is added (pushed) to capture information (CoS, Color, and S-VLAN ID[96]) that is useful for service implementation, but the S-Tag must be removed (popped) before the service frame is transmitted to the subscriber.

Per MEF 26.1, S-Tags are only required to support service hand off at ENNIs. However, operators commonly push and pop S-Tags at UNIs, as shown in the following figure.

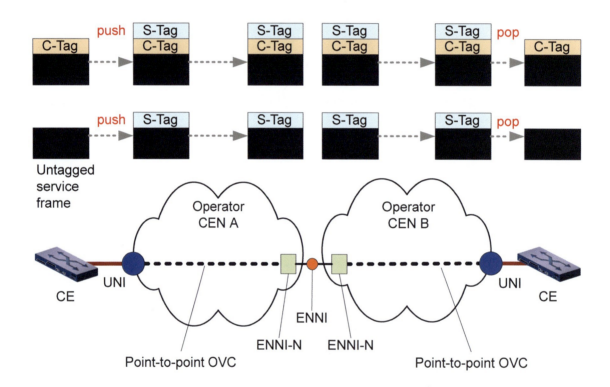

Operators do this in order to use the S-Tag information (CoS, Color, and S-VLAN ID) for service implementation within the Operator CEN (not just at the ENNI).

Note: *In single-CEN service applications, service providers also commonly push and pop S-Tags at UNIs for the same reason: to mark each service frame with an S-VLAN ID, a CoS identifier, and a Color identifier.*

---

[96] Used for OVC end point identification.

10.3
Operator Service Model

The MEF model for service across an Operator CEN is similar to the MEF model for the overall service, but it involves more service attributes and different stakeholders. The stakeholders are:

- **Service Provider**—The organization purchasing the service across the Operator CEN

- **Operator**—The organization providing the service across the Operator CEN

Just as MEF 6.2 uses service attributes to define an overall service, MEF 26.1 uses service attributes to define service across an Operator CEN. More service attributes are required, but the approach is basically the same: service across an Operator CEN is defined in terms of end point functionality (details of implementation are avoided).

In this document these services are called **operator services**, or **OVC-based services**, to distinguish them from UNI-to-UNI (EVC-based) Ethernet services.

Note: This lesson describes how the MEF defines OVC-based services in general. The next lesson describes two MEF-standarized OVC-based services (the **Access EPL** and the **Access EVPL**), which the MEF has defined to support industry standardization of Ethernet access service.

Related Links

E-Access Services on p. 232

10.4
Operator Service Attributes

In this section:

10.4.1 ENNI Service Attributes
10.4.2 OVC Service Attributes
10.4.3 OVC End Point per ENNI Service Attributes
10.4.4 Per UNI Service Attributes (Operator Service)
10.4.5 OVC per UNI Service Attributes

Each operator service attribute is associated to one of five categories (rather than the three categories used for UNI-to-Per UNI service attributes):

1. **ENNI** service attributes

2. **OVC** service attributes

3. **OVC End Point per ENNI** service attributes

4. **UNI** service attributes

5. **OVC per UNI** service attributes

Refer to MEF 26.1 for complete details on all operator service attributes.

 Attention: Most of the operator service attributes are similar to those previously described (for the overall service) and will not be reviewed in detail within this lesson. The following tables list the attributes to give you a general idea of what is involved. **They are not meant to be studied in detail.**

10.4.1
ENNI Service Attributes

For each ENNI, there are two sets of ENNI Service Attributes, one for each Operator CEN.

ENNI Service Attributes (Reference: Table 2 in MEF 26.1)		
Attribute Name	**Summary Description**	**Possible Values**
Operator ENNI Identifier	An identifier for the ENNI intended for management purposes	A string that is unique across the Operator CEN
Physical Layer	The physical layer of the links supporting the ENNI **Note:** ENNIs are defined to be high bandwidth (1 Gb/s or 10 Gb/s).	1000Base-SX, 1000Base-LX, 1000Base T, 10GBase-SR, 10GBase-LX4, 10GBase-LR, 10GBase-ER, 10GBase-SW, 10GBase-LW, 10GBase-EW
Frame Format	The format of the PDUs at the ENNI	Conforming to IEEE 802.1ad (2005)

ENNI Service Attributes (Reference: Table 2 in MEF 26.1)		
Attribute Name	Summary Description	Possible Values
Number of Links	The number of physical links in the ENNI	1 or 2
Protection Mechanism	The method for protection, if any, against a failure	Link Aggregation, None, or Other
ENNI Maximum Transmission Unit Size	The maximum length ENNI Frame in bytes are allowed at the ENNI	Integer ≥ 1526 bytes
End Point Map	The map that associates each S-Tagged ENNI Frame with an OVC End Point	A table with rows of the form <S-VLAN ID value, End Point Identifier, End Point Type>
Maximum Number of OVCs	The maximum number of OVCs that the Operator can support at the ENNI	Integer ≥ 1
Maximum Number of OVC End Points per OVC	The maximum number of OVC End Points that the Operator can support at the ENNI for an OVC.	Integer ≥ 1

Note: The MEF provides no option to assign bandwidth profiles per ENNI.

Related Links

Color-Aware Bandwidth Profiles at ENNI on p. 200
Protection at ENNI on p. 198
ENNI and OVC MTU Size on p. 197
End Point Map on p. 199

10.4.2
OVC Service Attributes

OVC Service Attributes (Reference: Table 5 in MEF 26.1)		
Attribute Name	Summary Description	Possible Values
OVC Identifier	Identifies the OVC for management purposes.	A string that is unique across the Operator CEN
OVC Type	Declares the OVC type.	Point-to-Point, Multipoint-to-Multipoint, or Rooted-Multipoint
OVC End Point List	Lists OVC End Points associated with the OVC.	A list of <OVC End Point Identifier, OVC End Point Role> pairs
Maximum Number of UNI OVC End Points	Bounds the number UNIs on which OVC End Points terminate.	Integer ≥ 0
Maximum Number ENNI OVC End Points	Bounds the number ENNIs on which OVC End Points terminate.	Integer ≥ 1

OVC Service Attributes (Reference: Table 5 in MEF 26.1)		
Attribute Name	Summary Description	Possible Values
OVC Maximum Transmission Unit Size	Declares the maximum size of frames supported over all OVC End Points.	Integer ≥ 1526 bytes
CE-VLAN ID Preservation	If Yes, the OVC preserves the value of the VLAN ID (VID) in the CE-VLAN tag.	Yes or No
CE-VLAN CoS Preservation	If Yes, the OVC preserves the value of the priority code point (PCP) bits in the CE-VLAN tag.	Yes or No
S-VLAN ID Preservation	If Yes, the OVC preserves the value of the VLAN ID (VID) in the S-Tag.	Yes or No
S-VLAN CoS Preservation	If Yes, the OVC preserves the value of the priority code point (PCP) bits in the S-Tag.	Yes or No
Color Forwarding	When Color Forwarding is Yes, the OVC cannot "promote" a frame from Yellow to Green.	Yes or No
Service Level Specification	Defines frame delivery performance definitions and objectives.	As described later in this lesson
Unicast Service Frame Delivery	Describes OVC delivery requirements for ingress frames with a unicast destination MAC address.	Deliver Unconditionally or Deliver Conditionally
Multicast Service Frame Delivery	Describes OVC delivery requirements for ingress frames with a multicast destination MAC address.	Deliver Unconditionally or Deliver Conditionally
Broadcast Service Frame Delivery	Describes OVC delivery requirements for ingress frames with a broadcast destination MAC address.	Deliver Unconditionally or Deliver Conditionally
Layer 2 Control Protocol Tunneling	The Layer 2 Control Protocols that are tunneled by the OVC	A list on Layer 2 Control Protocols

Related Links

Service Level Specification (OVC Service Attribute) on p. 206
Layer 2 Control Protocol Tunneling on p. 207
OVC End Point Role on p. 183
ENNI and OVC MTU Size on p. 197
Color Forwarding on p. 201

10.4.3
OVC End Point per ENNI Service Attributes

OVC End Point per ENNI Service Attributes (Reference: Table 17 in MEF 26.1)		
Attribute Name	Summary Description	Possible Values
OVC End Point Identifier	Identifies the OVC End Point for management purposes	A string that is unique across the Operator CEN

OVC End Point per ENNI Service Attributes (Reference: Table 17 in MEF 26.1)		
Attribute Name	Summary Description	Possible Values
Trunk Identifiers	For a Trunk OVC End Point, specifies the S-VLAN ID values used on the ENNI to distinguish frames originating at a Root UNI and frames originating at a Leaf UNI	<Root S-VLAN ID value, Leaf S-VLAN ID value> for Trunk OVC End Points; Not Applicable to Root or Leaf OVC End Points
Class of Service Identifiers	Determines CoS for ingress ENNI frames mapped to the OVC End Point	Non-overlapping sets S-Tag PCP values; one for each CoS
Ingress Bandwidth Profile Per OVC End Point	Determines per-OVC-End-Point policing for ingress ENNI Frames mapped to the OVC End Point	None or one set of bandwidth profile values (CIR, CBS, EIR, EBS, CF, CM)
Ingress Bandwidth Profile Per ENNI Class of Service Identifier	Determines per-CoS policing for ingress ENNI Frames mapped to the OVC End Point	None or one set of bandwidth profile values (CIR, CBS, EIR, EBS, CF, CM) for each CoS
Egress Bandwidth Profile Per End Point	Determines per-OVC-End-Point policing for egress ENNI Frames mapped to the OVC End Point	None or one set of bandwidth profile values (CIR, CBS, EIR, EBS, CF, CM)
Egress Bandwidth Profile Per ENNI Class of Service Identifier	Determines per-CoS policing for egress ENNI Frames mapped to the OVC End Point	None or one set of bandwidth profile values (CIR, CBS, EIR, EBS, CF, CM) for each CoS

Note: At ENNIs, bandwidth profiles (if used) must be color-aware.

Related Links

Trunk Identifiers on p. 213
Color-Aware Bandwidth Profiles at ENNI on p. 200

10.4.4
Per UNI Service Attributes (Operator Service)

The Per UNI service attributes for a service across an Operator CEN are identical to the Per UNI service attributes for the overall service.

Related Links

Per UNI Service Attributes on p. 60

10.4.5
OVC per UNI Service Attributes

Note: The term **OVC End Point per UNI** is equivalent to **OVC per UNI**. These terms are equivalent because an OVC can associated only one OVC End Point to a UNI.

OVC per Per UNI service attributes (Reference: Table 18 in MEF 26.1)		
Attribute Name	**Summary Description**	**Possible Values**
UNI OVC Identifier	Identifies the OVC at UNI for management purposes	A string formed by the concatenation of the UNI Identifier and the OVC Identifier
OVC End Point Map	The CE-VLAN ID(s) that map to the OVC End Point at the UNI	A list of one or more CE-VLAN ID values
Ingress Bandwidth Profile Per OVC End Point at a UNI	Determines policing for ingress frames mapped to the OVC End Point	None or one set of bandwidth profile values (CIR, CBS, EIR, EBS, CF, CM)
Ingress Bandwidth Profile Per Class of Service Identifier at a UNI	Determines per-CoS policing for ingress frames mapped to the OVC End Point	None or one set of bandwidth profile values (CIR, CBS, EIR, EBS, CF, CM) for each CoS
Egress Bandwidth Profile Per OVC End Point at a UNI	Determines policing for egress frames mapped to the OVC End Point	None or one set of bandwidth profile values (CIR, CBS, EIR, EBS, CF, CM)
Egress Bandwidth Profile Per Class of Service Identifier at a UNI	Determines per-CoS policing for egress frames mapped to the OVC End Point	None or one set of bandwidth profile values (CIR, CBS, EIR, EBS, CF, CM) for each CoS

10.5 Highlights of the Operator Service Model

In this section:

- 10.5.1 ENNI Frame Format
- 10.5.2 ENNI and OVC MTU Size
- 10.5.3 Protection at ENNI
- 10.5.4 End Point Map
- 10.5.5 Color-Aware Bandwidth Profiles at ENNI
- 10.5.6 Color Forwarding
- 10.5.7 Hairpin Switching
- 10.5.8 End Point Map Bundling
- 10.5.9 LOAM Requirement for ENNIs
- 10.5.10 Service Level Specification (OVC Service Attribute)
- 10.5.11 Layer 2 Control Protocol Tunneling

10.5.1 ENNI Frame Format

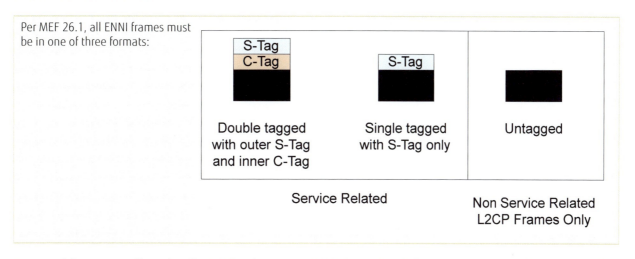

Per MEF 26.1, all ENNI frames must be in one of three formats:
- Double tagged with outer S-Tag and inner C-Tag (Service Related)
- Single tagged with S-Tag only (Service Related)
- Untagged (Non Service Related L2CP Frames Only)

Untagged frames are allowed at the ENNI only to support L2CPs, such as link aggregation control protocol (LACP), which are not service specific. All frames associated with a service require an outer S-Tag. This includes service-associated L2CP frames, such as spanning tree protocol (STP) bridge protocol data units (BPDUs).

10.5.2 ENNI and OVC MTU Size

Several operator service attributes specify MTU size:

Attribute Category	Attribute Name	Requirement
ENNI Service Attribute	ENNI Maximum Transmission Unit Size	≥ 1526 bytes (required) ≥ 2000 bytes (recommended)
OVC Service Attribute	OVC Maximum Transmission Unit Size	≥ 1526 bytes (required) ≥ 2000 bytes (recommended)
Per UNI service attribute	UNI MTU Size	≥ 1522 bytes

ENNIs and OVCs are required to support frames at least as large as 1526 bytes, which is 4 bytes larger than the same requirement at UNIs (1522 bytes). The difference (4 bytes) accounts for the S-Tag required at ENNIs.

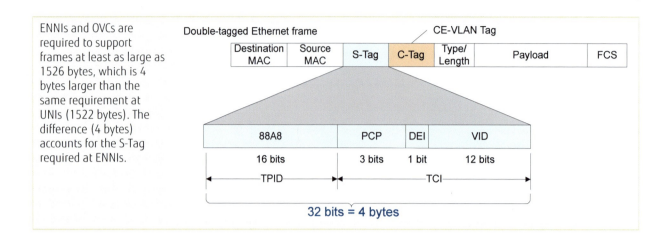

Related Links

Maximum Service Frame Size Service Attributes on p. 69
ENNI Service Attributes on p. 192
OVC Service Attributes on p. 193

10.5.3
Protection at ENNI

If an ENNI includes two physical links, it must be capable of implementing link aggregation, per IEEE 802.1AX, with one port active and one standby.

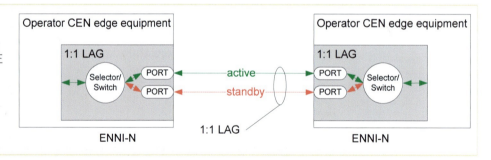

ENNI protection is specified by the value of the **Protection Mechanism** ENNI service attribute:

None—Applicable to ENNIs implemented with only one physical link

Link Aggregation—Indicates that the ENNI is implemented using two physical links, one active and one standby, as shown in the preceding figure

Other—Allows other unspecified protection mechanisms to be used by agreement

Related Links

ENNI Service Attributes on p. 192

10.5.4
End Point Map

The ENNI service attribute **End Point Map** specifies how ingress ENNI frames are assigned to OVC end points based on S-VLAN ID.

The following figure shows three services (red, green, and blue) implemented over three Operator CENs. The green and blue services are both point-to-point. The red service is multipoint-to-multipoint. Three services are shown to help you visualize service multiplexing at the circled ENNI. At this ENNI, Ethernet frames from all three services arrive to Operator CEN B mixed together in the same traffic stream. The End Point Map specifies how incoming Ethernet frames are sorted and distributed to OVC end points, based on S-VLAN ID. The zoom-in detail shows only one direction of traffic flow. In the other flow direction, a different End Point Map would apply (and govern distribution of traffic incoming to Operator CEN A from Operator CEN B).

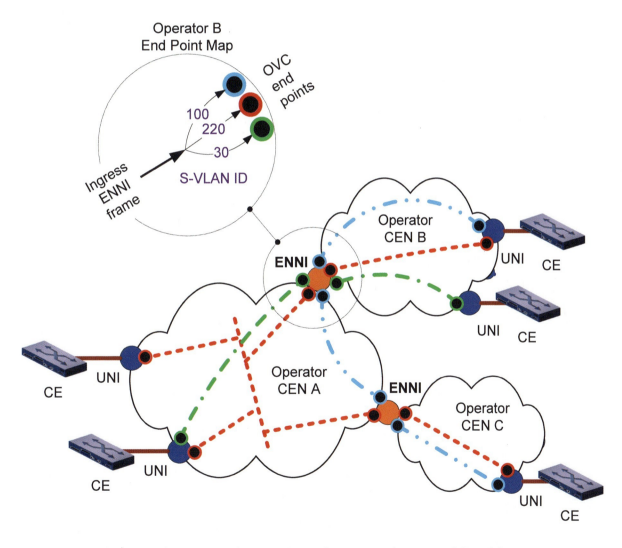

An S-VLAN ID can be mapped to no more than one OVC end point. It is the responsibility of the transmitting Operator CEN to set S-VLAN ID values appropriately for the receiving Operator CEN.

Test your understanding: *Assign true or false to each of the following statements and explain why:* ***(a)*** *An End Point Map is not needed if the ENNI is port-based.* ***(b)*** *Two End Point Maps are required at every ENNI.* ***(c)*** *To implement services within an Operator CEN, the operator needs to know only one of the two End Point Maps at each ENNI.* [97]

Related Links

ENNI Service Attributes on p. 192
End Point Map Bundling on p. 205

10.5.5
Color-Aware Bandwidth Profiles at ENNI

At ENNIs, ingress and egress bandwidth profiles are assigned per OVC end point. For each OVC end point, there are three options:

1. Assign no bandwidth profile.

2. Assign one bandwidth profile applicable to all ENNI frames that map to the OVC end point.

3. Assign a set of bandwidth profiles (per CoS) to all ENNI frames that map to the OVC end point.

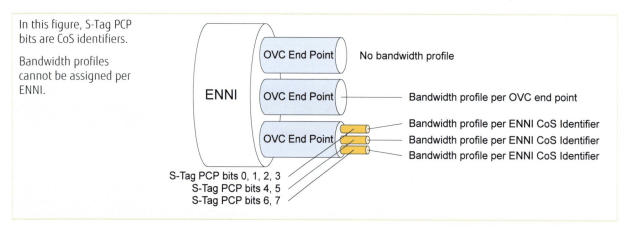

At ENNIs, bandwidth profiles are defined by six parameters, just as they are defined at UNIs. However, **at ENNIs, all bandwidth profiles must be color-aware.**[98]

Parameter		Units of Measure or Values
CIR	Committed Information Rate	Bits per second
CBS	Committed Burst Size	Bytes

---

[97] **Answers: (a)** False. There is no such thing as a port-based ENNI. **(b)** True. One End Point Map is required for each Operator CEN. **(c)** False. At each ENNI, the operator uses both End Point Maps. The operator uses one End Point Map to assign ingress ENNI frames to OVC end points. The operator uses the other End Point Map to assign S-VLAN IDs to egress ENNI frames.
[98] Per MEF 26.1 requirements [R89], [R91], [R93] and [R95].

Parameter		Units of Measure or Values
EIR	Excess Information Rate	Bits per second
EBS	Excess Burst Size	Bytes
CF	Coupling Flag	N or Y
CM	Color Mode	color-aware (color-blind not allowed at ENNI)

Note: At ENNIs, color can be encoded in the DEI bit of the S-Tag or in the PCP bits of the S-Tag.

The MEF does not require bandwidth profiles at ENNIs, but any bandwidth profiles used at an ENNI must be color-aware. Color-awareness of ENNI bandwidth profiles helps minimize the risk of recoloring service frames and of dropping green service frames as follows:

> Color-awareness ensures that yellow frames cannot be recolored to green, but <u>more importantly</u>, color-awareness ensures that yellow frames do not compete with green frames for CIR/CBS bandwidth. Color-awareness of an ingress bandwidth profile does not eliminate the possibility that a green frame will be recolored to yellow and/or dropped. It just reduces that possibility by ensuring that yellow frames do not compete with green frames for CIR/CBS bandwidth.

Note: Recall that Color reflects the service frame's compliance to the SLA (service-level agreement) bandwidth profile (implemented by policing at the ingress UNI) and should not be changed during transport through the service, UNI-to-UNI.

If bandwidth profiles are used at ENNIs, they should be carefully configured to ensure that green service frames are not dropped or recolored to yellow.

Related Links
ENNI Service Attributes on p. 192
Color Mode on p. 129
OVC End Point per ENNI Service Attributes on p. 194

10.5.6
Color Forwarding

The OVC service attribute *Color Forwarding* can be set to *Yes* or *No*. When Color Forwarding is Yes, the OVC cannot "promote" a frame from Yellow to Green.

Promoting a frame from Yellow to Green could have an undesired impact on EVC performance because newly promoted Green frames would compete for resources with frames that were marked Green at the ingress UNI.

If Color Forwarding is set to Yes, operators must ensure that:

- Color is encoded in the S-Tags of service frames prior to transmission across an ENNI

- Color is decoded from the S-Tags of service frames received from an ENNI

Related Links

OVC Service Attributes on p. 193
Encoding Information in S-Tags on p. 188
Color-Aware Bandwidth Profiles at ENNI on p. 200

10.5.7
Hairpin Switching

Note: *This example is based on Section 10.4, Example 3: Hairpin Switching in MEF 26.1.*

Recall that hairpin switching refers to functionality that returns an ingress ENNI frame across the ENNI with changes that cause the frame to be associated to a different OVC upon return.

In this example, hairpin switching is used to support the following EVP-LAN service.

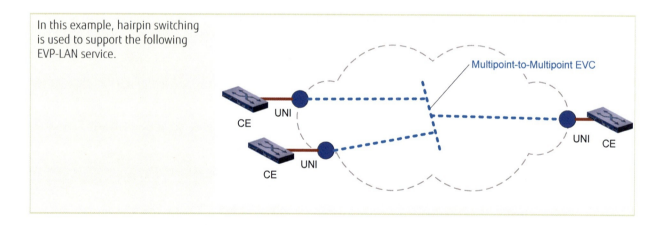

This EVP-LAN service is implemented with three OVCs: two point-to-point OVCs in Operator CEN A and one multipoint-to-multipoint OVC in Operator CEN B.

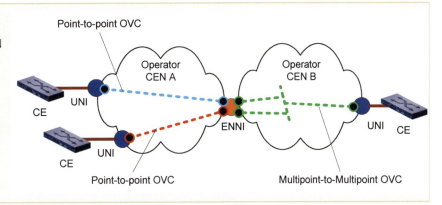

The multipoint-to-multipoint OVC in Operator CEN B includes two OVC end points at the ENNI. Two End Point Maps (ENNI service attributes), one in each operator CEN, govern the flow of service frames between OVC end points, as follows.

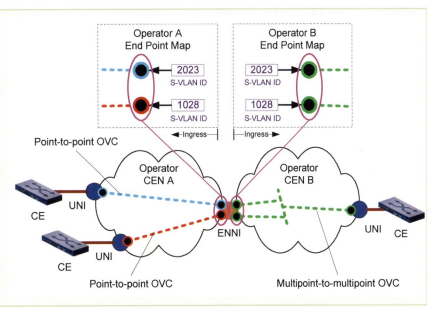

The End Point Maps, in effect, connect each point-to-point OVC to one endpoint of the multipoint-to-multipoint OVC.

The multipoint-to-multipoint OVC now in effect now has two connections through the ENNI, one for each point-to-point OVC.

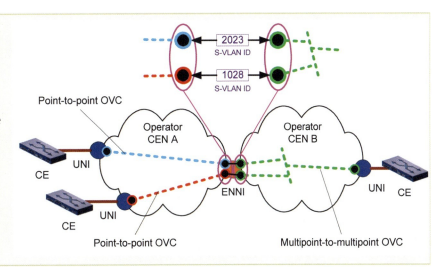

To implement a hairpin switch, the multipoint-to-multipoint OVC simply changes the S-VLAN ID on the ingress ENNI frame (from 2023 to 1028, in the example shown) and transmits it back through the ENNI.

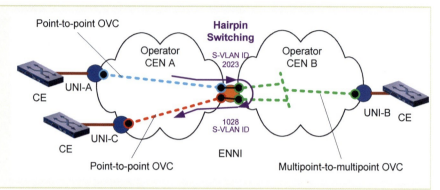

Data Loops

Improper use of hairpin switching can result in a data loop between two Operator CENs at a single ENNI, as shown in the following example.[99]

The service provider and operators are responsible for ensuring that such loops do not occur.

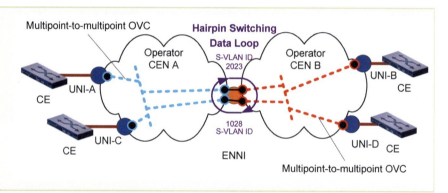

In this example, hairpin switching is not needed and should not be used. The two multipoint-to-multipoint OVCs should interconnect at the ENNI through one pair of OVC end points as shown.

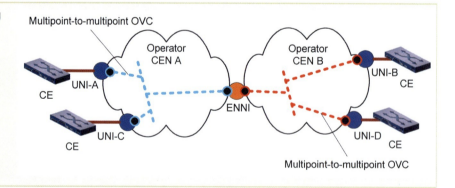

Related Links

Hairpin Switch on p. 185

---

[99] This example is based on *Section 10.5 Example 4: Data Loop at an ENNI with Hairpin Switching* in MEF 26.1.

10.5.8
End Point Map Bundling

An End Point Map associates a set of S-VLAN ID values to a set of OVC end points. Typically, the number of S-VLAN ID values equals the number of OVC end points, and each OVC end point is assigned one S-VLAN ID value.

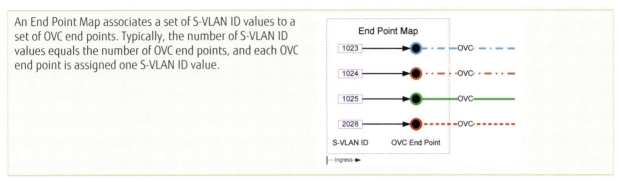

However, MEF 26.1 also permits End Point Maps to assign multiple S-VLAN ID values to one or more OVC endpoints, as shown in the following example.

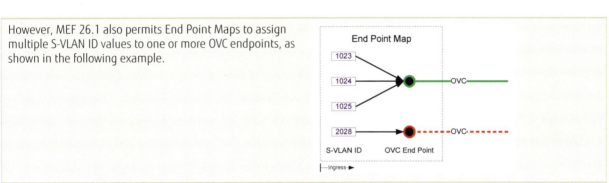

When multiple S-VLAN ID values map to a single OVC End Point, the End Point Map is said to have Bundling. End Point Map Bundling allows one OVC to support multiple services (S-VLAN ID values) as shown in the following example in which the green OVC through Operator CEN B supports two services.

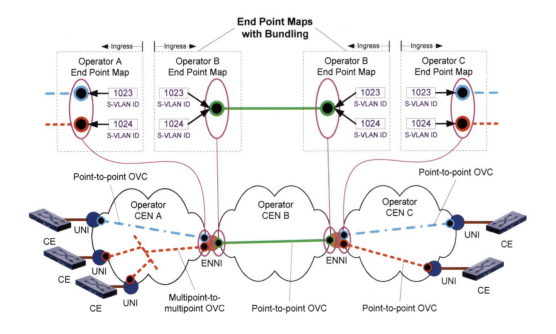

Per MEF 26.1, OVCs that support Bundling must meet the following requirements:

- The OVC must be point-to-point.
- The OVC must have its S-VLAN ID Preservation attribute set to Yes.
- The OVC must have its CE-VLAN ID Preservation attribute set to Yes.
- The OVC must have its CE-VLAN CoS Preservation attribute set to Yes.
- Both OVC end points must terminate at an ENNI.
- The OVC cannot support hairpin switching.

Note: *An OVC that supports Bundling can have its S-VLAN CoS Preservation attribute set to Yes or No.*

Related Links

Hairpin Switching on p. 202
OVC Service Attributes on p. 193
End Point Map on p. 199

10.5.9
LOAM Requirement for ENNIs

ENNIs are required to support Link OAM (Operation, Administration and Management) as defined in MEF 26.1, based on clause 57 of IEEE 802.3. LOAM allows operator on both sides of the ENNI to monitor and diagnose link-level connectivity issues.

Link OAM functionality is covered in a later lesson, within a larger context that includes all types of links (not just ENNI links). For now, just note that LOAM support is an important requirement for ENNIs.

Related Links

Link OAM on p. 253

10.5.10
Service Level Specification (OVC Service Attribute)

Per MEF 26.1, OVC service attribute **Service Level Specification** specifies frame delivery performance for an OVC-based operator service using 8 performance objectives:[100, 101]

---

[100] Not Specified (N/S) is an acceptable value for any of these performance objectives.
[101] The MEF addresses the problem of measuring OVC performance using SOAM Performance Management (as described in a later lesson). The focus here is on defining OVC performance.

1. One-way Frame Delay (FD)	5. One-way Frame Loss Ratio (FLR)
2. One-way Frame Delay Range (FDR)	6. One-way Availability (Availability)
3. One-way Mean Frame Delay (MFD)	7. One-way High Loss Intervals (HLI)
4. Inter Frame Delay Variation (IFDV)	8. One-way Consecutive High Loss Intervals (CHLI)

These performance objectives are similar to those defined for EVC Performance Attributes, except that frame delivery performance is defined EI-to-EI, rather than UNI-to-UNI. Recall that an EI (External Interface) is either a UNI or an ENNI.

Related Links

SOAM Performance Management on p. 270

OVC versus EVC Performance Objectives

When an EVC is composed of OVCs, the service provider is faced with the problem of defining performance objective values for each OVC as well as for the EVC. Conceptually, EVC performance results from the concatenation of the OVC performances. However, precise relationships between OVC and EVC performance can be hard to pin down.

The problem can be viewed from two perspectives:

> **Concatenation**— Determine EVC performance objectives, given OVC performance objectives
>
> **Segmentation**—Determine OVC performance objectives, given EVC performance objectives

In either case, the objective is to come up with a complete set of performance objective values (for each OVC and for the EVC) that is *consistent* in the sense that the OVC performance objectives will ensure that EVC performance objectives are met.

As a simple example, consider an EPL service supporting one class of service over two operator CENs. Mean frame delay (MFD) might be specified as follows:

```
MFD = 80 ms (for the EVC)
MFD = 10 ms (for OVC 1)
MFD = 50 ms (for OVC 2)
```

The methods, techniques, and negotiations needed to arrive at acceptable performance objectives are beyond the scope of MEF specifications and this lesson.

10.5.11
Layer 2 Control Protocol Tunneling

Note: L2CP handling requirements defined in MEF 26.1 are different from the new requirements defined in MEF 45. However, the MEF-CECP Exam Blueprint C, excludes portions of MEF 45 that apply to OVCs.

OVC service attribute **Layer 2 Control Protocol Tunneling** specifies a list of Layer 2 Control Protocols that are tunneled by the OVC.

MEF 26.1 defines two types of L2CP frames:

- **L2CP Service Frame**—A service frame[102] with a L2CP MAC address (one of the MAC addresses shown in the following table)

- **L2CP ENNI Frame**—An ENNI frame[103] with a L2CP MAC address (one of the MAC addresses shown in the following table)

List of Standardized Layer 2 Control Protocols (Table 3 in MEF 10.3 or Table 2 in MEF 45)	
L2CP Destination MAC Addresses	Description
01-80-C2-00-00-00 through 01-80-C2-00-00-0F	Bridge Block of protocols
01-80-C2-00-00-20 through 01-80-C2-00-00-2F	MRP (Multiple Registration Protocol) Block of protocols

Per MEF 26.1, when a *L2CP Service Frame* or *L2CP ENNI Frame* is tunneled:

1. The frame must be delivered to all OVC End Points, other than the ingress OVC End Point.

2. The frame format at egress must conform to requirements listed in the following table.

Format Relationships for Tunneled L2CP Service and ENNI Frames (Table 16 in MEF 26.1)		
Ingress Interface	Egress Interface	Egress Frame Format
UNI	UNI	Identical to the ingress frame
UNI	ENNI	Same as ingress frame, but with S-Tag added
ENNI	UNI	Same as ingress frame, but with S-Tag removed
ENNI	ENNI	Same as ingress frame, but with S-Tag possibly changed

Note: *If the egress frame differs from the ingress frame, the Frame Check Sequence in the egress frame is recalculated.*

---

102 A service frame is an Ethernet frame transmitted across the UNI.

103 An ENNI frame is an Ethernet frame transmitted across the ENNI.

10.6 Rooted-Multipoint OVCs

In this section:

10.6.1 Applications with Root and Leaf OVC End Points Only
10.6.2 Applications with Trunk OVC End Points

Rooted-multipoint OVCs are used to support rooted-multipoint EVCs for E-Tree services.

Each OVC end point in a rooted-multipoint OVC is assigned an OVC end point role (Root, Leaf, or Trunk) that is related to UNI designations (Root and Leaf) in the associated rooted-multipoint EVC:

OVC end point role **Root** – Indicates that all frames ingressing to the OVC end point originated at a Root UNI and can be forwarded to any OVC end point (Root, Leaf, or Trunk)
OVC end point role **Leaf** – Indicates that all frames ingressing to the OVC end point originated at a Leaf UNI and must not be forwarded to a Leaf OVC end point
OVC end point role **Trunk** – Indicates that frames ingressing to the OVC end point have mixed origins (some originate at a Root UNI and others originate at a Leaf UNI)

In MEF 26.1, *OVC end point role* is described as "a property of an OVC end point that determines the forwarding behavior between it and other OVC end points that are associated with the OVC end point by an OVC."

OVC end point roles appear in OVC service attribute *OVC End Point List*, which is a list of <OVC End Point Identifier, OVC End Point Role> pairs.

Related Links

OVC Service Attributes on p. 193
OVC End Point Role on p. 183

10.6.1 Applications with Root and Leaf OVC End Points Only

Example Application A

A rooted-multipoint EVC (for an E-Tree service) is implemented with 3 OVCs: a rooted-multipoint OVC in Operator CEN A, a multipoint-to-multipoint OVC in Operator CEN B, and a point-to-point OVC in Operator CEN C.

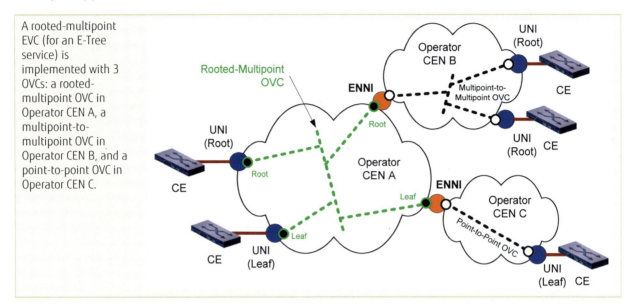

Observations:
1. The concatenation of OVCs results in a rooted-multipoint EVC that connects 5 UNIs (3 Root UNIs and 2 Leaf UNIs).
2. In Operator CEN B and Operator CEN C, OVC end point roles are not shown because the OVCs are not type rooted-multipoint.

   Note: For point-to-point and multipoint-to-multipoint OVCs, each OVC end point is assigned role Root, but that assignment is trivial. It is done for consistency only.
3. In Operator CEN A, OVC end point roles are assigned as follows:
   - At the UNIs, OVC end point roles simply match the UNI designation (Leaf or Root).
   - At the ENNIs, OVC end point roles match the designation of <u>all</u> UNIs that connect to it through the ENNI.

Test your understanding: *Suppose the UNI in Operator CEN C was a Root UNI (instead of a Leaf UNI). Which OVC end point role would you assign to the associated OVC end point (in Operator CEN A): Root, Leaf, or Trunk?* [104]

Test your understanding: *Suppose that the two UNIs in Operator CEN B were both Leaf UNIs (instead of Root UNIs). Which OVC end point role would you assign to the associated OVC end point (in Operator CEN A): Root, Leaf, or Trunk?* [105]

Test your understanding: *Under what conditions can a rooted-multipoint OVC connect to a multipoint-to-multipoint OVC through an ENNI?* [106]

Test your understanding: *A point-to-point OVC supports a rooted-multipoint EVC and connects to a UNI. What is the UNI designation?* [107]

---

[104] **Answer:** Root (to match the designation of all UNIs that connect to it through the ENNI)

[105] **Answer:** None of the suggested answers is correct because this scenario is invalid. The OVC in CEN B cannot support any Leaf UNIs because it is a multipoint-to-multipoint OVC (not a rooted-multipoint OVC). However, if the OVC in CEN B were a rooted-multipoint OVC (with Leaf end point roles at the two UNIs and Root end point role at the ENNI), then the associated end point (in Operator CEN A) would be Leaf.

[106] **Answer:** All UNIs that connect to the rooted-multipoint OVC through the multipoint-to-multipoint OVC must be Root UNIs.

Example Application B

A rooted-multipoint EVC (for an E-Tree service) is implemented with 4 OVCs: a rooted-multipoint OVC in Operator CEN A, 2 point-to-point OVCs in Operator CEN B, and 1 point-to-point OVC in Operator CEN C.

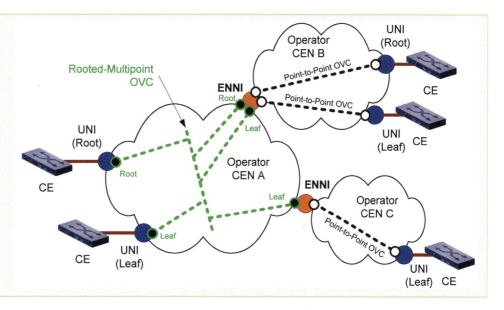

Observations:
1. The concatenation of OVCs results in a rooted-multipoint EVC that connects 5 UNIs (2 Root UNIs and 3 Leaf UNIs).
2. In Operator CEN B and Operator CEN C, OVC end point roles are not shown because the OVCs are not type rooted-multipoint.

   Note: For point-to-point and multipoint-to-multipoint OVCs, each OVC end point is assigned role Root, but that assignment is trivial. It is done for consistency only.
3. In Operator CEN A, OVC end point roles are assigned as follows:
   - At the UNIs, OVC end point roles simply match the UNI designation (Leaf or Root).
   - At the ENNIs, OVC end point roles match the designation of all UNIs that connect to it through the ENNI.
4. Hairpin switching in Operator CEN A is required to support traffic between the two UNIs in Operator CEN B.

Related Links

Hairpin Switching on p. 202

10.6.2
Applications with Trunk OVC End Points

OVC end point role Trunk is used when the source of ingress frames is ambiguous: when a frame ingressing to an OVC end point might have originated at a Root UNI or at a Leaf UNI. <u>This situation only occurs in applications that involve more than one rooted-multipoint OVC.</u> The following example includes two rooted-multipoint OVCs.

---

107 **Answer:** *The UNI can be either a Root UNI or a Leaf UNI. The example includes such a point-to-point OVC in Operator CEN C.*

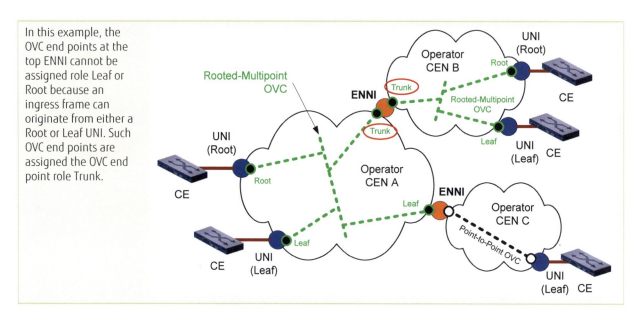

In this example, the OVC end points at the top ENNI cannot be assigned role Leaf or Root because an ingress frame can originate from either a Root or Leaf UNI. Such OVC end points are assigned the OVC end point role Trunk.

Assignment of role Trunk to such OVC end points does not fully resolve frame forwarding issues. It is only part of the solution.

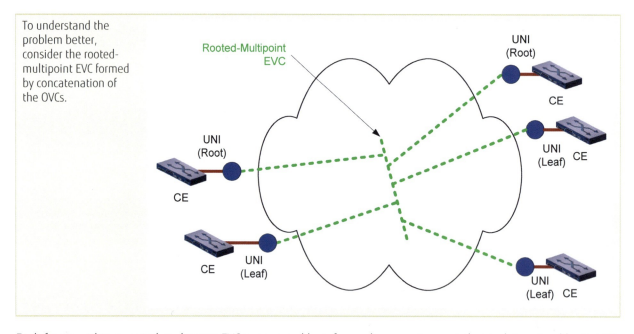

To understand the problem better, consider the rooted-multipoint EVC formed by concatenation of the OVCs.

Each frame within a rooted-multipoint EVC is governed by a forwarding requirement that is determined by its UNI of origin:

Frame Source	Forwarding Requirement
Leaf UNI	The frame must not be forwarded to another leaf UNI. It may be forwarded to any root UNI.
Root UNI	The frame may be forwarded to any leaf UNI or root UNI.

If an E-Tree service is implemented over multiple operator CENs, a mechanism is needed to propagate forwarding requirements through ENNIs.

If only one rooted-multipoint OVC is involved, this issue is fully resolved by assigning each OVC end point the role of Leaf or Root (as previously described):

> OVC end point role **Root** – Indicates that all frames ingressing to the OVC end point originated at a Root UNI and can be forwarded to any OVC end point (Root, Leaf, or Trunk)
>
> OVC end point role **Leaf** – Indicates that all frames ingressing to the OVC end point originated at a Leaf UNI and <u>must not</u> be forwarded to another Leaf OVC end point

However, this system for propagating forwarding requirements across an ENNI does not work for Trunk OVC end points, which have to support frames originating from both types of UNIs: Leaf UNIs and Root UNIs.

> OVC end point role **Trunk** – Indicates that frames ingressing to the OVC end point have mixed origin (some originating at a Root UNI and others originating at a Leaf UNI)

Trunk Identifiers

When the OVC end point role is Trunk, *Trunk Identifiers* are assigned to resolve the issue of propagating forwarding requirements across the ENNI.

The following two values constitute the *OVC End Point per ENNI* service attribute named **Truck Identifiers**:

> **Root S-VLAN ID value** – This value identifies ingress frames that originated at a **Root UNI**.
>
> **Leaf S-VLAN ID value** – This value identifies ingress frames that originated at a **Leaf UNI**.

Note: Trunk identifiers are only applicable to OVC end points with role Trunk.

Because Trunk Identifiers define S-VLAN ID values for Ingress frames, it is the responsibility of the transmitting Operator CEN to set them appropriately.

Note: *The method by which frame forwarding requirements are preserved as frames are forwarded through an Operator CEN depends upon the technology used within the Operator CEN and is beyond the scope of MEF specifications.*

When the OVC end point role is Trunk, the ENNI service attribute **End Point Map** associates two S-VLAN ID values to the OVC end point. When the OVC end point role is Leaf or Root, the ENNI End Point Map associates just one S-VLAN ID value to the OVC end point.

Related Links

End Point Map on p. 199

OVC End Point per ENNI Service Attributes on p. 194

Example Application C

A rooted-multipoint EVC (for an E-Tree service) is implemented with 3 OVCs: a rooted-multipoint OVC in Operator CEN A, a rooted-multipoint OVC in Operator CEN B, and a point-to-point OVC in Operator CEN C.

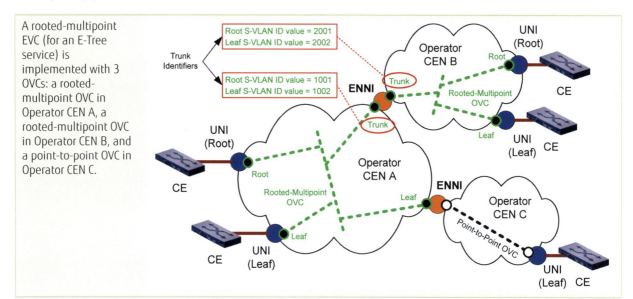

Observations:

1. The concatenation of OVCs results in a rooted-multipoint EVC that connects 5 UNIs (2 Root UNIs and 3 Leaf UNIs).
2. In Operator CEN C, OVC end point roles are not shown because the OVC is not type rooted-multipoint.

   Note: For point-to-point and multipoint-to-multipoint OVCs, each OVC end point is assigned role Root, but that assignment is trivial. It is done for consistency only.

3. In Operator CEN A, OVC end point roles are assigned as follows:

   - At the UNIs, OVC end point roles simply match the UNI designation (Leaf or Root).
   - At the ENNI connecting to Operator CEN C, the OVC end point role is set to Leaf, matching the UNI that connects to it through the ENNI.
   - At the ENNI connecting to Operator CEN B, the OVC end point role is set to Trunk because frames (ingressing from Operator CEN B) can originate from either a Root UNI or Leaf UNI.

4. In Operator CEN B, OVC end point roles are assigned as follows:

   - At the UNIs, OVC end point roles simply match the UNI designation (Leaf or Root).
   - At the ENNI, the OVC end point role is set to Trunk because frames (ingressing from Operator CEN A) can originate from either a Root UNI or Leaf UNI.

5. In Operator CEN A, the following Trunk Identifiers are assigned to the Trunk OVC end point:

   - Root S-VLAN ID value = 1001
   - Leaf S-VLAN ID value = 1002

6. In Operator CEN B, the following Trunk Identifiers are assigned to the Trunk OVC end point:

   - Root S-VLAN ID value = 2001
   - Leaf S-VLAN ID value = 2002

Test your understanding: *A frame with broadcast MAC address (FF-FF-FF-FF-FF-FF) is transmitted from the CE into Operator CEN C. When it gets to Operator CEN B, the frame includes an S-Tag. What is the value of S-VLAN ID?* [108]

Test your understanding: A frame with broadcast MAC address (FF-FF-FF-FF-FF-FF) and S-VLAN ID = 1001 enters Operator CEN A at the Trunk OVC end point. To which UNI(s) is it forwarded? [109]

Test your understanding: Suppose that the Root UNI in Operator CEN B is changed into a Leaf UNI (so that both UNIs in Operator CEN B are Leaf UNIs) and that the role of the associated OVC end point is also changed from Root to Leaf (because all ingress frames now originate at a Leaf UNI).

1. Are Trunk OVC end points still required at the ENNI?
2. If not, what OVC end point roles can be used in place of Trunk?

Answer:
1. No. Trunk OVC end points can still be used, but they are no longer required because the OVC end points no longer have to support two forwarding states.
2. As shown in the following figure:
   - The Trunk OVC end point in Operator CEN B can be changed to a Root OVC end point (because it now only has to support ingress frames that originate at a Root UNI).
   - The Trunk OVC end point in Operator CEN A can be changed into a Leaf OVC end point (because it now only has to support ingress frames that originate at Leaf UNIs).

Note: This solution is a more elegant (because it eliminates Trunk Identifiers), but it only works if all UNIs in Operator CEN B are Leaf UNIs.

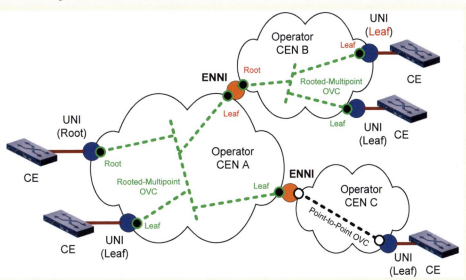

---

[108] *Answer:* 2002 (The frame originated at a Leaf UNI, so it should enter Operator CEN B with the Leaf S-VLAN ID value that is associated with the Trunk OVC Endpoint in Operator CEN B.)

[109] *Answer:* The frame is forwarded to both UNIs in Operator CEN A and to the UNI in Operator CEN C. S-VLAN ID = 1001 indicates that the frame originated at a Root UNI. It can therefore be forwarded to any Leaf UNI or Root UNI.

MEF-CECP Study Guide
3rd Edition - October 2015
Updated for MEF-CECP Certification Blueprint C

Example Application D

A rooted-multipoint EVC (for an E-Tree service) is implemented with 3 OVCs: a rooted-multipoint OVC in Operator CEN A, a bundled OVC in Operator CEN B, and a rooted-multipoint OVC in Operator CEN C.

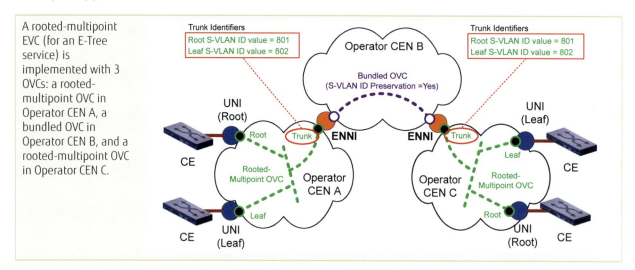

Observations:

1. The concatenation of OVCs results in a rooted-multipoint EVC that connects 4 UNIs (2 Root UNIs and 2 Leaf UNIs).
2. In Operator CEN B, OVC end point roles are not shown because the OVC is not type rooted-multipoint.

   Note: For point-to-point and multipoint-to-multipoint OVCs, each OVC end point is assigned role Root, but that assignment is trivial. It is done for consistency only.
3. In Operator CEN A and Operator CEN C, OVC end point roles are assigned as follows:

   - At the UNIs, OVC end point roles simply match the UNI designation (Leaf or Root).
   - At the ENNI, the OVC end point role is set to Trunk because frames (ingressing from Operator CEN B) can originate from either a Root UNI or Leaf UNI.
4. In Operator CEN A and Operator CEN C, the following Trunk Identifiers are assigned to the Trunk OVC end points:

   - Root S-VLAN ID value = 801
   - Leaf S-VLAN ID value = 802

Test your understanding: In this example, Trunk Identifier values (Root S-VLAN ID, Leaf S-VLAN) in Operator CEN A match those in Operator CEN C. Do they have to match? If so, why? [110]

Related Links

End Point Map Bundling on p. 205

---

[110] **Answer:** Yes, they have to match because the OVC in Operator CEN B is a bundled OVC (supporting multiple S-VLAN ID values), and bundled OVCs are required to have S-VLAN ID Preservation = Yes.

10.7 Review: Extending MEF Services over Multiple Operator CENs

1. Which entity delivers Ethernet frames between ENNIs and UNIs/ENNIs?

   a. Operator Virtual Connection
   b. Ethernet Virtual Circuit
   c. Intermediate Virtual Connection
   d. Operator Virtual Circuit
   e. Ethernet Virtual Connection

2. Per MEF 26.1, which three values are recognized for the *Protection Mechanism* ENNI service attribute? (Choose three.)

   a. LACP
   b. None
   c. Link Aggregation
   d. E-LMI
   e. Other

3. The *OVC End Points* of an operator virtual connection (OVC) must associate to:

   a. Exactly two UNIs and any number of ENNIs
   b. Exactly one ENNI and any number of UNIs
   c. UNIs only
   d. At least one ENNI
   e. Only ENNIs

4. Two or more operators can:

   a. connect through an ENNI
   b. be involved in an OVC
   c. be responsible for an EVC
   d. be involved in an EVC
   e. be responsible for an OVC

5. Which three frame formats are permitted at an ENNI? (Choose three.)

   a. Untagged
   b. C-Tag
   c. S-Tag and no C-Tag
   d. S-Tag and C-Tag
   e. Stacked S-Tags

6. How many EPL services can an ENNI support?

   a. One
   b. Two
   c. Up to 4094
   d. About 16 million
   e. Unlimited

7. Which statement about the External Network-to-Network Interface (ENNI) is true?

   a. The subscriber and service provider agree on its exact physical location so that responsibilities are clearly defined.
   b. It can only support one EPL service.
   c. Service provider is responsible for the service from the UNI to the ENNI, and then the organization in charge of the Operator CEN is responsible.
   d. It is a physical demarcation point between two Operator CENs.

8. An OVC requires which one of the following?

   a. A UNI
   b. Two or more UNIs
   c. Two or more EVCs
   d. An ENNI
   e. Two or more ENNIs

9. An *OVC End Point Map* has *bundling*. Which statement is true about the associated OVC?

   a. *S-VLAN ID Preservation* can be *Yes* or *No*.
   b. *CE-VLAN ID Preservation* can be *Yes* or *No*.
   c. *CE-VLAN CoS Preservation* can be *Yes* or *No*.
   d. *S-VLAN ID CoS Preservation* can be *Yes* or *No*.

10. In which category of operator service attributes is *Broadcast Service Frame Delivery*?

    a. OVC Service Attributes
    b. PVC End Point per ENNI Service Attributes
    c. ENNI Service Attributes
    d. Per UNI service attributes
    e. OVC per Per UNI service attributes

11. An *OVC End Point Map* has *bundling*. Which statement is <u>not</u> true about the associated OVC?

    a. The OVC cannot support hairpin switching.
    b. All end points of the OVC have bundling.
    c. *S-VLAN ID Preservation* is set to *Yes*.
    d. At least one end point of the OVC terminates at a UNI.
    e. The OVC is point-to-point.

12. Two Operator CENs connect through an ENNI. What is the advantage of using an ENNI with Link OAM?

    a. It provides link protection using two physical links, one active and one standby
    b. It allows the ENNI to support hairpin switching.
    c. It allows both operators to monitor and diagnose ENNI connectivity issues
    d. It allows two different types of physical layers to be connected at the ENNI
    e. It allows class of service (CoS) propagation through IEEE 802.1ad Ethernet Frames

13. Which OVC service attribute is <u>incompatible</u> with hairpin switching?

    a. CE-VLAN CoS Preservation = Yes
    b. S-VLAN ID Preservation = Yes
    c. S-VLAN CoS Preservation = Yes
    d. CE-VLAN ID Preservation = Yes

14. Which statement is <u>not</u> true about the service provider in the MEF 26.1 service model?

    a. The service provider is responsible for the service to the subscriber.
    b. The service provider is responsible for coordinating operators.
    c. The service provider may or may not be an operator.
    d. Two or more operators can collaboratively function as the service provider.

15. The smallest maximum transmission unit (MTU) size allowed for an operator virtual connection (OVC) is:

    a. 1522 bytes
    b. 1526 bytes
    c. 4094 bytes
    d. 4096 bytes
    e. None of the above

16. How many EVCs can be supported by one OVC?

    a. Exactly one
    b. Up to 4094 if the OVC is point-to-point between two ENNIs
    c. Up to 4094 if UNI is configured with *Service Multiplexing* = Yes
    d. Exactly one if the UNI is configured with *All to One Bundling* = Yes

17. Which three of the following statements are true? (Choose three.)

    a. At ENNIs, drop-eligibility can be encoded in the S-Tag DEI bit or in the S-Tag PCP value.
    b. At ENNIs, all frames require C-Tags.
    c. At an ENNI, both Operators are responsible for setting S-Tag values appropriately before transmitting frames across the ENNI.
    d. Ingress ENNI frames are mapped to OVC end points based on S-VLAN ID value.
    e. At ENNIs, CoS may be encoded in the C-Tag or in the S-Tag.

18. Which one of the following is **not** an ENNI requirement?

   a. ENNIs are required to support E-LMI.
   b. At ENNIs, all bandwidth profiles must be color-aware.
   c. ENNIs must support MTU sizes at least as large as 1526 bytes.
   d. If an ENNI includes two physical links, it must be capable of implementing link aggregation.
   e. ENNIs are required to support Link OAM.

19. Which one of the following is an ENNI service attribute?

   a. Bundling
   b. End Point Map
   c. Service Multiplexing
   d. All-to-one bundling

20. The *End Point Map* attribute:

   a. is inactive if the ENNI is provisioned with all-to-one bundling
   b. specifies how ingress ENNI frames are assigned to OVC end points based on S-VLAN ID
   c. lists the CE-VLAN IDs that map to the EVC
   d. is an *OVC End Point per ENNI* service attribute

21. A rooted-multipoint OVC has 5 OVC end points: 2 are designated Root, 2 are designated Leaf, and 1 is designated Trunk. A broadcast frame ingresses at a Leaf OVC end point. How many frames does the OVC deliver if OVC attribute *Broadcast Service Frame Delivery* is configured to *Deliver Unconditionally*?

   a. 1
   b. 2
   c. 3
   d. 4
   e. 5

22. Why is the minimum MTU size requirement at ENNIs (1526 bytes) four bytes larger than the minimum UNI Maximum Service Frame Size (1522 bytes)?

   a. Because ENNIs do not support all-to-one bundling.
   b. To allow hairpin switching.
   c. To account for the S-Tag.
   d. Because color-aware bandwidth profiles are required at ENNIs.

23. An EVPL service is implemented across three Operator CENs. How many UNIs, ENNIs, EVCs, and OVCs are involved?

   a. 2 UNIs, 2 ENNIs, 3 EVCs, and 1 OVC
   b. 2 UNIs, 3 ENNIs, 1 EVC, and 3 OVCs
   c. 2 UNIs, 2 ENNIs, 1 EVC, and 3 OVCs
   d. 2 UNIs, 3 ENNIs, 1 EVC, and 2 OVCs

24. An EPL service spans three Operator CENs and each OVC is configured with *S-VLAN ID Preservation = Yes*. Which of the following statements is true?

    a. The S-Tag VLAN identifier will match at both UNIs.
    b. The S-Tag VLAN identifier is preserved within each OVC, but can be translated at the ENNIs.
    c. The S-Tag VLAN identifier will match at both ENNIs.
    d. The S-Tag VLAN identifier will match at both UNIs and both ENNIs.

25. An EP-LAN service spans two Operator CENs that connect through one ENNI. At all UNIs, ingress bandwidth profiles are configured with CIR=0, CBS=0, EIR=20 Mb/s, and EBS=2,000 bytes. How should the service be configured to ensure that yellow frames are not "promoted" to green?

    a. At all OVC end points, configure ingress and egress bandwidth profiles with *Color Mode = Color Aware*.
    b. At those OVC end points that connect to the ENNI (not those connecting to UNIs), configure ingress and egress bandwidth profiles with *Color Mode = Color Aware*.
    c. For both OVCs, configure *Color Forwarding = Yes*.
    d. At those OVC end points that connect to UNIs (not those connecting to the ENNI), configure ingress bandwidth profiles with *Color Mode = Color Aware*. Also, do not configure any bandwidth profiles at the OVC end points that connect to the ENNI.

26. Which statement about CoS identification at ENNIs is <u>not</u> true?

    a. CoS is determined by S-Tag PCP bit values.
    b. At a given OVC end point, an S-Tag PCP bit value can map to more than one CoS.
    c. For each OVC end point, a CoS must be associated with each S-Tag PCP value.
    d. At a given OVC end point, two different S-Tag PCP bit values can map to the same CoS.
    e. The S-Tag supports up to eight classes of service.

27. A service is implemented over 3 Operator CENs. Which two statements are correct? (Choose two.)

    a. All three operators are responsible to the subscriber for the service.
    b. One of the operators can be the service provider.
    c. The subscriber has a business relationship with each operator.
    d. Each Operator CEN includes at least one ENNI-N.

28. An ENNI is to support many EVCs, including some EVCs configured with *EVC Maximum Service Frame Size* as large as 1800 bytes. What is the smallest value of the ENNI MTU Size that will support these EVCs?

    a. 1526 bytes
    b. 1800 bytes
    c. 1804 bytes
    d. 2000 bytes

29. For an Ethernet Virtual Private service that is implemented over multiple Operator CENs, which ENNI frame field(s) can be used to convey color across the ENNI?

    a. S-Tag DEI only
    b. C-Tag PCP or S-Tag DEI only
    c. S-Tag DEI or S-Tag PCP only
    d. C-Tag PCP or S-Tag DEI or S-Tag PCP only

11

MEF-Standardized Classes of Service

In this chapter:

11.1 Definitions and Requirements
11.2 Review: MEF-Standardized Classes of Service

EVC performance specification (or OVC service level specification), as previously described, requires the service provider and the subscriber (or the service provider and the operator) to reach a bilateral agreement with respect to many CoS details, including the following (for each CoS involved in the service):

> **CoS performance objectives** — values of performance metrics, such as Availability, High Loss Intervals (HLI), Consecutive High Loss Intervals (CHLI), Frame Loss Ration (FLR), Frame Delay (FD), Mean Frame Delay (MFD), Frame Delay Range (FDR), and Inter-Frame Delay Variation (IFDV), that represent agreed performance commitment
>
> **CoS performance parameters** — values, such as time intervals, required to derive and specify CoS performance objectives
>
> **CoS ID** — Class of Service Identifier. The mechanism and values used to identify CoS at UNIs (and ENNIs).
>
> **Color ID** — Color Identifier. The mechanism and values used to identify frame color at UNIs (and ENNIs).

So far, we have learned how these four items are used to define classes of service (what is allowed, how details are specified). We now look at some specific classes of service.

This lesson describes twelve classes of service defined in MEF 23.1 that conform to previously described requirements, but are much more prescribed. The purpose of these MEF-standardized classes of service is to establish a common baseline to help subscribers, service providers, and operators easily agree on CoS-related service attributes. MEF-standardized classes of service do not constrain CoS options offered by a service provider or operator. They are meant to help establish a common reference for communicating CoS performance requirements and capabilities.

The MEF-standardized classes of service described in this lesson can be applied in any MEF service application. They appear explicitly in mobile backhaul CoS requirements and in CE 2.0 certification.

Related Links

CE 2.0 Certification on p. 386

11.1
Definitions and Requirements

In this section:

- 11.1.1 CoS Labels and Performance Tiers
- 11.1.2 Ingress Bandwidth Profile Constraints (per CoS Label)
- 11.1.3 CoS Label and Color Identification Mechanisms
- 11.1.4 CoS Label and Color Identification Using PCP Bits, DEI Bit, and/or EVC/OVC End Point
- 11.1.5 CoS Label and Color Identification Using DSCP Values and/or EVC/OVC End Point
- 11.1.6 CoS Label Identification for L2CP Frames
- 11.1.7 Key Observations About CoS Label and Color Identification
- 11.1.8 Performance Metrics for CoS Labels
- 11.1.9 CoS Parameter Values (per CoS Label)
- 11.1.10 CPOs (per CoS Label and Performance Tier)

11.1.1
CoS Labels and Performance Tiers

Two values are used to identify the 12 classes of service defined in MEF 23.1:

> **CoS Label** – H, M, or L
>
> **Performance Tier** – PT1, PT2, PT3, or PT4

Each combination of two values (for example, M and PT3) identifies one of 12 classes of service.

Informally, the CoS Labels (L, M, H) indicate relative performance level (Low, Medium, High). Performance Tiers (PT1, PT2, PT3, PT4) indicate "field of use" or "area of applicability," which approximately aligns to network size, transmission distance, and/or propagation delay as shown in the following table.

Performance Tier	Field of Use (Area of Applicability)		
	Network Size	Transmission Distance	Propagation Delay
PT1	Metro	< 250 km	< 2 ms
PT2	Regional	< 1200 km	< 8 ms
PT3	Continental	< 7000 km	< 44 ms
PT4	Global	< 27500 km	< 172 ms

For each (CoS Label, Performance Tier) pair, MEF 23.1 specifies class of service details. As the naming convention suggests, these details were derived to represent realistic performance levels (Low, Medium, High) in different networking contexts (Metro, Regional, Continental, Global). However, these associations are informal; they place no limitations on how these MEF-standardized classes of service are used in practice.

This table (Table 36 in MEF 23.1) maps applications to values of CoS Label and Performance Tier.

Again, this table is only meant to provide helpful information; it does not limit how MEF-standardized classes of service are actually used in practice.

CoS Label	H				M				L			
Performance Tier	1	2	3	4	1	2	3	4	1	2	3	4
VoIP	X	X	X	X								
VoIP & videoconf signaling					X	X	X	X				
Videoconf data					X	X	X	X				
IPTV data					X	X	X					
IPTV control					X	X	X					
Streaming media									X	X	X	X
Interactive gaming	X	X			X	X						
SANs synch replication					X							
SANs asynch replication					X							
Network attached storage									X	X	X	X
Text & graphics terminals									X	X	X	X
T.38 fax over IP					X	X	X	X				
Database hot standby					X							
Database WAN replication					X							
Database client/server									X	X	X	X
Financial/Trading	X											
CCTV					X	X	X	X				
Telepresence	X	X	X									
Circuit Emulation	X											
Mobile BH H	X											
Mobile BH M					X							
Mobile BH L									X			

Reproduced with permission of the Metro Ethernet Forum

11.1.2
Ingress Bandwidth Profile Constraints (per CoS Label)

Per MEF 23.1, CoS Labels impose the following constraints on ingress bandwidth profiles.

CoS Label	Ingress Bandwidth Profile Constraints	
H	CIR > 0	EIR ≥ 0 (typically EIR=0)
M	CIR > 0	EIR ≥ 0
L	CIR ≥ 0	EIR ≥ 0

CoS Labels M and H require CIR > 0. Although CoS Label H allows EIR > 0, EIR is typically set to zero for CoS Label H. As stated in MEF 26.1, EIR>0 is allowed for CoS Label H to support "some situations for certain applications such as Mobile Backhaul."

Related Links
Single-Flow Bandwidth Profile on p. 126

11.1.3
CoS Label and Color Identification Mechanisms

Per MEF 23.1, CoS Label value (L, M, H) can be assigned to ingress frames using any of the usual mechanisms:

CoS Label Identification Mechanisms	
At UNIs	**At ENNIs**
Based on EVC (or OVC end point)	Based on OVC end point
Based on the value of PCP bits in C-Tag	Based on the value of PCP bits in S-Tag
Based on the value of the differentiated services code point (DSCP) in the IP header	
Based on Layer 2 Control Protocol	

Color value (Green, Yellow), if needed[111], can be assigned to ingress frames based on DEI bit value (in S-Tag), PCP bit value (in C-Tag or S-Tag), or DSCP value (in IP header).

Related Links

CoS ID Service Attributes on p. 114
Encoding Information in S-Tags on p. 188
Color-Aware Bandwidth Profiles at ENNI on p. 200
Color Forwarding on p. 201

11.1.4
CoS Label and Color Identification Using PCP Bits, DEI Bit, and/or EVC/OVC End Point

Note: *Values shown in the following tables are not example values. They are required per MEF 23.1.*

If CoS Labels are identified using PCP bits, PCP bits map to CoS Label and Color values as follows:

CoS Label	MEF-Specified PCP Bit Value			
	In C-Tag (or in S-Tag without DEI supported)		In S-Tag with DEI Supported	
	Color Green	Color Yellow	Color Green	Color Yellow
H	5	Not Supported	5 (with DEI=0)	Not Supported
M	3	2	3 (with DEI=0)	3 (with DEI=1)
L	1	0	1 (with DEI=0)	1 (with DEI=1)

---

111 Color identification is used for color forwarding and color-aware ingress bandwidth profiles.

If the S-Tag DEI bit is used to encode color, then PCP bits encode only CoS Label value. If CoS Labels are assigned per EVC or per OVC end point, PCP bits can encode Color as follows:

MEF-Specified PCP Bit Value in C-Tag	
Color Green	Color Yellow (CoS Label ≠H)
5, 3, or 1	2 or 0 **Note:** Color Yellow is not supported for CoS Label H.

In this case, PCP bits do not determine CoS Label value (L, M, H). They only determine Color.

11.1.5
CoS Label and Color Identification Using DSCP Values and/or EVC/OVC End Point

Note: Values shown in the following tables are not example values. They are required, per MEF 23.1.

Note: For reference, the following tables include IP per-hop behavior (PHB) for each differentiated services code point (DSCP) value. In the differentiated services (DiffServ) computer networking architecture, DSCP values determine PHB.

If CoS Labels are identified using DSCP values, DSCP values map to CoS Label and Color values as follows:

CoS Label	MEF-Specified PHB (DSCP Value)	
	Color Green	Color Yellow
H	EF (46)	Not Supported
M	AF31 (26)	AF32 (28) or AF33 (30)
L	AF11 (10)	AF12 (12), AF13 (14), or DF(0)

If CoS Labels are assigned per EVC or per OVC end point, DSCP values can encode Color as follows:

MEF-Specified PHB (DSCP Value)	
Color Green	Color Yellow (CoS Label ≠H)
EF (46), AF31 (26), or AF11 (10)	AF32 (28), AF33 (30), AF12 (12), AF13 (14), or DF(0) **Note:** Color Yellow is not supported for CoS Label H

In this case, DSCP values do not determine CoS Label value (L, M, H). They only determine Color.

11.1.6
CoS Label Identification for L2CP Frames

Per MEF 23.1, subscriber L2CP frames:

Can be assigned to any CoS Label value that is supported by the EVC/OVC
Should be assigned CoS Label M if M is supported. Otherwise, CoS Label H if H is supported. Otherwise, CoS Label L.

Note: As explained in MEF 23.1, "the M CoS Label is chosen for L2CP whenever available, based on its superior loss performance, and a desire to keep it separate from real-time applications."

11.1.7
Key Observations About CoS Label and Color Identification

Ingress frames are mapped to CoS Label values (L, M, H) using the usual mechanisms (based on EVC, OVC end point, PCP bits, DSCP value, or L2CP).
If PCP bits encode CoS Label only, values 5, 3, and 1 correspond to H, M, and L, respectively.
If PCP bits encode CoS Label and Color, values 5, 3, 2, 1, and 0 correspond to H (Green), M (Green), M (Yellow), L (Green), and L (Yellow), respectively.
Color Yellow is not supported for CoS Label H.
Color Yellow is not supported for CoS Label H.

11.1.8
Performance Metrics for CoS Labels

EVC/OVC performance for a CoS Label is defined using the usual set of 8 performance metrics:

1. One-way Frame Delay (FD)	5. One-way Frame Loss Ratio (FLR)
2. One-way Frame Delay Range (FDR)	6. One-way Availability (Availability)
3. One-way Mean Frame Delay (MFD)	7. One-way High Loss Intervals (HLI)
4. Inter Frame Delay Variation (IFDV)	8. One-way Consecutive High Loss Intervals (CHLI)

Per requirements [R18] and [R21] of MEF 23.1, an SLS that is based on a CoS Label must include at least one of either FD or MFD and at least one of either FDR or IFDV.

Related Links

EVC Performance Service Attribute on p. 148
CPOs (per CoS Label and Performance Tier) on p. 229

11.1.9
CoS Parameter Values (per CoS Label)

The following table from MEF 23.1 defines CoS Parameter values for CoS Labels H, M, and L.

Performance Metric	Parameter Name	Parameter Values for CoS Label H	Parameter Values for CoS Label M	Parameter Values for CoS Label L
FD	Percentile (P_d)	$\geq$ 99.9th	$\geq$ 99th	$\geq$ 95th
	Time Interval (T)	$\leq$ Month	$\leq$ Month	$\leq$ Month
MFD	Time Interval (T)	$\leq$ Month	$\leq$ Month	$\leq$ Month
IFDV	Percentile (P_v)	$\geq$ 99.9th	$\geq$ 99th or N/S[1]	N/S
	Time Interval (T)	$\leq$ Month	$\leq$ Month or N/S[1]	N/S
	Pair Interval (Δt)	$\geq$ 1sec	$\geq$ 1sec or N/S[1]	N/S
FDR	Percentile (P_r)	$\geq$ 99.9th	$\geq$ 99th or N/S[1]	N/S
	Time Interval (T)	$\leq$ Month	$\leq$ Month or N/S[1]	N/S
FLR	Time Interval (T)	$\leq$ Month	$\leq$ Month	$\leq$ Month
Availability	TBD	TBD	TBD	TBD
High Loss Interval	TBD	TBD	TBD	TBD
Consecutive High Loss Interval	TBD	TBD	TBD	TBD

[1] Parameters are N/S only when CPO is N/S
Note: each parameter value > 0

Reproduced with permission of the Metro Ethernet Forum

The inequalities in this table indicate that service providers and operators may provide more stringent values than the maximum and minimum values shown.

11.1.10
CPOs (per CoS Label and Performance Tier)

MEF 23.1 defines CoS Performance Objective (CPO) values for <u>point-to-point</u> EVCs and OVCs, as follows:[112]

CoS Label	H				M				L			
Performance Tier	PT1	PT2	PT3	PT4	PT1	PT2	PT3	PT4	PT1	PT2	PT3	PT4
FD (ms)	≤10	≤25	≤77	≤230	≤20	≤75	≤115	≤250	≤37	≤125	≤230	≤390
MFD (ms)	≤7	≤18	≤70	≤200	≤13	≤30	≤80	≤220	≤28	≤50	≤125	≤240
IFDV (ms)	≤3	≤8	≤10	≤32	≤8*	≤40*			N/S	N/S	N/S	N/S
FDR (ms)	≤5	≤10	≤12	≤40	≤10*	≤50*			N/S	N/S	N/S	N/S
FLR (%)	≤0.01		≤0.025	≤0.05	≤0.01		≤0.025	≤0.05	≤0.1			
Availability	TBD	TBD	TBD	TBD	TBD	TBD	TBD	TBD	TBD	TBD	TBD	TBD
HLI	TBD	TBD	TBD	TBD	TBD	TBD	TBD	TBD	TBD	TBD	TBD	TBD
CHLI	TBD	TBD	TBD	TBD	TBD	TBD	TBD	TBD	TBD	TBD	TBD	TBD

* Compliant services can leave this value unspecified.
N/S indicates Not Specified.

Additionally:

> The inequalities in this table indicate that service providers and operators may provide more stringent values than the maximum values shown.
>
> CPO values are not required for both FD and MFD (at least one must be specified).
>
> CPO values are not required for both IFDV and FDR (at least one must be specified).
>
> All CPO values apply to Green frames only.
>
> MEF 23.1 does not define CPO values for multipoint-to-multipoint (or rooted-multipoint) EVCs and OVCs.

Related Links

EVC Performance Service Attribute on p. 148
Service Level Specification (OVC Service Attribute) on p. 206
Performance Metrics for CoS Labels on p. 227

---

112   From Tables 6-9 in MEF 23.1

11.2
Review: MEF-Standardized Classes of Service

1. How many classes of service does MEF 23.1 define for Performance Tier 2?

   a. 2 classes of service
   b. 3 classes of service
   c. 4 classes of service
   d. 6 classes of service
   e. 12 classes of service

2. An *Ingress Bandwidth Profile Per ENNI Class of Service Identifier* is required at an OVC end point to police ingress ENNI frames marked with *CoS Label M*. Which one of the following ingress bandwidth profiles satisfies all MEF requirements?

   a. CIR=0, CBS=0 bytes, EIR=200 Mb/s, EBS=2000 bytes, CF=Y, CM=Y
   b. CIR=200 Mb/s, CBS=2000 bytes, EIR=200 Mb/s, EBS=2000 bytes, CF=N, CM=N
   c. CIR=200 Mb/s, CBS=2000 bytes, EIR=200 Mb/s, EBS=2000 bytes, CF=N, CM=Y
   d. CIR=0, CBS=0 bytes, EIR=200 Mb/s, EBS=2000 bytes, CF=Y, CM=N

3. A point-to-point service uses *CoS Label H*. Which CPO <u>must</u> be specified in the SLS?

   a. Both Frame Delay (FD) and Frame Delay Range (FDR)
   b. Both Mean Frame Delay (MFD) and Inter-Frame Delay Variation (IFDV)
   c. Frame Loss Ratio (FLR)
   d. High Loss Intervals (HLI)
   e. Consecutive High Loss Intervals (CHLI)

4. According to MEF 23.1, if CoS Label and Color are encoded in S-Tag PCP bits, PCP bit value 3 indicates...

   a. M, Yellow
   b. M, Green
   c. H, Green
   d. Nothing

5. Which two statements about Class of Service Performance Objectives (CPOs) are correct? (Choose two.)

   a. CPOs for *CoS Label L* are more demanding than CPOs for *CoS Label H*.
   b. CPOs for *Performance Tier 4* are more demanding than CPOs for *Performance Tier 3*.
   c. CPOs for *CoS Label M* are more demanding than CPOs for *CoS Label L*.
   d. CPOs for *Performance Tier 1* are more demanding than CPOs for *Performance Tier 3*.

6. How many performance tiers does MEF 23.1 define for CoS Label H?

   a. 3 performance tiers
   b. 4 performance tiers
   c. 6 performance tiers
   d. 12 performance tiers

7. For each of the following services, all service frames map to *CoS Label L*. Which service is subject to CPO values defined in MEF 23.1?

   a. *Performance Tier 1* EP-LAN service with ingress bandwidth profile CIR > 0.
   b. *Performance Tier 4* EVPL service with ingress bandwidth profile CIR > 0.
   c. *Performance Tier 1* EPL service with ingress bandwidth profile CIR = 0.
   d. *Performance Tier 4* EVP-LAN service with ingress bandwidth profile CIR = 0.

8. According to MEF 23.1, if CoS Label and Color is encoded in S-Tag PCP bits, PCP bit value 4 indicates…

   a. M, Yellow
   b. M, Green
   c. H, Green
   d. Nothing

9. A point-to-point service uses *CoS Label H*. If Frame Delay (FD) in not specified, which frame delay CPO <u>must</u> be specified in the SLS?

   a. Frame Delay Range (FDR)
   b. Mean Frame Delay (MFD)
   c. Inter-Frame Delay Variation (IFDV)

10. MEF 23.1 defines CoS Performance Objectives (CPOs) for …

    a. point-to-point services only
    b. point-to-point and multipoint-to-multipoint services only
    c. point-to-point, multipoint-to-multipoint, and rooted-multipoint services

Related Links

Answers: MEF-Standardized Classes of Service on p. 423

12
E-Access Services

In this chapter:

12.1 E-Access Service Applications
12.2 Access EPL and Access EVPL
12.3 E-Access Service Attributes
12.4 Highlights of E-Access Service Definitions
12.5 E-Access Service Applications
12.6 Review: E-Access Services

The previously described general framework for implementing Carrier Ethernet services across multiple Operator CENs supports the development of OVC-based services (services deployed by an operator and sold to the service provider). But this framework is very open, leaving it up to the service providers and operators to work out many service details.

In defining E-Access services, the MEF goes one step further: to define industry-standard OVC-based Ethernet services for Ethernet access applications.

Ethernet access is a critical topic in Carrier Ethernet because carrier networking has evolved into a tiered industry with separate businesses and networks operating at local, metro, regional, continental, and global levels. Large carriers that are well positioned to offer wholesale Ethernet services generally have to work with many access providers (providers that own and operate the first/last mile network connections) to acquire Ethernet access to subscriber sites. Access providers that are well positioned to offer Ethernet access services commonly work with more than one large carrier.

Today, global Ethernet service providers may have hundreds of interconnect agreements with many different access providers. Agreements that are unique and time consuming to procure will delay service deployments. E-Access services are designed to address this issue, making the Ethernet access business manageable for Ethernet service providers and Ethernet access providers alike. E-Access services allow access providers to mass market Ethernet access services similarly to how they currently sell standardized T1 or E1 access circuits. They also greatly simplify the purchasing process for large Ethernet service providers, allowing them to purchase standardized Ethernet access services similarly to how they have purchased standardized T1 or E1 access circuits for decades from any access provider they partner with.

12.1
E-Access Service Applications

An E-Access service can be used in two ways: **In combination with other OVC-based services** (to support EVC-based service, providing UNI-to-UNI connectivity between customer sites), and **Alone** (to connect a customer site to an IP network).

EVC-Based Service Application

In this application a service provider uses E-Access services to reach out-of-franchise subscriber locations.

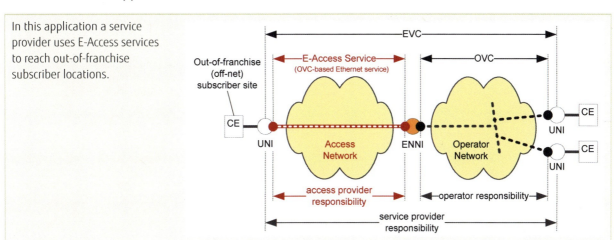

The business model has two principle stakeholders: [113]

- **Ethernet Access Provider** – the organization that operates the access network and offers the E-Access service to the service provider
- **Service Provider** – the organization that purchases the E-Access service to reach an out-of-franchise (off-net) subscriber site in order to deliver the end-to-end service to the subscriber

IP Network Access Application

In this application, an access provider uses E-Access services to connect customer sites to an IP network, for example, the network of an Internet service provider.

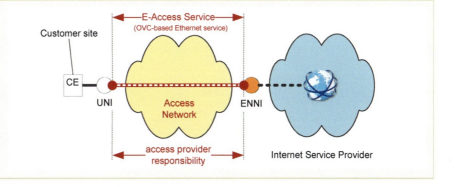

---

113 The subscriber has no business relationship with the Ethernet access provider and may be unaware of the E-Access service.

12.2 Access EPL and Access EVPL

MEF 33 defines two E-Access services: the **Access EPL** (Access Ethernet Private Line) and the **Access EVPL** (Access Ethernet Virtual Private Line). Both provide a point-to-point OVC between a UNI and an ENNI.

Access EPL

The Access EPL (Access Ethernet Private Line) is a point-to-point E-Access service that is port-based at the UNI.[114]

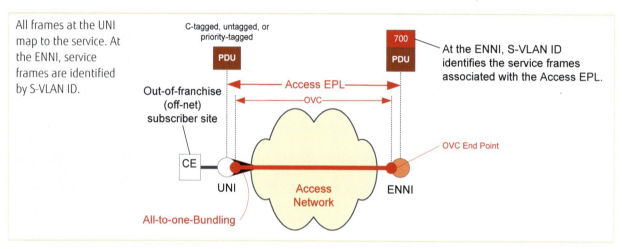

Access EVPL

The Access EVPL (Access Ethernet Virtual Private Line) is a VLAN-based point-to-point E-Access service.[115]

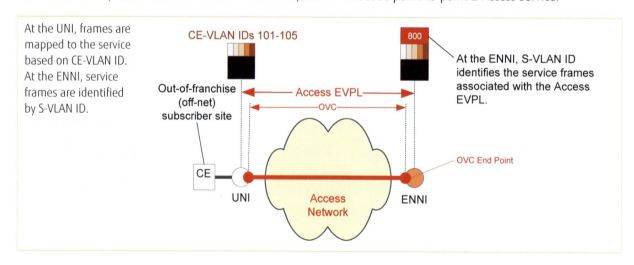

---

114   The UNI of an Access EPL implicitly supports all-to-one bundling. Services are never port-based at ENNIs.
115   The Access EVPL UNI implicitly supports bundling and service multiplexing. The OVC does not support CE-VLAN ID translation.

12.3
E-Access Service Attributes

In this section:

12.3.1 ENNI Service Attributes for E-Access
12.3.2 OVC Service Attributes for E-Access
12.3.3 OVC End Point per ENNI Service Attributes for E-Access
12.3.4 Per UNI Service Attributes for E-Access
12.3.5 OVC Per UNI service attributes for E-Access

MEF 33 defines E-Access services using a subset of MEF 26.1 service attributes (attributes used in MEF 26.1 to define general OVC-based operator services).

The following tables list MEF 26.1 service attributes and indicate how they are used and modified in MEF 33 to define E-Access services. These tables are meant for overview purposes only. Scanning them, you should notice that many attributes are unchanged from the general case and changes are often just the straight-forward consequence of specialization to point-to-point, port-based, or VLAN-based service.

Attributes shown in **bold** are explained later in this lesson.

Related Links

Operator Service Attributes on p. 192

12.3.1
ENNI Service Attributes for E-Access

General OVC-Based Operator Service Attribute (MEF 26.1)		E-Access Service Attribute (MEF 33)	
Name	Possible Values	Access EPL	Access EVPL
Operator ENNI Identifier	A string that is unique across the Operator CEN	No change	No change
Physical Layer	1000Base-SX, 1000Base-LX, 1000Base T, 10GBase-SR, 10GBase-LX4, 10GBase-LR, 10GBase-ER, 10GBase-SW, 10GBase-LW, 10GBase-EW	No change	No change
Frame Format	Conforming to IEEE 802.1ad (2005)	No change	No change
Number of Links	1 or 2	No change	No change
Protection Mechanism	Link Aggregation, None, or Other	No change	No change
ENNI Maximum Transmission Unit Size	Integer ≥ 1526 bytes	No change	No change
End Point Map	A table with rows of the form <S-VLAN ID value, End Point Identifier, End Point Type>	No change	No change

General OVC-Based Operator Service Attribute (MEF 26.1)		E-Access Service Attribute (MEF 33)	
Name	Possible Values	Access EPL	Access EVPL
Maximum Number of OVCs	Integer ≥ 1	No change	No change
Maximum Number of OVC End Points per OVC	Integer ≥ 1	No change	No change

Related Links

ENNI Service Attributes on p. 192

12.3.2
OVC Service Attributes for E-Access

General OVC-Based Operator Service Attribute (MEF 26.1)		E-Access Service Attribute (MEF 33)	
Name	Possible Values	Access EPL	Access EVPL
OVC Identifier	A string that is unique across the Operator CEN	No change	No change
OVC Type	Point-to-Point, Multipoint-to-Multipoint, Rooted-multipoint	Must be Point-to-Point	Must be Point-to-Point
OVC End Point List	A list of OVC End Point Identifiers	Exactly 2: one at UNI and one at ENNI	Exactly 2: one at UNI and one at ENNI
Maximum Number of UNI OVC End Points	Integer ≥ 0	Must be 1	Must be 1
Maximum Number ENNI OVC End Points	Integer ≥ 1	Must be 1	Must be 1
OVC Maximum Transmission Unit Size	Integer ≥ 1526 bytes	No change	No change
CE-VLAN ID Preservation	**Yes or No**	**Must be Yes**	**Must be Yes**
CE-VLAN CoS ID Preservation	**Yes or No**	**Must be Yes**	**Must be Yes**
S-VLAN ID Preservation	Yes or No	Not applicable (only one ENNI in the service)	Not applicable (only one ENNI in the service)
S-VLAN CoS Preservation	Yes or No	Not applicable (only one ENNI in the service)	Not applicable (only one ENNI in the service)
Color Forwarding	Yes or No	Should be Yes	Should be Yes
Service Level Specification	Same as for general OVC-based service. Eight performance metrics are specified, where Not Specified (N/S) is an acceptable value: FD, FDR, MFD, IFDV, FLR, Availability, HLI, and CHLI.		
Unicast Service Frame Delivery	Deliver conditionally or unconditionally	Must deliver unconditionally	Deliver conditionally or unconditionally

E-Access Services
E-Access Service Attributes

General OVC-Based Operator Service Attribute (MEF 26.1)		E-Access Service Attribute (MEF 33)	
Name	Possible Values	Access EPL	Access EVPL
Multicast Service Frame Delivery	Deliver conditionally or unconditionally	Must deliver unconditionally	Deliver conditionally or unconditionally
Broadcast Service Frame Delivery	Deliver conditionally or unconditionally	Must deliver unconditionally	Deliver conditionally or unconditionally
Layer 2 Control Protocol Tunneling	A list on Layer 2 Control Protocols that are tunnelled.	Processing of L2CP frames is for further study. Until defined in a future revision of MEF 33, processing of L2CP frames is agreed to by the two parties involved in the Access Service.	

Related Links

OVC Service Attributes on p. 193

Service Level Specification (OVC Service Attribute) on p. 206

12.3.3
OVC End Point per ENNI Service Attributes for E-Access

General OVC-Based Operator Service Attribute (MEF 26.1)		E-Access Service Attribute (MEF 33)	
Name	Possible Values	Access EPL	Access EVPL
OVC End Point Identifier	A string that is unique across the Operator CEN	No change	No change
Class of Service Identifiers	Non-overlapping sets of S-Tag PCP values; one for each CoS	All frames map to one CoS (regardless of S-Tag PCP value)	All frames map to one CoS (regardless of S-Tag PCP value)
Ingress Bandwidth Profile Per OVC End Point	None or one set of bandwidth profile values (CIR, CBS, EIR, EBS, CF, CM)	Supported per special requirements, as explained later in this lesson	Supported per special requirements, as explained later in this lesson
Ingress Bandwidth Profile Per ENNI Class of Service Identifier	None or one set of bandwidth profile values (CIR, CBS, EIR, EBS, CF, CM) for each CoS	Not supported	Not supported
Egress Bandwidth Profile Per End Point	None or one set of bandwidth profile values (CIR, CBS, EIR, EBS, CF, CM)	Not supported	Not supported
Egress Bandwidth Profile Per ENNI Class of Service Identifier	None or one set of bandwidth profile values (CIR, CBS, EIR, EBS, CF, CM) for each CoS	Not supported	Not supported

Related Links

OVC End Point per ENNI Service Attributes on p. 194

12.3.4
Per UNI Service Attributes for E-Access

General OVC-Based Operator Service Attribute (MEF 26.1)		E-Access Service Attribute (MEF 33)	
Name	Possible Values	Access EPL	Access EVPL
UNI Identifier	Arbitrary text string to identify the UNI	No change	No change
Physical Medium	UNI Type 2 Physical Interface	No change	No change
Speed	10 Mb/s, 100 Mb/s, 10/100 Mb/s Auto-negotiation, 10/100/1000 Mb/s Auto-negotiation, 1 Gb/s, or 10 Gb/s	No change	No change
Mode	Full Duplex	No change	No change
MAC Layer	IEEE 802.3-2005	No change	No change
UNI MTU Size	≥ 1522 bytes	No change	No change
Service Multiplexing	Yes or No. MUST be No if *All to One Bundling* is *Yes*.	Not applicable	Not applicable
Bundling	Yes or No. MUST be No if *All to One Bundling* is *Yes*.	Not applicable	Not applicable
All to One Bundling	Yes or No. MUST be No if *Bundling* or *Service Multiplexing* is *Yes*.	Not applicable	Not applicable
CE-VLAN ID for untagged and priority tagged Service Frames	MUST specify *CE-VLAN ID for untagged and priority tagged Service Frames* in the range of 1-4094. This requirement does not apply for services with all to one bundling at the UNI.	Not applicable	No change
Maximum number of EVCs	Integer ≥ 1	Must be 1	Integer ≥ 1
Ingress Bandwidth Profile Per UNI (optional)	If this attribute is supported, MUST specify CIR, CBS, EIR, EBS, CM, or CF. MUST NOT be combined with any other type of ingress bandwidth profile.	Must not specify	Must not specify
Egress Bandwidth Profile Per UNI (optional)	If this attribute is supported, MUST specify CIR, CBS, EIR, EBS, CM, or CF. MUST NOT be combined with any other type of egress bandwidth profile.	Must not specify	Must not specify
L2CP Processing	For each protocol, MUST specify one of the following: *Peer, Discard, Pass to EVC,* or *Peer and Pass to EVC*.	Processing of L2CP frames is for further study. Until defined in a future revision of MEF 33, processing of L2CP frames is agreed to by the two parties involved in the Access Service	

Related Links

Per UNI Service Attributes (Operator Service) on p. 195

12.3.5
OVC Per UNI service attributes for E-Access

General OVC-Based Operator Service Attribute (MEF 26.1)		E-Access Service Attribute (MEF 33)	
Name	Possible Values	Access EPL	Access EVPL
UNI OVC Identifier	A string formed by the concatenation of the UNI Identifier and the OVC Identifier	No change	No change
OVC End Point Map	A list of one or more CE-VLAN ID values	All service frames map to a single OVC.	A list of one or more CE-VLAN ID values
Ingress Bandwidth Profile Per OVC End Point at a UNI	None or one set of bandwidth profile values (CIR, CBS, EIR, EBS, CF, CM)	Supported per special requirements, as explained later in this lesson	Supported per special requirements, as explained later in this lesson
Ingress Bandwidth Profile Per Class of Service Identifier at a UNI	None or one set of bandwidth profile values (CIR, CBS, EIR, EBS, CF, CM) for each CoS	Not supported	Not supported
Egress Bandwidth Profile Per OVC End Point at a UNI	None or one set of bandwidth profile values (CIR, CBS, EIR, EBS, CF, CM)	Not supported	Not supported
Egress Bandwidth Profile Per Class of Service Identifier at a UNI	None or one set of bandwidth profile values (CIR, CBS, EIR, EBS, CF, CM) for each CoS	Not supported	Not supported

Related Links

OVC per UNI Service Attributes on p. 196

12.4
Highlights of E-Access Service Definitions

In this section:

12.4.1 Bundling and Multiplexing for E-Access Services
12.4.2 CE-VLAN ID Preservation for E-Access Services
12.4.3 CoS Identification for E-Access Services
12.4.4 CE-VLAN CoS ID Preservation for E-Access Services
12.4.5 Performance Objectives for E-Access Services
12.4.6 Bandwidth Profiles for E-Access Service

12.4.1
Bundling and Multiplexing for E-Access Services

E-Access services (unlike general OVC-based services) do not include Per UNI service attributes **Bundling**, **Service Multiplexing**, or **All to One Bundling**.

MEF 33 explains that these attributes are omitted because they are not relevant to the agreement between the Access Provider and the Service Provider. However, their values (were they to be included) would be as shown in the following table.

Per UNI service attribute	Access EPL	Access EVPL
Service Multiplexing	Disable	Enable
Bundling	Disable	Enable/Disable
All to One Bundling	Enable	Disable

Observe that the values shown for the Access EPL are consistent with the service being port-based at the UNI. The values shown for the Access EVPL are consistent with all MEF 33 requirements. In particular:

- The service being VLAN-based at the UNI

- The service supporting the association of multiple CE-VLAN IDs to the OVC at the UNI[116]

- The service requiring OVC service attribute *CE-VLAN ID Preservation=Yes*

Related Links

Bundling versus Service Multiplexing on p. 31
Service Multiplexing and Bundling Service Attributes on p. 70

---

116 To support more than one CE-VLAN ID, UNI attribute Bundling must be Enabled.

12.4.2
CE-VLAN ID Preservation for E-Access Services

MEF 33 requires OVC service attribute **CE-VLAN ID Preservation** = **Yes** for both kinds of E-Access service. For the Access EPL, this requirement is expected because the Access EPL is a port-based service. For the Access EVPL, this requirement represents a constraint compared to other VLAN-based services. Other VLAN-based services (EVPL, EVP-LAN, and EVP-Tree services) support CE-VLAN ID translation if UNI attribute *Bundling=No*. The Access EVPL, however, does not support CE-VLAN ID translation. Elimination of CE-VLAN ID translation support simplifies E-Access services, making them easier to manage.

Test your understanding: Can an Access EVPL support an EVC-based service that includes CE-VLAN ID translation? Explain why or why not. [117]

12.4.3
CoS Identification for E-Access Services

MEF 33 simplifies CoS identification for E-Access services compared to general OVC-based services, as summarized in the following table.

Location	CoS Identification Mechanisms	
	General OVC-Based Operator Service	Access EPL/EVPL
UNI	CoS identification based on EVC	All frames map to a single CoS
	CoS identification based on value of PCP bits in IEEE 802.1Q customer VLAN tag (CE-VLAN tag)	
	CoS identification based on the value of the differentiated services code point (DSCP) in the IP header	
	CoS identification based on Layer 2 Control Protocol	
ENNI	CoS identification based on S-Tag PCP bits	All frames map to a single CoS

All frames associated with an E-Access service instance map to the same CoS and get the same QoS treatment in the access network. Allowing only one CoS simplifies E-Access services, making them easier to manage.

Test your understanding: Can an Access EPL support an EVC-based service that includes more than one CoS? Explain why or why not. [118]

Related Links

CoS ID Service Attributes on p. 114

OVC End Point per ENNI Service Attributes on p. 194

---

[117] **Answer:** Yes. If the Access EVPL is deployed in combination with a general OVC-based operator service that includes CE-VLAN ID translation, the resulting EVC-based service would include CE-VLAN ID translation.

[118] **Answer:** Yes. If the Access EPL is deployed in combination with a general OVC-based operator service that includes more than one CoS, the resulting EVC-based service would include more than one CoS. In this scenario, all frames receive the same CoS treatment in the access network, but different CoS treatments in the other operator network.

12.4.4
CE-VLAN CoS ID Preservation for E-Access Services

MEF 33 requires OVC service attribute **CE-VLAN CoS ID Preservation** = **Yes** for both kinds of E-Access service. For the Access EPL, this requirement is expected because the Access EPL is a port-based service. For the Access EVPL, this requirement represents a constraint compared to other VLAN-based services. Other VLAN-based services (EVPL, EVP-LAN, and EVP-Tree services) support CE-VLAN CoS ID translation. The Access EVPL, however, does not support CE-VLAN CoS ID translation.

Elimination of CE-VLAN CoS ID translation support simplifies E-Access services, making them easier to manage.

Test your understanding: Can an Access EVPL support an EVC-based service that includes CE-VLAN CoS ID translation? Explain why or why not. [119]

12.4.5
Performance Objectives for E-Access Services

Up to 8 performance objectives (FLR, Availability, HLI, CHLI, FD, FDR, MFD, and IFDV) are specified for E-Access services using the OVC service attribute **Service Level Specification**, just as they are for general OVC-based services.

When an E-Access service is used to support an EVC-based service, performance objectives for the E-Access service are chosen to align with EVC performance objectives (as explained previously for general OVC-based services).

If an access provider offers a CE 2.0 certified E-Access service, performance objectives for that service will meet or exceed MEF-standardized CoS performance objectives (CPO's) for a particular CoS Label and Performance Tier.

Related Links

OVC Service Attributes for E-Access on p. 236
Service Level Specification (OVC Service Attribute) on p. 206
OVC versus EVC Performance Objectives on p. 207
CPOs (per CoS Label and Performance Tier) on p. 229

12.4.6
Bandwidth Profiles for E-Access Service

MEF 33 simplifies bandwidth profile support for E-Access services compared to general OVC-based services, as summarized in the following table.

---

[119] **Answer:** Yes. If the Access EVPL is deployed in combination with a general OVC-based operator service that includes CE-VLAN CoS ID translation, the resulting EVC-based service would include CE-VLAN CoS ID translation.

E-Access Services
Highlights of E-Access Service Definitions

Bandwidth Profile Attribute		Support	
Classification	Name	General OVC-Based Operator Service	Access EPL/EVPL
UNI	Ingress Bandwidth Profile Per UNI (optional)	If this attribute is supported, MUST specify CIR, CBS, EIR, EBS, CM, or CF. MUST NOT be combined with any other type of ingress bandwidth profile.	Must not specify
	Egress Bandwidth Profile Per UNI (optional)	If this attribute is supported, MUST specify CIR, CBS, EIR, EBS, CM, or CF. MUST NOT be combined with any other type of egress bandwidth profile.	Must not specify
OVC per UNI	Ingress Bandwidth Profile Per OVC End Point	None or one set of bandwidth profile values (CIR, CBS, EIR, EBS, CF, CM)	Supported as specified in MEF 33
	Ingress Bandwidth Profile Per Class of Service Identifier at a UNI	None or one set of bandwidth profile values (CIR, CBS, EIR, EBS, CF, CM) for each CoS	Not supported
	Egress Bandwidth Profile Per OVC End Point at a UNI	None or one set of bandwidth profile values (CIR, CBS, EIR, EBS, CF, CM)	Not supported
	Egress Bandwidth Profile Per Class of Service Identifier at a UNI	None or one set of bandwidth profile values (CIR, CBS, EIR, EBS, CF, CM) for each CoS	Not supported
OVC End Point per ENNI	Ingress Bandwidth Profile Per OVC End Point	None or one set of bandwidth profile values (CIR, CBS, EIR, EBS, CF, CM)	Supported as specified in MEF33
	Ingress Bandwidth Profile Per ENNI Class of Service Identifier	None or one set of bandwidth profile values (CIR, CBS, EIR, EBS, CF, CM) for each CoS	Not supported
	Egress Bandwidth Profile Per End Point	None or one set of bandwidth profile values (CIR, CBS, EIR, EBS, CF, CM)	Not supported
	Egress Bandwidth Profile Per ENNI Class of Service Identifier	None or one set of bandwidth profile values (CIR, CBS, EIR, EBS, CF, CM) for each CoS	Not supported

Key Observations:
1. Access EPL/EVPL services only support **ingress** bandwidth profiles (no egress bandwidth profiles).
2. Access EPL/EVPL services only support **per-OVC-end-point** ingress bandwidth profiles (no per-UNI or per-CoS-identifier bandwidth profiles).
3. Access EPL/EVPL services support two ingress bandwidth profiles (one at the UNI and one at the ENNI).
4. Access EPL/EVPL services are required to support ingress bandwidth profiles according to special rules, specified in MEF 33, which are described next.

Related Links

Single-Flow Bandwidth Profile on p. 126
Per UNI Service Attributes (Operator Service) on p. 195
OVC per UNI Service Attributes on p. 196
OVC End Point per ENNI Service Attributes on p. 194

Special Ingress Bandwidth Profile Requirements

Ingress bandwidth profiles for Access EPL and Access EVPL services are defined in the usual way, by specifying values for the six parameters listed in following table.

Bandwidth Profile Parameter		Units of Measure or Values	Requirements
CIR	Committed Information Rate	Bits per second	CIR ≥ 0
CBS	Committed Burst Size	Bytes	If CIR > 0, then CBS ≥ maximum MTU over all EVCs to which the bandwidth profile applies
EIR	Excess Information Rate	Bits per second	EIR ≥ 0
EBS	Excess Burst Size	Bytes	If EIR > 0, then EBS ≥ maximum MTU over all EVCs to which the bandwidth profile applies
CF	Coupling Flag	N or Y	none
CM	Color Mode	color-blind or color-aware	none

However, MEF 33 adds the following requirements, which ensure that services offered by all Ethernet access providers meet a common baseline standard for capability.

1. CIR must *be configurable* to each of the following 37 values:
   1, 2, 3, 4, 5, 6, 7, 8, 9, 10, 20, 30, 40, 50, 60, 70, 80, 90, 100, 200, 300, 400, 500, 600, 700, 800, 900 Mb/s,
   plus 1, 2, 3, 4, 5, 6, 7, 8, 9, 10 Gb/s
   Subject to the following limits:
   Up to 70% of **UNI** speed (for **Ingress Bandwidth Profile Per OVC End Point at UNI**)
   Up to 70% of **ENNI** speed (for **Ingress Bandwidth Profile Per OVC End Point at ENNI**)

   Note: *The service may support other values of CIR, but these values must be supported.*

   Note: *This requirement concerns capability, not the values of CIR used for a particular service instance.*

   Note: *As explained in Appendix A of MEF 33, CIR values are limited to 70% of UNI/ENNI speed because bandwidth profile algorithms do not count interframe overhead (interframe GAP + preamble bits), which consume UNI/ENNI bandwidth. Setting CIR too close to the bit rate of the physical layer of the UNI/ENNI has consequences, which may appear only under certain traffic conditions.*

   Example 1: *If UNI speed is 100 Mb/s, CIR in* **Ingress Bandwidth Profile Per OVC End Point at UNI** *must be configurable to 1, 2, 3, 4, 5, 6, 7, 8, 9, 10, 20, 30, 40, 50, 60, and 70 Mb/s.*

   Example 2: *If ENNI speed is 10 Gb/s,* **Ingress Bandwidth Profile Per OVC End Point at ENNI** *must be configurable to 1, 2, 3, 4, 5, 6, 7, 8, 9, 10, 20, 30, 40, 50, 60, 70, 80, 90, 100, 200, 300, 400, 500, 600, 700, 800, and 900 Mb/s, plus 1, 2, 3, 4, 5, 6, and 7 Gb/s.*

2. **Ingress Bandwidth Profile Per OVC End Point at UNI** must allow configuration of
   EIR=0, EBS=0, CF=N, CM="**color-blind**".

   Note: *The service may support other values of EIR, EBS, CF, and CM, but these values must be supported.*

E-Access Services
Highlights of E-Access Service Definitions

Note: *This requirement concerns capability, not the values of EIR, EBS, CF, and CM used for a particular service instance.*

3. **Ingress Bandwidth Profile Per OVC End Point at ENNI** must allow configuration of
   EIR=0, EBS=0, CF=N, CM="**color-aware**".

Note: *The service may support other values of EIR, EBS, CF, and CM, but these values must be supported.*

Note: *This requirement concerns capability, not the values of EIR, EBS, CF, and CM used for a particular service instance.*

4. CBS must be ≥ 12176 bytes for both bandwidth profiles:
   Ingress Bandwidth Profile Per OVC End Point at UNI
   Ingress Bandwidth Profile Per OVC End Point at ENNI

Note: *This requirement concerns the actual value of CBS used in any service instance.*

Note: *The value 12176 is equal to 8 times 1522 (the minimum value of **UNI Maximum Service Frame Size** and **EVC Maximum Service Frame Size** attributes).*

5. If **Ingress Bandwidth Profile Per OVC End Point at UNI** has CIR>0 and EIR=0, egress frames at ENNI must be marked green (via S-Tag).

Related Links

Maximum Service Frame Size Service Attributes on p. 69
About Line Rate and CIR on p. 143

12.5
E-Access Service Applications

In this section:

12.5.1   E-Access Services Applied in EVC-Based Services
12.5.2   E-Access Services Applied for IP Network Services
12.5.3   E-Access Compared to E-Line

12.5.1
E-Access Services Applied in EVC-Based Services

E-Access services are designed to support any EVC-based service (EPL, EVPL, EP-LAN, EVP-LAN, EP-Tree, or EVP-Tree service), regardless of how the EVC-based service is defined.

Access EPLs and Access EVPLs, on their own, have limited capability compared to EVC-based services:

No support for multipoint-to-multipoint functionality
No support for rooted-multipoint functionality
No support for multiple CoS
No support for CE-VLAN ID translation
No support for CE-VLAN CoS ID translation

However, these limitations do not restrict their ability to support EVC-based services that include these capabilities. Conceptually, Access EPL and Access EVPLs are role players, designed to provide point-to-point connectivity to out-of-franchise (off-net) customer sites. To support general EVC-based services, Access EPL/EVPLs are combined with general OVC-based operator services, which have general capability.

Example 1

A subscriber requires an EP-LAN service supporting 3 CoS levels (Low, Medium, and High) between five sites, three of which are off-net. To support this service, the service provider:

1. Purchases three Access EPLs, each supporting all traffic with 1 CoS (High), from two different Ethernet access providers.

2. Deploys a multipoint-to-multipoint OVC-based operator service within their own network supporting three CoS (Low, Medium, and High).

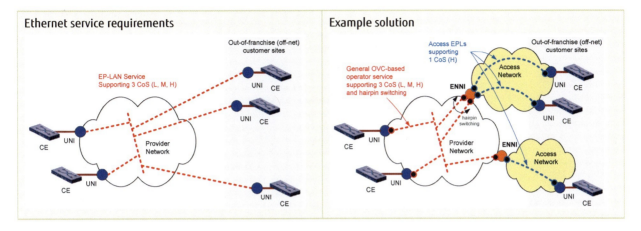

The Access EPLs are purchased with CoS level High in order to support all three CoS levels (Low, Medium, and High) that are supported by the EP-LAN service, in particular the most demanding CoS level (High).

Note: *In this example, the general OVC-based operator service requires a multipoint-to-multipoint OVC with multi-CoS support and hairpin switching support.*

Example 2

A subscriber requires two services involving four sites, two of which are off-net: an EVP-Tree service with CE-VLAN ID translation and an EVPL service supporting CE-VLAN IDs 100–120.

To support these services, the service provider:

1. Purchases four Access EVPLs.

2. Deploys a point-to-point OVC-based operator service within their own network to support the EVPL service.

3. Deploys a rooted-multipoint OVC-based operator service within their own network to support the EVP-Tree service.

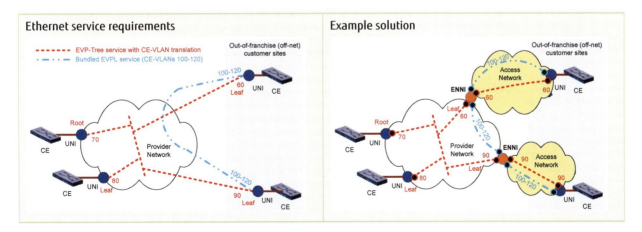

Note: *In this example, the rooted-multipoint OVC provides all CE-VLAN ID translation support.*

12.5.2
E-Access Services Applied for IP Network Services

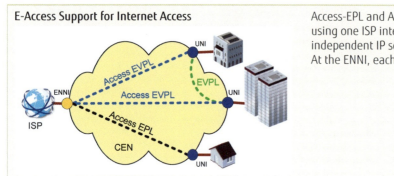

E-Access Support for Internet Access

Access-EPL and Access-EVPL services support this application using one ISP interface (ENNI) to support multiple independent IP service connections for different subscribers. At the ENNI, each Access EPL/EVPL is identified by S-VLAN ID.

Note: A single ENNI can support up to 4094 Access EPL and/or Access EVPL service connections.

Note: Each Access EVPL can support any set of CE-VLAN ID values at the ENNI. CE-VLAN ID values need not be distinct, as would be required for EVPLs multiplexing to an ISP UNI.

12.5.3
E-Access Compared to E-Line

Key Similarities:

- Access EPL, Access EVPL, EPL, and EVPL services are all point-to-point.
- Access EPL and EPL are both port based at UNI(s).
- Access EVPL and EVPL are both VLAN-based at UNI(s).

Key Differences:

Access EPL / EVPL	EPL / EVPL
OVC-based	EVC-based
UNI-to-ENNI	UNI-to-UNI
ENNI supports multiplexing of Access EPLs and/or Access EVPLs	UNI configured with Service Multiplexing = Enabled supports multiple EVPLs UNI configured with Service Multiplexing = Disabled supports one EPL or one EVPL
No support for CE-VLAN ID translation	EVPL supports CE-VLAN ID translation if only one CE-VLAN ID maps to the EVC.
Supports one CoS only	Supports multiple CoS

12.6
Review: E-Access Services

1. Both the Access EVPL and the Access EPL... (Choose two.)

   a. Allow CE-VLAN ID translation
   b. Associate each service instance to one S-VLAN ID value at the ENNI
   c. Are point-to-point OVCs
   d. Connect one ENNI and one UNI

2. Two access providers establish an ENNI connection between their networks. What types of EVC-based services can they offer subscribers using only Access EPL and Access EVPL services? Assume that one of the access providers takes the role of service provider.

   a. E-Line only
   b. E-Line and E-LAN only
   c. E-Line and E-Tree only
   d. E-Line, E-LAN, and E-Tree

3. Access EVPL differs from EVPL in that...

   a. Access EVPL supports multiple CoS, while EVPL supports only one CoS.
   b. Access EVPL is VLAN-based, while EVPL is port-based.
   c. Access EVPL is OVC-based, while EVPL is EVC-based.
   d. Access EVPL supports CE-VLAN ID Preservation, while EVPL does not.

4. Which service supports CE-VLAN ID translation?

   a. Access EVPL
   b. Access EPL
   c. EVPL
   d. EPL

5. E-Access services and E-Line services both include at least one...

   a. UNI
   b. ENNI
   c. OVC
   d. EVC

6. A service provider has been using four Access EPLs to support an EP-LAN for a subscriber. The subscriber now wants to convert the EP-LAN service to an EP-Tree service. How are the Access EPLs impacted by this change?

   a. They can no longer be used.
   b. The must be converted to Access EVPLs.
   c. They must now filter traffic.
   d. They are not impacted.

7. Both Access EVPL and Access EPL…

   a. Support hairpin switching
   b. Can connect a customer site to an Internet service provider
   c. Support multiple CoS
   d. Are EVC-based services

8. If an E-Access service is applied to reach an off-net customer site in an EVC-based service application, the EVC-based service…

   a. Can support only one class of service
   b. Cannot support CE-VLAN ID translation
   c. Must be point-to-point
   d. Must involve at least one ENNI

9. As a service provider you have agreed to provide an EPL service supporting IP packets up to 2000 bytes in length. However, one customer site is off-net, so you need to purchase an Access EPL service to reach that customer site. The access provider offers Access EPLs with ingress bandwidth profiles at the ENNI supporting the following values of CBS. Which value do you choose if you want to minimize CBS?

   a. CBS = 2000 bytes
   b. CBS = 2010 bytes
   c. CBS = 2020 bytes
   d. CBS = 2030 bytes

10. Which of the following statements is false?

    a. A UNI can support up to 4094 Access EVPLs.
    b. A UNI can support up to 4094 Access EPLs.
    c. An ENNI can support up to 4094 Access EPLs.
    d. An ENNI can support up to 4094 Access EVPLs.

11. Which two services are used to reach off-net customer sites? (Choose two.)

    a. Access EVPL
    b. EVPL
    c. Access EPL
    d. EPL

12. Access EPL is similar to EPL in that… (Choose two.)

    a. Both support untagged frames and C-Tagged frames at the UNI.
    b. Both support CE-VLAN ID translation.
    c. Both support CE-VLAN CoS ID preservation.
    d. Both are OVC-based services.

Related Links

Answers: E-Access Services on p. 426

13
Ethernet OAM

In this chapter:

13.1 Link OAM
13.2 Service OAM Overview
13.3 SOAM-Related Service Attributes
13.4 SOAM Connectivity Fault Management
13.5 SOAM Performance Management
13.6 Review: Ethernet OAM

Operations, administration, and maintenance (OAM) is a vital component of the Service Management attribute of Carrier Ethernet.

MEF specifications are designed to provide Carrier-Class OAM at all levels of service application: locally, regionally, and globally.

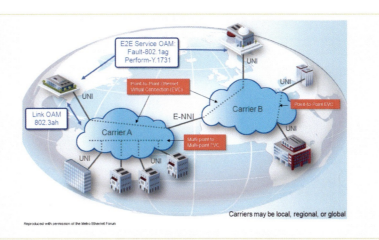

OAM can be broken down into two categories:

- **Link OAM (LOAM)** — Applies to the physical link interconnecting two devices (conforms to IEEE 802.3ah)

- **Service OAM (SOAM)** — Applies to the end-to-end Carrier Ethernet service (conforms to MEF 17, ITU-T Y.1731, and IEEE 802.1Q[12])

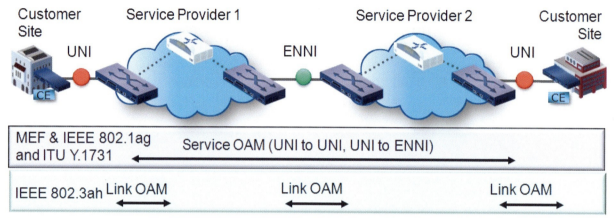

Reproduced with permission of the Metro Ethernet Forum

Although LOAM can be applied to any physical link, LOAM support is especially important at UNIs and ENNIs, where link issues typically occur. LOAM functions only at the physical link level and cannot be extended to the service level.

SOAM provides per-service OAM functionality, end-to-end, across the network and distributes that functionality between administrative organizations (subscribers, service providers, and operators).

LOAM and SOAM are independent (have no effect on each other). However, at the link level, LOAM and SOAM can have some overlapping functionality. LOAM and SOAM are both important for a comprehensive fault management solution.

---

12 IEEE 802.1ag-2007 (the original source of IEEE SOAM standards, referenced in older MEF specifications) has been incorporated into and superseded by IEEE 802.1Q-2011.

13.1
Link OAM

MEF requirements for LOAM are based on clause 57 (OAM) of the IEEE 802.3ah standard.

LOAM is used to monitor and troubleshoot individual Ethernet links.

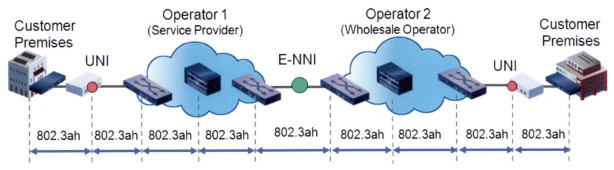

Reproduced with permission of the Metro Ethernet Forum

Although LOAM can be applied to any Ethernet link, it is most relevant to links between administrative organizations (at UNIs and ENNIs). LOAM allows operators to troubleshoot link issues with access from only one side of the link.

LOAM support is required for Type 2.2 UNIs (per MEF 20) and at ENNIs (per MEF 26.1).

LOAM functionality includes:

> **Link Discovery**—After activation, LOAM goes into discovery mode to identify the LOAM capability of its peer on the other side of the link.
>
> **Link Monitoring**—After LOAM is operating, each side periodically sends a LOAM frame to its peer and expects to periodically receive a LOAM frame from its peer. LOAM frames are normally sent at 1-second intervals (per the IEEE 802.3ah standard). If one side stops receiving LOAM frames from its peer, it raises an alarm condition (locally) and sends a remote defect indication (RDI) to its peer (encoded within outgoing LOAM frames).
>
> **Remote Failure Indication**—RDI from a peer indicates that the peer is not receiving frames sent.
>
> **Loopback**—LOAM loopback triggers creation of a port-based loopback in the peer across the link. The loopback redirects all Ethernet traffic (except LOAM control packets) back to the local NE.

 Caution: *LOAM loopback is service disrupting. For this reason (per MEF 26.1), if LOAM is enabled at an ENNI-N, the LOAM loopback capability should be disabled.*

Related Links

LOAM Requirement for Type 2.2 UNIs on p. 171
LOAM Requirement for ENNIs on p. 206

13.2
Service OAM Overview

In this section:

13.2.1 The MEF Service Life Cycle
13.2.2 SOAM Domains
13.2.3 SOAM Frames
13.2.4 SOAM Components
13.2.5 SOAM MEG Levels

Service OAM (SOAM) requirements are based on IEEE® 802.1Q[121], ITU-T Y.1731, and ITU-T G.8021 standards. MEF 17 and MEF 30.1 define the SOAM framework and requirements for Carrier Ethernet.

MEF 17 and MEF 35 specify the SOAM requirements for **Performance Management (PM)**, including the measurement of frame loss and frame delay for the calculation of performance metrics. MEF 30.1 specifies SOAM requirements for **Connectivity Fault Management (CFM)**, including continuity check message (CCM), remote defect indication (RDI), alarm indication signal (ETH-AIS), lock signal (ETH-LCK), test signal (ETH-Test), loopback, and link trace.

SOAM functionality is based on the exchange of Ethernet frames between SOAM components provisioned within network elements (NEs) across the network.

Related Links

SOAM Requirement for Type 2 UNIs on p. 170

13.2.1
The MEF Service Life Cycle

The MEF identifies Performance Management (PM) and Fault Management (FM) as critical components of a Carrier Ethernet service life cycle. Both are based on SOAM.

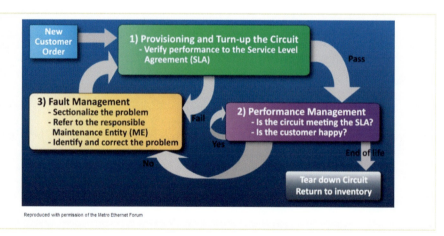

---

[121] IEEE 802.1ag-2007 (the original source of IEEE SOAM standards, referenced in older MEF specifications) has been incorporated into and superseded by IEEE 802.1Q-2011.

13.2.2
SOAM Domains

A SOAM domain is an Ethernet network or subnetwork that is of interest to, or the responsibility of, an administrative entity, such as the subscriber, the service provider, or an operator.

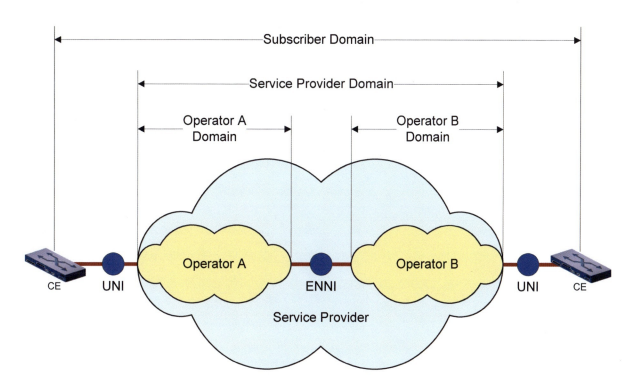

SOAM domains are defined, as required, subject to the following constraints:

- SOAM domains form a hierarchy with the subscriber domain at the highest level.
- Lower-level domains nest within higher-level domains.
- SOAM domains cannot overlap.

If service fails, the hierarchy of SOAM domains provides a framework for locating the failure and identifying the administrative organization that is responsible for fixing the fault.

SOAM provides each organization with the information it needs to perform its function without sharing privileged internal information with other organizations.

13.2.3
SOAM Frames

The term **SOAM frame** refers to any Ethernet frame injected into the network to support a SOAM function. SOAM frames are defined, as required, per SOAM function and have function-specific names, as shown in the following table.

SOAM Area	SOAM Function	SOAM Frame Name
Connectivity Fault Management	Connectivity Monitoring **Note:** RDI (Remote Defect Indication) is encoded in CCM frames.	CCM (Continuity Check Message)
		AIS (Alarm Indication Signal)
		LCK (Locked Signal)
		Test (Test Signal)
	Loopback	LBM (Loopback Message)
		LBR (Loopback Reply)
	Link Trace	LTM (Link Trace Message)
		LTR (Link Trace Reply)
Performance Management	Single-Ended Delay Measurement	DMM (Delay Measurement Message)
		DMR (Delay Measurement Reply)
	Single-Ended Synthetic Frame Loss Measurement	SLM (Synthetic Loss Message)
		SLR (Synthetic Loss Reply)
	Dual-Ended Delay Measurement	1DM (One-Way Delay Measurement)
	Single-Ended Service Frame Loss Measurement	LMM (Loss Measurement Message)
		LMR (Loss Measurement Reply)

Note: The terms **OAM frame**, **SOAM PDU**, and **SOAM frame** are used interchangeably in MEF 17, MEF 30.1, and MEF 35. The term **SOAM frame** is used in these lessons.

13.2.4
SOAM Components

The following table provides a summary of SOAM component definitions as they appear in MEF 30.1. These definitions follow ITU-T Y.1731 terminology. The last column indicates equivalent terminology from IEEE 802.1Q[122].

 Attention: If you are not already familiar with SOAM components, the definitions in the following table may be hard to follow. More friendly descriptions follow.

---

[122] IEEE 802.1ag-2007 (the original source of IEEE SOAM standards, referenced in older MEF specifications) has been incorporated into and superseded by IEEE 802.1Q-2011.

Ethernet OAM
Service OAM Overview

Component		Definition	IEEE 802.1Q Term
MEP	MEG End Point	An actively managed SOAM entity associated with a specific service instance that can generate and receive SOAM frames and track any responses. It is an end point of a single MEG and is an endpoint of a separate ME for each of the other MEPs in the same MEG.	Equivalent to a Maintenance association End Point (MEP) in IEEE 802.1Q
MIP	MEG Intermediate Point	A SOAM entity, associated with a single maintenance domain, that can generate SOAM frames, but only in response to received SOAM frames.	Equivalent to a Maintenance domain Intermediate Point (MIP) in IEEE 802.1Q
ME	Maintenance Entity	A point-to-point relationship between two MEPs within a single MEG.	Equivalent to a Maintenance Entity (ME) in IEEE 802.1Q.
MEG	Maintenance Entity Group	A set of MEs that exists in the same administrative boundary with the same MEG Level and MEG ID.	Equivalent to a Maintenance Association (MA) in IEEE 802.1Q

MEPs and MIPs

SOAM functionality is based on the exchange of SOAM frames between MEPs and MIPs provisioned within NEs across the network.

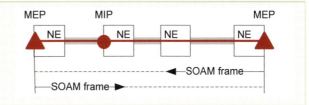

A **MEP (MEG End Point)** is a provisioned component that can initiate and terminate SOAM frames/processes and can also react to SOAM frames.

A **MIP (MEG Intermediate Point)** is a provisioned component that can only react to SOAM frames (for example, to support loopback or link trace). A MIP cannot initiate an SOAM process, but it can generate an SOAM frame in response to a received SOAM frame.

MEPs are always provisioned in pairs. One pair, plus any number of optional MIPs, is dedicated to a segment of the path of Carrier Ethernet service flow. The MEPs define endpoints for the path segment. MIPs, if used, are positioned between the MEPs.

SOAM frames are forwarded through the network like service frames, using the same Layer 2 infrastructure and forwarding mechanisms. However, unlike service frames, SOAM frames are subject to processing at MEPs and MIPs.

Maintenance Entity (ME)

The ME is a higher-level SOAM component, associated to a segment of the path of Carrier Ethernet service flow.

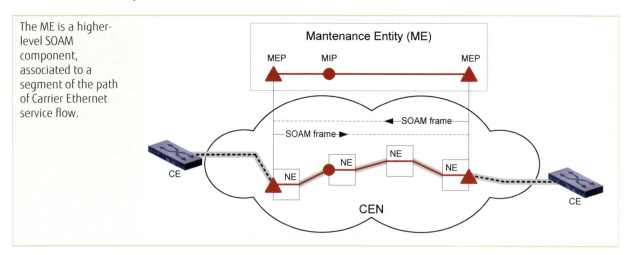

Every ME includes exactly two MEPs, defining endpoints for the ME, plus any number of (optional) MIPs.

Maintenance Entity Group (MEG)

The MEG is the highest-level SOAM component. It associates a set of MEs to a particular service and SOAM domain.

This figure illustrates a MEG supporting the service provider domain for a multipoint-to-multipoint EVC with three UNIs. This MEG includes three MEs (one for each combination of UNIs).

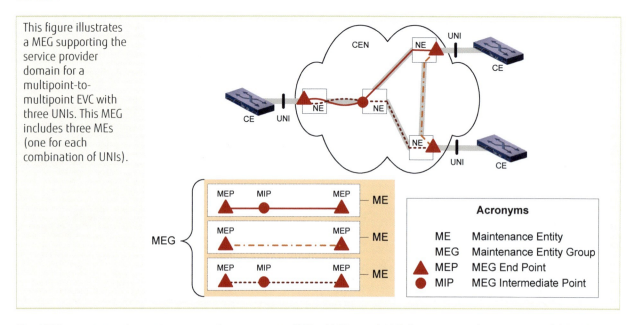

The MEG associates the entire group of components (MEs, MEPs, and MIPs) to a particular service and SOAM domain. A Carrier Ethernet service can have many MEGs.

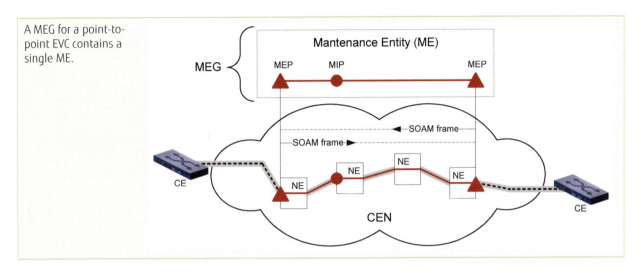

A MEG for a point-to-point EVC contains a single ME.

The MEG for a multipoint-to-multipoint EVC with n UNIs contains n*(n-1)/2 MEs.

Test your understanding: *(a)* Which SOAM components can initiate an SOAM process? *(b)* How many MIPs can an ME contain? *(c)* How many MEPs can an ME contain? *(d)* Can a point-to-point service have more than one ME? [123]

Up MEPs and Down MEPs

Every MEP is located at a specific network element (NE) interface and is provisioned to be either an Up MEP or a Down MEP. If the MEP's peer lies in the direction outward from the interface (away from the NE), it is provisioned as a **Down MEP**. If the MEP's peer lies in the opposite direction (inward toward the NE), it is provisioned as an **Up MEP**.

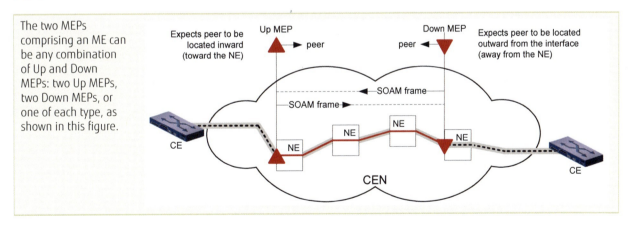

The two MEPs comprising an ME can be any combination of Up and Down MEPs: two Up MEPs, two Down MEPs, or one of each type, as shown in this figure.

---

[123] **Answers:** *(a)* Only the MEP. *(b)* Any number. *(c)* 2. *(d)* Yes. Any service, including any point-to-point service, can contain many MEGs. Each MEG in a point-to-point service has only one ME, but there can be many MEGs, so there can be many MEs.

13.2.5
SOAM MEG Levels

Per ITU-T Y.1731, SOAM supports eight MEG levels (0–7), which are used to differentiate SOAM traffic per administrative organization (subscriber, service provider, and operator).

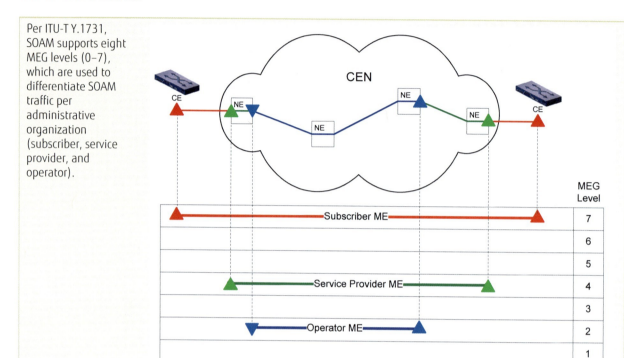

Lower-level MEGs are nested within higher-level MEGs.

 Important: With proper provisioning, each SOAM frame is confined to the MEG in which it originates. Lower-level MEGs allow SOAM frames for higher-level MEGs to pass through transparently (they do not react to, or change, higher-level frames; they simply forward them).

Suggested MEs and Default MEG Levels

MEG levels are allocated between administrative organizations (subscriber, service provider, and operators) based on mutual agreement.

MEF 17 suggests the following assignments as a baseline[124]:

- Subscriber uses MEG Level 7, 6, or 5.

- Service Provider uses MEG Level 3 or 4.

- Operators use MEG Levels 2, 1, or 0.

---

[124] This baseline allocation of MEG levels follows default MEG level assignments specified in ITU-T Y.1731.

MEF 30.1 further refines suggested ME allocation as illustrated in the following figure (Figure 1 in MEF 30.1).

Note: This is only an example. Not all MEs are required for every application.

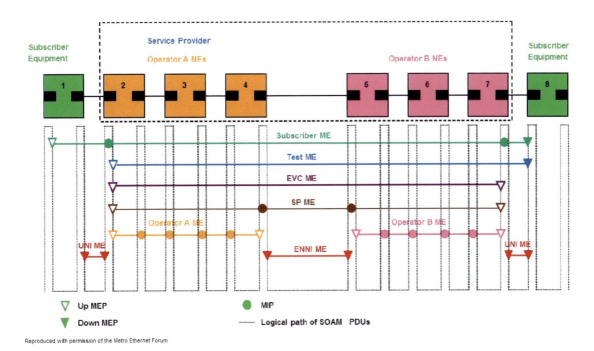

Per MEF 30.1, default MEG levels must conform to the following table (from Table 3 in MEF 30.1).

MEG	Suggested Usage	Default MEG Level
Subscriber MEG	Subscriber monitoring of a Carrier Ethernet service	6
Test MEG	Service Provider isolation of subscriber-reported problems	5
EVC MEG	Service Provider monitoring of EVC	4
Service Provider MEG	Service Provider Monitoring of Service Provider network	3
Operator MEG	Network Operator monitoring OVC	2
UNI MEG	Service Provider monitoring of a UNI	1
ENNI MEG	Network Operators' monitoring of an ENNI	1

The default allocation of the MEG Level space can be changed by mutual agreement of the parties involved (subscribers, service providers, and operators).

Test your understanding: For a given Carrier Ethernet service, can a service provider and an operator use the same MEG level? [125]

---

[125] **Answer:** In general no. But as shown in the preceding table, UNI MEGs (used by the service provider) and ENNI MEGs (used by operators) can be at the same MEG level.

13.3
SOAM-Related Service Attributes

In this section:

13.3.1 Attribute: UNI MEG
13.3.2 Attribute: Test MEG
13.3.3 Attribute: Subscriber MEG MIP

Prior to MEF 10.3 and MEF 6.2, no service attributes addressed SOAM functionality. MEF 10.3 and MEF 6.2 introduced three service attributes to specify basic SOAM functionality in EVC services.

Service Attribute		Requirement					
		Port-Based Service			VLAN-Based Service		
Cat.	Name	EPL	EP-LAN	EP-Tree	EVPL	EVP-LAN	EVP-Tree
Per UNI	UNI MEG	Enabled / Disabled					
EVC per UNI	Test MEG	Enabled / Disabled					
	Subscriber MEG MIP	Enabled / Disabled					

Related Links

Logically Related Service Attributes on p. 62

13.3.1
Attribute: UNI MEG

If attribute *UNI MEG = Enabled* (for a particular UNI), the UNI must be able to support a UNI MEG as specified in Section 7.9 of MEF 30.1.

To meet requirements, the UNI-C and the UNI-N must both be able to support a MEP on the UNI MEG, regardless of whether any EVC is configured for the UNI.

Enabling this attribute ensures that UNI connectivity can be tested, independently from any service(s) that may or may not be provisioned over it.

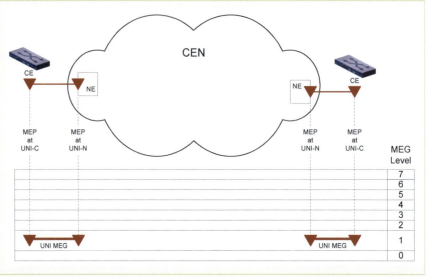

13.3.2
Attribute: Test MEG

If attribute *Test MEG* = *Enabled* (for a particular UNI and EVC), the service must be able to support a Test MEG as specified in Section 7.5 of MEF 30.1. A Test MEG involves one MEP located at the UNI-C and another MEP located somewhere in the service provider network.

The figure shows two Test MEGs, one for each UNI. Every Test MEG is associated with a particular EVC and includes one UNI.

Test MEGs are assigned to the service provider and are used for isolating subscriber-reported problems and activation testing.

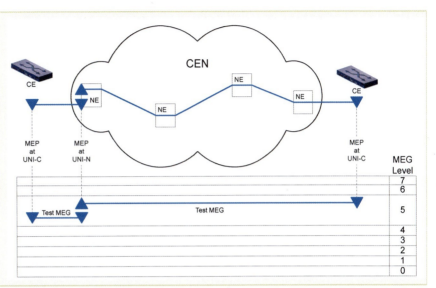

13.3.3
Attribute: Subscriber MEG MIP

If attribute *Subscriber MEG MIP* = *Enabled* (for a particular UNI and EVC), the service must instantiate a subscriber level MIP as specified in MEF 30.1. The MIP is located at the UNI-N (of the particular UNI) and is associated with the particular EVC.

In the example shown, two Subscriber MEG MIPs are instantiated, one for each UNI.

Instantiation of subscriber level MIPs at UNI-Ns can help subscribers troubleshoot connectivity issues using SOAM Link Trace.

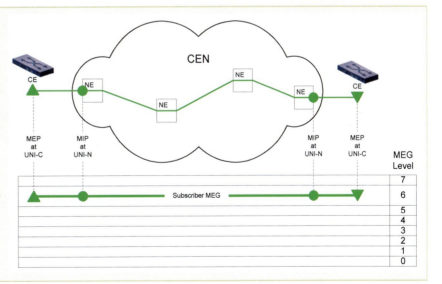

Related Links

SOAM Link Trace on p. 269

13.4
SOAM Connectivity Fault Management

In this section:

13.4.1	Continuity Check Message (CCM)	13.4.5	Test Signal (ETH-Test)
13.4.2	Remote Defect Indication (RDI)	13.4.6	SOAM Loopback
13.4.3	Alarm Indication Signal (ETH-AIS)	13.4.7	SOAM Link Trace
13.4.4	Locked Signal (ETH-LCK)		

SOAM connectivity fault management (CFM) is implemented per IEEE 802.1Q[126], ITU-T Y.1731 and ITU-T G.8021.

Note: Requirement [R2f] in MEF 17 states that **SOAM frames for connectivity SHOULD be transmitted at the highest priority permissible for the service**. This requirement is meant to ensure that SOAM frames for connectivity are less likely to be discarded in conditions of congestion.

13.4.1
Continuity Check Message (CCM)

A CCM is a type of SOAM frame. MEF 30.1 requires MEPs to support CCM messages and processes as defined in IEEE 802.1Q.

The MEPs within an ME exchange CCMs across the network to detect loss of continuity (LOC) and misprovisioning. Each MEP periodically sends a CCM to its peer and expects to periodically receive a CCM from its peer.

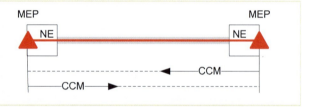

Per MEF 30.1, CCMs can be administratively turned on and off, but compliant NEs <u>must</u> support CCM intervals of 1 second and 10 seconds and <u>should</u> support intervals of 3.33 ms, 10 ms, and 100 ms.

If a MEP fails to receive a CCM within a provisioned time interval (3 times the CCM interval, by default), the MEP raises an LOC alarm.

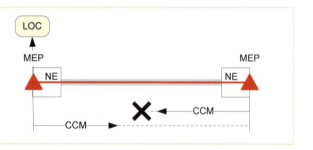

For connectivity monitoring, the CCM interval is commonly set to 1 second (or 10 seconds), which results in 3-second (or 30-second) LOC detection. For protection switching, the CCM interval is commonly set to 10 ms or 3.33 ms. For sub-50ms protection switching, the CCM interval can be set to 3.33 ms, which provides 10 ms LOC detection.

---

126   IEEE 802.1ag-2007 (the original source of IEEE SOAM standards, referenced in older MEF specifications) has been incorporated into and superseded by IEEE 802.1Q-2011.

13.4.2
Remote Defect Indication (RDI)

MEF 30.1 requires MEPs to support RDI as defined in IEEE 802.1Q[127] (equivalent to ETH-RDI in ITU-T Y.1731 and ITU-T G.8021).

A MEP uses RDI to inform its peer of LOC. When a MEP raises an LOC condition, the MEP encodes RDI in all outgoing CCMs (sets bit 8 of the CCM flags field to 1) until the LOC defect clears.

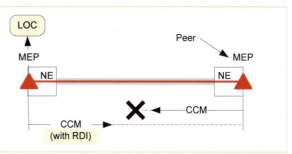

13.4.3
Alarm Indication Signal (ETH-AIS)

AIS is a type of SOAM frame that is used to support LOC condition suppression. Per MEF 30.1, MEPs should support ETH-AIS as defined in ITU-T Y.1731 and ITU-T G.8021. Per MEF 30.1, ETH-AIS is not intended for, or recommended for, multipoint services.

Without LOC condition suppression, a connectivity failure generally results in multiple levels of LOC, one for each MEG spanning the point of failure.

Several administrative domains are alerted to the fault, but each has no immediate way of knowing whether the fault originated at their level, so they can fix it, or at a lower level, which is the responsibility of another organization.

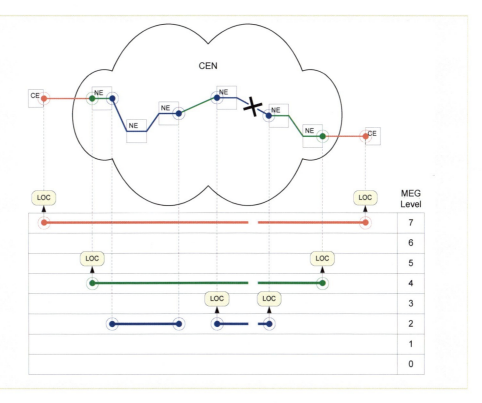

---

127 IEEE 802.1ag-2007 (the original source of IEEE SOAM standards, referenced in older MEF specifications) has been incorporated into and superseded by IEEE 802.1Q-2011.

AIS and LOC condition suppression resolves this issue by masking higher-level conditions, leaving only root-level LOC conditions in the network.

When an LOC condition occurs, MEPs send AIS frames away from their peers, causing higher-level MEPs in remote NEs to suppress LOC conditions. Now, if an unsuppressed LOC condition occurs, the organization knows that the fault originated at their level and that they need to fix it.

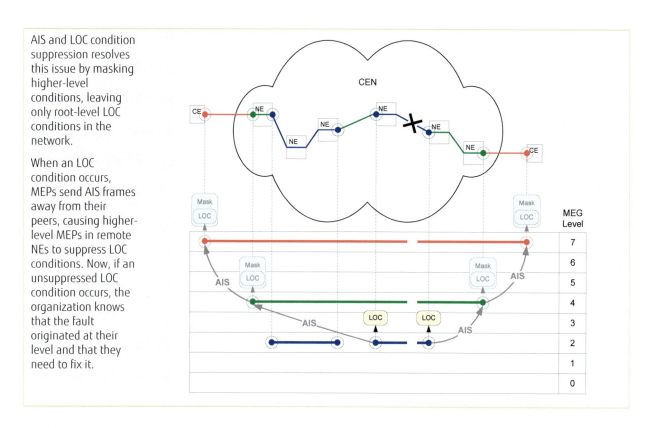

13.4.4
Locked Signal (ETH-LCK)

The ETH-LCK function is an administrative function that does two things when applied to a MEP:

1. Locks the MEP (stops it from forwarding data traffic)

2. Causes the MEP to send LCK signals to higher-level MEGs, indicating that traffic has been interrupted for administrative purposes (rather than by a defect)

Per MEF 30.1, MEPs should support ETH-LCK as defined in ITU-T Y.1731 and ITU-T G.8021.

Note: *Per MEF 30.1, ETH-LCK is not intended for, or recommended for, multipoint services.*

The ETH-LCK function allows an operator to stop traffic flow through a MEP for any purpose, but is generally used to support out-of-service testing (using ETH-Test, for example).

Ethernet OAM
SOAM Connectivity Fault Management

Without LCK signaling, a locked MEP would look like a fault to each higher-level MEG spanning the locked MEP. As shown in the following figure, LOCs would occur because CCMs would not be forwarded through the locked MEP.

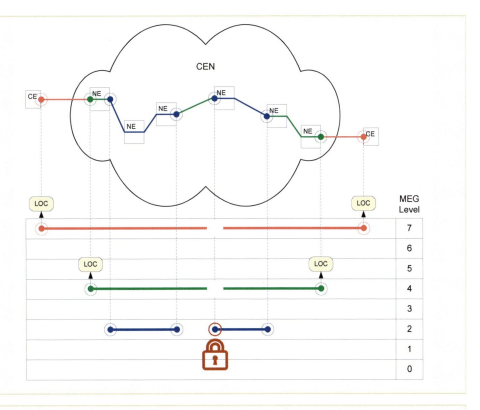

However, when the ETH-LCK function is applied to a MEP, the MEP stops forwarding traffic and begins sending LCK frames (a type of SOAM frame) periodically in both directions. These LCK frames support LOC condition suppression as shown in the figure.

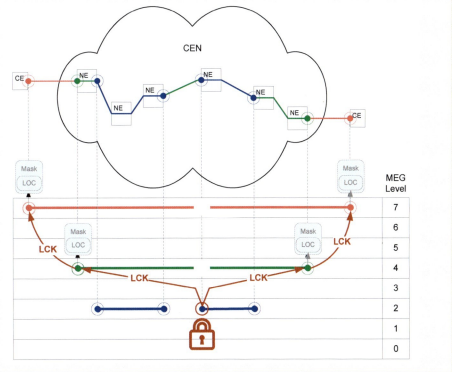

Note: LCK frames, like AIS frames, support LOC condition suppression. However, LCK frames indicate that traffic interruption is due to administrative locking, rather than due to a defect condition.

13.4.5
Test Signal (ETH-Test)

The ETH-Test function is an administrative function that is applied to a MEP to trigger one-way in-service or out-of-service diagnostic tests between itself and its peer MEP. The ETH-Test function causes the MEP to send test frames with specified throughput, test patterns, and frame size to its peer MEP. It also causes the peer MEP to monitor received test frames, detect errors, and report errors (such as bit error rates).

Per MEF 30.1, MEPs can support ETH-Test as defined in ITU-T Y.1731 and ITU-T G.8021.

If the MEP is configured for **out-of-service ETH-Test testing**, the MEP is locked (stops forwarding data traffic) and sends LCK frames, as previously described for the ETH-LCK function. If the MEP is configured for **in-service ETH-Test testing**, the MEP is not locked (continues to forward data traffic). In this case, care must be taken to ensure that bandwidth consumed by test frames is limited (so that services are not unacceptably impacted).

13.4.6
SOAM Loopback

SOAM loopback, defined by IEEE 802.1Q[128], is different from the traditional loopback, which redirects existing traffic flow back toward its source. SOAM loopback is more similar to an Internet Control Message Protocol (ICMP) **ping**, which tests target reachability. SOAM loopback sends a stream of test frames from a source MEP to a target MEP/MIP with instructions to return a reply to the sender. SOAM loopback also offers options to set frame characteristics, such as size, CoS, and drop-eligibility (green/yellow).

SOAM Loopback uses two types of SOAM frames, loopback messages (LBMs) and loopback replies (LBRs).

An LBM is sent from a MEP towards its peer targeting a specific MIP or MEP in the same ME. If the target MIP/MEP receives the LBM, it immediately returns an LBR.

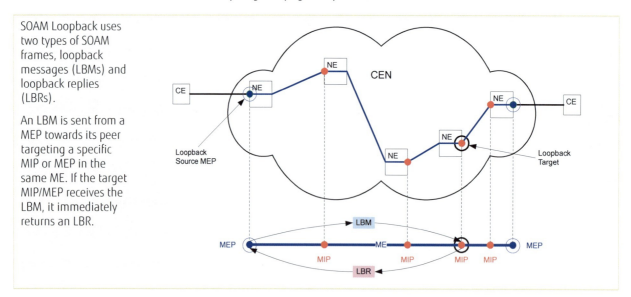

LBMs are sent as a loopback session of N (default is 3) consecutive LBMs in a predefined time interval. If an LBR is not received within a given time interval (default is 5 seconds), the MEP declares a reachability fault.

Unlike LOAM loopback, SOAM Loopback is not service disrupting.

---

128 IEEE 802.1ag-2007 (the original source of IEEE SOAM standards, referenced in older MEF specifications) has been incorporated into and superseded by IEEE 802.1Q-2011.

13.4.7
SOAM Link Trace

SOAM Link Trace, defined by IEEE 802.1Q[129], is used to test connectivity and to troubleshoot connectivity issues.

Note: *SOAM Link Trace is analogous to Internet Control Message Protocol (ICMP)* **traceroute**.

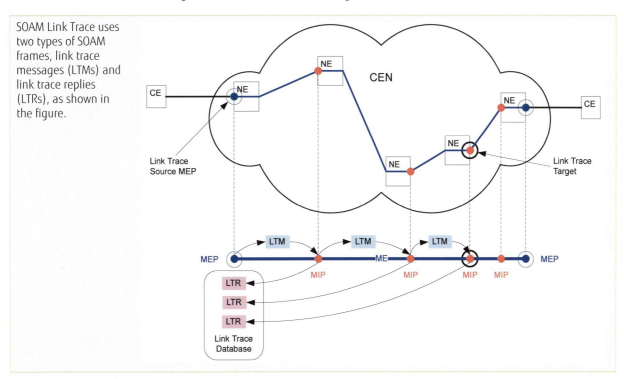

SOAM Link Trace uses two types of SOAM frames, link trace messages (LTMs) and link trace replies (LTRs), as shown in the figure.

An LTM is sent from a MEP towards its peer targeting a specific MIP or MEP in the same ME.

The LTM travels to the first MIP/MEP encountered with a matching MEG level (in the same ME). There it triggers the MIP/MEP to send a link trace reply (LTR) back to the source and (if it is not the target MEP/MIP) to forward the LTM onward toward the target MEP/MIP. The process continues in this way until the target is reached or until TTL (time to live) terminates the process. LTR data, collected at the source MEP, can then be analyzed to troubleshoot connectivity issues.

---

[129] IEEE 802.1ag-2007 (the original source of IEEE SOAM standards, referenced in older MEF specifications) has been incorporated into and superseded by IEEE 802.1Q-2011.

13.5
SOAM Performance Management

In this section:

13.5.1	SOAM Framework for Measuring Performance Metrics	13.5.4	Single-Ended Delay
13.5.2	Synthetic Frames versus Service Frames	13.5.5	Single-Ended Synthetic Loss
13.5.3	Single-Ended versus Dual-Ended PM Functions	13.5.6	Dual-Ended Delay
		13.5.7	Single-Ended Service Loss
		13.5.8	The Performance Monitoring Process

SOAM Performance Management (PM) addresses the problem of measuring EVC/OVC performance, for example, to verify that performance objectives specified in the SLS are met.

From previous lessons, recall that:

- Frame delivery performance for an EVC-based service is specified using the **EVC Performance** service attribute.

- Frame delivery performance for an OVC-based service is specified using the **Service Level Specification** service attribute.

In either case, performance is specified per CoS in the SLS using eight performance objectives (limiting values for eight performance metrics). As shown in the following table, four of the performance metrics are related to frame loss, and the other four are related to frame delay.

Frame Loss – Related Performance Metrics	Frame Delay – Related Performance Metrics
• Frame Loss Ratio (FLR) • Availability • High Loss Intervals (HLI) • High Loss Intervals (CHLI)	• Frame Delay (FD) • Frame Delay Range (FDR) • Mean Frame Delay (MFD) • Inter-Frame Delay Variation (IFDV)

SOAM PM defines techniques for measuring these performance metrics.

Note: For clarity, you may want to quickly review the **EVC Performance** service attribute (for EVC-based service) and the **Service Level Specification** service attribute (for OVC-based service), which were described in an earlier lesson.

Related Links

Service Level Specification (OVC Service Attribute) on p. 206
EVC Performance on p. 147

13.5.1
SOAM Framework for Measuring Performance Metrics

The MEF framework for SOAM PM, initially defined in MEF 17, has been extended in MEF 35.

Note: *The initial MEF-CECP exam did not include extensions to SOAM PM introduced in MEF 35.*

The extended framework, defined in MEF 35, is based on the concept of a *PM Solution*.

> **PM Solution** — A set of related requirements that when implemented allow a given set of performance metrics to be measured using a given set of PM functions

As shown in the following figure[130], a PM Solution can involve components at three layers: the Network Element (NE) layer, the Element Management Systems (EMS) layer, and the Network Management System (NMS) layer.

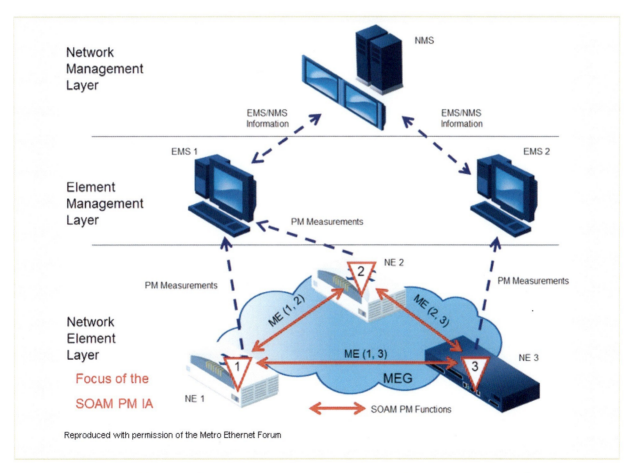

The NE layer is responsible for conducting performance measurements, while the EMS and NMS layers are responsible for configuring, collecting, and processing performance measurements to determine one or more performance metrics for the MEG.

---

130   Figure 4 in MEF 35.

MEF 35 focuses on the NE layer and defines requirements for three PM solutions (PM-1, PM-2, and PM-3) <u>at the NE layer only</u>.

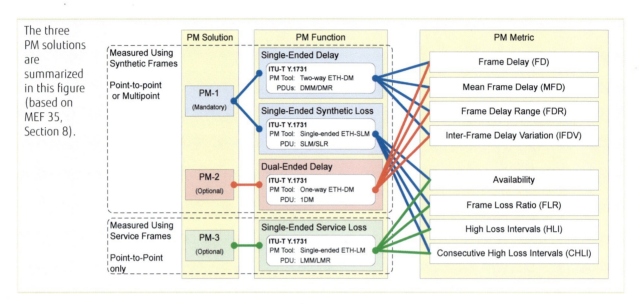

The three PM solutions are summarized in this figure (based on MEF 35, Section 8).

As shown in the figure, each PM solution supports the determination of four or eight PM metrics using one or two *PM functions*. Support for PM-1 is mandatory, while PM-2 and PM-3 are optional.

PM Function – A MEP capability specified for performance monitoring purposes.

MEF 35 defines four PM functions: *Single-Ended Delay*, *Single-Ended Synthetic Loss*, *Dual-Ended Delay*, and *Single-Ended Service Loss*

As shown in the following table[131], each PM Function is implemented using an ITU-T–defined **PM Tool** that uses one or two ITU-T–defined **PDUs**.

PM Function	ITU-T Y.1731	
	PM Tool	PDU(s)
Single-Ended Delay	Two-Way ETH-DM	DMM (Delay Measurement Message)
		DMR (Delay Measurement Reply)
Single-Ended Synthetic Loss	Single-Ended ETH-SLM	SLM (Synthetic Loss Message)
		SLR (Synthetic Loss Reply)
Dual-Ended Delay	One-Way ETH-DM	1DM (One-Way Delay Measurement)
Single-Ended Service Loss	Single-Ended ETH-LM	LMM (Loss Measurement Message)
		LMR (Loss Measurement Reply)

---

131 Based on Table 3 in MEF 35

13.5.2
Synthetic Frames versus Service Frames

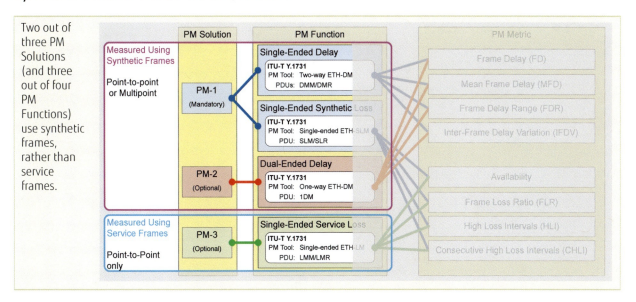

Two out of three PM Solutions (and three out of four PM Functions) use synthetic frames, rather than service frames.

Synthetic frames are Ethernet frames that are created to emulate service traffic for performance measurement purposes. They are not service frames, but they are treated in the network like service frames. Synthetic frames are used in place of service frames because they can carry additional information, such as time stamp and/or identification data, which may be needed or useful for calculating frame delay or frame loss.

As shown in the previous figure, PM-3 (which uses service frames) has limited utility compared to PM-1 and PM-2 (which use synthetic frames):

- PM-3 only supports MEGs with two MEPs (point-to-point MEGs), while PM-1 and PM-2 can support MEGs with two or more MEPs (multipoint MEGs).
- PM-3 can only determine frame loss-related metrics (not frame delay-related metrics).

These limitations are due to the limited utility of service frames (compared to synthetic frames) in measuring PM metrics.

13.5.3 Single-Ended versus Dual-Ended PM Functions

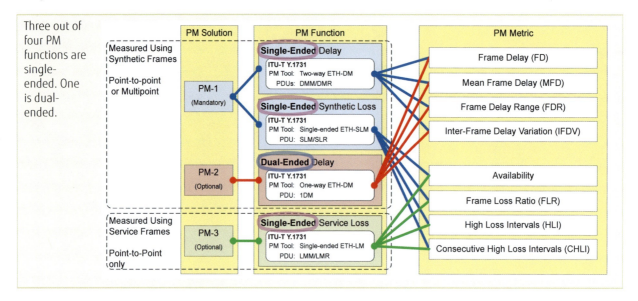

Per MEF 35, the following definitions apply:

Single-ended — A type of process where a MEP sends a measurement request and the peer MEP replies with the requested information so the originating MEP can calculate the measurement

Dual-ended — A type of process where a MEP sends measurement information to a peer MEP that will perform the calculations.

Each of the three single-ended PM functions use two SOAM PDUs (a message PDU and a reply PDU). The dual-ended PM function (Dual-ended Delay) uses only one SOAM PDU.

Ethernet OAM
SOAM Performance Management

13.5.4
Single-Ended Delay

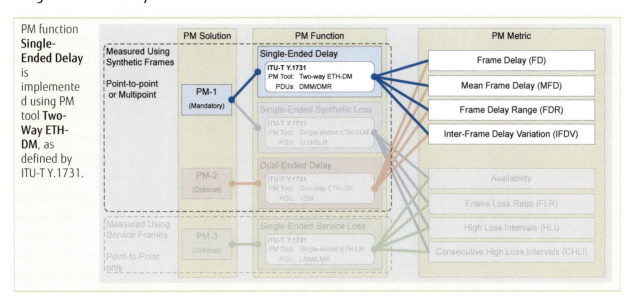

PM function **Single-Ended Delay** is implemented using PM tool **Two-Way ETH-DM**, as defined by ITU-T Y.1731.

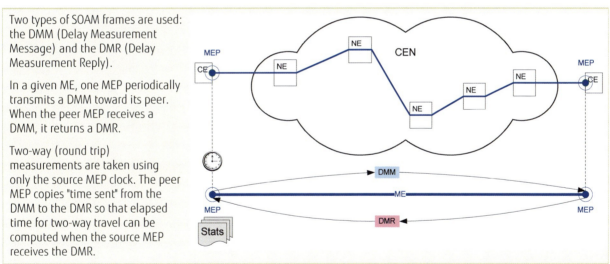

Two types of SOAM frames are used: the DMM (Delay Measurement Message) and the DMR (Delay Measurement Reply).

In a given ME, one MEP periodically transmits a DMM toward its peer. When the peer MEP receives a DMM, it returns a DMR.

Two-way (round trip) measurements are taken using only the source MEP clock. The peer MEP copies "time sent" from the DMM to the DMR so that elapsed time for two-way travel can be computed when the source MEP receives the DMR.

Single-Ended Delay measurement:

- Measures the delay of synthetic frames (not service frames)
- Provides data for computing frame delay-related PM metrics (FD, MFD, FDR, and IFDV)
- Can be applied to point-to-point MEGs and multipoint MEGs

In multipoint-to-multipoint and rooted-multipoint service applications, multiple MEs may be involved because PM metrics are measured over an agreed subset of ordered UNI pairs, as specified in the SLS. Separate measurements are made per CoS.

13.5.5
Single-Ended Synthetic Loss

PM function **Single-ended Synthetic Loss** is implemented using PM tool **Single-ended ETH-SLM**, as defined by ITU-T Y.1731.

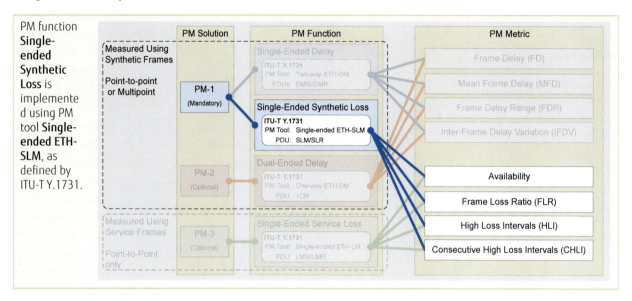

Two types of SOAM frames are used: the SLM (Synthetic Loss Message) and the SLR (Synthetic Loss Reply).

In a given ME, one MEP periodically transmits an SLM toward its peer. When the peer MEP receives an SLM, it returns an SLR. Both MEPs keep count of synthetic frames sent and received.

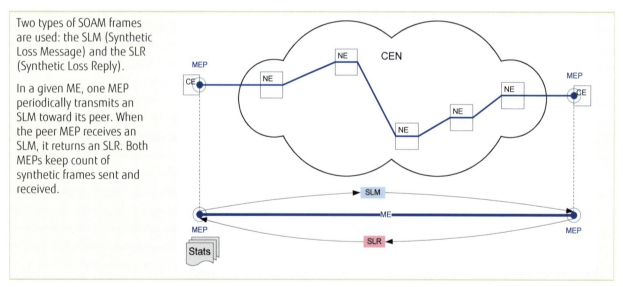

Single-Ended Synthetic Loss measurement:

- Measures the loss of synthetic frames (not service frames)
- Provides data for computing frame loss-related PM metrics (Availability, FLR, HLI, and CHLI)
- Can be applied to point-to-point MEGs and multipoint MEGs

In multipoint service applications, multiple MEs may be involved because PM metrics are measured over an agreed subset of ordered UNI pairs, as specified in the SLS. Separate measurements are made per CoS.

13.5.6
Dual-Ended Delay

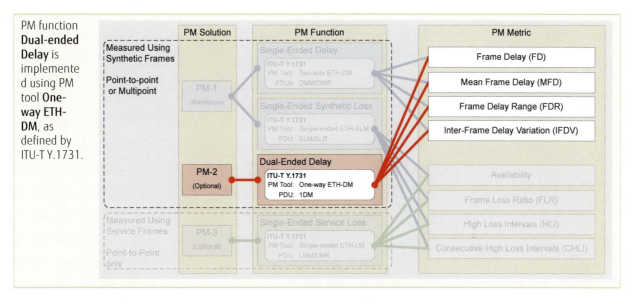

PM function **Dual-ended Delay** is implemented using PM tool **One-way ETH-DM**, as defined by ITU-T Y.1731.

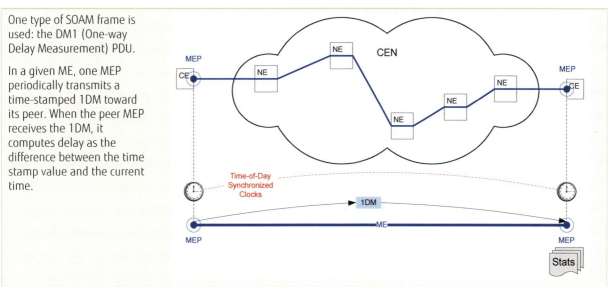

One type of SOAM frame is used: the DM1 (One-way Delay Measurement) PDU.

In a given ME, one MEP periodically transmits a time-stamped 1DM toward its peer. When the peer MEP receives the 1DM, it computes delay as the difference between the time stamp value and the current time.

The clocks at the two MEPs must be **time-of-day synchronized**. If delay measurement is required for both directions, a second instance of Dual-ended Delay measurement is applied in the opposite direction.

Dual-Ended Delay measurement:

- Measures the delay of synthetic frames (not service frames)
- Provides data for computing frame delay-related PM metrics (FD, MFD, FDR, and IFDV)
- Can be applied to point-to-point MEGs and multipoint MEGs

In multipoint service applications, multiple MEs may be involved because PM metrics are measured over an agreed subset of ordered UNI pairs, as specified in the SLS. Separate measurements are made per CoS.

Related Links

Frequency, Phase, and Time-of-Day Synchronization on p. 371

13.5.7
Single-Ended Service Loss

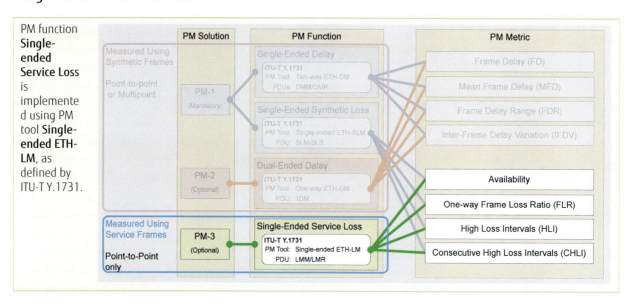

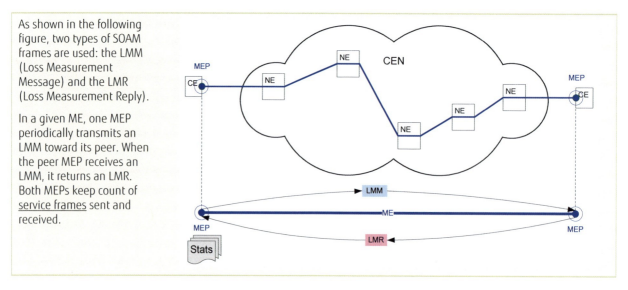

> Single-Ended Service Loss measurement:
> - Measures the loss of service frames (not synthetic frames)
> - Provides data for computing frame loss-related PM metrics (Availability, FLR, HLI, and CHLI)
> - Is applicable to MEGs with two MEPs (point-to-point MEGs) only

Separate measurements are made per CoS.

13.5.8 The Performance Monitoring Process

Per MEF 35, the performance monitoring process is made up of a number of performance monitoring instances, known as PM Sessions.

> **PM Session** — an instance of a PM Solution between a given pair of MEPs using a given CoS frame set over a given (possibly indefinite) period of time

A PM Session is initiated on a MEP to take performance measurements for a given CoS frame set in conjunction with its peer MEP. A PM Session can be classified as either a loss measurement session or a delay measurement session, depending on the PM function used.

Various parameters define a PM session, including start time, end time, and frequency of SOAM frame transmission. Time within a PM session is divided into discrete, non-overlapping periods of time called measurement intervals.

> **Measurement Interval** — A period of time within a PM session in which PM session measurements are performed and results are gathered. Measurements initiated during one measurement interval are kept separate from measurements taken during other measurement intervals.

Note: A measurement interval is different from T (the time interval over which a performance objective is defined).

Results for loss measurement sessions are stored directly, per measurement interval, as shown in this example (Figure 8 in MEF 35). This example is for a MEP running a Single-Ended Synthetic Loss PM function that measures loss separately for each direction.

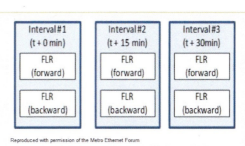

Results for delay measurement sessions are stored, per measurement interval, using measurement bins.

> **Measurement Bin** — a counter that stores the number of delay measurements falling within a specified range during a measurement interval

This figure (Figure 7 in MEF 35) illustrates the relationship between measurement intervals and measurement bins.

Interval #1 (t + 0 min)	Interval #2 (t + 15 min)	Interval #3 (t + 30 min)
FD Bin #0	FD Bin #0	FD Bin #0
FD Bin #1	FD Bin #1	FD Bin #1
FD Bin #2	FD Bin #2	FD Bin #2
FD Bin #3	FD Bin #3	FD Bin #3
MFD	MFD	MFD

Reproduced with permission of the Metro Ethernet Forum

Each bin is defined by a configurable threshold value, as illustrated in this example (Table 5 in MEF 35).

Bin	Threshold	Range
bin 0	0 µs	0 µs ≤ measurement < 5,000 µs
bin 1	5,000 µs	5,000 µs ≤ measurement < 10,000 µs
bin 2	10,000 µs	10,000 µs ≤ measurement < 15,000 µs
bin 3	15,000 µs	15,000 µs ≤ measurement < ∞

Reproduced with permission of the Metro Ethernet Forum

Measurement intervals and measurement bins reduce that amount of memory that an NE needs for storing PM data:

- Rather than store the time at which the measurement is made (individually for each measurement), each measurement is simply associated to a predefined measurement interval.

- Rather than store values individually for each delay measurement, each delay measurement simply increments the counter for a predefined measurement bin.

Each PM Session uses a PM Function. Each PM Function uses a specific ITU-T PM Tool which in turn uses specific ITU-T PDU(s).

Multiple PM Sessions can be run simultaneously between the MEPs, allowing for multiple classes of service to be tested.

PM Sessions define how PM data is measured and stored at the NE layer. As previously explained, the NE layer is responsible for conducting performance measurements, while the EMS and NMS layers are responsible for configuring, collecting, and processing performance measurements to determine performance metrics.

Related Links
SOAM Framework for Measuring Performance Metrics on p. 271

13.6
Review: Ethernet OAM

1. Which one of the following statements describes how frame loss ratio (FLR) is measured for an EPL service?

    a. For each EVC CoS, count all green and yellow frames sent and received over an agreed time interval.
    b. For each EVC CoS, count all green frames sent and received over an agreed time interval.
    c. For an EVC, count all frames sent and received (regardless of CoS) over an agreed time interval.
    d. For an EVC, count all green and yellow frames sent and received over an agreed time interval.

2. NE A and NE B are connected by an Ethernet link. Brian, an operator, has access only to NE B (NE B is in Brian's domain of operations, but NE A is not). Which two options below can be available (with correct provisioning) to Brian? (Choose two.)

    a. Use SOAM loopback to redirect all traffic at NE A back toward NE B.
    b. Use SOAM loopback to verify link connectivity.
    c. Use LOAM loopback to redirect all traffic at NE B back toward NE A.
    d. Use LOAM loopback to redirect all traffic at NE A back toward NE B.
    e. Use RDI to initiate LOAM link discovery.

3. Which one of the following is not an SOAM frame?

    a. Connectivity Check Message (CCM)
    b. Alarm Indication Signal (AIS)
    c. Remote defect indication (RDI)
    d. Loss Measurement Message (LMM)

4. Which two of the following statements are correct ? (Choose two.)

    a. LOAM support is required for Type 2.1 UNIs and at ENNIs.
    b. SOAM CCMs can support 50 ms protection switching.
    c. SOAM domains can overlap.
    d. An ME can include more than two MEPs.
    e. An ME can include any number of MIPs.

5. If a MEP sends a Loss Measurement Message (LMM), where does it go?

    a. To all MEPs in every ME
    b. To peer MIPs in the same ME
    c. To all MIPs in every ME
    d. To all MEPs in the MEG
    e. To the peer MEP in the same ME

6. Per MEF 30.1, to whom does the EVC MEG belong?

   a. Subscriber
   b. Service Provider
   c. Operator
   d. Subscriber and Operator
   e. Operator and Service Provider

7. Which PM function requires time-of-day synchronization of MEP clocks?

   a. Single-Ended Delay
   b. Dual-Ended Delay
   c. Single-Ended Service Loss
   d. Dual-Ended Service Loss

8. To isolate a fault within a point-to-point OVC, an operator can:

   a. Inspect all continuity check messages (CCMs) for the appropriate ME.
   b. Initiate SOAM Loopback over the appropriate ME.
   c. Send a frame loss measurement message (LMM) to the appropriate peer MEP.
   d. Process the most recent remote defect indicator (RDI) per IEEE 802.1Q.
   e. Initiate SOAM Link Trace over the appropriate ME.

9. Which Maintenance Entity (ME) should the service provider use to monitor the performance of an Ethernet service that spans two Operator CENs?

   a. Subscriber ME
   b. EVC ME
   c. Operator ME
   d. ENNI ME
   e. UNI ME

10. Which two SOAM frames are used for performance monitoring? (Choose two.)

    a. CCM (Continuity Check Message)
    b. LMM (Loss Measurement Message)
    c. LBM (Loopback Message)
    d. LTM (Link Trace Message)
    e. DMM (Delay Measurement Message)

11. One-way frame delay for a service frame in an EVC-based service... (Choose two.)

    a. Measures time of travel, CE-to-CE, for the first bit in the service frame.
    b. Includes the time of transmission between the UNI-C and the UNI-N at both UNIs.
    c. Includes the time that the service frame waits in queue at the CE to be scheduled for transmission.
    d. Depends on the length of the service frame.

12. Which four of the following items are connectivity fault management (CFM) functions? (Choose four.)

    a. Remote defect indication (RDI)
    b. Link Trace
    c. Frame Delay Measurement
    d. Alarm Indication Signal (AIS)
    e. Loopback
    f. Frame Loss Measurement

13. How many ordered UNI pairs are in a multipoint-to-multipoint EVC containing three UNIs?

    a. Two
    b. Three
    c. Six
    d. Nine

14. Which two statements about SOAM frames are true? (Choose two.)

    a. AIS frames are sent away from the direction of failure.
    b. AIS frames are sent toward the direction of failure.
    c. CCM frames containing RDI are sent away from the direction of failure.
    d. CCM frames containing RDI are sent toward the direction of failure.

15. A PM function requires two SOAM PDUs (a message PDU and a reply PDU) to calculate a performance measurement. In MEF 35, this type of PM function is called a ...

    a. Single-ended PM function
    b. Dual-ended PM function
    c. Loopback PM function
    d. Reciprocal PM function

16. Which two PM functions can be used to measure High Loss Intervals (HLIs)? (Choose two.)

    a. Single-Ended Delay
    b. Single-Ended Synthetic Loss
    c. Dual-Ended Delay
    d. Single-Ended Service Loss

17. Which service attribute is important to subscribers who anticipate using Link Trace to troubleshoot connectivity issues?

    a. Subscriber MEG MIP
    b. Test MEG
    c. UNI MEG
    d. Link OAM

18. Among the following MEs, which has the highest default MEG level?

    a. Operator ME
    b. EVC ME
    c. Test ME
    d. ENNI ME

Related Links

Answers: Ethernet OAM on p. 429

14
Access Technologies

In this chapter:

14.1 Access versus Transport Technology
14.2 Ethernet over Optical Fiber
14.3 Ethernet over PDH
14.4 Ethernet over Copper
14.5 Ethernet over Wireless Network
14.6 Ethernet over HFC
14.7 Summary: Access Technologies
14.8 Review: Access Technologies

Service providers need to support subscribers through a wide variety of access technologies, which are also called "first-mile" or "last-mile" technologies.

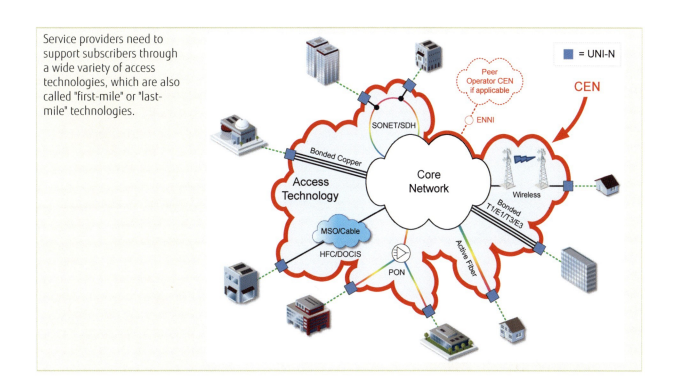

The Access Technologies

The following table, taken from the MEF white paper *Delivering Ubiquitous Ethernet Services using an Array of Access Technologies*, provides a summary of Carrier Ethernet access technologies.

 Hint: In the MEF White Papers area of the MEF Web site (mef.net), the link to this white paper is titled Carrier Ethernet – the Technology of Choice for Access Networks.

Summary of Carrier Ethernet Access Technologies

Carrier Ethernet Access Method	Technology Alternatives	Deployment Scenarios (When to use the technology)	Advantages
Ethernet over Fiber	- Active Ethernet - Ethernet over SONET/SDH - Passive Optical Network	- On-net buildings - Greenfield - Dense Metro area - 1Gbit/s or greater bandwidth requirements	- Highest bandwidth - Noise immunity - Security - Long reach - SONET/SDH leverage existing - Growth potential via xWDM
Ethernet over PDH	- Bonded T1/E1 - DS3/E3 and bonded DS3/E3	- Remote branch offices - Off-net customer locations (out of region, type 2) - SMB	- Leverage existing transport - Universally deployable - Lower CAPEX - No reach limitations - Well understood provisioning - Resiliency through bonding
Ethernet over Copper	- 2BASE-TL - 10PASS-TS	- Remote branch offices - On-net or off-net - SMB - Campus settings - Traffic monitoring	- Ubiquitous copper availability - Rapid deployment - Low cost unbundled local loop - Resiliency through bonding
Wireless Ethernet	- Terrestrial microwave - WiMAX - Broadband wireless - Free space optics - WiFi	- Remote branch office - Campus setting - No fiber or copper available - Mobility required	- Installation requires no trenching - Rapid deployment - Some alternatives offer mobility
Hybrid Fiber Coax	DOCSIS 2.x/3.x	- Work at home - SOHO/SMB - Remote branch office	- Extensive coverage - High performance options - Deep penetration into residential and suburban geographies

Reproduced with permission of the Metro Ethernet Forum. From white paper " "Delivering Ubiquitous Ethernet Services using an Array of Access Technologies".

For the MEF-CECP exam, it is important to know how each technology operates and their merits. Given an application scenario, you should also be able to identify which access technologies meet stated requirements.

 Hint: Consider jumping ahead to preview Summary: Access Technologies, which may help you to visualize what you are expected to take away from this lesson.

Key Areas for Comparing the Access Technologies

The access technologies differ in the following key areas:

- **Transmission Medium**—Through what substance is traffic supported? For example, is traffic carried over optical fiber, copper wire, or coaxial cable, or is it transmitted through the air?

- **Infrastructure Availability**—Does the technology use infrastructure that is already in place (commonly available), or does it require new infrastructure to be deployed?

- **Bandwidth (Speed and Symmetry)**—What speeds of Carrier Ethernet service can the technology support (for example, 10 Mb/s, 1 Gb/s, or 40 Gb/s)? Is the technology neutral with respect to upstream versus downstream bandwidth support, or is it inherently asymmetric?

- **Distance**—Over what distances can the technology operate?

- **Reliability**—Does the technology support protection/resiliency mechanisms?

- Cost

Attention: By necessity, this lesson makes generalizations about relative cost and performance characteristics, such as maximum bandwidth and distance capabilities. These generalizations align with technology at the time the initial MEF-CECP exam was developed (circa 2010). These generalizations are not meant to capture performance records or to be perfectly current.

14.1
Access versus Transport Technology

The MEF-CECP exam tests for general knowledge of technologies that service providers and operators may use to implement a Carrier Ethernet Service. In this context, the CEN or Operator CEN is understood to include:

1. A core network that is implemented with **Transport Technology**, and

2. Access links that are implemented with **Access Technology**. Here, **access link** refers to the connection between the UNI-N to the core network.

The term *Access* or *Transport* declares the *role* that a technology serves in a Carrier Service implementation, not an inherent property of the technology itself.

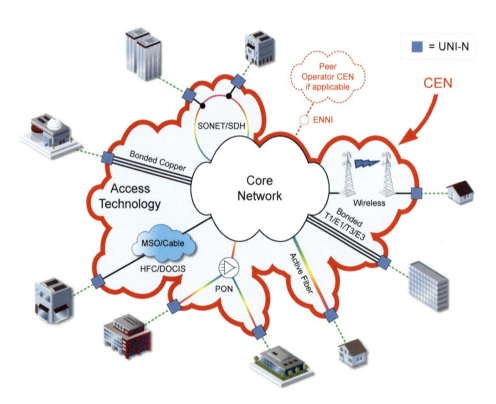

MEF standards do not preclude any technology from either role (access or transport).[132] Classification of technologies (as access or transport) is based on the current MEF-CECP Certification Exam Blueprint and reference materials, which reflects conventional practice (not what is theoretically viable or required by standard).

This lesson identifies and describes technologies that are well suited to the access role. The next lesson identifies and describes technologies that are well suited to the transport role.

---

[132] Carrier Ethernet services are defined to be agnostic with respect to technology (excluding technologies used to implement UNIs and ENNIs, such as IEEE 802.3 Ethernet).

14.2 Ethernet over Optical Fiber

In this section:

14.2.1 Ethernet over Active Fiber
14.2.2 Ethernet over SONET/SDH
14.2.3 Ethernet over PON

\multicolumn{4}{c}{Summary of Carrier Ethernet Access Technologies}			
Carrier Ethernet Access Method	Technology Alternatives	Deployment Scenarios (When to use the technology)	Advantages
Ethernet over Fiber	- Active Ethernet - Ethernet over SONET/SDH - Passive Optical Network	- On-net buildings - Greenfield - Dense Metro area - 1Gbit/s or greater bandwidth requirements	- Highest bandwidth - Noise immunity - Security - Long reach - SONET/SDH leverage existing - Growth potential via xWDM

Reproduced with permission of the Metro Ethernet Forum. From white paper " "Delivering Ubiquitous Ethernet Services using an Array of Access Technologies".

14.2.1 Ethernet over Active Fiber

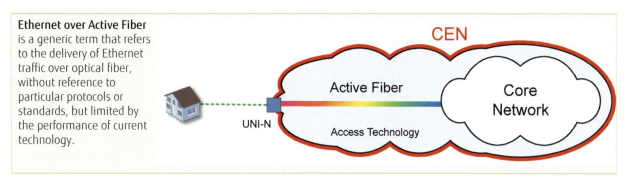

Ethernet over Active Fiber is a generic term that refers to the delivery of Ethernet traffic over optical fiber, without reference to particular protocols or standards, but limited by the performance of current technology.

Ethernet over fiber technologies can support very high bandwidth (exceeding 100 Gb/s)[133] over great distances (exceeding 150 km using standard optics without amplification/regeneration).

---

[133] As of March 2012, a single optical fiber can support 100 Gb/s without wavelength division multiplexing (WDM). With WDM, a single fiber-optic cable can support up to 88 DWDM wavelengths (at 100 Gb/s each) or 8.8 Tb/s.

14.2.2 Ethernet over SONET/SDH

Ethernet over SONET/SDH (EoS) is a point-to-point technology that uses fixed-size TDM time slots to transport Ethernet frames over fiber-optic cables. The time slots can be concatenated together to match bandwidth requirements.

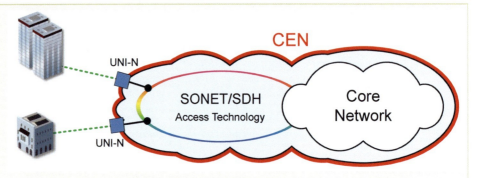

Advantages of EoS include:

- Widely deployed and available worldwide
- Highly reliable and traditionally regarded as the "gold standard" for resiliency (sub-50 ms protection/restoration, Layer 1 security)
- Fully standardized OAM tools for performance monitoring and fault detection
- Capable of simultaneously supporting both TDM and Ethernet
- Capable of supporting a wide range of bandwidths from 1.5 Mb/s (using subrate virtual tributary signals) up to 40 Gb/s
- No distance limitation

Note: SONET/SDH is described in more detail in the Transport Technology lesson.

Related Links

SONET/SDH (Synchronous Optical Network / Synchronous Digital Hierarchy) on p. 308

14.2.3 Ethernet over PON

A **passive optical network (PON)** is a point-to-multipoint optical fiber technology that uses unpowered optical splitters to enable a single optical fiber to serve multiple UNIs.

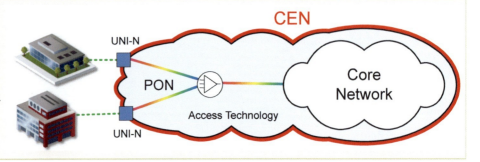

Access Technologies
Ethernet over Optical Fiber

There are two PON standards:

- **EPON** (Ethernet Passive Optical Network)—Developed by the IEEE, this standard supports 1 Gb/s symmetrical communication over distances up to at least 20 km (per the IEEE standard) or up to about 40 km in commercial application[134].

- **GPON** (Gigabit Passive Optical Network)—Developed by ITU-T, this standard supports 1.25 Gb/s upstream and 2.5 Gb/s downstream over distances up to at least 20 km (per the ITU-T standard) or up to about 40 km in commercial application.

Additionally, 10 Gb/s versions of both standards (10G-EPON and 10G-PON) are now available.

A PON consists of an optical line terminal (OLT) at the service provider's central office and a number of optical network terminals (ONTs) at customer premises. A PON reduces the amount of fiber and central office equipment required compared with point-to-point architectures.

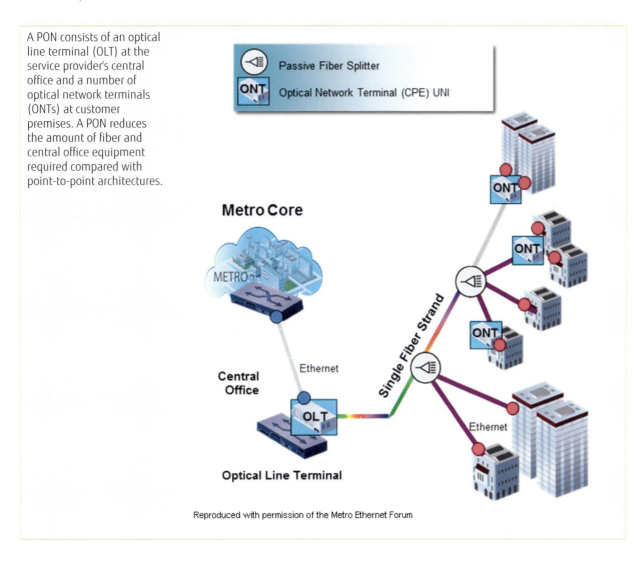

Reproduced with permission of the Metro Ethernet Forum

---

13 Per the MEF access technologies white paper *Delivering Ubiquitous Ethernet Services using an Array of Access Technologies*, in the 4 MEF White Papers area of the MEF Web site (mef.net), under the link titled *Carrier Ethernet – the Technology of Choice for Access Networks*.

Downstream signals are broadcast to all ONTs sharing the same OLT fiber. Each ONT then filters the downstream signal appropriately (encryption can prevent eavesdropping), as shown in the figure illustrating downstream broadcast.

This figure also illustrates how PON naturally supports multicasting: the video is multicast to three of the four subscribers.

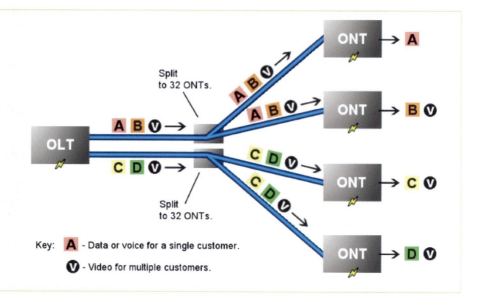

Upstream signals are combined using a multiple access protocol, usually TDMA (time division multiple access).

Advantages of PON include:

- High bandwidth capability compared to legacy copper technologies
- Lower deployment and operational costs compared to active optical networks
- Reduced fiber requirements due to point-to-multipoint topology
- More efficient multicasting

14.3
Ethernet over PDH

Summary of Carrier Ethernet Access Technologies			
Carrier Ethernet Access Method	Technology Alternatives	Deployment Scenarios (When to use the technology)	Advantages
Ethernet over PDH	- Bonded T1/E1 - DS3/E3 and bonded DS3/E3	- Remote branch offices - Off-net customer locations (out of region, type 2) - SMB	- Leverage existing transport - Universally deployable - Lower CAPEX - No reach limitations - Well understood provisioning - Resiliency through bonding

Reproduced with permission of the Metro Ethernet Forum. From white paper " "Delivering Ubiquitous Ethernet Services using an Array of Access Technologies".

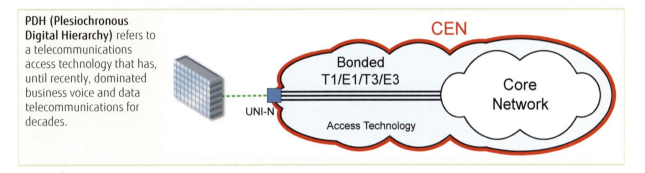

PDH (Plesiochronous Digital Hierarchy) refers to a telecommunications access technology that has, until recently, dominated business voice and data telecommunications for decades.

Ethernet over PDH leverages the telecommunications infrastructure that supports the following carrier signals:

- **T1 and T3 lines**—Used in the US and Canada

    Note: *DS designations (DS1 and DS3) are used in connection with T1 and T3. Strictly speaking, a DS1/DS3 is the data carried on a T1/T3 circuit, but in practice the terms are used interchangeably.*

- **E1 and E3 lines**—Used in the rest of the world

Ethernet over PDH (EoPDH) can support a wide variety of Carrier Ethernet service speeds (up to approximately 100 Mb/s) and with no distance limitations using bonded signals, as shown in the following table.

Carrier Type	Number of Bonded Signals	Maximum Bandwidth	Distance Limitation
T1 (E1)	1	1.5 Mb/s (2.0 Mb/s)	None
	2	3.0 Mb/s (4.0 Mb/s)	
	3	4.5 Mb/s (6.0 Mb/s)	
	4	6.0 Mb/s (8.0 Mb/s)	
	5	7.5 Mb/s (10.0 Mb/s)	
	6	9.0 Mb/s (12.0 Mb/s)	
	7	10.5 Mb/s (14.0 Mb/s)	
	8	12.0 Mb/s (16.0 Mb/s)	
T3 (E3)	1	45 Mb/s (34 Mb/s)	
	2	90 Mb/s (68 Mb/s)	

Note: Bonding is the aggregation of multiple lines/circuits to provide additional bandwidth and resiliency through load sharing. If an individual line/circuit fails in a bonded group, the service remains active, but with less bandwidth. EoPDH is deployed predominately with bonded T1/E1 signals. It is rarely deployed with bonded T3/E3 signals.

Advantages of PDH include:

- Widely deployed and available worldwide
- Reliable and well understood technology
- Supports rapid turn-up
- Supports access over any distance
- Supports resiliency through bonding

Access Technologies
Ethernet over Copper

14.4 Ethernet over Copper

In this section:

14.4.1 2BASE-TL (G.SHDSL)
14.4.2 10PASS-TS (VDSL)
14.4.3 Bonded Copper Pairs
14.4.4 EoCu versus EoPDH

Summary of Carrier Ethernet Access Technologies			
Carrier Ethernet Access Method	Technology Alternatives	Deployment Scenarios (When to use the technology)	Advantages
Ethernet over Copper	- 2BASE-TL - 10PASS-TS	- Remote branch offices - On-net or off-net - SMB - Campus settings - Traffic monitoring	- Ubiquitous copper availability - Rapid deployment - Low cost unbundled local loop - Resiliency through bonding

Reproduced with permission of the Metro Ethernet Forum. From white paper " "Delivering Ubiquitous Ethernet Services using an Array of Access Technologies".

Ethernet over Copper (EoCu) allows fast deployment of resilient Ethernet access links over existing voice-grade copper infrastructure, providing a very economical alternative to fiber. There are two standardized alternatives: 2BASE-TL and 10PASS-TS.

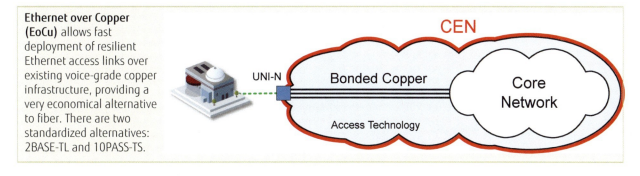

14.4.1 2BASE-TL (G.SHDSL)

2BASE-TL for Ethernet over Copper combines two technologies:

2BASE-TL (2 Mb/s, baseband, twisted pair, long reach) technology based on IEEE 802.3 (physical layer Ethernet)

SHDSL (symmetric high-speed digital subscriber line) technology based on ITU-T G.991.2 (commonly known by its draft name: ITU-T **G.SHDSL**)

Note: G.SHDSL is a type of digital subscriber line (DSL) technology.[135]

In the MEF-CECP exam, either term, **2-BASE-TL** or **G.SHDSL**, may refer to this combination of technologies.

MEF-CECP Study Guide
3rd Edition - October 2015
Updated for MEF-CECP Certification Blueprint C

2Base-TL (G.SHDSL) can support either of two bandwidths over a single copper pair:

- 2 Mb/s (symmetric bandwidth) over distances up to 6 km (3.7 miles)
- 5.69 Mb/s (symmetric bandwidth) over distances up to 3 km (1.9 miles)

14.4.2
10PASS-TS (VDSL)

10PASS-TS for Ethernet over Copper, combines two technologies:

> **10PASS-TS** (10 Mb/s, twisted pair, short reach) technology based on IEEE 802.3 (physical layer Ethernet)
>
> **VDSL** (very-high-bit-rate digital subscriber line) technology based on ITU-T G.993.1

In the MEF-CECP exam, either term, **10PASS-TS** or **VDSL**, may refer to this combination of technologies.

10PASS-TS (VDSL) supports high bandwidth asymmetrical data communication over short distances of voice grade phone line. For distances up to 0.75 km (about 0.5 miles), 10PASS-TS over a single copper pair supports 10 Mb/s downstream and 1-2 Mb/s upstream.

14.4.3
Bonded Copper Pairs

Both EoCu technologies (2BASE-TL and 10PASS-TS) support bonding of multiple copper pairs to provide higher bandwidth and resiliency. Bonded 10PASS-TS can provide bandwidth in excess of 100 Mb/s (downstream).

Note: Bonding is the aggregation of multiple lines/circuits to provide additional bandwidth and resiliency through load sharing. If an individual line/circuit fails in a bonded group, the service remains active, but with less bandwidth.

14.4.4
EoCu versus EoPDH

Ethernet over Copper and **Ethernet over PDH** use the same transport medium: voice-grade copper wire.

EoPDH is a TDM (time division multiplexing) technology. EoCu is not.

EoCu is generally cheaper than EoPDH, but has significant distance limitations (EoPDH has no distance limitations).

---

[135] G.SHDSL technology differs from ADSL (asymmetric digital subscriber line) technology, which is used in residential applications. ADSL supports asymmetric data communication over phone lines in parallel with analog, plain old telephone service (POTS), voice communication using a frequency splitter (DSL filter) to separate ADSL data frequencies from POTS frequencies. G.SHDSL supports higher bandwidth symmetrical data communication over phone lines using all frequencies, including POTS frequencies. Unlike ADSL, G.SHDSL cannot be used together with POTS on the same copper pair. G.SHDSL is a popular choice for business applications.

14.5 Ethernet over Wireless Network

Summary of Carrier Ethernet Access Technologies			
Carrier Ethernet Access Method	Technology Alternatives	Deployment Scenarios (When to use the technology)	Advantages
Wireless Ethernet	- Terrestrial microwave - WiMAX - Broadband wireless - Free space optics - WiFi	- Remote branch office - Campus setting - No fiber or copper available - Mobility required	- Installation requires no trenching - Rapid deployment - Some alternatives offer mobility

Reproduced with permission of the Metro Ethernet Forum. From white paper " "Delivering Ubiquitous Ethernet Services using an Array of Access Technologies".

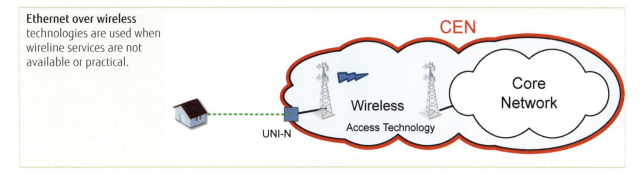

Ethernet over wireless technologies are used when wireline services are not available or practical.

Example applications include:

- Across rugged terrain

- Where mobility is required, such as to support a laptop computer with a broadband (WiFi) capability

- To establish a quick connection (without wire/cable deployment)

A variety of wireless technologies are available. The following table lists representative examples.

Technology	Transmission Medium	Description	Bandwidth over Distance
Free Space Optical	Light	Line of sight, point-to-point communication using light in place of electromagnetic signals	1.25 Gb/s over 11 km (7 miles) is supported.
Terrestrial Microwave	High frequency electromagnetic radiation (Microwave*)	Line of sight, point-to-point communication using either licensed spectrum (allocated and regulated by government agencies) or low-power unlicensed spectrum (within unlicensed regulatory limits)	100 Mb/s can be achieved reliably up to 19 km (12 miles).

Technology	Transmission Medium	Description	Bandwidth over Distance
WiMAX	High frequency electromagnetic radiation	IEEE 802.16 standards for point-to-multipoint wireless broadband communication	1 Gb/s is shared between users over a 50 km (30 mile) signal radius.
WiFi	High frequency electromagnetic radiation	IEEE 802.11 standards for point-to-multipoint wireless local area connection (WLAN) communication	IEEE 802.11n supports four streams of 150 Mb/s over a 250 m (820 ft) signal radius outdoors.

*Microwave communication uses high-frequency (> 1 GHz) electromagnetic signals.

Note: Numbers in this table are generalizations selected to align with the MEF-CECP exam, which tests for a general understanding of the relative strengths of each technology at the time the initial MEF-CECP exam was developed (circa 2010). The actual capabilities of each wireless technology advance over time and depend on many factors.

Advantages of wireless Ethernet include:

- Deployable where no fiber or copper infrastructure is available
- Easily installed (no wires or cables)
- Rapidly deployed

14.6 Ethernet over HFC

| Summary of Carrier Ethernet Access Technologies ||||
Carrier Ethernet Access Method	Technology Alternatives	Deployment Scenarios (When to use the technology)	Advantages
Hybrid Fiber Coax	DOCSIS 2.x/3.x	- Work at home - SOHO/SMB - Remote branch office	- Extensive coverage - High performance options - Deep penetration into residential and suburban geographies

Reproduced with permission of the Metro Ethernet Forum. From white paper " "Delivering Ubiquitous Ethernet Services using an Array of Access Technologies".

Hybrid Fiber Coax (HFC) is a broadband network that combines optical fiber and coaxial cable and has been commonly deployed by MSO/Cable TV operators since the early 1990s.

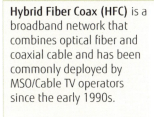
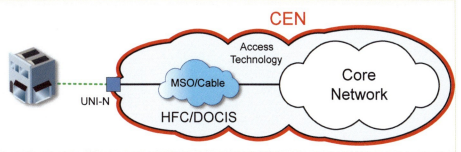

The fiber-optic network extends from the cable operators' regional head-end to a neighborhood's node, which serves anywhere from 25 to 2000 homes through coaxial cables. As shown in the following figure, a master head-end will usually have satellite dishes, antennas, and/or fiber-optic connections to other video sources for reception of distant video signals. Some master head-ends also house telephony equipment for providing telecommunications services.

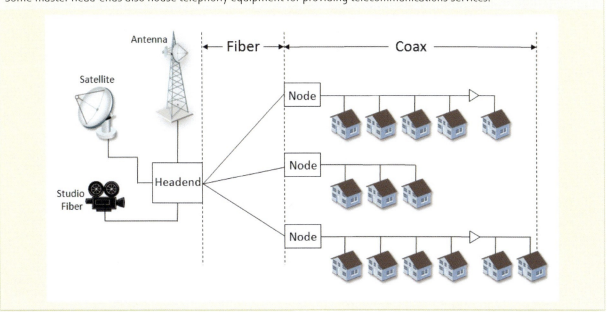

MEF-CECP Study Guide
3rd Edition - October 2015
Updated for MEF-CECP Certification Blueprint C

Using frequency division multiplexing, an HFC network may carry a variety of services simultaneously, including analog TV, digital TV (standard definition and HDTV), telephony, and high-speed data services.

Cable modems connect to the HFC plant to provide always-on, high-speed access to the Internet. The DOCSIS (Data Over Cable Service Interface Specifications) standard for cable modems have enabled low-cost, interoperable cable modems. DOCSIS 3.0 provides a peak downstream rate of approximately 350 Mb/s and a peak upstream rate of approximately 125 Mb/s.

Ethernet over HFC/DOCSIS can support MEF services. However, most HFC deployments today do not support Ethernet over DOCSIS, but only IP services over DOCSIS.

Advantages of HFC include:

- Supports bandwidth up to 350 Mb/s downstream per user (subject to lower performance if many users are on the network at the same time)
- Widely available in many major markets

14.7 Summary: Access Technologies

The MEF-CECP exam includes questions to test your ability to choose an access technology for a given set of requirements. These questions usually include speed and distance requirements.

The following figure places the access technologies on a graph showing approximate maximum distance and speed capabilities.

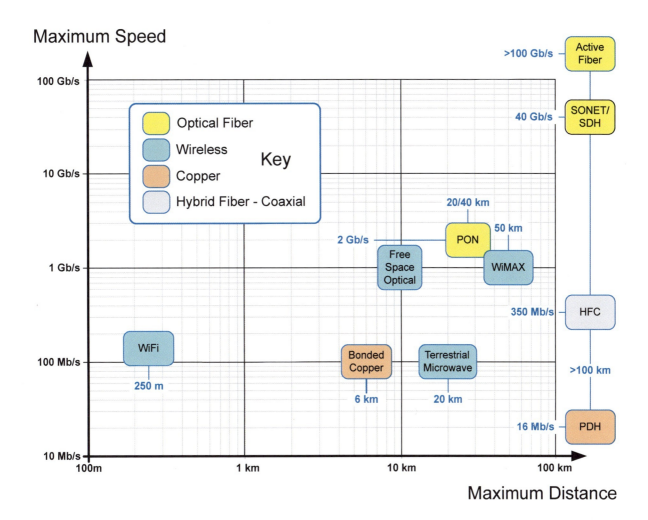

Note: Values shown in the preceding figure are approximations and are selected to align with the MEF-CECP exam, which tests for a general understanding of the relative strengths of each technology at the time the initial MEF-CECP exam was developed (circa 2010). The values shown are based principally on MEF access technologies white paper.[136] The actual capabilities of each technology advance over time and depend on many factors.

---

[136] *Delivering Ubiquitous Ethernet Services using an Array of Access Technologies*, in the MEF White Papers area of the MEF Web site (mef.net), under the link titled *Carrier Ethernet – the Technology of Choice for Access Networks*.

Many other factors can also influence the choice of access technology, including those listed in the following table.

Highlights of Carrier Ethernet Access Technologies

Access Technology		Transmission Medium	Other Characteristics
Ethernet over Optical Fiber	Active fiber	Fiber-optic cable	High performance
	SONET/SDH	Fiber-optic cable	Widely deployed Excellent reliability
	PON	Fiber-optic cable	Low cost Efficient multicast Asymmetric bandwidth
Ethernet over PDH		Voice-grade copper wire	Widely deployed Resiliency through bonding Bandwidth may be asymmetric
Ethernet over Copper		Voice-grade copper wire	Low cost Widely deployed Resiliency through bonding Bandwidth may be asymmetric
Wireless Ethernet	Free space optics	Light	Rapid deployment No wire/fiber infrastructure WiMAX and WiFi are point-to-multipoint technologies.
	Terrestrial microwave	Microwave	
	WiMAX	Microwave	
	WiFi	Microwave	
Ethernet over HFC		Hybrid fiber - coaxial cable	Asymmetric bandwidth Widely deployed in some markets

14.8 Review: Access Technologies

1. What are three advantages offered by *Ethernet over Bonded Copper*? (Choose three.)

   a. Easy to deploy in rugged terrain
   b. Low cost
   c. No distance limitation
   d. Supports rates up to 1 Gb/s through bonding of additional copper pairs
   e. Resiliency through bonding copper pairs
   f. Widely available copper infrastructure

2. An office, located 3 miles (4.8 km) from the core service provider network, requires 2 Mb/s of symmetric connectivity to an EVP-LAN service. A single copper pair is available. Which of the following access technologies is most appropriate?

   a. Ethernet over DOCSIS
   b. G.SHDSL
   c. Ethernet over PDH
   d. 10PASS-TS

3. What is the advantage of having Ethernet service over WiMAX?

   a. Bandwidth split among multiple users
   b. No cabling
   c. Resilience
   d. No reach limitation

4. Which access technology can support Ethernet services in parallel with TV services as commonly deployed by MSO/Cable TV operators?

   a. Ethernet over GPON
   b. Ethernet over Bonded Copper
   c. Ethernet over HFC
   d. Ethernet over PDH
   e. Ethernet over Terrestrial Microwave

5. A mobile backhaul operator needs to reach a cell tower located in an undeveloped rural area. Which two of the following technologies could be most quickly deployed? (Choose two.)

   a. Ethernet over PDH
   b. Ethernet over Terrestrial Microwave
   c. Ethernet over Free Space Optics
   d. Ethernet over SONET/SDH
   e. Ethernet over bonded copper pairs
   f. Ethernet over Fiber

6. What are two advantages of *Ethernet over SONET/SDH*? (Choose two.)

   a. Supports multiple classes of service
   b. Highly reliable
   c. Supports multipoint services (EP-LAN, EP-Tree)
   d. Provides dedicated bandwidth that is not impacted by other user traffic
   e. Supports circuit emulation

7. An incumbent provider (ILEC/PTT) wants to provide an Ethernet service at 6 Mb/s over its existing copper network infrastructure. The UNI will be 20 km (12.4 miles) away from the nearest switching office. Which technology do you recommend for this application?

   a. Ethernet over bonded copper pairs (2BASE-TL)
   b. Ethernet over HFC/DOCSIS
   c. Ethernet over bonded T1/E1 PDH circuits
   d. Ethernet over bonded T3/E3 PDH circuits

8. What is an advantage of *Ethernet over PDH* compared to *Ethernet over Copper*?

   a. Uses widely deployed infrastructure
   b. Easy, low-cost, and rapid to deploy
   c. Supports eight classes of service
   d. Supports resiliency through bonding
   e. No distance limitation

9. Which two of the following access technologies support rates over 1 Gb/s? (Choose two.)

   a. Ethernet over SONET/SDH
   b. Ethernet over PDH
   c. Ethernet over HFC/DOCSIS
   d. Ethernet over Active Fiber

10. Which wireless access technology uses licensed frequency spectrum in high-power applications?

    a. Ethernet over DOCSIS
    b. Ethernet over terrestrial microwave
    c. Ethernet over free space optical
    d. Ethernet over WiFi

11. Which of the following access technologies has the shortest reach?

    a. Ethernet over Terrestrial Microwave
    b. Ethernet over Bonded Copper
    c. Ethernet over PDH
    d. Ethernet over HFC/DOCSIS
    e. Ethernet over Active Fiber

Access Technologies
Review: Access Technologies

12. Which of the following is a disadvantage of *Ethernet over Active Fiber*?

    a. Distance limited to under 40 km
    b. Lack of widespread availability for fiber infrastructure
    c. Speed limited to 100 Mb/s
    d. Dated technology
    e. Poor bandwidth granularity

13. What are two advantages of using *Ethernet over GPON* versus *Ethernet over copper*? (Choose two.)

    a. The physical media is widely deployed.
    b. Higher bandwidth
    c. Supports efficient multicasting
    d. Resiliency through bonding

Related Links

Answers: Access Technologies on p. 433

15

Transport Technologies

In this chapter:

15.1 Layer 1 Transport Technologies
15.2 Layer 2 Transport Technologies
15.3 Layer 2.5 Technologies (Multiprotocol Label Switching)
15.4 Ethernet Service Protection Technologies
15.5 Summary
15.6 Review: Transport Technologies

Several technologies can be used to transport MEF services. Some are simple Layer 1 technologies, some are Layer 2 technologies, and some are Layer "2.5" technologies (a "shim" between Layers 2 and 3). The following transport technologies are reviewed in this lesson:

OSI Model Layer	Transport Technology
Layer 1	• Synchronous Optical Network (SONET)/Synchronous Digital Hierarchy (SDH) • Optical Transport Network (OTN)—ITU-T G.709 • Wavelength Division Multiplexing (WDM)
Layer 2	• Bridging—IEEE 802.1D and 802.1Q–2005 • Provider Bridging (PB)—IEEE 802.1ad • Provider Backbone Bridging (PBB)—IEEE 802.1ah • Provider Backbone Bridging with Traffic Engineering extensions (PBB-TE)—IEEE 802.1Qay • Ethernet Tag Switching—Fujitsu implementation of connection-oriented Ethernet (COE) leveraging the IEEE 802.1ad frame format
Layer "2.5"	• Multiple Protocol Label Switching Virtual Private Wire Service (MPLS VPWS) • Multiple Protocol Label Switching Virtual Private LAN Service (MPLS VPLS) • Multiple Protocol Label Switching Transport Profile (MPLS-TP)

All of these technologies can operate over any physical network topology: mesh, partial mesh, tree, or a set of rings.

For the MEF-CECP exam, it is important to have a basic understanding of how each technology operates and a clear understanding of the support capabilities, advantages, and disadvantages of each technology.

Hint: *Consider jumping ahead to preview the study aid that appears in the summary to this lesson. This study aid will not make much sense at this time, but it may help you to visualize what you are expected to take away from this lesson.*

Key Areas for Comparing the Transport Technologies

The transport technologies differ in their ability to support Carrier Ethernet services in the following key areas:

- **Multipoint capability**—Multipoint capability (typically, with MAC learning) is required to support EP-LAN, EVP-LAN, EP-Tree, and EVP-Tree services. Some technologies are designed to support only point-to-point services (EPL, EVPL, Access EPL, and Access EVPL).

- **CE-VLAN awareness**—CE-VLAN awareness is required to support EVPL, EVP-LAN, EVP-Tree, and Access EVPL services.

- **S-VLAN awareness**—S-VLAN awareness is required to support ENNIs and OVC-based services, including Access EPL and Access EVPL services.

- **CoS support**—Some technologies support CoS, while others do not. Technologies that do not support CoS treat all service frames identically, providing the same quality of service (QoS) to all service frames.

- **Bandwidth**—Technologies differ in terms of maximum bandwidth capability and in their ability to support service bandwidths of arbitrary size (granularity).

- **Scalability**—Layer 2 and Layer "2.5" technologies differ in the number of Ethernet services they allow a single network to support (this is scalability). For some technologies, scalability is limitless. For other technologies, various factors limit scalability, such as the number of unique service identifiers and/or vulnerability to MAC table overflow.

- **Service protection mechanisms**—Transport technologies differ in fault detection and protection switching mechanisms. Sub-50 ms protection switching/restoration is an important benchmark for real-time communications.

Note: *A brief overview of basic Ethernet service protection technologies appears near the end of this lesson.*

Related Links
Access versus Transport Technology on p. 288
Ethernet Service Protection Technologies on p. 333

15.1
Layer 1 Transport Technologies

In this section:

15.1.1   SONET/SDH (Synchronous Optical Network / Synchronous Digital Hierarchy)
15.1.2   OTN (Optical Transport Network)
15.1.3   WDM (Wavelength Division Multiplexing)

Three Layer 1 transport technologies provide sufficient bandwidth to support Carrier Ethernet services:

> **SONET/SDH** — Synchronous Optical Network/Synchronous Digital Hierarchy
> **OTN** — Optical Transport Network
> **WDM** — Wavelength Division Multiplexing

These fiber-optic technologies can be used alone or in combination[137] to provision highly reliable, fixed-bandwidth circuits for the transparent transport of Ethernet service frames in port-based point-to-point applications.

 Important: When a Layer 1 transport technology supports an Ethernet service, a fixed amount of network bandwidth is consumed by the service, regardless of actual service traffic. Bandwidth in a Layer 1 network is shared using time division multiplexing (TDM). Each service is allocated fixed bandwidth (dedicated time slots), end-to-end, through the network. That bandwidth is consumed by the service, regardless of actual data throughput (another service cannot use that bandwidth).

Layer 1 technologies are not VLAN aware and do not support frame-based routing/switching, CoS, or multicasting. They only support port-based point-to-point EVC-based services (EPL services).

SONET/SDH and OTN include OAM functions and protection mechanisms. WDM does not include OAM functions or protection mechanisms because it is typically used in combination with SONET/SDH and/or OTN, which already provide that functionality.

15.1.1
SONET/SDH (Synchronous Optical Network / Synchronous Digital Hierarchy)

SONET and SDH are similar technologies, but developed with different standards. Both are widely deployed today. SONET is used in the U.S. and Canada, and SDH is used in the rest of the world.

SONET/SDH technology was originally designed to support circuit-switched real-time voice communication, but has evolved to support a wide variety of payload types, including Ethernet frames.

The following figure shows an EPL service implemented using Ethernet over SONET/SDH (EoS).

---

137   When used together, they are used in one of the following combinations: (1) SONET/SDH within OTN, (2) OTN within WDM, or (3) SONET within OTN, then both within WDM.

Transport Technologies
Layer 1 Transport Technologies

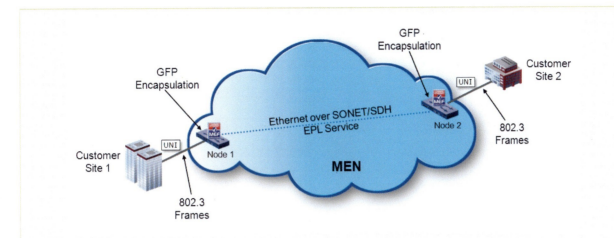

In this application, Ethernet frames are transported as follows:
1. Customer Site 1 sends 802.3-compliant Ethernet frames to the service provider's Node 1.
2. Node 1 encapsulates the Ethernet frames in GFP (generic framing procedure) frames.
3. GFP frames are cross connected into a SONET payload.
4. The SONET network sends the encapsulated Ethernet frame to Node 2.
5. Node 2 de-encapsulates the Ethernet frame (removes the Ethernet frame from the GFP frame) and sends it out on the UNI to Customer Site 2.

Transport in the opposite direction is similar.

Bandwidth

Bandwidth in a SONET/SDH network is shared through time division multiplexing (TDM). Each service is allocated fixed bandwidth (dedicated time slots), end-to-end, through the network, and that bandwidth is consumed by the service, regardless of usage. As shown in the following table, standard SONET/SDH signals do not provide much flexibility with respect to the size of payload bandwidth. For example, a service requiring 100 Mb/s would use an OC-3 SONET signal, providing 150 Mb/s, 50% more bandwidth than needed.

SONET Optical Carrier Level	SONET Frame Format	SDH Frame Format	Payload (kb/s)	Line Rate (kb/s)	Standard Ethernet Speed Supported
OC-1	STS-1	STM-0	50,112	51,814	10 Mb/s
OC-3	STS-3	STM-1	150,336	155,520	100 Mb/s
OC-12	STS-12	STM-4	601,344	622,080	n/a
OC-24	STS-24	n/a	1,202,688	1,244,160	1 Gb/s
OC-48	STS-48	STM-16	2,405,376	2,488,320	n/a
OC-192	STS-192	STM-64	9,621,504	9,953,280	10 Gb/s*
OC-768	STS-768	STM-256	38,486,016	39,813,120	40 Gb/s*

* Cannot be transported at full rate transparently

Bandwidth flexibility can be increased using **virtual concatenation (VCAT)**, which permits bandwidth to be custom sized in any multiple of the basic rate (STS-1, or 50 Mb/s, for SONET) or in any multiple of a smaller VT (virtual tributary) subrate (VT1.5, or 1.5 Mb/s, for SONET low-order VCAT). This greatly increases the range of bandwidth sizes that the service provider can offer. SDH provides support for virtual concatenation that is similar to SONET's support for virtual concatenation, but using different bandwidth container sizes.

Protection and OAM

SONET/SDH includes OAM performance monitoring and fault detection and supports 1+1, UPSR (unidirectional path-switched ring) protection, and BLSR (bidirectional line-switched ring) protection switching, each with sub-50 ms protection switching/restoration.

SONET/SDH Summary

Advantages	Limitations / Issues
Rapid service turn-up: • Leverages widely deployed equipment and optical fiber • Ubiquitous availability world wide Highly resilient and secure: • Sub-50ms protection/restoration • Layer 1 security Flexible bandwidth options: • STS-3/STM-1 (155 Mb/s) up to STS-768/STM-256 (39.8 Gb/s) • Sub-rate and NxSTS/STM available with bonding using VCAT circuits Comprehensive OAM: • Performance monitoring • Fault detection and isolation	Larger, less granular, fixed bandwidth increments may not correlate well with Ethernet bandwidth requirements. The maximum rate of any SONET/SDH interface is 40 Gb/s. Only EPL service is supported (no VLAN awareness). Only single-CEN applications are supported (no ENNI or OVC support). Because only Layer 1 functionality is supported, SONET/SDH: • Is not frame aware • Does not support classes of service (supports one CoS) • Does not support multicasting or any other Layer 2 functions

Related Links

Ethernet over SONET/SDH on p. 290

15.1.2
OTN (Optical Transport Network)

The ITU-T developed OTN to provide SONET/SDH-like functionality for narrowband optical channels within WDM (wavelength division multiplexing) technology. OTN, also called G.709 digital-wrapper technology, has expanded beyond WDM into a generic, independent technology for switching, multiplexing, and aggregating any traffic type (not just within WDM applications).

Similar to Ethernet over SONET/SDH, Ethernet service frames are encapsulated with GFP, prior to OTN encapsulation.

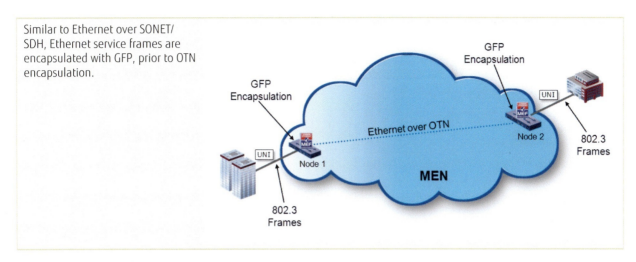

Like SONET/SDH, OTN provides channel bonding, similar to SONET/SDH virtual concatenation, using a technology called ODUflex that allows concatenation of ODUs to create different bandwidth options. Additionally, SONET/SDH entities (including subrate/bonded VCAT entities) can be encapsulated and transported within the OTN entity to support more granular service bandwidth.

Bandwidth

OTN supports higher bandwidths compared to SONET/SDH as shown in the following table. Notice that OTU signals are sized to align well with standard Ethernet speeds.

OTN Level	OTU Rate (Gb/s)	ODU Rate (Gb/s)	OPU Rate (Gb/s)	Payload Rate (Gb/s)	Standard Ethernet Speed Supported
OTU1	2.66	2.4999	2.489	2.488	2 x 1 Gb/s
OTU2	10.709	10.037	10.001	9.995	n/a
OTU2e	11.096	10.400	10.361	10.356	10 Gb/s
OTU3	43.018	40.319	40.171	40.151	40 Gb/s
OTU4	111.809	104.794	104.410	104.356	100 Gb/s

Protection and OAM

OTN includes OAM performance monitoring and fault detection and supports 1+1, 1:1, and 1:N optical protection switching with sub-50 ms protection switching/restoration. OTN supports forward error correction (FEC), which increases OTN's tolerance to physical-layer transmission errors, allowing longer transmission distances compared to all other Carrier Ethernet transport options.

OTN Summary

Advantages	Limitations / Issues
Highly resilient and secure: • Sub-50ms protection/restoration • Layer 1 security Higher bandwidth (up to 100 Gb/s) compared to SONET/SDH Superior OAM: • Stronger forward error correction than other Carrier Ethernet transport technologies • Supports up to 6 TCM (Tandem Connection Monitoring) levels that provide connectivity fault management (similar to SOAM) • Enhanced performance monitoring at multiple layers	Larger, less granular, fixed bandwidth increments may not correlate well with Ethernet bandwidth requirements. Only EPL service is supported (no VLAN awareness). Only single-CEN applications are supported (no ENNI or OVC support). Because only Layer 1 functionality is supported, OTN: • Is not frame aware • Does not support classes of service (supports one CoS) • Does not support multicasting or any other Layer 2 functions

15.1.3
WDM (Wavelength Division Multiplexing)

WDM (wavelength division multiplexing) technology allows a single fiber-optic cable to support multiple data streams, with each data stream assigned a different wavelength (or "color") of laser light. Each wavelength in a WDM link has capacity equivalent to an individual fiber-optic cable (using a single standard wavelength) or to an individual OTN signal. Thus, WDM greatly improves fiber utilization and reduces the need for new fiber installation. Within a WDM network, wavelengths can be individually added, dropped, or rerouted at NEs using optical splitting, filtering, and blocking. These mechanisms allow narrowband wavelength signals to follow independent paths through the WDM network. WDM wavelengths use the G.709 OTN frame.

The ITU-T defines two types of WDM technologies, CWDM (coarse wavelength division multiplexing) and DWDM (dense wavelength division multiplexing), which are compared in the following table.

Attribute	CWDM	DWDM
Cost	Less expensive	More expensive
Transmission distance	Short range	Long-range
Spacing between wavelengths	Wide (20 nm) providing 1 GHz frequency spacing	Narrow (0.4 nm) providing 50 GHz frequency spacing
Number of channels	16 or fewer (typical)	Up to 88 (typical)
Laser precision	Less precise	More precise
Laser rate	Up to 10 Gb/s (typical)	Up to 100 Gb/s (typical)
Maximum capacity per fiber-optic cable	160 Gb/s (10 Gb/s x 16 wavelengths per fiber)	8.8 Tb/s (100 Gb/s x 88 wavelengths per fiber)

Bandwidth

WDM provides the highest transport capacity of all Carrier Ethernet transport options: Up to 88 DWDM wavelengths (at 100 Gb/s each) per fiber-optic cable (as of March 2012). If more granular service bandwidth is required, it can be supported using OTN and/or SONET/SDH subsignals within the WDM wavelength signal, as shown in the following example:

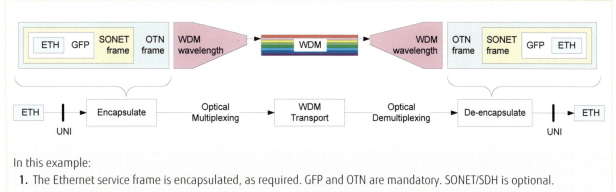

In this example:

1. The Ethernet service frame is encapsulated, as required. GFP and OTN are mandatory. SONET/SDH is optional.
2. The OTN frame is converted to a narrowband WDM wavelength and optically multiplexed into the WDM signal.
3. Data is transported across the WDM network.
4. The WDM wavelength is optically demultiplexed and converted to an OTN frame.
5. The ETH service frame is de-encapsulated from OTN, SONET/SDH, and GFP frames, as required.

Protection and OAM: WDM wavelengths use the G.709 OTN frame for optical-layer OAM functions and protection. WDM networks provide the same OAM features and protection functions as OTN.

WDM Summary

Advantages	Limitations / Issues
Most efficient fiber-optic cable utilization: • Enables multiple wavelengths per fiber-optic cable • Economical use of fiber-optic cable • Provides highest capacity transport—Up to 88 DWDM wavelengths (at 100 Gb/s each) per fiber optic cable (as of March 2012). • Minimizes new fiber-optic cable installs Cost effective: • Small form-factor pluggable (SFP) transceivers, multiplexers, and media converters enable WDM wavelengths with existing infrastructure equipment Flexibility: • Wavelengths can support different network protocols, for example, a mix of Ethernet and TDM services over the same fiber-optic cable Superior OAM and protection (identical to OTN)	Only EPL service is supported (no VLAN awareness). Only single-CEN applications are supported (no ENNI or OVC support). Because only Layer 1 functionality is supported, WDM: • Is not frame aware • Does not support classes of service • Does not support multicasting or any other Layer 2 functions

15.2
Layer 2 Transport Technologies

In this section:

15.2.1   Bridging
15.2.2   PB (Provider Bridging)
15.2.3   PBB (Provider Backbone Bridging)
15.2.4   PBB-TE (Provider Backbone Bridge Traffic Engineering)
15.2.5   ETS (Ethernet Tag Switching)

Layer 2 transport technologies are based on IEEE 802.1 standards:

- **Bridging**—IEEE 802.1Q-2005

- **PB** (Provider Bridging)—IEEE 802.1ad

- **PBB** (Provider Backbone Bridging)—IEEE 802.1ah

- **PBB-TE** (Provider Backbone Bridging with Traffic Engineering extensions)—IEEE 802.1Qay

- **Ethernet Tag Switching**—IEEE 802.1ad

 Important: *The IEEE standards shown in the preceding list are now obsolete, superseded by IEEE 802.1Q-2011. IEEE 802.1Q-2011 updated IEEE 802.1Q-2005 and incorporated many amendments to IEEE 802.1Q-2005, including IEEE 802.1ad (Provider Bridging), IEEE 802.1ah (Provider Backbone Bridging), and IEEE 802.1Qay (Provider Backbone Bridging with Traffic Engineering Extensions). IEEE 802.1Q-2011 is now the proper current reference for all of these technologies. This lesson references the older, now obsolete, IEEE standards for purposes of continuity.*

Note: *Ethernet tag switching is a Fujitsu implementation of connection-oriented Ethernet (COE) that leverages the IEEE 802.1ad frame format to forward/route Ethernet frames.*

Layer 2 transport technologies fall naturally into two groups:

1. **Bridging**, **PB**, and **PBB** technologies support multipoint services using MAC learning.

2. **PBB-TE** and **Ethernet Tag Switching** are connection-oriented Ethernet (COE) technologies designed to support point-to-point services.

15.2.1
Bridging

Bridging supports multipoint-to-multipoint and rooted-multipoint Ethernet services based on two standards:

> **IEEE 802.1D bridging** — MAC addressing, MAC bridging, MAC learning, and Spanning Tree Protocol (STP)
>
> **IEEE 802.1Q Customer VLAN tagging** — C-Tag or CE-VLAN tag

Recall that all Ethernet service frames are either untagged or include an IEEE 802.1Q customer tag (CE-VLAN tag) in the Ethernet header.

Untagged Ethernet frame

| Destination MAC | Source MAC | Type/Length | Payload | FCS |

The VLAN identifier (VID) includes 12 bits representing one of 4094 values that are used to identify the VLAN to which the Ethernet frame belongs. (Although 12 bits permit 4096 values, two values, 0 and FFF, are reserved for other uses)

C-Tagged Ethernet frame

| Destination MAC | Source MAC | C-Tag | Type/Length | Payload | FCS |

Drop Eligibility Indicator (DEI)

> Prior to IEEE 802.1Q (2011), the DEI bit was called the Canonical Format Indicator (CFI) bit and was used for a different purpose.

C-Tag fields: 16 bits (8100) = TPID; 3 bits (PCP), 1 bit (DEI), 12 bits (VID) = TCI

TPID=8100 indicates that this tag is a C-Tag

Since IEEE 802.1Q (1998), these three bits are called User Priority bits. In IEEE 802.1Q (2005), they were called PCP bits. They are also commonly called P-bits, or 802.1p bits.

Bridging technology is widely available and familiar but is difficult to apply in Carrier Ethernet networks because the service provider must repurpose the 802.1Q customer VLAN tag (used by subscribers for CE-VLAN tagging at UNIs) to support service identification, CoS identification, and drop-eligibility identification within the CEN. In addition, L2CP frame tunneling becomes difficult to support, and ENNIs are not supported because S-Tags are unsupported.

If bridging is used for transport within the CEN, every transported Ethernet service frame must include an 802.1Q customer VLAN tag, and that tag is used within the CEN as follows:

- The VID is used to identify the service (service identifier).

- The PCP bits are used to identify both CoS and drop-eligibility (green/yellow).

This usage limits the service provider's ability to support Ethernet services, as defined by the MEF, in several ways. First, the subscriber cannot use the CE-VLAN tag at the UNI in any way that conflicts with the service provider's system of usage.

Service type	Conflict	Implications
Port-based (EPL, EP-LAN, and EP-Tree)	The service provider uses the VLAN-ID to identify the service in the CEN, so the subscriber must ensure that all service frames are either untagged or share the same CE-VLAN ID.	All-to-one bundling is not supported. The service can support one VLAN, at most, in the subscriber domain, making it equivalent to an unbundled VLAN-based service.
VLAN-based (EVPL, EVP-LAN, EVP-Tree)	The service provider uses the VLAN-ID to identify the service in the CEN, so the subscriber can associate only one CE-VLAN ID with a service.	Bundling is not supported.
	The subscriber cannot use a CE-VLAN ID that conflicts with the VLAN-IDs used by other services in the CEN.	The subscriber and service provider must coordinate the value of CE-VLAN ID in some way, such as one of the following: • The service provider assigns the CE-VLAN ID value. • The subscriber chooses a CE-VLAN ID value from a limited set of currently unused VLAN ID values. • The service provider translates the CE-VLAN ID value at CEN ingress and restores it at CEN egress.
All	The subscriber cannot use PCP bits in the CE-VLAN tag in any way that conflicts with the service provider's system of usage.	Subscribers conforms to a compromise, such as one of the following: • The subscriber does not use PCP bits in CE-VLAN tags. • The subscriber conforms to the service provider's system for PCP bit usage. • The subscriber allows the service provider to overwrite the PCP bits at CEN ingress (this implies that the CE-VLAN CoS preservation service attribute must be No).

Additionally, the service provider's usage of VLAN tags makes it difficult to support tunneling of L2CP frames. To tunnel L2CP frames within a service, the service provider must push a C-Tag (802.1Q customer VLAN tag) onto each L2CP frame at CEN ingress and pop the C-Tag at CEN egress. However, it becomes difficult to distinguish L2CP frames from other service frames at CEN egress because they all have C-Tags.

Scalability

Bridging transport technology is not very scalable. The number of services a CEN can support is limited to approximately 4K, which is the number of unique VLAN IDs supported by the 802.1Q–2005 Ethernet frame.

MAC table growth is another factor limiting scalability. At each network bridge, MAC tables grow and may overflow as services are added and MAC addresses multiply.

Note: *One way service providers deal with MAC address scalability is to place a router, rather than a bridge, at the CE. The router "hides" all of the MAC addresses in the local subscriber network from the service provider network so that the service provider network sees only router interface MAC addresses.*

Protection

Bridging supports protection with xSTP (any variant of Spanning Tree Protocol). However, restoration time is limited by the speed of spanning tree convergence (sub-50 ms protection switching can be difficult to achieve, depending on network size).

Bridging Summary

Considering all of its limitations, bridging transport technology is only suitable for small-scale CEN applications.

Advantages	Limitations / Issues

• Supports all types of MEF services, excluding Access EPL and Access EVPL (with limitations)
• Widely available and familiar technology
	• MEF service support is limited (and implementation is complicated) because the service provider must repurpose CE-VLAN tags to support transport within the CEN.
	• There is no support for CE-VLAN bundling or all-to-one bundling.
	• Increased coordination (between subscriber and service provider) is needed for CE-VLAN tagging.
	• There is no support for ENNIs due to the lack of S-Tag support. This technology cannot support OVCs, Access EPLs, Access EVPLs, or multi-Operator CEN service applications.
	• Scalability is very limited because:
	  • The maximum number of services supported per CEN is approximately 4K.
	  • MAC tables grow with service addition, leading to possible overflow (unless routers are used at CEs).
	• Sub-50 ms protection switching can be difficult to achieve with xSTP (depending on network size).

15.2.2
PB (Provider Bridging)

Provider Bridging, also called "Q-in-Q" or VLAN tag stacking, was developed to address the limitations of Bridging. PB uses the same IEEE 802.1D bridging standard (for MAC addressing, MAC bridging, MAC learning, and STP) used by Bridging, but it replaces the VLAN tagging standard (IEEE 802.1Q–2005) with IEEE 802.1ad, which adds a second VLAN tag to the Ethernet frame, as follows:

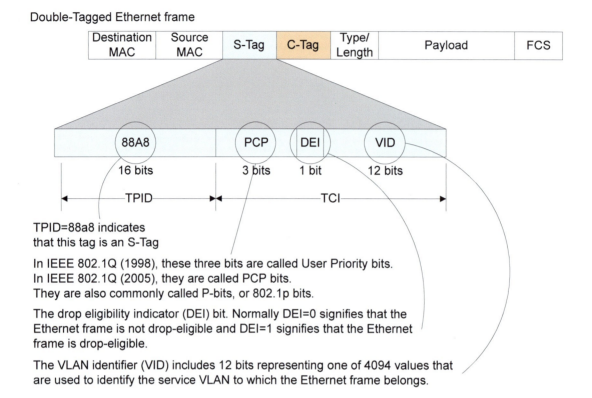

Double-Tagged Ethernet frame

TPID=88a8 indicates that this tag is an S-Tag

In IEEE 802.1Q (1998), these three bits are called User Priority bits.
In IEEE 802.1Q (2005), they are called PCP bits.
They are also commonly called P-bits, or 802.1p bits.

The drop eligibility indicator (DEI) bit. Normally DEI=0 signifies that the Ethernet frame is not drop-eligible and DEI=1 signifies that the Ethernet frame is drop-eligible.

The VLAN identifier (VID) includes 12 bits representing one of 4094 values that are used to identify the service VLAN to which the Ethernet frame belongs.

By now, this frame format should be familiar. The C-Tag corresponds to the CE-VLAN tag used at UNIs. The S-Tag is the additional tag required at ENNIs to capture CoS, Color, and OVC end-point mapping information.

Used as a transport technology within a CEN (or Operator CEN), PB overcomes the inherent limitations of Bridging. The service provider no longer needs to use the C-Tag to support service identification, CoS identification, and drop-eligibility within the CEN. All of this information is instead captured in the S-Tag, which is added (pushed) to each service frame at CEN ingress and removed (popped) at CEN egress. The C-Tag now more truly belongs to the subscriber[138]. The service provider is able to transport and preserve CE-VLAN tags, support all types of MEF service (including bundling) without limitations, and support ENNIs (multi-Operator CEN applications) Additionally, L2CP frames in port-based services (EPL, EP-LAN, and EP-Tree services) can be tunneled with the service (using the S-Tag).

Scalability

Provider Bridging is more scalable than Bridging, but is still not highly scalable. If services are identified within the CEN based on S-VLAN ID alone, PB supports approximately 4K services (the number of unique S-VLAN IDs supported by 802.1ad). Although this same number is supported by Bridging, S-VLAN IDs (unlike C-VLAN IDs) do not have to be coordinated with subscribers.

MAC table growth is another factor limiting scalability. At each network bridge, MAC tables grow and may overflow as services are added and MAC addresses multiply.[139]

---

138 Of course, even using PB, the service provider may use the C-Tag at CEN ingress to identify which service frames belong to a VLAN-based service and/or to identify CoS.

Protection

PB supports two protection options:

- **xSTP** (some variant of Spanning Tree Protocol) – Can be applied over any network topology. Restoration time is limited by the speed of spanning tree convergence, which can make sub-50 ms protection switching difficult to achieve (depending on network size).

- **G.8032** (ITU-T Ethernet Ring Protection Switching) – Can be applied over ring topologies only. Provides sub-50 ms protection switching.

Provider Bridging Summary

Advantages	Limitations / Issues

• Supports all types of MEF services
• Widely available and familiar technology
• Supports bundling
• S-Tag supports CoS and drop-eligibility with no impact on subscriber CE-VLAN tag
• Supports ENNIs
• Supports sub-50 ms protection switching with G. 8032 ERPS
	• Scalability is limited:
	  • A maximum of approximately 4K services per CEN is supported.
	  • MAC tables grow with service addition, leading to possible overflow (unless routers are used at CEs).
	• Sub-50 ms protection switching can be difficult to achieve using only xSTP (depending on network size).

15.2.3
PBB (Provider Backbone Bridging)

Provider Backbone Bridging (IEEE 802.1ah), also called "MAC-in-MAC," was developed to address scalability limitations of Provider Bridging (802.1ad), including the following:

- **Service instance scalability** – PB can only support about 4K services (limited by the number of unique S-VLAN ID values).

- **MAC address scalability** – MAC tables in a PB network grow and may overflow as services are added and MAC addresses multiply.

To address these problems, PBB defines the 802.1ah Ethernet frame, which adds a second MAC header to the 802.1ad Ethernet frame:

---

139 One way service providers deal with MAC address scalability is to place a router, rather than a bridge, at the CE. The router "hides" all of MAC addresses in the local subscriber network from the service provider network so that the service provider network sees only router-interface MAC addresses.

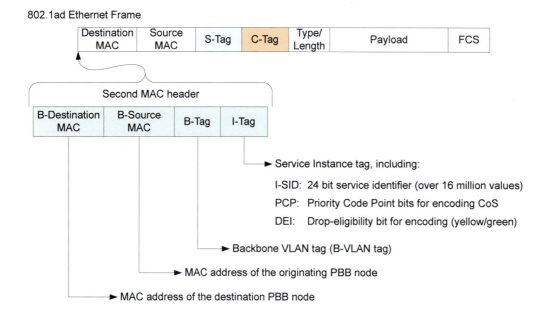

The second MAC header is used as follows:

1. At Ingress to the PBB network CEN or Operator CEN, a Provider Edge Bridge encapsulates each incoming Ethernet frame (802.1Q–2005 or 802.1ad), adding a second MAC header.
2. Within the PBB network, Provider Core Bridges forward 802.1ah Ethernet frames based solely on the second MAC header.
3. On egress from the PBB network, the original Ethernet frame is de-encapsulated from the 802.1ah Ethernet frame.

The I-Tag is used for service identification.

The B-Tag (which is identical to an S-Tag in format and TPID) supports B-VLAN functionality within the PBB network. B-VLANs are used to confine services to a virtual subnetwork within the PBB network as illustrated by the following example. It is not used for service identification.

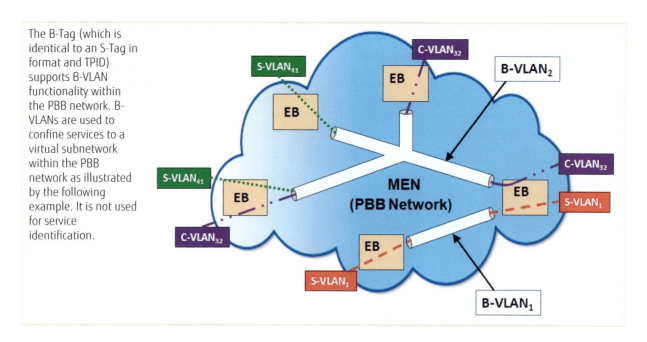

CoS and drop-eligibility information can be encoded in the I-Tag.

 Important: *The second MAC header isolates subscriber BPDUs from service provider BPDUs, improving security.*

Scalability

The 24-bit service identifier (I-SID, within the I-Tag) makes service instance scalability virtually unlimited. The I-SID provides over 16 million unique identifiers, each of which can be associated with over 4K unique S-VLAN IDs (and over 4K unique C-VLAN IDs).

Provider Core Bridges within the PBB network are completely unaware of subscriber-level MAC addresses. Switching and learning (except at the network edge) are based on the B-VLAN tag and B-MAC addresses only. Isolation from subscriber-level MAC addresses protects the PBB network from MAC table overflow, making it scalable with respect to MAC addressing.

Example of Subscriber-Level MAC Learning

This example explains how the PBB network learns to switch subscriber traffic using subscriber-level MAC learning at network-edge bridges only.

The PBB network shown in the following figures has been operating for some time, PBB-level xSTP has converged, and B-MAC learning is complete. An EP-LAN service, connecting four subscriber locations (Denver, Atlanta, Boston, and Chicago), is in operation.

Host 1 in Denver, now sends an Ethernet frame to Host 3 (in Boston). The PBB network has not previously seen traffic from Host 1 or Host 3. The following steps explain how the PBB network supports the unknown unicast (Host 1 to Host 3) and the reply (Host 3 to Host 1) and learns to connect the two hosts without broadcasting. The first figure illustrates Steps 1 through 4. The second figure illustrates Steps 5 through 9.

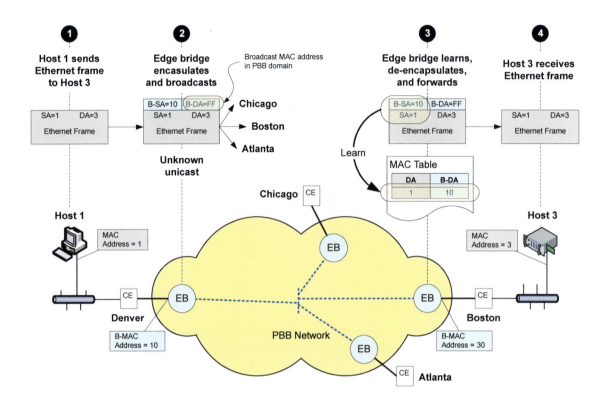

1. Host 1 initiates an unknown unicast to host 3 addressed with SA=1 and DA=3.

2. The PBB edge bridge (EB) in Denver receives this frame through port 10 (the UNI), but has no entry for Host 3 in its MAC tables. So it treats the frame as an unknown unicast:

    a. It applies a second MAC header to the frame with:

    - B-Tag and I-Tag set appropriately for the service

    - B-SA=10 (the B-MAC address of the originating port, port 10)

    - B-DA=FF (FF represents *FFFF,FFFF,FFFF*, the broadcast MAC address)

    b. It forwards the frame out of all ports associated with the service, flooding the service domain.

3. Edge bridges in Atlanta, Boston, and Chicago each receive the frame. Each of these bridges then:

    a. Learns, for future reference, that DA=1 traffic should be addressed to B-DA=10

    b. De-encapsulates the subscriber frame

    c. Forwards the subscriber frame out the appropriate subscriber port (UNI)

4. Host 3 in Boston receives the frame.

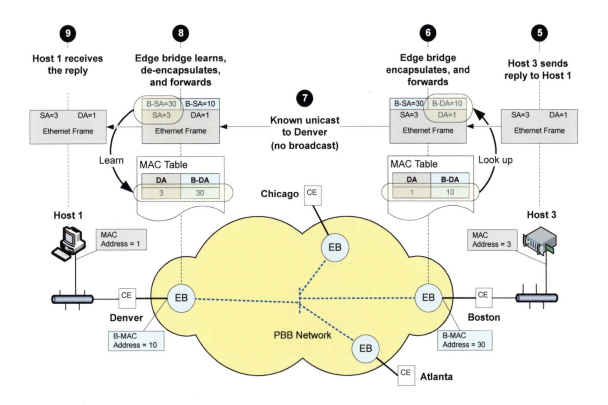

5. Host 3 sends a reply with SA=3 and DA=1.

6. The edge bridge in Boston receives the reply frame through the UNI and knows where to send it based on previous learning (Step 3a), so it treats the frame as a known unicast:

    a. It applies a second MAC header to the frame with:

    - B-Tag and I-Tag set appropriately for the service

    - B-SA=30 (the B-MAC address of the originating port)

    - B-DA=10 (the B-MAC address of the target port, learned in Step 3a)

    b. It forwards the frame out the port associated with B-DA=10.

7. The frame travels through the PBB network directly to Denver because it is a known unicast frame. Based on previous learning, all bridges receiving the frame (with B-DA=10) know which port to use for forwarding.

8. The edge bridge in Denver receives the frame and then:

    a. Learns, for future reference, that DA=3 traffic should be addressed to B-DA=30

    b. De-encapsulates the subscriber frame

    c. Forwards the subscriber frame out the appropriate subscriber port (UNI)

9. Host 1 in Denver receives the reply.

The PBB network can now support unicast traffic between Host 1 and Host 3 without broadcasting. Subscriber-level MAC addresses were learned only at the network edge.

Protection

PBB supports two protection options:

> **xSTP** (some variant of Spanning Tree Protocol) — Can be applied over any network topology. Restoration time is limited by the speed of spanning tree convergence, which can make sub-50 ms protection switching difficult to achieve (depending on network size). However, fast protection switching and restoration may be easier to achieve in a PBB network (compared to a PB or Bridging network) because the spanning tree is isolated from subscriber networks and changes less frequently.
>
> **G.8032** (ITU-T Ethernet Ring Protection Switching) — Can be applied over ring topologies only. Provides sub-50 ms protection switching.

PBB Summary

Advantages	Limitations / Issues
• Supports all types of MEF services • Unlimited scalability • Can coexist in the same network with PBB-TE • Subscriber L2CP frames are isolated from service-provider L2CP frames, improving security. • Supports sub-50 ms protection switching with G.8032 ERPS • PBB simplifies network operations and troubleshooting by isolating/protecting the service provider's network from the subscribers' networks.	• PBB is more complex than PB or Bridging • Sub-50 ms protection switching may be difficult to achieve, using only xSTP (depending on network size)

15.2.4
PBB-TE (Provider Backbone Bridge Traffic Engineering)

PBB-TE (defined by IEEE 802.1Qay) is based on PBB but is designed to support high-performance, traffic-engineered, connection-oriented Ethernet (COE) services.

PBB-TE can be deployed with PBB in the same network (using a separate PBB-TE domain) and uses the same IEEE 802.1ah Ethernet frame structure as PBB.

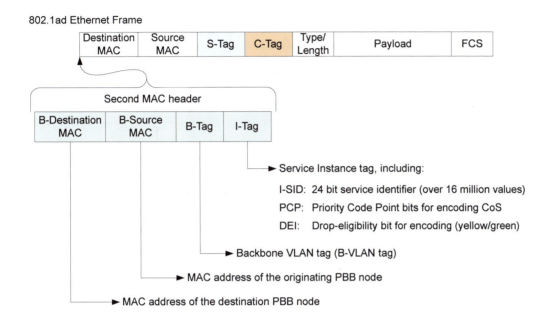

Unlike PBB, PBB-TE only supports point-to-point services (EPL, EVPL, Access EPL, and Access EVPL services).

PBB-TE supports provisioning that explicitly selects traffic engineered paths within 802.1ah networks, disabling bridging behavior such as flooding (unknown unicast), MAC address learning, and xSTP.

Compared to bridging technologies (Bridging, PB, or PBB), PBB-TE behaves more predictably, and its behavior can be more easily controlled by provisioning connections at each bridge along the forwarding path. This creates a point-to-point tunnel, or Ethernet Switched Path (ESP), that is accessed using the B-VLAN ID and the source and destination B-MAC addresses.

Scalability: The second MAC header gives PBB-TE unlimited scalability, just like PBB.

Protection and OAM: PBB-TE supports resource reservation across the ESP (Ethernet Switched Path) to guarantee EVC bandwidth, OAM performance monitoring and fault detection, and G.8031 Ethernet protection switching with sub-50 ms protection switching/restoration.

PBB-TE Summary

Advantages	Limitations / Issues
• Supports sub-50 ms protection switching and restoration with G.8031 EPS • Unlimited scalability • Can co-exist in the same network with PBB • Subscriber L2CP frames are isolated from service provider L2CP frames, improving security.	• Supports only point-to-point services (EPL, EVPL, Access EPL, and Access EVPL)

15.2.5
ETS (Ethernet Tag Switching)

 Important: ETS is not included in the MEF-CECP exam. However, ETS is interesting, not difficult to understand, and highlights the fact that service implementation is not limited to the transport technologies covered in the MEF-CECP exam (any transport technology that can support MEF-compliant services can be used).

Ethernet Tag Switching (ETS) is Fujitsu's implementation of connection-oriented Ethernet (COE). It supports high-performance, traffic-engineered, point-to-point, MEF-compliant services (EPL and EVPL services) similar to PBB-TE, but using simpler mechanisms. ETS uses 802.1ad frame format (used by PB), rather than the more complex 802.1ah frame format used by PBB-TE.

As with PB, an S-Tag is pushed onto service frames at CEN ingress and is used to capture transport information. The VID is used for service identification (but, unlike PB, only locally). PCP bits encode CoS. DEI bit encodes drop-eligibility (green/yellow). As with PBB-TE, bridging behavior, such as flooding (unknown unicast), MAC address learning, and xSTP Frames, are all disabled.

Frames are forwarded based on S-VLAN IDs and/or C-VLAN IDs, rather than the MAC address. VLAN "cross-connects" are explicitly provisioned through the network with the aid of an element management system (EMS), and frames are forwarded (switched) based on these VLAN "cross-connects."

Scalability: Scalability is unlimited because VLAN tags have only local significance and may be swapped along the path.

Protection and OAM: Similar to PBB-TE, ETS supports resource reservation through the network to guarantee EVC bandwidth, service-level OAM performance monitoring and fault detection, and G.8031 protection switching with sub-50 ms protection switching/restoration.

Ethernet Tag Switching Summary

Advantages	Limitations / Issues
• Supports sub-50 ms protection switching and restoration (G.8031) • Provides unlimited scalability • Provides COE functionality similar to PBB-TE using only the 802.1ad frame format and simpler mechanisms	• Supports only point-to-point services (EPL, EVPL, Access EPL, and Access EVPL)

15.3
Layer 2.5 Technologies (Multiprotocol Label Switching)

In this section:

15.3.1   MPLS VPWS (MPLS Virtual Private Wire Service)
15.3.2   MPLS VPLS (MPLS Virtual Private LAN Service)
15.3.3   MPLS-TP (MPLS Transport Profile)

Three transport technologies are based on MPLS (Multiprotocol Label Switching) technology:

- **MPLS VPWS**—MPLS Virtual Private Wire Service

- **MPLS VPLS**—MPLS Virtual Private LAN Service

- **MPLS-TP**—MPLS Transport Profile

MPLS operates at a layer that is generally considered to lie between Layers 2 and 3 and thus is often called a Layer "2.5" protocol. It was designed to provide a unified data-carrying service for both circuit-based clients and packet-switching clients and supports many different kinds of traffic, including IP, ATM, SONET, and Ethernet frames.

MPLS uses an MPLS label (or a stack of MPLS labels) inserted between Layer 2 and Layer 3 of the PDU. The following figure shows MPLS labels inserted into an Ethernet frame.

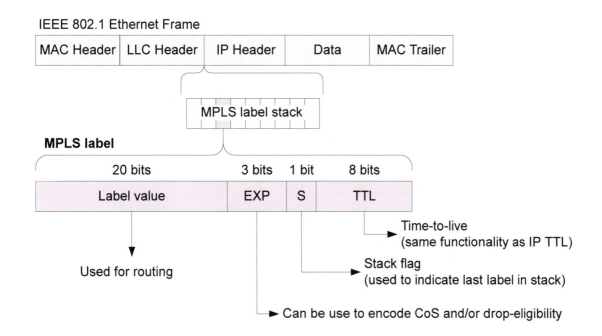

Attention: *MPLS can use one or more labels. Stacks of labels are used to support hierarchical routing and are not considered going forward in this lesson.*

The MPLS label value governs packet routing but is only locally significant. At each router, the MPLS label value determines where the packet is sent next, but each router swaps the MPLS label value before forwarding the packet. The following figure shows an example of MPLS packet routing (the figure also introduces some MPLS terminology).

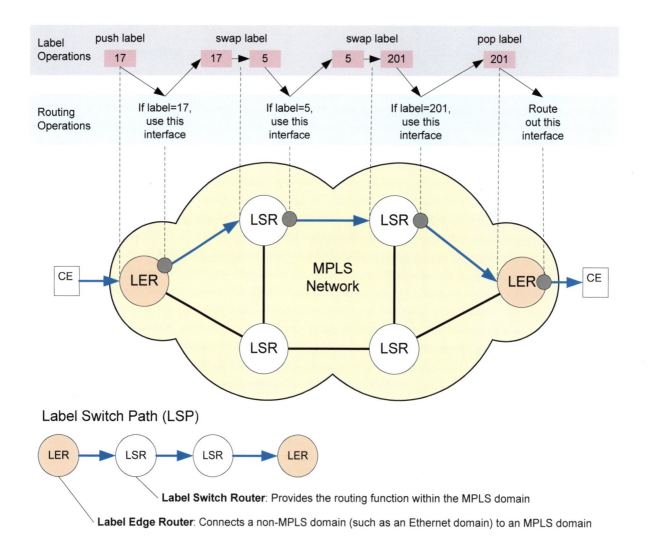

In this example, the PDU (Ethernet frame, for example) enters the MPLS network from the left. At ingress, the Label Edge Router (LER) pushes label 17 onto the PDU, and this binds the PDU to a specific Label-Switched Path (LSP). Along the LSP, each router uses the incoming label to make a routing decision and then swaps the label before forwarding the PDU. Eventually the PDU reaches the egress LER, which pops the label and routes the PDU out the appropriate interface.

Key Points of MPLS Operation

1. Prior to use, the MPLS network is provisioned to support many Label-Switched Paths (LSPs), like the one shown in the figure.
2. When a PDU enters the network, it is assigned an MPLS label value (Label Value=17, in the example), and this value binds the PDU to a specific LSP.
3. Because there are more than 1 million unique MPLS label values (20 bits), a Label Edge Router (LER) can provide gateway to more than 1 million LSPs.
4. Service instance scalability is limitless because:
   - The MPLS network can include many LERs.
   - Each LER can terminate more than 1 million LSPs.
   - Each LSP can support more than 16 million EVCs/OVCs (based on the number of unique combinations of C-VLAN IDs and S-VLAN IDs) or more than 4,000 EVCs/OVCs (based on unique S-VLAN IDs only).

This explains how MPLS works after LSPs are established. But how are LSPs established? Establishment of LSPs is a complex topic that is mostly beyond the scope of this lesson. An LSP can be set up (planned) manually or automatically using an algorithm such as OSPF (Open Shortest Path First). LDP (Label Distribution Protocol) allows MPLS routers to exchange label mapping information and to maintain forwarding databases. For the MEF-CECP exam, it is enough to understand that there are practical methods for planning and creating LSPs in the network, both manually and automatically.

All three types of MPLS transport technologies (MPLW VPWS, MPLS VPLS, and MPLS-TP) route PDUs in this way.

15.3.1
MPLS VPWS (MPLS Virtual Private Wire Service)

MPLS VPWS (Virtual Private Wire Service) is used to deliver EPL and EVPL services, providing point-to-point EVCs between two UNIs. In VPWS applications, a pseudowire emulates a simplex Ethernet link (wire) between two UNIs. Therefore, two pseudowires are configured to provide duplex operation, one in the "forward" direction and one in the "reverse" direction, as shown in the following figure.

Two LSPs are required to establish the VPWS, one for each direction. Because LSPs can support multiple pseudowires (as well as other MPLS traffic), suitable LSPs may already exist in the network. Otherwise, they have to be created.

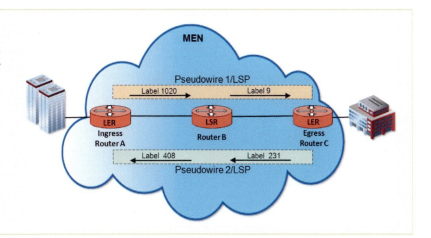

The unidirectional pseudowires are associated to LSPs by provisioning Label Edge Routers (LERs) appropriately. At ingress, the LER is provisioned to recognize service frames and to push the appropriate MPLS label onto them, binding them to the appropriate LSP. At egress, the LER is provisioned to pop MPLS labels and forward service frames out the appropriate interface. Service frames are routed through the network using the previously described MPLS routing mechanism.

Scalability: MPLS VPWS has unlimited service instance scalability, like all MPLS transport technologies.

Protection: Protection can be provided using MPLS Fast Reroute (FRR).[140]

MPLS VPWS Summary

Advantages	Limitations / Issues
• Unlimited scalability • Can coexist in the same network with MPLS VPLS	• Only point-to-point services (EPL, EVPL, Access EPL, and Access EVPL) are supported. • Service-level OAM performance monitoring and fault detection are limited compared to Ethernet-centric OAM, such as Y.1731 and 802.1Q (SOAM).

15.3.2
MPLS VPLS (MPLS Virtual Private LAN Service)

MPLS Virtual Private LAN Service (VPLS) is used to deliver all MEF services (E-Line, E-LAN, and E-Tree), providing multipoint-to-multipoint EVCs between two or more UNIs and MAC learning. VPLS is "private" in that customer equipment (CE) devices that belong to different VPLSs cannot interact. VPLS is "virtual" in that multiple VPLSs can be offered over a common packet-switched network.

Because pseudowires and LSPs are point-to-point and unidirectional, a full mesh is required to create a multipoint-to-multipoint service, as shown.

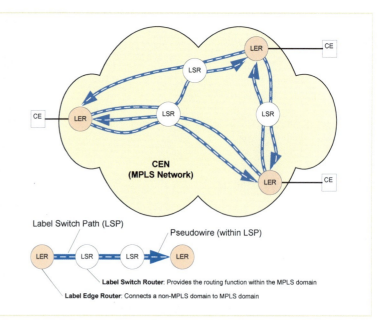

---

[140] MPLS FRR provides segment-based protection. Each LSP passing through a facility is protected by a backup path that originates at the node immediately upstream to that facility.

Six pseudowires/LSPs are needed to create a full mesh between three UNIs.

> To support bridging, LERs keep MAC tables and support MAC learning as follows:
>
> 1. If an unknown unicast is received from the CE domain, the LER broadcasts the frame out all pseudowires/LSPs associated with the service.
> 2. Each LER receiving the broadcast, forwards it out the appropriate UNI and adds a MAC table entry associating the SA of the unknown unicast with the appropriate pseudowire/LSP (not the one it arrived from, but its partner going in the opposite direction).
> 3. When the target (host) replies, the ingress LER recognizes the DA of the reply unicast frame because of the MAC learning described previously, so it will not broadcast it. The reply is assigned to the correct pseudowire/LSP and goes directly to where it is supposed to go.
> 4. The LER receiving the unicast reply, forwards it out the appropriate UNI and adds a MAC table entry associating the SA of the unknown unicast reply with the appropriate pseudowire/LSP (not the one it arrived from, but its partner going in the opposite direction).
>
> A connection has now been established between the two hosts.
>
> Observe the similarity between this description of MAC learning and the explanation of MAC learning for PBB.

Scalability: MPLS-VPLS has unlimited service instance scalability, like all MPLS transport technologies. Similar to PBB, MAC learning is confined to the network edge (LERs), improving MAC address scalability and reducing its vulnerability to MAC table overflow.

Protection: Protection can be provided using MPLS Fast Reroute (FRR).[141]

MPLS VPLS Summary

Advantages	Limitations / Issues
• Supports all types of MEF services • Unlimited scalability • Can coexist in the same network with MPLS VPWS	• Service-level OAM performance monitoring and fault detection are limited compared to Ethernet-centric OAM, such as Y.1731 and 802.1Q (SOAM).

15.3.3
MPLS-TP (MPLS Transport Profile)

MPLS-TP (Transport Profile) is a traffic-engineered transport that was developed to simplify MPLS and make it more like a Layer 1 transport protocol. MPLS-TP technology does not typically use control plane protocols to establish connections. Instead, it uses the management plane (an external Network Management System) to establish LSPs. Paths are traffic engineered, resulting in a highly predictable, connection-oriented services.

---

141 MPLS FRR provides segment-based protection. Each LSP passing through a facility is protected by a backup path that originates at the node immediately upstream to that facility.

Like MPLS VPWS, MPLS-TP supports only EPL and EVPL services. However, unlike VPWS, MPLS-TP supports bidirectional pseudowires and LSPs (in addition to unidirectional pseudowires and LSPs).

MPLS-TP services are also engineered (they are not automatically created using a protocol such as OSPF) and can provide higher performance.

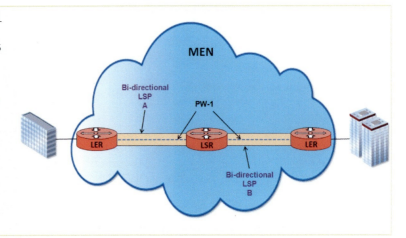

Scalability: MPLS-VPLS has unlimited service instance scalability, like all MPLS transport technologies.

Protection and OAM: MPLS-TP supports COE functionality similar to PBB-TE (or ETS, Fujitsu's COE implementation), including resource reservation through the network to guarantee EVC bandwidth, Service-level OAM performance monitoring and fault detection, and Linear protection per RFC 6378 and ring protection.

MPLS-TP Summary

Advantages	Limitations / Issues
• Supports sub-50 ms protection switching and restoration • Unlimited scalability • Support for traffic engineered paths • Simplifies MPLS to make it more like a Layer 1 transport protocol	• Only point-to-point services (EPL, EVPL, Access EPL, and Access EVPL) are supported. • Service-level OAM performance monitoring and fault detection are limited compared to Ethernet-centric OAM, such as Y.1731 and 802.1Q (SOAM).

15.4
Ethernet Service Protection Technologies

In this section:

15.4.1 1+1 Linear Protection
15.4.2 1:1 Linear Protection
15.4.3 xSTP-Based Protection
15.4.4 1:1 Ring Protection
15.4.5 Protection Mechanisms and Transport Technologies

Networks offer protection through redundancy by providing alternative resources when working resources fail.

15.4.1
1+1 Linear Protection

1+1 linear protection supports point-to-point connectivity only.

Unidirectional traffic from A to B is protected as follows:
1. Ingress traffic at A is duplicated and sent to B along two distinct network paths.
2. Two copies of the traffic are received at B.
3. At B, one of the two copies is selected for forwarding.
4. Failure in the active signal is detected at B and triggers switching.

To protect bidirectional traffic, this scheme is used in both directions.

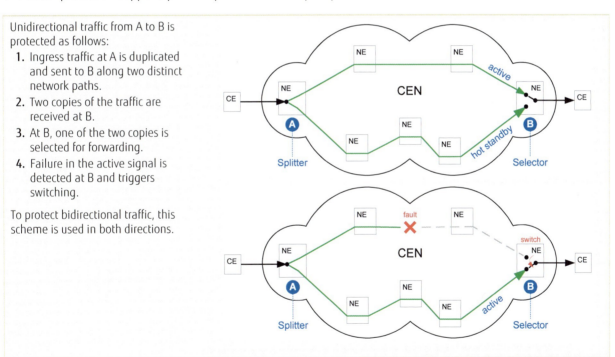

Examples of 1+1 linear protection include:

- UPSR (unidirectional path-switched ring) protection used by SONET

- Och-DPRING (optical channel dedicated protection ring) used by OTN/WDM

15.4.2
1:1 Linear Protection

1:1 linear protection supports point-to-point connectivity only.

Unidirectional traffic from A to B is protected as follows:
1. Two distinct network paths from A to B are provisioned: a working path and a protect path.
2. In normal operation, the working path is active. The protect path is on standby.
3. If network failure occurs, the protect path becomes active.

To protect bidirectional traffic, this scheme is used in both directions.

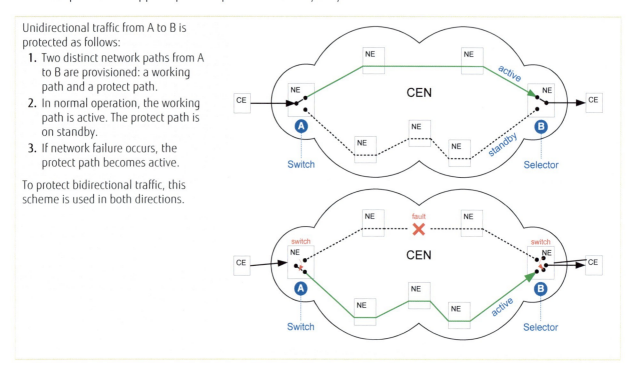

Note: *Because the standby path does not carry replicated traffic, it can potentially carry other traffic.*

ITU-T G.8031 Ethernet Linear Protection Switching is an example of 1:1 linear protection.

15.4.3
xSTP-Based Protection

The network of bridging NEs that supports a multipoint service must be loop-free by design or must be controlled be loop-free (to avoid broadcast storms). All variations of spanning tree protocol (xSTP)[142] artificially block links, such that the active topology is loop-free.

---

142 For example: STP (Spanning Tree Protocol per IEEE 802.1D), RSTP (Rapid Spanning Tree Protocol per IEEE 802.1w), and MSTP (Multiple Spanning Tree Protocol per IEEE 802.1s).

If a fault occurs in the active network, the xSTP algorithm converges to a new loop-free topology. However, re-convergence can take time.

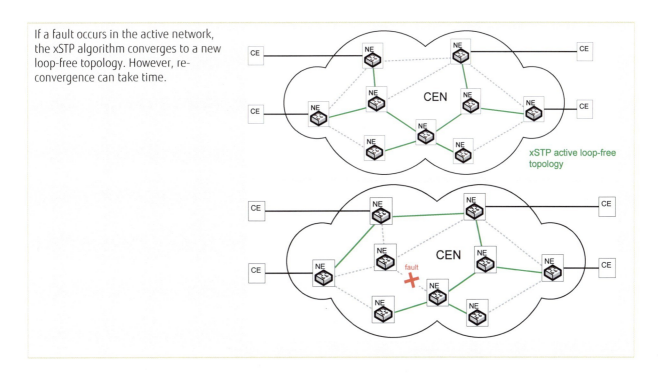

15.4.4
1:1 Ring Protection

1:1 ring protection (such as ITU-T G.8032) provides functionality similar to xSTP in that links are artificially blocked to produce an active topology that is loop-free. However, in contrast to xSTP, 1:1 ring protection applies only to ring-based network topologies.

If a fault occurs in an active link, the ring containing the faulty link opens its blocked link, producing a new loop-free topology.

Protection switching for 1:1 ring protection is faster and more predictable than for xSTP protection.

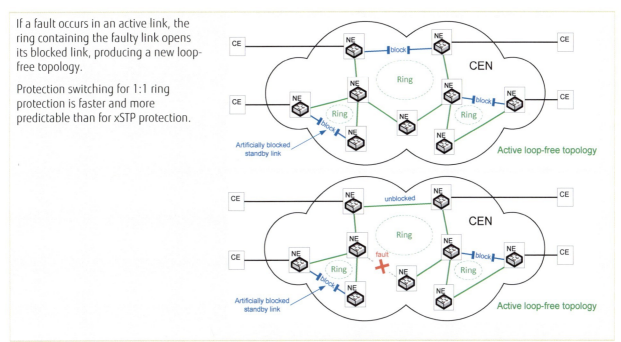

15.4.5 Protection Mechanisms and Transport Technologies

Different transport technologies rely on different protection mechanisms as shown in the following table. Also note that an Ethernet service can be protected by several mechanisms (operating at different OSI layers, for example).

Summary of Protection and Resiliency Mechanisms

Layer	Protection Mechanism	Description	Applicable Transport Technologies	50 ms Switchover Support
"2.5"	**FRR** (MPLS fast reroute)—per RFC 7490 (IETF)	1:1 segment protection Creates local bypass to faulty node or link.	MPLS VPWS and MPLS VPLS	Yes
	MPLS-TP Ring Protection—under development (IETF) or ITUT-G.3132 (draft)	1:1 ring protection	MPLS-TP	Yes
	MPLS-TP Linear Protection—per RFC 6378 (IETF) or ITU-T G.8131	1:1 linear path protection	MPLS-TP	Yes
2	**xSTP**—any variant of spanning tree protocol: • STP—per IEEE 802.1D • RSTP—per IEEE 802.1w • MSTP—per IEEE 802.1s	Creates loop-free topology that automatically reconfigures in the event of node/port/link failure	Bridging, PB, or PBB over any topology	Depends*
	G.8032—ERPS (Ethernet ring protection switching, ITU-T)	1:1 ring protection Uses Y.1731 CCMs for fault detection.	Bridging, PB, or PBB over ring topology	Yes
	G.8031—ELPS (Ethernet linear protection switching, ITU-T)	1:1 linear path protection Uses Y.1731 CCMs for fault detection.	PBB-TE or Ethernet Tag Switching	Yes
1	**OCh-DPRING** (optical channel dedicated protection ring)	1+1 linear path protection	OTN or WDM	Yes
	BLSR (bidirectional line-switched ring)	1:1 ring protection	SONET	Yes
	UPSR (unidirectional path-switched ring)	1+1 linear path protection	SONET	Yes
0	**1:1 LAG**—link aggregation, per clause 43 of IEEE 802.3	1:1 link protection ENNIs and Type 2.2 UNIs require 1:1 LAG support.	All	Yes

* xSTP switchover time depends on the speed of spanning tree convergence.

15.5 Summary

This lesson has provided an overview of eleven transport technologies:

OSI Model Layer	Transport Technology
Layer 1	• Synchronous Optical Network (SONET)/Synchronous Digital Hierarchy (SDH) • Optical Transport Network (OTN)—ITU-T G.709 • Wavelength Division Multiplexing (WDM)
Layer 2	• Bridging—IEEE 802.1D and 802.1Q–2005 • Provider Bridging (PB)—IEEE 802.1ad • Provider Backbone Bridging (PBB)—IEEE 802.1ah • Provider Backbone Bridging with Traffic Engineering extensions (PBB-TE)—IEEE 802.1Qay • Ethernet Tag Switching—Fujitsu implementation of connection-oriented Ethernet (COE) leveraging S-Tags
Layer "2.5"	• Multiple Protocol Label Switching Virtual Private Wire Service (MPLS VPWS) • Multiple Protocol Label Switching Virtual Private LAN Service (MPLS VPLS) • Multiple Protocol Label Switching Transport Profile (MPLS-TP)

For the MEF-CECP exam, it is important to understand the advantages and limitations of each technology.

Note: *Different technologies rely on different protection mechanisms, as previously summarized in* Protection Mechanisms and Transport Technologies.

The following study aid arranges the transport technologies into three groups: Group A, Group B, and Group C.

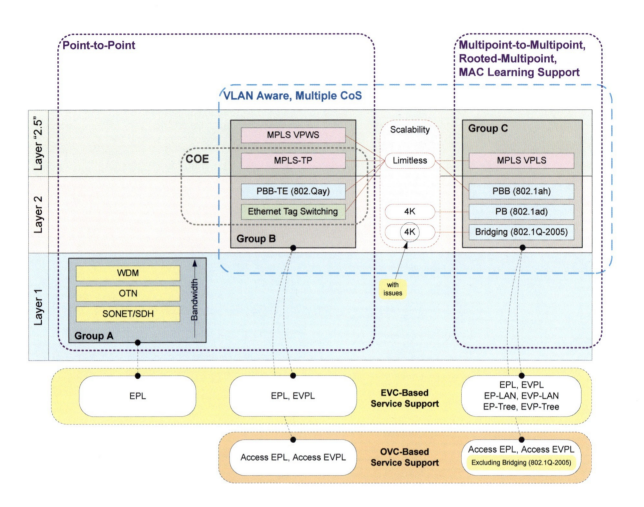

All Layer 1 transport technologies (SONET/SDH, OTN, and WDM) are placed in Group A. These technologies are point-to-point, are VLAN unaware, do not support multiple CoS, support only the EPL service, and differ from each other in bandwidth granularity.

Layer 2 and "2.5" technologies are divided into Groups B and C. Group B technologies (MPLS VPWS, MPLS TE, PBB-TE, and Ethernet Tag Switching) are point-to-point, are VLAN aware, support multiple CoS, and support EPL, EVPL, Access EPL, and Access EVPL services. All are COE technologies, except MPLS VPWS, which is not considered a COE technology. Scalability is unlimited for all Group B technologies.

Group C technologies (MPLS VPLS, PBB, PB, and Bridging) are VLAN aware and support multiple CoS, MAC learning, and all MEF services with one exception: 802.1Q-2005 bridging does not support E-Access services (due to lack of S-Tag support). Scalability for MPLS VPLS and PBB technologies is unlimited. The scalability of PB is limited by 4K unique S-VLAN IDs. The scalability of 802.1Q–2005 bridging technology is severely limited because the service provider has only 4K unique C-VLAN IDs, and they are shared among subscribers.

Note: In the previous paragraph and figure, the number 4K is an approximation. The exact number of VLAN IDs is 4094. The 12-bit VID field allows 4096 values, but only 4094 values can be used for VLAN identification because, per IEEE standards, values 0 and FFF are reserved for other uses.

15.6
Review: Transport Technologies

1. How many service instances can Multi-Protocol Label Switching (MPLS) support in one network?

   a. 16,777,216
   b. 16 million
   c. Unlimited
   d. 4094

2. Which two technologies forward traffic over an explicitly provisioned traffic-engineered path (similar to Layer 1) without bridging or a control plane? (Choose two.)

   a. Ethernet over MPLS-TP
   b. Ethernet over MPLS VPWS
   c. Ethernet over MPLS VPLS
   d. Ethernet over PBB-TE
   e. Ethernet over PBB

3. Which two of the following statements describe an advantage of *Provider Bridging* compared to *Bridging*? (Choose two.)

   a. It allows customer VLAN Identifiers to be separated from service provider VLAN Identifiers.
   b. It can coexist in the same network with PBB-TE.
   c. It has unlimited scalability.
   d. It supports ENNIs.
   e. It can support multipoint-to-multipoint services and MAC learning.

4. Which three of the following technologies can support an EVPL service? (Choose three.)

   a. PB
   b. SONET/SDH
   c. PBB-TE
   d. WDM
   e. MPLS VPLS
   f. OTN

5. Which two of the following protection mechanisms use CCMs? (Choose two.)

   a. ITU-T G.8031, Ethernet linear protection switching
   b. RSTP (Rapid Spanning Tree Protocol)
   c. 1:1 link aggregation, per clause 43 of IEEE 802.3
   d. ITU-T G.8032, Ethernet ring protection switching
   e. FRR (MPLS Fast Reroute)
   f. SONET UPSR protection

6. What is the advantage of MPLS-TP compared to MPLS VPWS?

   a. It provides unlimited scalability.
   b. It supports multipoint-to-multipoint services, such as EVP-LAN and EVP-Tree.
   c. It supports traffic engineered paths, resulting in a highly predictable, connection-oriented service.
   d. It supports both EPL and EVPL services.

7. Which three of the following terms are related to a network's ability to detect and recover from faults without impacting subscribers? (Choose three.)

   a. Bandwidth
   b. Resiliency
   c. G.8031
   d. Scalability
   e. Protection
   f. VLAN awareness

8. Which three of the following technologies can support an Access EPL service? (Choose three.)

   a. PBB-TE
   b. OTN
   c. Bridging
   d. PBB
   e. PB
   f. SONET/SDH

9. Which two of the following technologies support MAC address learning? (Choose two.)

   a. MPLS VPWS
   b. PBB-TE
   c. PBB
   d. MPLS VPLS
   e. OTN

10. Which technology is also known at MAC-in-MAC?

    a. Provider Bridging
    b. MPLS VPLS
    c. Provider Backbone Bridging
    d. PBB-TE
    e. WDM

11. Which transport technology supports the highest bandwidth per optical fiber?

    a. OTN
    b. WDM
    c. SONET
    d. SDH

12. Which two of the following technologies can support multipoint-to-multipoint Ethernet services? (Choose two.)

    a. MPLS VPWS
    b. MPLS VPLS
    c. MPLS-TP
    d. PBB-TE
    e. PBB
    f. SONET/SDH

13. Which technology is also referred to as Q-in-Q?

    a. Provider Backbone Bridging
    b. OTN
    c. MPLS VPLS
    d. Provider Bridging
    e. PBB-TE

14. Which two of the following technologies support EP-LAN services? (Choose two.)

    a. MPLS-TP
    b. Provider Bridging
    c. PBB-TE
    d. SONET/SDH
    e. MPLS VPLS

15. Provider Backbone Bridging allows a single Carrier Ethernet network to accommodate a total of how many subscribers?

    a. Unlimited
    b. 4094
    c. 16 million
    d. 16,777,216

16. Which two of the following technologies support multicasting? (Choose two.)

    a. SONET/SDH
    b. Provider Bridging
    c. MPLS-TP
    d. MPLS VPLS
    e. OTN over WDM

17. Which two of the following technologies can support EP-LAN services? (Choose two.)

   a. PB
   b. PBB-TE
   c. MPLS-TP
   d. MPLS VPWS
   e. MPLS VPLS

18. Which one of the following technologies cannot support an Access EVPL service?

   a. PBB-TE
   b. Bridging
   c. MPLS-TP
   d. MPLS VPWS

Related Links

Answers: Transport Technologies on p. 436

16 Applications

In this chapter:

16.1 Target Applications
16.2 Comparing and Positioning Carrier Ethernet Services with Legacy Services
16.3 Mobile Backhaul Services
16.4 Circuit Emulation Services over Ethernet
16.5 Review: Applications

This lesson provides a survey of applications that can be supported by MEF services.

Hint: In preparing for the MEF-CECP exam, your first objective should be to become deeply familiar with MEF service definitions in the abstract (the subject of previous lessons) because most MEF-CECP exam questions are focused on that material. However, the material in this lesson is also very important because many MEF-CECP exam questions are presented in the context of an application, which may be difficult to interpret if you are not familiar with it.

16.1
Target Applications

In this section:

16.1.1 Wholesale Access Service
16.1.2 Ethernet Access to IP Services
16.1.3 Retail Commercial/Business Services
16.1.4 Mobile Backhaul

The following table lists target applications that are referenced in the MEF-CECP exam. Become familiar with each application so that, given a scenario, you can choose a Carrier Ethernet solution that meets end-user specifications.

Target Application	Description
Wholesale access services	First/last-mile Carrier Ethernet services enabling service providers to reach out-of-franchise (off-net) customer premises
Ethernet access to IP services	Ethernet access to IP-managed IP VPNs
	Ethernet access to Internet
	Ethernet access to cloud services
	Ethernet backhaul of IP video from DSLAM, GPON, or CMTS aggregator
Retail commercial/ business services	Connectivity between enterprise campuses/locations/sites
	Ethernet access to IP services
	Can involve a mixture of many requirements, including: • Multipoint-to-multipoint connectivity between enterprise sites (L3 VPN, L2 VPN) • Hub and spoke connectivity of branch offices with headquarters • Connectivity to partner businesses (supplier, credit agency, etc.) • Ethernet access to IP services
Mobile backhaul services	Interconnection of mobile operator's cell sites and on-net aggregation sites through Carrier Ethernet infrastructure
Support for legacy services	Support for TDM private line services, such as T1/E1 or SONET/SDH, over a Carrier Ethernet infrastructure
	Replacement for Frame Relay services

16.1.1
Wholesale Access Service

A wholesale access service is a first/last-mile service that enables service providers to reach out-of-franchise (off-net) customer premises. Typically, a retail service provider operates a carrier network and makes business agreements with one or more access providers to provide Ethernet connections between the carrier network and customer premises, as required, to support the Carrier Ethernet services that they offer. The MEF defines this type of provider as an Ethernet Access Provider (MEF 33).

The following figure illustrates MEF service implementation involving one retail service provider and two wholesale access providers.

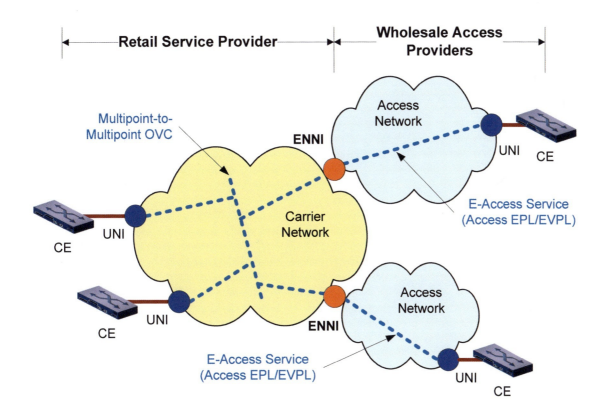

In this figure, the wholesale access providers furnish OVC-based E-Access services, as required, to support EVCs offered by the retail service provider. The figure shows only one E-Access service in each access network. Each ENNI would normally support many E-Access services, one for each service that the retail service provider orders from the wholesale access provider.

16.1.2
Ethernet Access to IP Services

Carrier Ethernet services can be used as a method for accessing IP services, such as Hosted Voice over IP (VoIP), the Internet, or IP virtual private networks (VPNs). This access method is analogous to using a T1 private line or Frame Relay. One of the key benefits of using Carrier Ethernet is much higher bandwidth. Ethernet's role in IP access applications is to provide connectivity to the IP service or ISP (Internet Service Provider) point of presence (POP) with appropriate bandwidth and performance attributes.

E-Line, E-Tree, and E-Access service types are appropriate for this application. For E-Access services, handoff to the ISP is through an ENNI. For EVC-based services (E-Line and E-Tree services), handoff is through a UNI.

Note: *Each of the following solutions ensures that subscribers cannot see each other's traffic. Communication between subscribers using applications such as e-mail is supported, but each e-mail must go to the ISP before it is forwarded to the appropriate subscriber.*

Port-Based Solutions

For port-based customer access, three services can be considered: EPL, EP-Tree, and Access EPL.

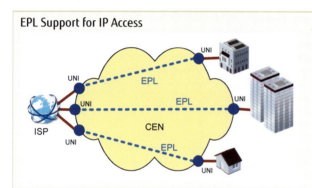

EPL Support for IP Access

EPL service supports this application, but requires a separate ISP interface (UNI) for each IP service connection.

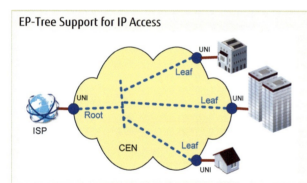

EP-Tree Support for IP Access

The EP-Tree service supports multiple IP service connections through a single ISP interface (UNI) and provides traffic separation for each connection (leaf-to-root path).

Note: *A potential security issue (involving unknown unicast frames as explained in an earlier lesson) may exist for E-Tree services, but the use of routers as CEs (typical in IP service applications) helps to circumvent this issue.*

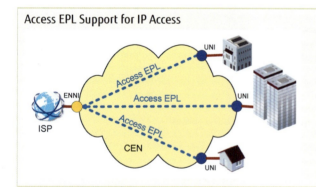

Access EPL Support for IP Access

Access-EPL supports this application using one ISP interface (ENNI) to support multiple independent IP service connections. At the ENNI, each Access EPL is identified by an S-VLAN ID.

Related Links

Security Considerations for E-Tree Services on p. 86

VLAN-Based Solutions

For VLAN-based customer access, three services can be considered: EVPL, EVP-Tree, and Access EVPL.

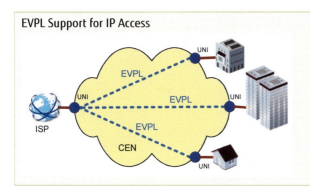

EVPL Support for IP Access

EVPL service supports this application and allows one ISP interface (UNI) to support multiple independent IP service connections. However, coordination is required because each EVPL is identified by CE-VLAN ID (not S-VLAN ID) at the ISP UNI.

Note: CE-VLAN ID values for EVPLs cannot overlap at the ISP UNI. The values used by each EVPL must be distinct from those used by every other EVPL multiplexing to the ISP UNI.

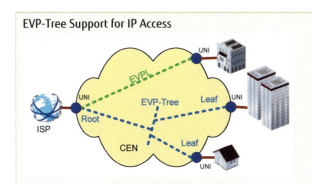

EVP-Tree Support for IP Access

EVP-Tree support for IP services is similar to EP-Tree support for IP services, except that the service is VLAN-based, rather than port-based. Unlike the EP-Tree service, the EVP-Tree service can be multiplexed with other VLAN-based services.

Note: A potential security issue (involving unknown unicast frames as explained in an earlier lesson) may exist for E-Tree services, but the use of routers as CEs (typical in IP service applications) helps to circumvent this issue.

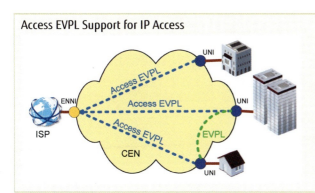

Access EVPL Support for IP Access

Access EVPL support for IP services is similar to Access EPL support for IP services, except that the service is VLAN-based, rather than port-based. Again, one ISP interface (ENNI) supports multiple independent IP service connections, each identified at the ENNI by an S-VLAN ID. However, as a VLAN-based service, the Access EVPL can be multiplexed with other VLAN-based services at the subscriber UNIs.

Note: Each Access EVPL can support any set of CE-VLAN ID values at the ENNI. CE-VLAN ID values need not be distinct, as is required for EVPLs multiplexing to an ISP UNI.

Related Links

Security Considerations for E-Tree Services on p. 86

16.1.3
Retail Commercial/Business Services

Carrier Ethernet provides scalable, easily managed solutions for a wide variety of business applications. Requirements vary widely, but often include one of more of the following goals:

- Support for wide area networking (virtual networking) between sites

- Cost reduction by consolidating services (new and/or legacy) over a shared Ethernet-based infrastructure

- Data center storage replication for disaster recovery

- Performance guarantees for certain types of traffic

- Security requirements

Some business applications naturally map to a single MEF service and are straightforward to define. Others can involve multiple requirements that can be satisfied in more than one way by different combinations of MEF services.

 Hint: Deep familiarity with MEF service definitions is your best resource for creating good solutions and judging which one is best.

The following examples illustrate some Carrier Ethernet solutions for business applications.

Example Business Application 1:

An enterprise has a headquarters and two branch offices and requires:

- Transparent, wide-area networking functionality between all three locations

- Connection to the Internet for all three locations through a firewall located at the headquarters

Question: Which of the two solutions shown best meets requirements?

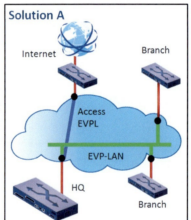
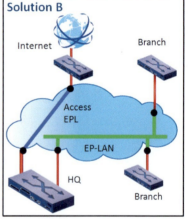

Answer: Solution B, shown with the firewall in the following figure, is the better solution for the following reasons:

- Internet connection through a dedicated port (UNI) with firewall provides excellent security.
- The EP-LAN service requires no CE-VLAN ID coordination between service provider and subscriber.
- The EP-LAN service supports transparency, including tunneling of BPDUs for STP.

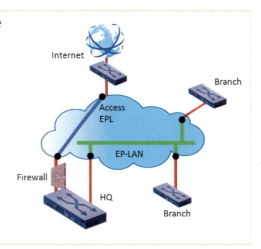

Example Business Application 2

Turbo 2000, an Internet service provider (ISP), uses the architecture shown.

1. Why does Turbo 2000 support customers using EVPLs, rather than EPLs? [143]

2. Why is VLAN ID set to 2000 at each customer site? [144]

3. What value is required for Per EVC service attribute *CE-VLAN ID Preservation*? [145]

4. Does this architecture allow customers to use the same port (UNI) for other services? [146]

---

[143] So that Turbo 2000 (using service multiplexing) can support multiple customers with a single router port (UNI), rather than one router port (UNI) per customer.

[144] To standardize configuration of customer sites.

[145] *CE-VLAN ID Preservation* must be *No* to allow translation of the CE-VLAN ID.

Alternatively, Turbo 2000 might support customers using a single EVP-Tree service. In this case, the Turbo 2000 UNI would be designated as the only root, and each customer UNI would be designated as a leaf (to ensure that customers cannot see each other's traffic). This EVP-Tree service option would offer improved scalability (one service, rather than many EVPLs). However, it would be more complex to implement and would share bandwidth between subscribers, potentially allowing customers to impact each other's quality of service.

Example Business Application 3

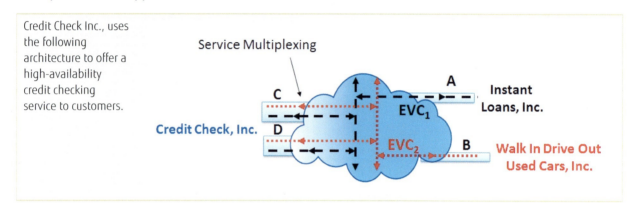

Credit Check Inc., uses the following architecture to offer a high-availability credit checking service to customers.

1. What type of MEF service are EVC1 and EVC2? [147]

2. How does this architecture support high-availability for Credit Check Inc.? [148]

3. How does this architecture make efficient use of router ports at Credit Check Inc.? [149]

4. Does this architecture provide security for customers? [150]

16.1.4
Mobile Backhaul

Mobile communication (cellular/wireless communication) involves connections through several networks.

---

14 Yes, this architecture allows service multiplexing at customer UNIs.
6
14 Both are EVP-LAN services.
7
14 Each EVC provides redundant points of access to Credit Check, Inc.
8
14 EVP-LANs allow service multiplexing at both routers (C and D).
9
15 Yes, customers cannot see each other's traffic.
0

Applications
Target Applications

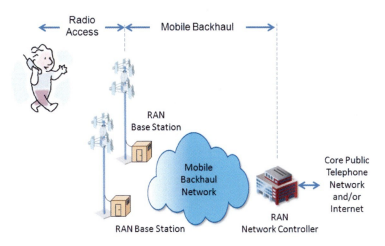

The first link, by radio wave, is between the smart phone (or similar device) and the cell tower. The second link is through a mobile backhaul network connecting one or more cell towers (RAN base stations) to a RAN network controller. The RAN network controller, in turn, provides a gateway to the core public phone network and/or Internet.

Mobile backhaul refers to the network that interconnects RAN base stations with RAN network controllers.

A **mobile backhaul service** is something that an access provider offers to a mobile/cellular service provider (also known as a wireless operator). It supports numerous end users. It is not offered to individual end users (cell phone users).

Mobile backhaul services are described in more detail later in this lesson. For now just recognize the role of mobile backhaul in cellular/wireless communication.

Related Links
Mobile Backhaul Services on p. 362

16.2
Comparing and Positioning Carrier Ethernet Services with Legacy Services

In this section:

16.2.1 Support for TDM Private Lines
16.2.2 Replacement of Frame Relay Service
16.2.3 Internet Access
16.2.4 Virtual Private Networks (VPNs)

16.2.1
Support for TDM Private Lines

Time division multiplexing (TDM) services have dominated voice and data telecommunications for decades. The following table lists example Carrier signals for TDM services.[151]

System	Signal Type (approximate bandwidth)	
	US and Canada	Rest of the World
PDH (Plesiochronous Digital Hierarchy)	T1 (1.5 Mb/s)	E1 (2.0 Mb/s)
	T3 (45 Mb/s)	E3 (34 Mb/s)
SONET/SDH	OC-3 (150 Mb/s)	STM-1 (150 Mb/s)
	OC-12 (600 Mb/s)	STM-4 (600 Mb/s)

Traditionally, telecommunication service providers have supported TDM services through a TDM network as shown.

In this example, the service provider uses a SONET network to support a T1 private line between two PBXs (private branch exchanges), which are owned and operated by the subscriber.

---

151 DS designations (DS1 and DS3) are used in connection with T1 and T3. Strictly speaking, a DS1/DS3 is the data carried on a T1/T3 circuit, but in practice the terms are used interchangeably.

Applications
Comparing and Positioning Carrier Ethernet Services with Legacy Services

This figure shows the Carrier Ethernet solution for the same service.

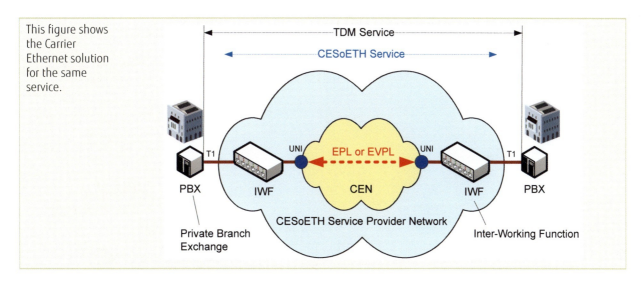

The Carrier Ethernet solution includes two parts:

- A point-to-point service (EPL or EVPL) providing Ethernet transport through the CEN

- Two IWFs (Inter-Working Functions) located on both ends (to mediate between the TDM network and the Carrier Ethernet network)

The MEF calls this combination of technologies **Circuit Emulation Service over Ethernet (CESoETH)**.

Requirements for CESoETH are presented later in this lesson. For now, just recognize that the Carrier Ethernet service (EPL or EVPL) is subsumed within the CESoETH service. In the TDM domain, CESoETH provides a service that is equivalent to a switched-circuit TDM service, but the service is implemented by "tunneling" TDM traffic through the Carrier Ethernet Network. The EPL/EVPL service functions like a virtual wire between IWFs within the CESoETH service.

Overall, CESoETH enables TDM services to be transported across a Carrier Ethernet network, recreating the TDM circuit in the TDM network.

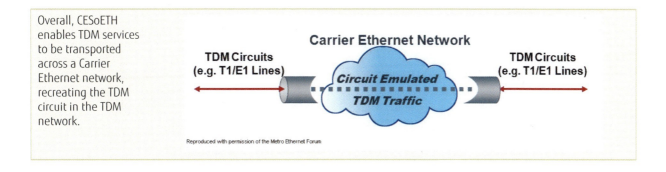

Related Links
Circuit Emulation Services over Ethernet on p. 374

16.2.2
Replacement of Frame Relay Service

Frame Relay services are widely deployed by telecommunications service providers to support wide area networking (WAN).

Frame Relay

This figure shows an example deployment of Frame Relay service equipment. The following equipment is involved:

- **DTE (data terminal equipment)**—Frame Relay router located at the subscriber site
- **DCE (data communications equipment)**—Frame Relay switch located in the provider network

The access links, connecting DTEs to DCEs, are standard leased lines (for example, T1/E1 service lines).

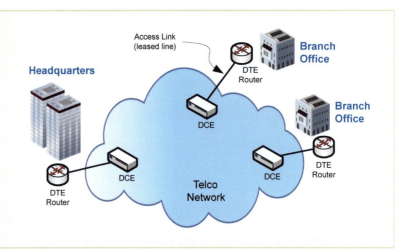

After DTE routers are deployed and connected, WAN connectivity between sites is established using **PVCs (permanent virtual circuits)**. PVCs are point-to-point virtual connections between sites that the subscriber purchases as needed.

The subscriber in this example might purchase two PVCs, creating a hub-and-spoke WAN topology:

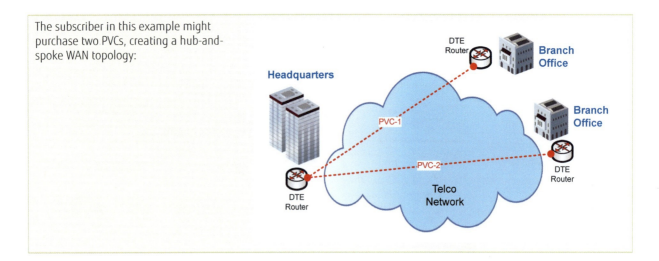

Or, the subscriber might purchase three PVCs, creating a fully meshed WAN topology:

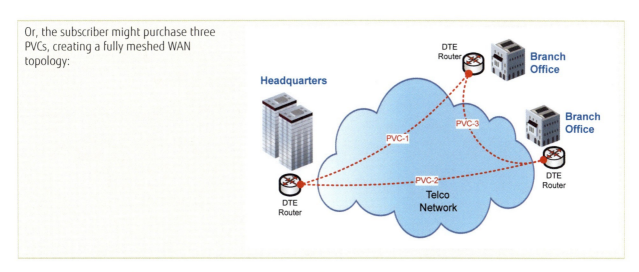

After PVCs are established, the subscriber provisions the DTE routers to associate service frames to PVCs. DTE routers insert a Frame Relay header into each service frame, and that header includes a **DLCI (data link connection identifier)** that binds the service frame to a PVC. The DCE switches service frames based on the DLCI value.

A key benefit of Frame Relay over point-to-point leased lines (TDM private lines) is Frame Relay's ability to support multiple point-to-point links (PVCs) on a single interface (DTE router port).

From this description, do you see similarity between Frame Relay and MEF EVPL services?

Frame Relay Replacement by EVPLs

To make the analogy more explicit, compare the previous figures with the following MEF service figures.

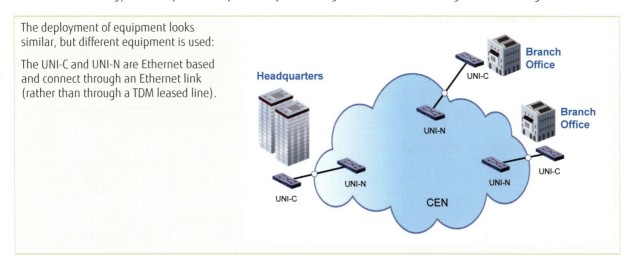

After the UNI-C and UNI-N equipment are deployed and connected, WAN connectivity is established using EVPL services that the subscriber purchases as needed (similar to Frame Relay PVCs).

The subscriber in this example might purchase two EVPLs, creating a hub-and-spoke WAN topology:

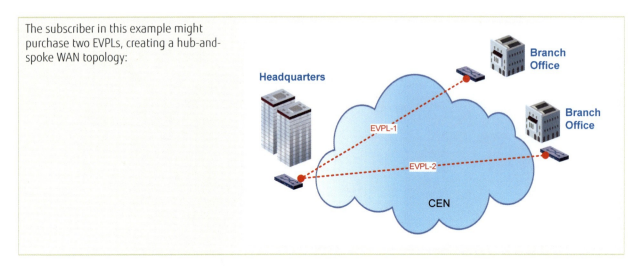

Or, the subscriber might purchase three EVPLs, creating a fully meshed WAN topology:

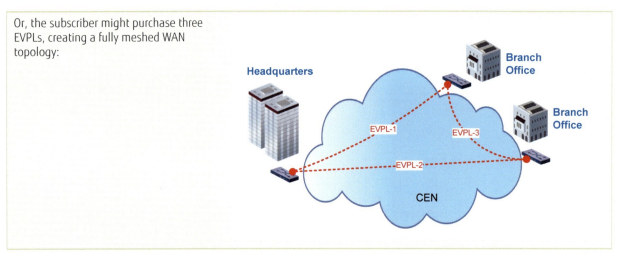

After EVPLs are established, the subscriber provisions the UNI-Cs (bridges or routers) to associate service frames on the customer premises equipment to EVPLs. The UNI-C inserts a CE-VLAN tag into the Ethernet header of each service frame. The CE-VLAN ID within the CE-VLAN tag binds the service frame to a specific EVPL.

Think again about the similarity between Frame Relay and MEF EVPL services:

- Both provide point-to-point connections.

- Both permit a single interface to support multiple point-to-point connections (unlike TDM private line services).

Frame Relay Replacement by an Ethernet Tree or Ethernet LAN Services

Although EVPL services closely resemble Frame Relay services, they are not necessarily the best option for service replacement. Multipoint-to-multipoint Ethernet Tree and LAN services should also be considered, especially for the support of multipoint services.

For example, if the service objective is to provide fully meshed WAN connectivity between three or more sites, an EP-LAN or EVP-LAN service may be better solution.

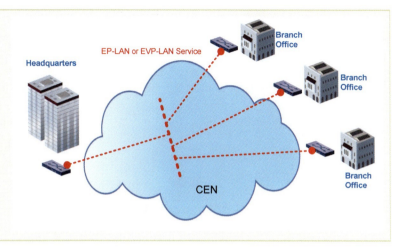

Potential advantages include:

- EP-LAN and EVP-LAN services connect all participating sites without explicit point-to-point provisioning.

    Note: Complete meshing of four sites would require six EVPLs (or six Frame Relay PVCs). Complete meshing of N sites would require N*(N-1)/2 EVPLs (or the same number of Frame Relay PVCs).

- EP-LAN service requires no coordination of CE-VLAN IDs between the service provider and the subscriber.

- EP-LAN service allows tunneling of Layer 2 control protocol frames (including STP BPDUs).

If the application also requires some sites to be isolated from each other (as, for example, in a hub-and-spoke deployment of Frame Relay service), the EP-Tree or EVP-Tree service may be best.

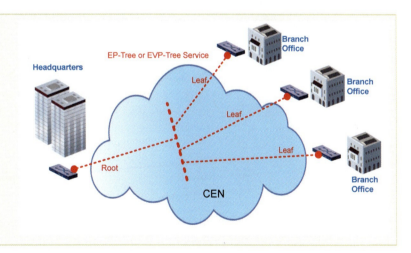

Ethernet LAN and Tree services can also simplify subscriber-side provisioning compared to meshed EVPL services:

- Service frames are forwarded based on MAC learning (or broadcast), rather than CE-VLAN IDs.

- Customer-edge equipment (CE) does not have to be provisioned to assign CE-VLAN IDs, as required, to bind service frames to EVPLs.

16.2.3
Internet Access

TDM private lines, Frame Relay services, and other legacy methods for accessing the Internet can be replaced by Carrier Ethernet services, such as EVPL or E-Access services.

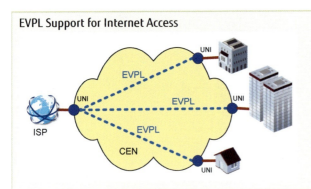

EVPL Support for Internet Access

EVPL service supports this application and allows one ISP interface (UNI) to support multiple independent IP service connections. However, coordination is required because each EVPL is identified by CE-VLAN ID (not S-VLAN ID) at the ISP UNI.

Note: CE-VLAN ID values for EVPLs cannot overlap at the ISP UNI. The values used by each EVPL must be distinct from those used by every other EVPL multiplexing to the ISP UNI.

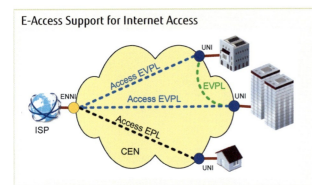

E-Access Support for Internet Access

Access-EPL and Access-EVPL services support this application using one ISP interface (ENNI) to support multiple independent IP service connections. At the ENNI, each Access EPL/EVPL is identified by S-VLAN ID.

Note: Each Access EVPL can support any set of CE-VLAN ID values at the ENNI. CE-VLAN ID values need not be distinct, as is required for EVPLs multiplexing to an ISP UNI.

A key benefit of these solutions over TDM private lines is their ability to support multiple point-to-point connections at the shared interface between networks (UNI or ENNI). Frame Relay also has this ability, but at lower bandwidths compared to Carrier Ethernet service.

To support the E-Access solutions, the Ethernet service provider and the ISP must both be able to support S-VLAN tagging at the shared interface (ENNI). The EVPL solution requires support for C-VLAN tagging at the shared interface (UNI):

- A UNI supports multiple EVPLs (distinguished by CE-VLAN ID at the UNI).

- An ENNI supports multiple Access EPL/EVPLs (distinguished by S-VLAN ID at the ENNI).

Related Links

Ethernet Access to IP Services on p. 345

16.2.4
Virtual Private Networks (VPNs)

A **virtual private network (VPN)** is a network formed by interconnecting two or more (geographically separate) networks into a single network through a public or third-party communication infrastructure.

If each network connects through an Ethernet bridge (Layer 2), the VPN is called a Layer 2 VPN.

If each network connects through a router (Layer 3), the VPN is called a Layer 3 VPN.

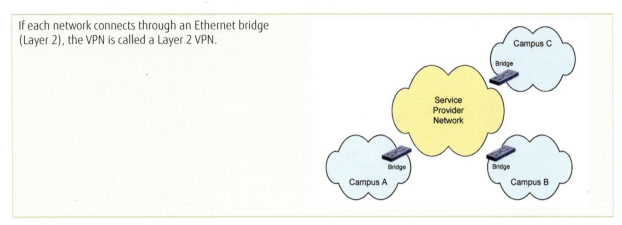

Service Provider Options for VPN Connectivity

For a Layer 2 VPN, the service provider can only offer connectivity at Layer 2:

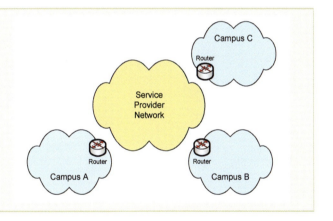

However, for a Layer 3 VPN, the service provider can offer connectivity at Layer 2:

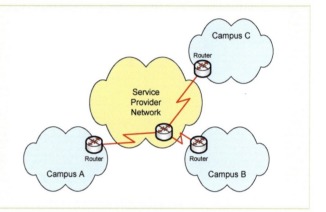

Or, the service provider can offer connectivity at Layer 3:

This option (Layer 3 connectivity) is not considered further (going forward in this lesson) because Carrier Ethernet services do not support it (nor do Frame Relay or TDM Private Line services). It is included here for contextual completeness. If an enterprise uses this type of service, it must coordinate IP addressing within their network with the service provider.

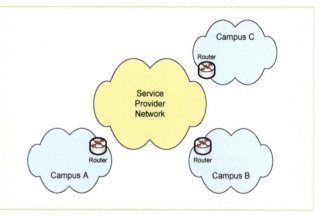

Building a Layer 3 VPN with Layer 2 Service

An enterprise with three campuses wants to build a Layer 3 VPN with Layer 2 connectivity between the campuses.

A service provider can offer a variety of Layer 2 services to support this application: a full mesh of Frame Relay PVCs, a full mesh of EVPLs, a full mesh of EPLs, an EP-LAN service, or an EVP-LAN service. Each of these solutions involves only Layer 2 services: Frame Relay is a Layer 2 service as are all Carrier Ethernet services.

Note: *Because routers terminate STP bridging domains, Layer 3 VPN applications never require the service provider to tunnel BPDUs.*

Building a Layer 2 VPN with Layer 2 Service

An enterprise includes three campuses. Each campus has a managed network. The enterprise wants to build a Layer 2 VPN to interconnect the three campuses.

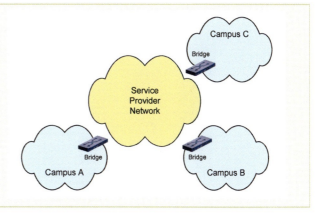

Frame Relay cannot be used in this application because the campuses interconnect through bridges (not routers).

Interconnection can be accomplished using the following Carrier Ethernet solutions: a full mesh of EVPLs, a full mesh of EPLs, an EP-LAN service, or an EVP-LAN service. If transparent support of BPDUs is required, the port-based solutions (EPL and EP-LAN) are best.

This figure illustrates a full mesh of EPLs.

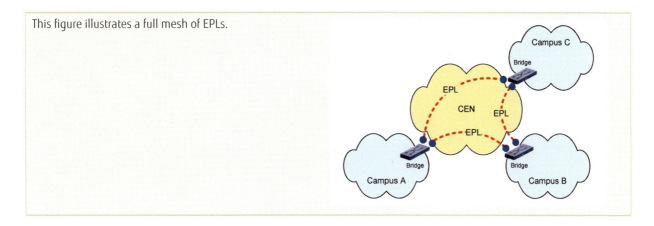

16.3
Mobile Backhaul Services

In this section:

16.3.1	Mobile Backhaul Reference Model	16.3.5	MEF Service Definitions for Mobile Backhaul
16.3.2	Mobile Backhaul Use Cases	16.3.6	MEG Levels in Mobile Backhaul
16.3.3	Mobile Backhaul for LTE	16.3.7	Mobile Backhaul Synchronization
16.3.4	Mobile Backhaul CoS and Performance Requirements		

Mobile communication (cellular/wireless communication) involves connections through several networks.

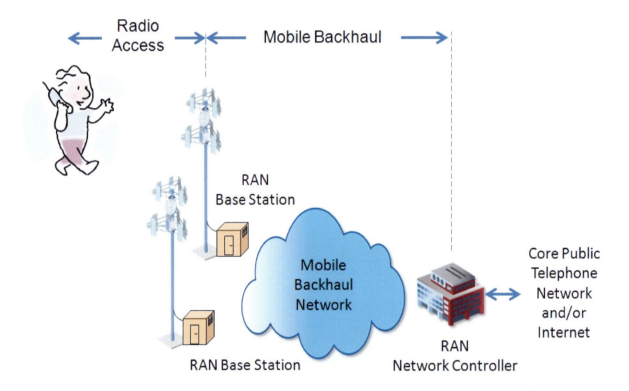

The first link, by radio wave, is between a smart phone (or similar device) and the cell tower. The second link is through a mobile backhaul network connecting one or more cell towers (RAN base stations) to a RAN network controller. The RAN network controller, in turn, provides a gateway to the core public phone network and/or Internet.

Mobile backhaul refers to the network that interconnects RAN base stations with RAN network controllers.

A **mobile backhaul service** is something that an access provider offers to a mobile/cellular service provider (also known as a wireless operator). It supports numerous end users. It is not offered to individual end users (cell phone users).

Mobile backhaul networks have traditionally used TDM and ATM technologies, but the latest generation of equipment and networks is based on Ethernet.

Mobile Backhaul Technologies

Generation	Technologies
2G	TDM
3G	ATM, Ethernet (GSMA/HSPA, CDMA/EVDO)
4G	IP, Ethernet (LTE, WiMAX)

This trend toward Ethernet technology makes Carrier Ethernet a natural fit for mobile backhaul applications going forward.

MEF 22.1, Mobile Backhaul Phase 2 Implementation Agreement specifies requirements for mobile backhaul.

16.3.1 Mobile Backhaul Reference Model

MEF 22.1 uses the following basic reference model and terminology:

Reproduced with permission of the Metro Ethernet Forum

Term		Description
RAN	Radio Access Network	The wireless access network, including the mobile backhaul network connecting RAN CEs
RAN CE	RAN Customer Edge	A generic term that identifies a mobile network node/site (RAN NC or RAN BS)
RAN BS	RAN Base Station	A cell tower/site
RAN NC	RAN Network Controller	A node that aggregates traffic from multiple base stations and provides a gateway to the public phone network and/or Internet

Similar to the MEF reference model for EVC-based service, this reference model involves two stakeholders:

- **Service Provider**—The organization providing the mobile backhaul service

- **Mobile Operator (Subscriber/Customer)**—The organization purchasing the mobile backhaul service

However, the mobile backhaul service is not required to be purely Carrier Ethernet:

- The mobile backhaul service may involve a TDM-based (legacy) component operating in parallel with a Carrier Ethernet component.

- The Carrier Ethernet service component may connect indirectly to the RAN CE through an Inter-working Function (IWF).

For this reason, the previous figure does not include UNIs and does not indicate that the service provider network is a CEN.

16.3.2
Mobile Backhaul Use Cases

MEF 22.1 presents four uses cases to illustrate how Carrier Ethernet services can be applied in mobile backhaul applications.

Use Case	RAN CE Interface Type	In-Parallel Deployment with Legacy Network
Use Case 1a	Non-Ethernet	Yes

Reproduced with permission of the Metro Ethernet Forum

Applications
Mobile Backhaul Services

Use Case	RAN CE Interface Type	In-Parallel Deployment with Legacy Network
Use Case 1b	Non-Ethernet	No
Use Case 2a	Ethernet	Yes
Use Case 2b	Ethernet	No

These four use cases outline a path of evolution from in-parallel deployment with legacy circuit-based equipment to solo deployment with Ethernet-based equipment.

In Use Cases 1a and 1b, the RAN CEs cannot be directly connected to UNIs because they have non-Ethernet–based interfaces, such as ATM or TDM. In these cases, the RAN CE connects to what the MEF calls an Generic Inter-

Working Function (GIWF) or Inter-Working Function (IWF)[152], which in turn connects to the UNI. Use Cases 2a and 2b illustrate deployments with RAN CE equipment that can be connected directly to the UNI through an Ethernet interface, eliminating the need for a GIWF.

Note: *The GIWFs encapsulate synchronous TDM circuits into Ethernet frames for transport across the asynchronous CEN using Circuit Emulation Services over Ethernet (CESoETH). CESoETH is explained later in this lesson.*

Use Cases 1a and 2a show split access scenarios where the CEN is deployed in parallel with a legacy network. These two use cases are used when an operator wants to continue to support low-bandwidth voice traffic with an existing legacy network but offload high-bandwidth data traffic to the CEN, thereby reducing demand on the legacy network. In Use Cases 1b and 2b, the CEN supports all traffic between RAN CEs.

Related Links

Circuit Emulation Services over Ethernet on p. 374
Inter-Working Function on p. 375

16.3.3
Mobile Backhaul for LTE

Note: *The initial MEF-CECP exam did not include this material. It was introduced in MEF 22.1.*

Mobile technologies such as GSM, WCDMA, and CDMA use a centralized *hub-and-spoke* network topology for mobile backhaul. As shown by examples in the following figure, multiple RAN base stations (BTS's or Node B's) connects to a single RAN network controller (BSC or RNC) in hub-and-spoke fashion.

Example GSM and WCDMA Mobile Backhaul Networks (Fig 1, in MEF 22.1)

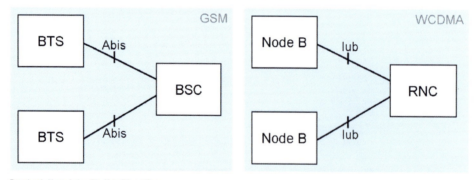

Reproduced with permission of the Metro Ethernet Forum

More recent mobile technologies such as LTE and WiMAX support decentralized control. LTE, for example, supports meshed connectivity between mobile backhaul network elements, as shown by example in the following figure.

---

152 Some MEF specifications use the term GIWF (Generic Inter-Working Function). Others use the term Inter-Working Function (IWF). They are essentially the same thing.

This example includes four network elements: two RAN base stations (eNB's) and two RAN network controllers (one S-GW and one MME). The S-GW terminates data plane traffic (solid lines), while the MME terminates signal and control plane traffic (dashed lines). Each eNB has an X2 connection with a set of neighboring eNB's to support radio handovers.

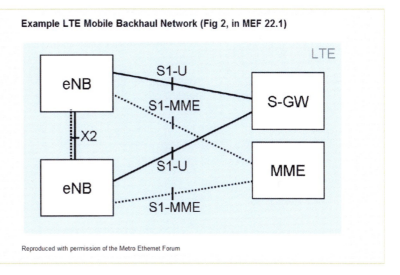

The main point is that mobile backhaul for recent technologies, such as LTE, can involve meshed connectivity, in contrast to earlier technologies that involve only hub-and-spoke connectivity. As a consequence, recent technologies, such a LTE, tend to use a broader range of Carrier Ethernet services.

16.3.4
Mobile Backhaul CoS and Performance Requirements

The evolution in mobile backhaul toward Ethernet-based technology is driven by the explosive growth of high-bandwidth, best-effort data traffic, compared to low-bandwidth, real-time voice traffic. Under these conditions, support for differentiated quality of service (QoS) —supported by Carrier Ethernet— is key to efficient network utilization. With priority-based traffic management, the mobile backhaul service provider can realize better (more profitable) network utilization without compromising end-user experience. This is accomplished by forwarding voice traffic, synchronization traffic, and control traffic ahead of best-effort data traffic.

Per [R42] in MEF 22.1, a mobile backhaul EVC must support at least two classes of service (CoS). The following table (Table 7 in MEF 22.1) provides examples on how mobile backhaul traffic classes might be mapped into four, three, or two CoS Names.

In this table, CoS Names H, M, and L correspond to CoS Labels defined in MEF 23.1. Each value (H, M, or L), used in combination with a performance tier (PT1, PT2, PT3, or PT4), implies specific values of CoS performance objectives (CPOs). Per MEF 22.1, a MEF-compliant mobile backhaul service should conform to performance tier PT1, but may conform to PT2 or PT3.

CoS Names	Generic Traffic Classes[2] mapping to CoS Names			
	4 CoS Names	3 CoS Names	2 CoS Names	2 CoS Names
Very High (H⁺) Defined in this IA	Synchronization	-	-	-
High (H) Defined in [18]	Conversational, Signaling, Network Management and Control	Synchronization, Conversational, Signaling, Network Management and Control	Synchronization, Conversational, Signaling, Network Management Control, and Streaming media	Synchronization, Conversational, Signaling, Network Management, Control, and Streaming media
Medium (M) Defined in [18]	Streaming media	Streaming media	-	Interactive and Background
Low (L) Defined in [18]	Interactive and Background	Interactive and Background	Interactive and Background	

Reproduced with permission of the Metro Ethernet Forum

CoS Name H⁺ is a special CoS Name defined to support packet-based synchronization traffic that requires more stringent performance than is offered by CoS Label H. This table (Table 8 from MEF 22.1) includes CPOs for CoS Name H⁺.

CoS Name	Ingress Bandwidth Profile**	One Way CPO for Mobile Backhaul Service {S, CoS ID, PT}							
		FD	MFD	IFDV	FDR	FLR	Availability	L	B
Very High (H⁺)	CIR>0 EIR=0	≤10 ms	≤7 ms	N/S	A_{FDR}	≤.01% (i.e., 10^{-4})	≥A_{Avail}	≤A_{HLI}	≤A_{CHLI}
High (H)	CIR>0 EIR≥0	For CPO values across PT1 see Table 6 of MEF CoS IA [18].							
Medium (M)	CIR>0 EIR≥0	For CPO values across PT1 see Table 6 of MEF CoS IA [18].							
Low (L)	CIR≥0 EIR≥0*	For CPO values across PT1 see Table 6 of MEF CoS IA [18].							

Notes:
- A_{FDR} values and parameters for H⁺ to be included in a future phase of this IA. Values for FD and MFD might change depending on values for FDR.
- For Synchronization traffic class (see Section 11.4.1) A_{IFDV} for H⁺ = N/S since FDR is used. Also, either MFD or FD needs to be used in SLS.
- (*) both CIR = 0 and EIR = 0 is not allowed as this results in no conformant Service Frames. CIR=0 and EIR>0 results in non-specified objectives.
- (**) Ingress Bandwidth Profile for CoS Labels (H, M and L) are from Table 2 of MEF 23.1 [18].
- CBS, EBS ≥ 8xMTU per MEF 13 [11]
- See Table 5 of MEF CoS IA [18] for Parameters and values for H, M and L

Reproduced with permission of the Metro Ethernet Forum

Note: MEF 22.1, Mobile Backhaul Implementation Agreement – Phase 2, uses resiliency performance metrics HLI and CHLI to quantify "short term disruptions" in mobile backhaul services.

Related Links

Resiliency Performance on p. 157
CoS Labels and Performance Tiers on p. 223
Mobile Backhaul Synchronization on p. 371
Overview of Traffic and Performance Management on p. 104

16.3.5
MEF Service Definitions for Mobile Backhaul

Per MEF 22.1, a case can be made for each EVC-based service (EPL, EVPL, EP-LAN, EVP-LAN, EP-Tree, or EVP-Tree) in mobile backhaul applications.

MEF Service	Mobile Backhaul Application Notes	Example Illustration
Ethernet Private Line (EPL)	The EPL service might be preferred in cases where there is a desire for a 1:1 correspondence between RAN NC UNIs and RAN BS UNIs. However, this solution is not very scalable.	
Ethernet Virtual Private Line (EVPL)	The Ethernet Virtual Private Line (EVPL) service may be used to emulate existing service offerings with a point-to-point relationship between each RAN NC site and each RAN BS site. EVPL supports multiplexing at the UNI. This allows services between the RAN BS and RAN NC to be multiplexed at the RAN NC UNI.	
Ethernet Private LAN (EP-LAN)	Mobile operators with multiple RAN NC sites or deployments where inter RAN BS communication is permitted may want to interconnect them at high speeds so all sites appear to be on the same Local Area Network (LAN) and have equivalent performance. The EP-LAN service is defined to provide All to One bundling at each UNI, CE-VLAN ID preservation, CE-VLAN CoS preservation, and tunneling of key Layer 2 Control Protocols. A key advantage of this approach is that if the mobile operator has outsourced its backhaul network to another service provider or different company (for example, transport/transmission network organization), the mobile operator can configure VLANs at the RAN NCs and the RAN BSs without any need to coordinate with the other Service Provider.	

MEF Service	Mobile Backhaul Application Notes	Example Illustration
Ethernet Virtual Private LAN (EVP-LAN)	Some mobile operators commonly desire an E-LAN service type to connect their UNIs in a Carrier Ethernet network, while at the same time accessing other services from one or more of those UNIs. An example of such a UNI is a mobile operator site that has co-siting of RAN BS of different technologies, such as legacy GSM and WiMAX. Each technology may have a specific EVC assigned to transport mobile backhaul traffic and different UNI peers. The EVP-LAN service may provide similar transparency as the EP-LAN case. For example, bundling may or may not be used on the UNIs in the Multipoint-to-Multipoint EVC. As such, CE-VLAN ID preservation, CE-VLAN CoS preservation, and tunneling of certain Layer 2 Control Protocols may or may not be provided.	
Ethernet Private Tree (EP-Tree)	Mobile operators with multiple sites may want to interconnect them to provide services other than those that resemble a LAN. These services may be distributed from a single or several centralized sites where the distribution sites are designated as roots and all the remaining sites are designated as leaves. Traditionally in mobile backhaul, the RAN BS sites only need to exchange Service Frames with the RAN NC sites and not with other RAN BSs. This behavior is possible in an Ethernet Private Tree (EP-Tree) service, where the RAN NC sites would be roots and the RAN BS sites would be leaves. The EP-Tree service is defined to provide All to One bundling, CE-VLAN ID preservation, CE-VLAN CoS preservation, and tunneling of key Layer 2 Control Protocols. A key advantage of this approach is that the mobile operator can configure VLANs across the sites without any need to coordinate with the Service Provider.	
Ethernet Virtual Private Tree (EVP-Tree)	Some mobile operators desire to keep the root-leaf relationship between RAN NC and RAN BS sites, but also want to multiplex services at one or more of the interconnected UNIs. For such cases, the EVP-Tree service is used. Bundling may or may not be used on the UNIs in the Rooted-Multipoint EVC. As such, CE-VLAN ID preservation, CE-VLAN Cos preservation, and tunneling of certain Layer 2 Control Protocols may or may not be provided. In the example, an EVP-Tree service is used to transport mobile voice and data traffic, while the EVP-LAN service offers an inter-site connection for node and site management.	

16.3.6
MEG Levels in Mobile Backhaul

Per MEF 22.1, if Service OAM (SOAM) is used to monitor a mobile backhaul service:

- The *Subscriber* MEG level is used by the Mobile Operator.

- The *EVC*, *Service Provider*, and *Operator* MEG levels are used by the Service Provider.

- The *UNI* MEG level is used to monitor connectivity between the UNI-C and the UNI-N.

16.3.7
Mobile Backhaul Synchronization

Clock synchronization is required to support voice traffic in mobile backhaul networks. Unlike TDM networks (which are synchronous by design), Ethernet-based networks are asynchronous (nodes have no common clock). So, to support mobile backhaul voice traffic, Carrier Ethernet services must be deployed in combination with a mechanism to distribute timing for clock synchronization.

Frequency, Phase, and Time-of-Day Synchronization

Clock synchronization deals with the problem of ensuring that internal clocks across the network keep the same time in some sense (at least to ensure that clocks tick at the same frequency). Requirements vary with application. Three levels of clock synchronization are broadly recognized: frequency synchronization, phase synchronization, and time-of-day synchronization (also called time synchronization).

Frequency synchronization only ensures that clocks tick at the same rate. They can be out of phase.

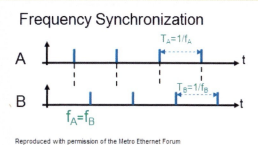

Reproduced with permission of the Metro Ethernet Forum

Phase synchronization ensures that clocks tick at the same rate and are in phase. In other words, all clocks across the network tick at the same time. However, it does not imply that clocks across the network assign the same value of time (or any value of time) to each clock tick.

Note: Phase synchronization implies frequency synchronization.

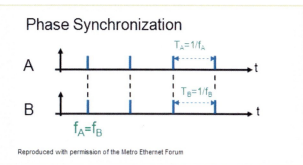

Reproduced with permission of the Metro Ethernet Forum

Time-of-day synchronization (also called Time synchronization) ensures that clocks tick at the same rate, are in phase, and assign the same value of time to each clock tick.

Note: Time-of-day synchronization implies frequency synchronization and phase synchronization.

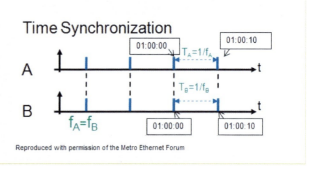

Related Links

Synchronization on p. 376

Mobile Backhaul Synchronization Requirements

Synchronization requirements for mobile backhaul depend on which technology is used.

Mobile Network Architecture	Frequency Sync	Time-of-day / Phase Sync
CDMA2000		✓
GSM	✓	
UMTS-FDD	✓	
LTE-FDD	✓	
UMTS-TDD	✓	✓
LTE-FDD with MBMS-Single Freq. Network	✓	✓
LTE-TDD	✓	✓
Mobile WiMAX	✓	✓
TD-SCDMA	✓	✓

Reproduced with permission of the Metro Ethernet Forum

Mobile Backhaul Synchronization Methods

MEF 22.1 lists four methods for distributing timing from a primary reference clock to slave clocks at RAN BS sites.

Method	Description	Notes
1	Use GPS at RAN BS sites	MEF 22.1 mentions this as a possible method.
2	Distribute timing using a legacy TDM network.	Only viable for mobile backhaul Use Cases 1a and 2a, which include a legacy TDM network operating in parallel with the CEN.
3	Distribute timing over the Ethernet physical layer using synchronous Ethernet (SyncE).	SyncE follows the same approach used for traditional TDM (PDH/SONET/SDH) synchronization. It uses physical layer line signals and is implemented with similar engineering rules and principles. SyncE delivers frequency, but not phase or time of day synchronization.
4	Distribute timing by a packet-based method, such as through Circuit Emulation Services over Ethernet (CESoETH).	CESoETH is required for mobile backhaul Use Case 1b. *Note:* *CESoETH is explained later in this lesson.*

MEF 22.1 addresses frequency synchronization only. Time and phase synchronization are for further study.

CESoETH is required to distribute timing for mobile backhaul Use Case 1b.

In this use case, synchronous TDM circuits (which carry timing) are encapsulated into Ethernet frames and transported across the asynchronous CEN using CESoETH.

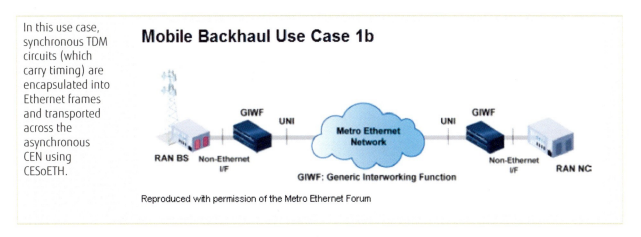

Note: *CESoETH (Circuit Emulation Services over Ethernet) is explained later in this lesson.*

Related Links

Mobile Backhaul Use Cases on p. 364
Circuit Emulation Services over Ethernet on p. 374

16.4
Circuit Emulation Services over Ethernet

In this section:

16.4.1   CEN Requirements for CESoETH
16.4.2   Inter-Working Function
16.4.3   Synchronization

Circuit Emulation Services over Ethernet (CESoETH) services are designed to support TDM circuits, such T1 or E1 lines, over an Ethernet network CEN.

CESoETH uses an EPL or EVPL service in combination with two Inter-Working Functions (IWFs).[153]

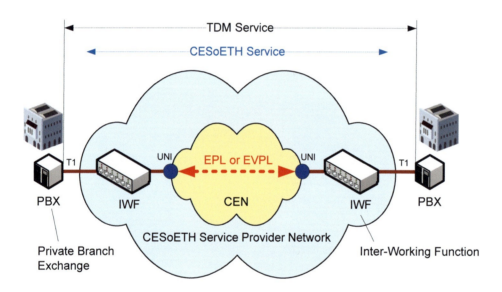

The EPL or EVPL service carries the TDM traffic through the CEN. The IWFs on each end mediate between the asynchronous Carrier Ethernet service (inside the CEN) and the synchronous TDM service (outside the CEN). The resulting service is called a CESoETH service.

CESoETH technology allows a CEN service provider to support synchronous TDM traffic in the same CEN with asynchronous Ethernet traffic.

Three MEF specifications are related to CESoETH:

MEF 3 – Circuit Emulation Service Definitions, Framework and Requirements in Metro Ethernet Networks
MEF 8 – Implementation Agreement for the Emulation of PDH Circuits over Metro Ethernet Networks
MEF 18 –Tests for compliance of CESoETH system – 334 tests for T1/E1 and DS3/E3, including tests of clock recovery

---

[153] In some MEF specifications, the term GIWF (Generic Inter-Working Function) is used in place of IWF. They are essentially the same thing.

16.4.1
CEN Requirements for CESoETH

The Carrier Ethernet service that carries CESoETH must be a point-to-point service (either EPL or EVPL) and should deliver all service frames with high reliability and appropriate performance:

- Bandwidth profiles should include only CIR and CBS components (no EIR or EBS components).

- All service frame delivery attributes should be *Deliver Unconditionally*.

- Class of service performance objectives (CPOs) should be specified to meet TDM standards.

Bandwidth requirements for a TDM circuit, such as a T1 or E1 line, are well defined. The bit rate is constant, and the circuit is always on.

Related Links
CPOs (per CoS Label and Performance Tier) on p. 229

16.4.2
Inter-Working Function

At both ends, the CESoETH service presents a TDM interface to the subscriber (for example a T1 or E1 interface). In the CEN, the CESoETH service traffic is carried as payload within an EPL or EVPL service between two Ethernet interfaces (UNIs). The **Inter-Working Functions (IWFs)** are responsible for all the functions required for the emulated service to function, including all adaptation functions between the TDM interface and the UNI interface. UNI-N functionality within the CEN is unchanged. UNI-C functionality in the customer network is subsumed within the IWF.

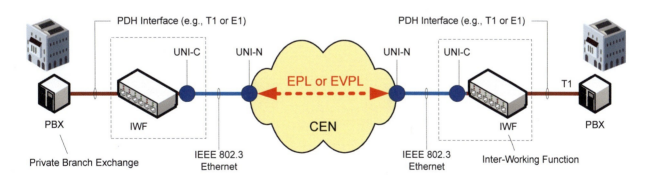

Per MEF 8, IWF functionality includes:

- Encapsulation and de-encapsulation
- Payload formation and extraction
- Synchronization
- Carriage of TDM signaling and alarms
- Error Response and Defect Behaviour
- TDM performance monitoring

16.4.3
Synchronization

Synchronization is the generic concept of distributing common time/frequency references to nodes within a network. Synchronization is required in both mobile backhaul and CESoETH service applications.

In CESoETH service applications, synchronization is required to ensure that the egress clock (used to clock the transmission of TDM bits at the egress IWF) is frequency synchronized with the ingress clock (defined at the ingress IWF).

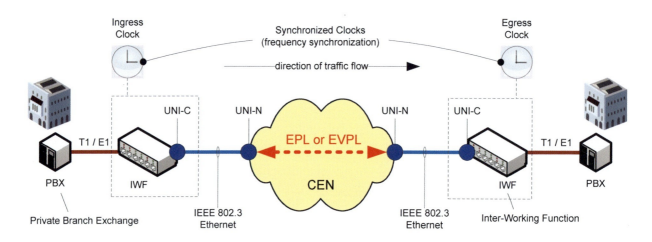

In a TDM network, synchronization is accomplished using TDM technology to keep all clocks across the network in sync. However, Carrier Ethernet services are asynchronous, providing no inherent means for synchronizing clocks.

This problem can be solved using an **external reference source**, such as a TDM line clock or GPS to synchronize the two IWF clocks, but this solution relies on an external system (outside CEN) which may be unavailable or impractical.

Other solutions distribute timing through the CEN using one of two approaches:

1. Distribute timing over the Ethernet physical layer using SyncE.

    - **SyncE** (Synchronous Ethernet) — provides a mechanism to deliver a network traceable physical layer clock over IEEE 802.3 PHYs with *Ethernet Equipment Clock* (EEC) as specified in ITU-T G.8262. The SyncE model follows the same approach that was adopted for traditional TDM (PDH/SDH) synchronization (i.e. utilizing the physical layer line signals) and implemented with similar engineering rules and principles.

2. Distribute timing by a packet-based method, such as using one or more of the following:

    - **ACR** (Adaptive Clock Recovery) is a general method whereby a constant bit rate source stream is packetized and transmitted into the CEN at a precisely known bit rate (the ingress clock frequency). At CEN egress, the bit stream is de-packetized and the frequency of the ingress clock is recovered from the signal using adaptive signal processing to filter out timing deviations that occur due to CEN transport.

ACR is predicated on the existence of a constant bit rate source stream and low loss, low latency transport through the CEN. ACR is most commonly used for CESoETH.

- **NTP** (Network Time Protocol) is defined in RFC 1305 (NTPv3) or RFC 5905 (NTPv4). Operationally, NTP is quite simple: the NTP client polls the NTP server at regular intervals and the server responds with a time stamp. The disadvantage of using NTP for precise timing applications is that there is no allowance to account for network delays other than through multiple poll time averaging techniques and buffering. So NTP, even in the latest implementation, may not meet the higher precision requirements for 3G/4G mobile backhaul.

- **IEEE-1588 v2 / PTP** (Precision Time Protocol) was originally designed to provide precise timing for critical industrial automation applications. It is now providing the highest level of accurate frequency, phase, and time of day to wireless backhaul networks. PTP overcomes the NTP latency and delay variation issues, providing accuracy in the nanosecond range.

Both NTP and PTP (IEEE-1588 v2) can provide time-of-day synchronization. SyncE and ACR can provide frequency synchronization, but cannot provide time-of-day synchronization.

Related Links

Frequency, Phase, and Time-of-Day Synchronization on p. 371

16.5
Review: Applications

1. Why is CESoETH sometimes used in Carrier Ethernet mobile backhaul networks?

   a. For performance monitoring
   b. To support voice traffic and/or to distribute timing
   c. To multiplex traffic from multiple RAN base stations to the RAN network controller
   d. To support CoS

2. A mobile operator approaches a Service Provider to provide mobile backhaul service using a hub-and-spoke topology with a single Ethernet UNI at the hub site where the RAN Network Controller is located. Which of the following is most appropriate?

   a. Use one EPL service between each RAN Base Station and the RAN Network Controller.
   b. Use one EVP-LAN service interconnecting all RAN Base Stations.
   c. Use one EVPL service between each RAN Base Station and the RAN Network Controller.
   d. Use one EVP-Tree service with the RAN base station designated as root and the RAN network controllers designated as leaves.

3. A customer wants to replace a T1 private line with a Carrier Ethernet service. Which of the following bandwidth profiles is most appropriate?

   a. CIR=1.5 Mb/s, CBS=0 bytes, EIR=0, EBS=0
   b. CIR=2 Mb/s, CBS=10,000 bytes, EIR=2 Mb/s, EBS=10,000
   c. CIR=2 Mb/s, CBS=10,000 bytes, EIR=0, EBS=0
   d. CIR=0, CBS=0 bytes, EIR=2 Mb/s, EBS=10,000

4. Which two of the following functions are required to support CESoETH? (Choose two.)

   a. ITU-T G.8031 Ethernet linear protection switching
   b. Synchronization
   c. Internet access
   d. Link OAM (LOAM)
   e. Encapsulation and de-encapsulation

5. Which two of the following services can be used, in conjunction with CESoETH, in the replacement of a TDM private line service? (Choose two.)

   a. EP-LAN
   b. EPL
   c. EP-Tree
   d. EVPL
   e. EVP-LAN

6. LANs at three sites are to be interconnected. Which two of the following service scenarios can be configured to tunnel bridge protocol data units (BPDUs) so that spanning tree protocol (STP) works across the aggregation of connected LANs? (Choose two.)

   a. Each site has one UNI. All three sites are interconnected by an EP-LAN service.
   b. Each site has two UNIs. Each pair of sites is interconnected by an EVPL service.
   c. Each site has one UNI. Each pair of sites is interconnected by an EVPL service.
   d. Each site has one UNI. All three sites are interconnected by an EVP-LAN service.
   e. Each site has two UNIs. Each pair of sites is interconnected by an EPL service.

7. Which two of the following clock synchronization methods transmit timing packets across the Carrier Ethernet network? (Choose two.)

   a. Free run timing
   b. NTP (Network Time Protocol)
   c. SyncE (Synchronous Ethernet)
   d. TDM line timing
   e. PTP (Precision Time Protocol)
   f. External timing

8. A service provider wants to offer very transparent LAN connectivity, while limiting broadcast traffic. Which service solution is best?

   a. EVP-LAN service with EVC attribute *Broadcast Service Frame Delivery* set to *Deliver Conditionally*
   b. EP-LAN service with EVC attribute *Broadcast Service Frame Delivery* set to *Deliver Conditionally*
   c. EVP-LAN service with EVC attribute *Broadcast Service Frame Delivery* set to *Deliver Unconditionally*
   d. EP-LAN service with EVC attribute *Broadcast Service Frame Delivery* set to *Deliver Unconditionally*

9. A hospital has three clinics that need to connect to it. The three clinics are independent companies that must not be allowed to share information with each other. Which two service arrangements are suitable? (Choose two.)

   a. EP-LAN service
   b. EP-Tree service
   c. An EVPL service from each clinic to a service multiplexed UNI at the hospital
   d. An EVP-LAN service

10. Which EVC-based Ethernet services can be used for mobile backhaul?

    a. Any
    b. EVPL or EVP-Tree only
    c. EP-LAN or EP-Tree only
    d. EVP-Tree, EVP-LAN, or EVPL only

11. A sporting goods retailer has two data centers and numerous stores throughout the country. Each store needs to regularly exchange inventory, sales, and payroll information with both data centers. Stores should not exchange data with each other. Which two service arrangements are suitable? (Choose two.)

    a. A full mesh of EVPL services interconnecting all sites
    b. A single EP-LAN service interconnecting all sites
    c. A single EP-Tree service with root UNIs at the data centers and leaf UNIs at the stores
    d. A single EVP-LAN service interconnecting all sites
    e. One EPL service connecting the two data centers and one EVPL service connecting each store to each data center

12. An ISP wants to deliver Internet access services to up to 100 customers through a single 1 Gb/s UNI with each customer allowed up to 10 Mb/s of bandwidth. Which two the following service solutions are viable? (Choose two.)

    a. One EVPL service between each customer and the ISP
    b. One EVP-LAN service connecting all UNIs
    c. One EP-Tree service connecting all UNIs with the ISP UNI designated as a Root and all other UNIs designated as leaves
    d. One EP-LAN service between each customer and the ISP

13. MEF 22.1 defines four use cases for transporting mobile backhaul traffic over Carrier Ethernet services. When is CESoETH (Circuit Emulation Services over Ethernet) required?

    a. When RAN CE can connect to the Ethernet UNI through an Ethernet interface, eliminating the need for a Generic Inter-Working Function (GIWF)
    b. When the RAN CE cannot connect to the Ethernet UNI and there is no legacy network operating in parallel to deliver timing
    c. When timing is distributed over the Ethernet physical layer using synchronous Ethernet (SyncE)
    d. When the operator needs to support voice traffic via an existing legacy network and offload data to a Carrier Ethernet network

14. A customer wants to replace a T1 private line service between two PBXs (private branch exchanges) with a Carrier Ethernet service. Which technology is required to carry the customer's traffic over a Carrier Ethernet Network (CEN)?

    a. SONET/SDH
    b. CESoETH
    c. ATM
    d. Frame Relay

15. An enterprise has a headquarters (HQ) and four branch offices. Each branch office requires access to the Internet through a firewall at HQ, but no access to each other. In addition, HQ requires connection to the Internet service provider (ISP). Which two of the following service arrangements supports these requirements using only one physical connection at each site? (Choose two.)

    a. One EP-Tree service with HQ and ISP designated as roots and branch offices designated as leaves
    b. Four EVPL services connecting branch offices to HQ, plus one EVPL service connecting HQ with ISP
    c. One EVP-LAN service interconnecting the branch offices and HQ, plus one EVPL service between HQ and ISP
    d. One EVPL service between HQ and ISP, plus one EVP-Tree service with HQ designated as the root and branch offices designated as leaves

16. A subscriber needs a single EVP-LAN service to connect numerous sites to three applications. All three applications use a different VLAN. All other VLANs should be blocked. Which two attribute settings are required? (Choose two.)

    a. Service Multiplexing = Disabled
    b. Bundling = Enabled
    c. Service Multiplexing = Enabled
    d. CE VLAN ID Preservation = Enabled
    e. Bundling = Disabled

17. A subscriber requires an EP-LAN service between 6 sites: 3 in Los Angeles and 3 in Miami. The LA sites are on-net (reachable by the Service Provider's network). The Miami sites are off-net and only reachable through an Ethernet Access Provider that has no connectivity to the Service Provider. To deliver this service, the Service Provider purchases three Access EPLs from the Miami Ethernet Access Provider and one point-to-point OVC from an Interstate Operator. The Interstate Operator shares one ENNI with the LA Service Provider and one ENNI with the Miami Ethernet Access Provider. Which of the following statements is not consistent with this service scenario?

    a. The OVC in the Interstate Operator network uses end point map bundling.
    b. The OVC in the Service Provider network is multipoint-to-multipoint.
    c. The OVC in the Interstate Operator network provides hairpin switching.
    d. Three OVC end points in the Ethernet Access Provider network interconnect (through the ENNI) to a single OVC endpoint in the Interstate Operator network.
    e. Three OVC end points in the Service Provider network interconnect (through the ENNI) to a single OVC endpoint in the Interstate Operator network.

18. An Ethernet Mobile Backhaul Service provides:

    a. Radio access between cell phone users and cell tower base stations
    b. Temporary Ethernet services through a mobile WiMAX network
    c. Connectivity between two or more mobile phone users
    d. Connectivity between RAN base stations and RAN network controllers
    e. A gateway between the public mobile phone network and the Internet

19. A service provider uses Carrier Ethernet as the access network technology to deliver an IP service. What functionality does Ethernet access provide for the service provider?

    a. A Layer 3 (IP) VPN
    b. Layer 2 connectivity to a Layer 3 service or an Internet Service Provider (ISP)
    c. Connection to the Internet through a Layer 2 (Ethernet) firewall
    d. Layer 2 emulation of a Layer 3 (IP) access service
    e. A virtual private gateway to the Internet

20. A company wants to connect two remote campuses to its corporate headquarters, extending all corporate VLANs across all three locations. Which two properties make the EP-LAN service a good choice for this application? (Choose two.)

   a. The service provider can forward frames without MAC address learning.
   b. The company does not have to coordinate CE-VLAN IDs with the service provider.
   c. The service can perform CE-VLAN ID translation if desired.
   d. The company can run STP across all locations if desired.
   e. The UNIs can support service multiplexing if desired.

21. Which two statements concerning Carrier Ethernet mobile backhaul are true? (Choose two.)

   a. A mobile backhaul service must support at least 2 classes of service.
   b. A mobile operator using SOAM uses the Subscriber MEG level.
   c. If LTE technology is used, the mobile backhaul service topology must be "hub and spoke."
   d. CoS Label H$^+$ must be used for packet-based synchronization traffic.

22. A mobile operator requests mobile backhaul services for a 4G LTE network that includes base stations (called eNodeBs) with Ethernet interfaces. Which of the following options would you recommend for interconnecting the eNodeBs to the Carrier Ethernet mobile backhaul service?

   a. Generic Inter-Working Function (GIWF)
   b. Circuit Emulation Services over Ethernet (CESoETH)
   c. GIWF in combination with CESoETH
   d. None of the above

23. A subscriber has 10 sites with one UNI at each site. The 10 sites are interconnected by an EVP-LAN service that supports multiple VLANs between the sites. Each UNI also supports one EVPL service that connects the site to an Internet service provider (ISP). Which one of the following configuration options is not required?

   a. Configure all UNIs with *Bundling* set to *Enabled*.
   b. Configure *CE-VLAN ID Preservation* for each EVPL service to *Enabled*.
   c. Configure *CE-VLAN ID Preservation* for the EVP-LAN service to *Enabled*.
   d. Configure all UNIs with *Service Multiplexing* set to *Enabled*.

24. Which one of the following technologies interconnects a PDH interface and an Ethernet UNI?

   a. Inter-Working Function (IWF)
   b. Circuit Emulation Service over Ethernet (CESoETH)
   c. Long-Term Evolution (LTE)
   d. IEEE-1588 v2 Precision Time Protocol (PTP)

25. Time of day synchronization can be achieved using which two technologies? (Choose two.)

a. IEEE-1588 v2 Precision Time Protocol (PTP)
b. Adaptive Clock Recovery (ACR)
c. Network Time Protocol (NTP)
d. Synchronous Ethernet (SyncE)

26. An enterprise needs Carrier Ethernet services that give two branch offices access to critical business applications located at corporate headquarters, but not to each other. The critical business applications use VLAN IDs 10 and 20. CE devices do not support translation of CE VLAN IDs. All other VLANs should be blocked. Both branch offices need access to both critical business applications. Which service arrangement will support this application?

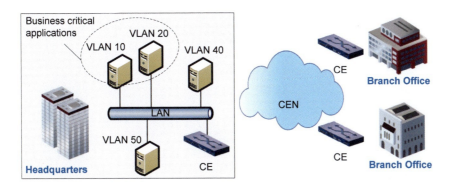

a. One Ethernet Private Line (EPL) service between each branch and the headquarters.
b. One Ethernet Virtual Private Line (EVPL) service between each branch and the headquarters. At the headquarters CE, both EVCs terminate on one UNI that is configured for service multiplexing.
c. One Ethernet Virtual Private Line (EVPL) service between each branch office and the headquarters. At the headquarters CE, the EVPLs terminate on different UNIs, which are both configured to support bundling.
d. One Ethernet Private Tree (EP-Tree) service with the headquarters UNI designated as the root and branch offices designated as leaves and with the root UNI configured to support bundling.

Related Links

Answers: Applications on p. 440

17
MEF Certification Program

In this chapter:

17.1 Equipment and Services Certification
17.2 Professional Certification
17.3 Review: MEF Certification

The MEF defines and administers a threefold certification program to confirm compliance with and/or knowledge of Carrier Ethernet specifications:

- **Equipment Certification**—Confirms that the equipment offered by an equipment vendor complies with MEF standards and is fully capable of supporting high-performance Carrier Ethernet services

- **Service Certification**—Confirms that the service offered by a service provider conforms to MEF standards of quality and performance

- **Professional Certification**—Confirms that the individual awarded the certificate has proven knowledge and the skills to support the explosive growth of Carrier Ethernet across the world's markets

For both equipment and services, the MEF has two categories of certification:

- **CE 1.0 Certification** – Introduced in 2005 and discontinued in 2015.[154] Certifies compliance with MEF 9 and/or MEF 14. Applicable to EPL, EVPL, EP-LAN, and EVP-LAN services only.

- **CE 2.0 Certification** – Introduced in 2013. Certifies compliance with *MEF Carrier Ethernet 2.0 Certification Blueprint*. Applicable to EPL, EVPL, EP-LAN, EVP-LAN, EP-Tree, EVP-Tree, Access EPL, and Access EVPL services.

For professional certification, the MEF offers MEF-CECP (MEF Carrier Ethernet Certified Professional) certification.

---

15 As of March 31st, 2015, the MEF no longer offers CE 1.0 certifications. However, CE 1.0 certifications already obtained continue to be
4 valid and recognized.

17.1
Equipment and Services Certification

In this section:

17.1.1 CE 1.0 Certification
17.1.2 CE 2.0 Certification
17.1.3 Equipment Certification
17.1.4 Service Certification

The *MEF Carrier Ethernet 2.0 Services Technical Foundation Document*, available from the MEF Web site (mef.net), provides tables such as the following comparing CE 2.0 and CE 1.0 requirements. For each service, CE 2.0 certification includes all CE 1.0 requirements. So, CE 2.0 certification implies compliance with CE 1.0.

E-Line - EVC per UNI Service Attributes and SOAM Frames Handling

EVC per UNI Service Attributes	What's new in Carrier Ethernet 2.0	EPL 1.0	EPL 2.0	EVPL 1.0	EVPL 2.0
UNI EVC ID	Carrier Ethernet 1.0 and 2.0 require the UNI EVC ID to be a string formed by the concatenation of the UNI ID and the EVC ID.	✔	✔	✔	✔
CE-VLAN ID / EVC Map	Carrier Ethernet 2.0 requires that all Service Frames at the UNI map to a single point-to-point EVC for EPL and to specify mapping table of CE-VLAN IDs to EVC ID for EVPL.	✔	✔ Enh.	✔	✔ Enh.
Ingress BWP Per EVC	If ingress BWP per EVC is supported, Carrier Ethernet 2.0 requires configuration granularities per UNI Type 1 IA.	✔	✔ Enh.	✔	✔ Enh.
Ingress BWP Per CoS ID	If ingress BWP per CoS ID is supported, Carrier Ethernet 2.0 requires configuration granularities per UNI Type 1 IA.	✔	✔ Enh.	✔	✔ Enh.
Egress BWP Per EVC	Carrier Ethernet 2.0 requires to not specify Egress BWP per EVC.	✘	✘	✘	✘
Egress BWP Per CoS ID	Carrier Ethernet 2.0 requires to not specify Egress BWP per CoS ID.	✘	✘	✘	✘
SOAM Frames Handling	**What's new in Carrier Ethernet 2.0**	**1.0**	**2.0**	**1.0**	**2.0**
Connectivity Check messages	Carrier Ethernet 2.0 requires that all CCM frames at the default Test and Subscriber MEG levels be tunneled.	✘	✔ New	✘	✔ New
Linktrace messages with at least one MIP configured	Where at least one MIP is configured at the default Test or Subscriber MEG level, Carrier Ethernet 2.0 requires that Linktrace frames with the corresponding target MAC DA and MEG level be peered or discarded.	✘	✔ New	✘	✔ New
Linktrace messages without any MIPs configured	Where no MIPs are configured at the default Test or Subscriber MEG level, Carrier Ethernet 2.0 requires that Linktrace frames with the corresponding target MAC DA and MEG level be tunneled.	✘	✔ New	✘	✔ New
Unicast Loopback messages with at least one MIP configured	Where at least one MIP is configured at the default Test or Subscriber MEG level, Carrier Ethernet 2.0 requires that Loopback frames with the corresponding target unicast MAC DA and MEG level be peered or discarded.	✘	✔ New	✘	✔ New
Unicast Loopback messages with at least one MIP configured	Where at least one MIP is configured at the default Test or Subscriber MEG level, Carrier Ethernet 2.0 requires that Loopback frames with the corresponding MEG level and a target unicast DA not equal to the MAC address of any MIPs be tunneled.	✘	✔ New	✘	✔ New
Multicast Loopback messages	Carrier Ethernet 2.0 requires that all multicast Loopback frames at the default Test and Subscriber MEG levels be tunneled.	✘	✔ New	✘	✔ New

✔ New — New attribute introduced in CE 2.0
✔ — Attribute introduced in CE 1.0 and still applicable as is in CE 2.0
✔ Enh. — Attribute introduced in CE 1.0 and enhanced in CE 2.0
✘ — Attribute not specified

Reproduced with permission of the Metro Ethernet Forum

17.1.1
CE 1.0 Certification

 CE 1.0, introduced in 2005 and discontinued in 2015, certifies that equipment (or service) complies with MEF 9 and/or MEF 14.

MEF Test Specification	Description
MEF 9 (Ethernet Services at the UNI)	244 Test Cases to verify that Carrier Ethernet EPL, EVPL, and E-LAN services comply with the functional specifications defined by the MEF for each service.
MEF 14 (Traffic Management Phase 1)	183 Test Cases to verify that Carrier Ethernet EPL, EVPL, and E-LAN services adhere to a strict set of MEF service performance objectives.

CE 1.0 certification applies to EPL, EVPL, EP-LAN and EVP-LAN services only. CE 1.0 certification is based on technical specifications MEF 6 and MEF 10. CE 1.0 service certification requires use of CE 1.0–certified equipment.

Note: As of March 31st, 2015, the MEF no longer offers CE 1.0 certifications. However, CE 1.0 certifications already obtained continue to be valid and recognized.

17.1.2
CE 2.0 Certification

 CE 2.0 certification, introduced in 2013, certifies compliance with the *MEF Carrier Ethernet 2.0 Certification Blueprint*, available from the MEF Web site (mef.net).

CE 2.0 certification is per service—The equipment manufacturer (or service provider) can apply for certification for any one or more of 8 Carrier Ethernet services: EPL, EVPL, EP-LAN, EVP-LAN, EP-Tree, EVP-Tree, Access EPL, and/or Access EVPL. There is no requirement to get certified for all eight services.

CE 2.0 certification tests CPOs for point-to-point services only—Because MEF 23.1 does not define CoS performance objectives (CPOs) for multipoint EVCs and OVCs, CE 2.0 certification tests CPOs for E-Line and E-Access services only.

CPO testing (if applicable) is per MEF-standardized CoS Label and Performance Tier—Point-to-point services can be certified with respect to any selection of CoS Labels and Performance Tiers defined in MEF 23.1. There is no requirement to certify a service with respect to all CoS Labels and Performance Tiers.

As shown in the following table, CE 2.0 certification verifies that the equipment (or service) supports all applicable service attributes, plus certain Service OAM frame handling requirements.

Note: CE 2.0 certification verifies that all CCM frames at the default Test and Subscriber MEG levels are tunneled.

Attributes and Requirements Verified by CE 2.0 Certification	
EPL, EVPL, EP-LAN, EVP-LAN, EP-Tree or EVP-Tree	Access EPL or Access EVPL
1. Per UNI service attributes 2. EVC per UNI service attributes 3. Per EVC service attributes 4. Service OAM Frame Handling	1. Per UNI service attributes 2. ENNI Service Attributes 3. OVC Per UNI service attributes 4. OVC End Point Per ENNI Service Attributes 5. OVC Service Attributes 6. Service OAM Frame Handling

CE 2.0 certification is based on MEF 6.1, MEF 10.2, MEF 23.1, MEF 26.1, and MEF 33. For details, refer to the *MEF Carrier Ethernet 2.0 Certification Blueprint* available from the MEF Web site (mef.net).

CE 2.0 Certification Deliverables

CE 2.0 companies receive a set of marketing and technical materials designed to be included in product documentation, Web site content, press releases, product launches, and RFP responses. Additional deliverables, per certification, include:

- **CE 2.0 Certificate**—Official statement of CE 2.0 certification principally used as proof of compliance in response to customer requests. Certificates are delivered in soft and hard copies.
- **CE 2.0 Test Report**—Provides a comprehensive technical description of the CE 2.0 services that are tested together with a full set of test results. Reports are the property of the CE 2.0 Company and are distributed at its discretion.
- **CE 2.0 Certified Compliant Logo**—Delivered in print and publishing formats, the logo provides instant recognition of CE 2.0 companies, services, and equipment.
- **MEF Certification Registry**—New certifications are added to the official on-line registry of MEF certified companies and services. Posted on the MEF Web site, this directory is widely consulted in the industry.

Related Links

CPOs (per CoS Label and Performance Tier) on p. 229

17.1.3
Equipment Certification

MEF Equipment Certification ensures that products conform to MEF global Carrier Ethernet specifications. Equipment vendors apply for equipment certification through an independent streamlined process, with testing conducted by **Iometrix**, the official MEF certification lab. If equipment achieves certification, the equipment vendor receives a certificate that can be used in product documentation, Web site content, press releases, product launches, and RFP responses. The MEF public Web site provides a complete listing of certified products, per vendor, so that customers can validate certification.

MEF equipment certification also benefits service providers, helping them to confidently select equipment and systems appropriate for MEF service implementation.

CE 1.0 Certification testing is no longer available, but CE 1.0 certifications already obtained continue to be valid and recognized. **CE 2.0 Certification**, introduced in 2013, certifies compliance with *MEF Carrier Ethernet 2.0*

Certification Blueprint, and is applicable to EPL, EVPL, EP-LAN, EVP-LAN, EP-Tree, EVP-Tree, Access EPL, and Access EVPL services.

Prerequisite: Any equipment manufacturer with a Carrier Ethernet product can apply for certification of its products <u>providing it is a MEF member at the time of the actual certification testing</u>.[155]

CE 2.0 Equipment Certification:

- **Is per service**—The equipment manufacturer can apply for certification with respect to any one or any combination of 8 Carrier Ethernet services: EPL, EVPL, EP-LAN, EVP-LAN, EP-Tree, EVP-Tree, Access EPL, and/or Access EVPL. Equipment is not required to support all 8 services.
- **Does not require CE 1.0 equipment certification**— There is no requirement for equipment to already have CE 1.0 certification (MEF 9 and/or MEF 14 certification) in order to be tested for CE 2.0 equipment certification.
- **Ensures compliance** to the *MEF Carrier Ethernet 2.0 Certification Blueprint*, available from the MEF Web site (mef.net).
- **Provides deliverables** to the equipment manufacturer, as previously explained for CE 2.0 Certification.

The Equipment Certification Process

Equipment certification is carried out by the MEF-approved test lab, Iometrix, according to the following three-phase process:

1. **Qualification**—The equipment manufacturer conducts a detailed review of the candidate equipment for certification by telephone and email with Iometrix. A thorough and effective Qualification phase reduces effort required by the equipment manufacturer for the subsequent Configuration phase.
2. **Configuration**—Once the Qualification phase is complete, the equipment manufacturer configures the equipment according to recommendations by Iometrix in order to prepare the equipment for live testing. Again, an effective Configuration phase minimizes the time and effort required by the equipment manufacturer for the Testing phase.
3. **Testing**—The equipment manufacturer <u>sends the product accompanied by suitably trained staff</u> to the Iometrix test lab in San Francisco. Testing continues until certification is achieved.

For more information about equipment certification, refer to the MEF Web site (mef.net) and the Iometrix Web site (Iometrix.com).

17.1.4
Service Certification

MEF Service Certification is designed for service providers and validates compliance of Carrier Ethernet services to MEF specifications through an independent streamlined process. Testing is conducted on live services provisioned across the service provider production network by **Iometrix**, the official MEF certification lab. If a service achieves certification, the service provider receives a certificate that can be used in service documentation, Web site content, press releases, service launches, and RFP responses. The MEF public Web site provides a complete listing of certified services, per vendor, so that customers can validate certification.

CE 1.0 Certification testing is no longer available, but CE 1.0 certifications already obtained continue to be valid and recognized. **CE 2.0 Certification**, introduced in 2013, certifies compliance with *MEF Carrier Ethernet 2.0 Certification Blueprint*, and is applicable to EPL, EVPL, EP-LAN, EVP-LAN, EP-Tree, EVP-Tree, Access EPL, and Access EVPL services.

---

[155] *Once equipment certification is granted, it remains forever valid, regardless of MEF membership status.*

Prerequisite: Any service provider with a Carrier Ethernet service can apply for certification of its service - providing it is a MEF member at the time of the actual certification testing.[156]

CE 2.0 Service Certification:

- **Is per service**—The service provider can apply for certification with respect to any one or any combination of 8 Carrier Ethernet services: EPL, EVPL, EP-LAN, EVP-LAN, EP-Tree, EVP-Tree, Access EPL, and/or Access EVPL. The service provider is not required to get all 8 services certified.
- **Tests CPOs for E-Line and E-Access services only**—Because MEF 23.1 does not define CoS performance objectives (CPOs) for multipoint EVCs and OVCs, CPO testing only occurs for E-Line and E-Access services.
- **CPO testing (if applicable) is per MEF-standardized CoS Label and Performance Tier**—The service provider will indicate the CoS Label(s) and Performance Tier(s) that the service under certification supports.
- **Does not require CE 1.0 service certification**—There is no requirement for a service to already have CE 1.0 certification (MEF 9 and/or MEF 14 certification) in order to be tested for CE 2.0 service certification.
- **Does not require CE 2.0 certified equipment**—As stated on the MEF web site: "*It is not mandatory to use CE 2.0 certified network equipment for the CE 2.0 certified service – however it is strongly recommended by the MEF in order to maximize the efficiency of the process of certifying the CE 2.0 service.*"
- **Ensures compliance** to the *MEF Carrier Ethernet 2.0 Certification Blueprint*, available from the MEF Web site (mef.net).
- **Provides deliverables** to the service provider, as previously explained for CE 2.0 Certification.

The Service Certification Process

Service certification is carried out by the MEF-approved test lab, Iometrix, according to the following three-phase process:

1. **Qualification**— The service provider conducts a detailed review of the candidate services for certification by telephone and email with Iometrix. A thorough and effective Qualification phase reduces effort required by the service provider for the subsequent Configuration phase.
2. **Configuration**— Once the Qualification phase is complete, the service provider configures its service according to recommendations by Iometrix in order to prepare the service for live testing. Again, an effective Configuration phase minimizes the time and effort required by the service provider for the Testing phase.
3. **Testing**—Iometrix provides two or more network probes to the service provider, which are then attached by the service provider in pre-defined locations to enable remote testing by Iometrix of the service to be certified.

Services are tested remotely, *in situ* in the service provider network wherever it is located. For EVC-based services, testing is UNI-to-UNI. For Access EPL and Access EVPL services, testing is UNI-to-ENNI.

For more information about service certification, refer to the MEF Web site (mef.net) and the Iometrix Web site (Iometrix.com).

Related Links

CPOs (per CoS Label and Performance Tier) on p. 229

---

156 Once service certification is granted, it remains forever valid, regardless of MEF membership status.

17.2 Professional Certification

Reproduced with permission of the Metro Ethernet Forum

The MEF professional certification program is designed for professionals seeking to validate their expertise, skills, and knowledge of Carrier Ethernet technologies, standards, services, and applications.

MEF-CECP certification is awarded to individuals who pass the MEF-CECP exam, which covers material listed in the current MEF-CECP Certification Exam Blueprint published on the *MEF Reference Wiki* at the time the exam is taken.

Individuals who pass the MEF-CECP exam are awarded:

1. An official MEF-CECP certificate

2. A listing, as being MEF-CECP certified, on the online Directory of MEF Certified Professionals posted at the widely visited EthernetAcademy.net Web site

3. Qualification to use the MEF-CECP logo (for example, in e-mail signatures, business cards, and CVs) for instant recognition of their status

The MEF-CECP exam is open to anyone (you need not be an MEF member) and may be taken online from your home or office, or from an MEF Accredited Training Provider, such as Fujitsu. Refer to the EthernetAcademy.net Web site for more details.

Related Links

About MEF-CECP Certification on p. 15

17.3
Review: MEF Certification

1. Which two services can include CE 2.0 certified support for CoS Label H at Performance Tier 2? (Choose two.)

   a. EPL
   b. EVP-LAN
   c. EP-Tree
   d. Access EVPL

2. Which two are required for an equipment vendor to participate in MEF CE 2.0 testing? (Choose two.)

   a. The equipment vendor must supply the equipment to Iometrix (the official MEF certification lab).
   b. The equipment vendor must attend MEF quarterly member meetings.
   c. The equipment vendor must be ISO 9001 compliant.
   d. The equipment vendor must be a member of the MEF.

3. For MEF CE 2.0 service certification, where does testing occur?

   a. At the Iometrix lab (the official MEF certification lab)
   b. On the service provider's production network
   c. On a representative network using MEF-certified networking equipment
   d. At an MEF testing facility

4. Which one of the following is true for MEF CE 2.0 service certification?

   a. The service provider must provide on-site engineering support at the Iometrix lab during of testing.
   b. The service provider must be a member of the MEF.
   c. The service must terminate on MEF-certified equipment.
   d. Certification is lost if MEF membership is not renewed annually.

5. Where is equipment tested for MEF CE 2.0 equipment certification?

   a. At the Iometrix lab (the official MEF certification lab)
   b. On the service provider's production network
   c. On the MEF service certification network
   d. At the equipment vendor's facility

6. CE 2.0 Certification allows <u>equipment</u> to be certified with respect to:

   a. Link OAM (per clause 57 of IEEE 802.3) at the UNI
   b. Any one or more of 8 services: EPL, EVPL, EP-LAN, EVP-LAN, EP-Tree, EVP-Tree, Access EPL, and/or Access EVPL
   c. CESoETH (per ITU-T G.8261, G.823 and G.824)
   d. The following service only: EPL, EVPL, and/or E-LAN (EP-LAN together with EVP-LAN)

Related Links

Answers: MEF Certification on p. 447

18
Answers to Review Questions

In this chapter:

- 18.1 Answers: Carrier Ethernet Services
- 18.2 Answers: Ethernet Frames and Service Frames
- 18.3 Answers: How Carrier Ethernet Services are Defined
- 18.4 Answers: Service Connectivity Attributes
- 18.5 Answers: Traffic and Performance Management
- 18.6 Answers: Bandwidth Profiles
- 18.7 Answers: EVC Performance Attributes
- 18.8 Answers: UNI Requirements
- 18.9 Answers: Extending MEF Services over Multiple Operator CENs
- 18.10 Answers: MEF-Standardized Classes of Service
- 18.11 Answers: E-Access Services
- 18.12 Answers: Ethernet OAM
- 18.13 Answers: Access Technologies
- 18.14 Answers: Transport Technologies
- 18.15 Answers: Applications
- 18.16 Answers: MEF Certification

18.1
Answers: Carrier Ethernet Services

1. The interface between an Operator CEN and the subscriber is called a(an):

   a. ENNI
   b. OVC
   c. UNI
   d. EVC
   e. CE

   Note: Refer to General Reference Model.

2. Service multiplexing allows:

   a. Multiple services on one EVC
   b. Multiple EVCs on one UNI
   c. Multiple UNIs on one EVC
   d. Bundling
   e. Multiple CE-VLAN IDs to be mapped to an EVC

   Note: Refer to Service Multiplexing.

3. What is the MEF definition of a UNI?

   a. The logical representation of a service connection between two or more EVCs
   b. The physical demarcation point between the responsibility of the Service Provider and the responsibility of the Subscriber
   c. All functions required to connect the CE to the CEN
   d. The interface between two Operator CENs

   Note: Refer to Basic Reference Model.

4. Equipment on the subscriber side of the UNI that connects to the CEN is called the:

   a. Carrier edge
   b. Subscriber edge
   c. User network interface
   d. Consumer edge
   e. Customer edge
   f. Network edge

   Note: Refer to Basic Reference Model.

5. Which two Carrier Ethernet service combinations can be offered simultaneously at a given UNI?

   a. EP-LAN and EVPL
   b. EVP-Tree and EPL
   c. EVPL and EVP-LAN
   d. EPL and EP-Tree

   Note: Refer to Port-Based versus VLAN-Based Services.

6. A UNI is configured to support all-to-one bundling. Which statement is NOT true?

   a. Service multiplexing is not supported at the UNI.
   b. **Any number of EVCs can be bundled to this UNI.**
   c. Bundling is not supported at the UNI.
   d. At this UNI, all CE-VLAN IDs map to the same EVC.

   Note: Refer to Bundling.

7. Which three service types are defined in MEF 6.2? (Choose three.)

   a. Ethernet Virtual Connection (EVC)
   b. **Ethernet Line (E-Line)**
   c. **Ethernet Tree (E-Tree)**
   d. Ethernet Access (E-Access)
   e. **Ethernet LAN (E-LAN)**
   f. TDM Line (T-Line)

   Note: Refer to Taxonomy of EVC-Based Services.

8. An enterprise needs to connect three branch offices with its two payroll processing data centers. The two data centers require interconnectivity for data mirroring (protection). The service should not allow the branch offices to communicate directly with each other. Which two of the following service arrangements supports this application? (Choose two.)

   a. An EP-Tree service with the payroll data center UNIs designated as leaves and the branch office UNIs designated as roots
   b. **An EP-Tree service with payroll data center UNIs designated as roots and branch office UNIs designated as leaves**
   c. One EP-LAN service connecting all five sites
   d. **One EVPL service from each branch office to each payroll data center (six EVPLs in all), plus an EPL between the two payroll centers**

   Note: (a) Allows branches to see each other's payroll data. (b) Works. (c) Does not prevent communication between branch offices. (d) Works. Requires two UNIs at both payroll centers.

9. A UNI is configured without bundling or all-to-one bundling and is also configured to support service multiplexing. How many EVCs can terminate at this UNI?

   a. 0
   b. 0 or 1
   c. Up to 64
   d. **Up to 4094**

   Note: There are 4094 distinct VLAN identifiers (VIDs) in a VLAN tag. Per IEEE 802.1Q, the maximum number of VLANs that can be supported by the 12-bit VID field is 4094 rather than 4096 because VID values 0 and FFF are reserved. Refer to Service Frames.

10. Which kind of UNI-to-UNI connectivity is used for the Ethernet Private Line (EPL) service?

   a. Ethernet Private Circuit
   b. Point-to-point Ethernet Private Connection
   c. Point-to-point Ethernet Virtual Connection
   d. Point-to-point Ethernet Virtual Circuit

   *Note: Refer to EPL Service and recall that **EVC** stands for **Ethernet Virtual Connection**. All three incorrect answers are red herrings: the MEF does not use the terms "Ethernet Private Circuit," "Ethernet Private Connection," or "Ethernet Virtual Circuit."*

11. A customer with three locations requests a Carrier Ethernet service that provides the most transparent connectivity for all PDU types between sites. Which service is most suitable?

   a. A single Ethernet Private LAN (EP-LAN)
   b. A single Ethernet Virtual Private LAN (EVP-LAN)
   c. A single Ethernet Private Tree (EP-Tree)
   d. A single Ethernet Virtual Private Tree (EVP-Tree)

   Note: (a) Works and provides the most transparency. (b) Works, but with less transparency. (c) and (d) All E-Tree service types limit connectivity between sites with Leaf UNIs (one of the site UNIs must be designated as a Root UNI). Refer to Matrix of Service Distinctions.

12. McBary's, a business enterprise with numerous independently-owned restaurant franchises, wants to connect each franchise to the corporate data center to obtain daily sales information. Which two of the following service arrangements do you recommend for this application? (Choose two.)

   a. A single Ethernet Virtual Private LAN (EVP-LAN) service
   b. One Ethernet Virtual Private Line (EVPL) service between each franchise and the corporate data center
   c. A single Ethernet Private Tree (EP-Tree) service with the corporate data center UNI designated as the root and franchise UNIs designated as leaves
   d. One Ethernet Private Line (EPL) service between each franchise and the corporate data center

   Note: (a) Works, but also interconnects franchises which is not desirable because each franchise is independently owned (they are different businesses). (b) Works. (c) Works. (d) Works, but is impractical because a separate UNI is required at the corporate data center for each franchise.

13. Which two statements about a VLAN-based (virtual private) service are true? (Choose two.)

   a. All UNIs must be configured to support service multiplexing.
   b. All UNIs must be configured to support bundling.
   c. All UNIs must be configured to support all-to-one bundling.
   d. All UNIs may be configured to support service multiplexing.
   e. All UNIs may be configured to support bundling.
   f. All UNIs may be configured to support all-to-one bundling.

   Note: Refer to Port-Based versus VLAN-Based Services.

14. A UNI is configured without bundling or all-to-one bundling and is also configured to support service multiplexing. What is the maximum number of CE-VLAN IDs that can be mapped to a given EVC at the UNI?

    a. 0
    b. <u>1</u>
    c. 256
    d. 4094
    e. 4096

    Note: Without bundling or all-to-one bundling, only one CE-VLAN ID can be mapped to an EVC. Refer to Bundling and Bundling versus Service Multiplexing.

15. Which Carrier Ethernet services typically forward Ethernet frames based on MAC address learning? (Choose all answers that are correct.)

    a. EPL
    b. EVPL
    c. **EP-LAN**
    d. **EVP-LAN**
    e. **EP-Tree**
    f. **EVP-Tree**

    Note: E-LAN and E-Tree services typically support bridging. E-Line (and E-Access) services do not. Refer to Matrix of Service Distinctions.

16. The MEF refers to an Ethernet frame transmitted across a UNI towards the subscriber as a (an):

    a. L2CP frame
    b. Subscriber frame
    c. **Service frame**
    d. UNI frame

    Note: An Ethernet frame transmitted across the UNI toward the CEN is also called a service frame. Refer to Service Frames.

Related Links

Review: Carrier Ethernet Services on p. 41

18.2
Answers: Ethernet Frames and Service Frames

1. MEF service definitions require that physical connectivity between CEs and the CEN at the UNI...

   a. **be IEEE 802.3-compliant**
   b. be IEEE 802.1-compliant
   c. be IEEE 802.1Q-compliant
   d. be implemented with link aggregation per clause 43 of IEEE 802.3
   e. support Link OAM per clause 57 of IEEE 802.3

   Note: Refer to Ethernet Frames and Service Frames.

2. Per IEEE 802.1Q (2011), which field is NOT in the customer VLAN tag (C-Tag):

   a. Tag protocol identifier (TPID) with value 8100
   b. VLAN identifier (VID)
   c. Drop eligibility indicator (DEI)
   d. **Canonical format indicator (CFI)**

   Note: Refer to C-Tagged Ethernet Frames.

3. Per MEF 10.3, a priority-tagged service frame must have ... (Choose two.)

   a. **Tag protocol identifier (TPID) = 8100**
   b. Drop eligibility indicator (DEI) = 0.
   c. **VLAN identifier (VID) = 0**
   d. Tag protocol identifier (TPID) = 88a8

   Note: Refer to Service Frame Tag Recognition.

4. An Ethernet frame is transmitted from the CE to the CEN. Its source MAC address is followed by a TPID field with value 88e7. Per MEF 10.3, that Ethernet frame is:

   a. **Untagged**
   b. Priority-Tagged
   c. Undefined / Out of scope
   d. S-Tagged
   e. VLAN-Tagged
   f. C-Tagged

   Note: It is an untagged service frame because the TPID value is not 8100 or 88a8. Refer to Service Frame Tag Recognition.

5. Egress service frames are transmitted ...

   a. from CE to CEN
   b. **from CEN to CE**
   c. from UNI to CEN
   d. from CE to UNI

   Note: Refer to Ingress and Egress Service Frames.

6. A Service frame includes all fields from...

   a. **Destination MAC Address to FCS, including any Ethernet tags (if present)**
   b. Destination MAC Address to FCS, excluding any Ethernet tags (if present)
   c. Interframe GAP to FCS, including any Ethernet tags (if present)
   d. Interframe GAP to FCS, excluding any Ethernet tags (if present)

   Note: Refer to Exclusion of Layer 1 Components.

7. Three UNIs (UNI A, UNI B and UNI C) are connected by an EP-LAN service. At UNI A, an IEEE 802.3-compliant Ethernet frame is transmitted from the CE to the CEN. Its source MAC address is followed by a TPID field with value 88a8. According to MEF 10.3, how should the EP-LAN service treat this service frame?

   a. It should be discarded.
   b. It should be delivered like any other service frame.
   c. It should be delivered like any other service frame, however performance objectives do not apply to it.
   d. **Its delivery is undefined.**

   Note: Because TPID = 88a8, the frame is recognized as an S-Tagged service frame. However, the behavior for S-Tagged Service Frames is beyond the scope of MEF 10.3. Refer to Service Frame Tag Recognition.

8. Using MEF 10.3 service frame definitions, which two of the following statements are false? (Choose two.)

   a. A service frame tagged with PVID=88a8 and VID=0 is an S-tagged service frame.
   b. A service frame tagged with PVID=88e7 and VID=0 is an untagged service frame.
   c. **A service frame tagged with PVID=8100 and VID=0 is an untagged service frame.**
   d. **A service frame tagged with PVID=88a8 and VID=0 is priority-tagged service frame.**
   e. A service frame tagged with PVID=8100 and VID=0 is a priority-tagged service frame.

   Note: Refer to Service Frame Tag Recognition.

Related Links

Review: Ethernet Frames and Service Frames on p. 56

18.3
Answers: How Carrier Ethernet Services are Defined

1. Which one of the following service attributes is an *EVC per UNI* attribute?

   a. Maximum number of EVCs
   b. **Ingress Bandwidth Profile per CoS Identifier**
   c. CE VLAN ID Preservation
   d. CE-VLAN ID / EVC Map
   e. Bundling

   Note: Refer to EVC per UNI Service Attributes

2. Which one of the following statements is false?

   a. The SLS is considered part of the SLA.
   b. The SLS contains technical details in engineering terms.
   c. The SLA includes all business agreements related to the service.
   d. **The SLA is considered part of the SLS.**

   Note: Refer to The MEF Service Agreement Framework (SLA and SLS).

3. A Service Level Agreement (SLA) is which one of the following?

   a. **A contract between the subscriber and service provider specifying a business agreement**
   b. An agreement stating service-level commitments in engineering terms
   c. A technical specification for the service
   d. A specification of service levels offered by the service provider
   e. An agreement about service performance attributes, including frame delay, inter-frame delay variation, frame loss ratio, and availability

   Note: Refer to The MEF Service Agreement Framework (SLA and SLS).

Related Links

Review: How Carrier Ethernet Services are Defined on p. 66

18.4
Answers: Service Connectivity Attributes

1. An EVC is configured with EVC Maximum Service Frame Size set to 1526 bytes. A service frame containing 1530 bytes is transmitted to the UNI from the CE. Which statement is correct?

   a. **The frame should be discarded.**
   b. The frame should be marked yellow (drop-eligible) and forwarded.
   c. The service level specification (SLS) applies to the frame.
   d. The frame should be truncated to 1526 bytes and forwarded.

   Note: Per [D1] and [D2] in MEF 10.3. Refer to Maximum Service Frame Size Service Attributes.

2. A broadcast service frame is transmitted from the subscriber to a UNI that is provisioned to support service multiplexing. Where will the service frame be delivered, assuming that it is not discarded?

   a. To all UNIs of each EVC multiplexed at the UNI
   b. To all UNIs in the EVC
   c. To all EVCs multiplexed at the UNI
   d. **To all UNIs in the EVC, except the ingress UNI**
   e. To all UNIs in the EVC, except the egress UNI

   Note: An Ethernet frame cannot be assigned to more than one EVC. Refer to Assigning Service Frames to EVCs.

3. Which two services cannot tunnel L2CP service frames containing Bridge Protocol Data Units (BPDUs) to support Spanning Tree Protocol (STP)? (Choose two.)

   a. **EVP-LAN**
   b. EP-LAN
   c. **EVPL**
   d. EPL

   Note: Tunneling is the process by which an L2CP service frame is passed through the service provider network without being processed and is delivered unchanged to the proper UNI(s).

   Note: VLAN-based services are not allowed to tunnel L2CP frames containing BPDUs. EVP-Tree service would also be correct if it were an option. Refer to L2CP Requirements for Spanning Tree Protocols.

4. A EVPL service has to support an application that uses IP packets of length up to 800 bytes. What is the smallest value of attribute *EVC Maximum Service Frame Size* that can be specified for this service?

   a. 800 bytes
   b. 818 bytes
   c. 822 bytes
   d. 1500 bytes
   e. 1518 bytes
   f. **1522 bytes**

   Note: A C-Tagged Ethernet frame contains 22 bytes more than its payload (Size of Untagged and C-Tagged Ethernet Frames). In this scenario the largest payload is an IP packet of length 800 bytes. So the service must support frames up to length 800+22=822 bytes. Additionally, the MEF requires that **EVC Maximum Service Frame Size** ≥1522 bytes (Maximum Service Frame Size Service Attributes). The smallest value meeting both requirements is 1522 bytes.

5. Which statement is true for a UNI that is configured with bundling?

   a. All CE-VLAN IDs are mapped to a single EVC.
   b. The UNI must be configured to support service multiplexing.
   c. Only VLAN-based services can be provisioned on it.
   d. More than one EVC must terminate at the UNI.

   Note: (a) False. (b) False. Service multiplexing is optional. If service multiplexing is off, the UNI can support only one EVC, but that EVC can be bundled. (c) True. Bundling is only supported on VLAN-based services. (d) False. Not required. If you chose this answer, you may be confused about the difference between bundling and service multiplexing. Refer to Bundling versus Service Multiplexing.

6. A UNI is configured without bundling or all-to-one bundling and is also configured to support service multiplexing. What is the maximum number of CE-VLAN IDs that can be mapped to a given EVC at the UNI?

   a. 4095
   b. 4094
   c. 64
   d. 1

   Note: Without bundling or all-to-one bundling, only one CE-VLAN ID can be mapped to an EVC. Refer to Service Multiplexing and Bundling Service Attributes.

7. A UNI is configured with service multiplexing. Which statement is <u>not</u> true?

   a. The UNI can support up to 4094 EVCs.
   b. Bundling is optional at the UNI.
   c. At the UNI, at least one CE-VLAN ID must be mapped to each EVC.
   d. At the UNI, all-to-one bundling is permitted.

   Note: (a) True. There are 4094 unique CE-VLAN IDs. 4094 EVCs can be supported if only one CE-VLAN ID is mapped to each. (b) True. (c) True. (d) False. All-to-one bundling and service multiplexing are mutually exclusive. Refer to Service Multiplexing and Bundling Service Attributes.

8. Which statement is <u>not</u> true for a UNI configured with all-to-one bundling?

   a. Service multiplexing is Disabled.
   b. Bundling is Disabled.
   c. CE-VLAN ID preservation is Enabled.
   d. CoS Preservation is Enabled.
   e. The UNI can support up to 4094 EVCs.

   Note: Refer to Service Multiplexing and Bundling Service Attributes, CE-VLAN ID Preservation, and CE-VLAN CoS Preservation.

9. An EPL service has to support jumbo frames with payload of up to 3000 bytes. What is the smallest value of attribute *EVC Maximum Service Frame Size* that can be specified for this service?

   a. 3000 bytes
   b. 3018 bytes
   c. 3022 bytes
   d. 3026 bytes
   e. 3030 bytes

   Note: A C-Tagged Ethernet frame contains 22 bytes more than its payload (Size of Untagged and C-Tagged Ethernet Frames). In this scenario the largest payload is 3000 bytes. So the service must support frames up to length 3000+22=3022 bytes. Additionally, the MEF requires that **EVC Maximum Service Frame Size** ≥1522 bytes (Maximum Service Frame Size Service Attributes). The smallest value meeting both requirements is 3022 bytes.

10. The *CE-VLAN ID for Untagged and Priority Tagged Service Frames* service attribute applies to which three of the following services? (Choose three.)

    a. EPL services
    b. EVPL services
    c. EP-LAN services
    d. EVP-LAN services
    e. EP-Tree services
    f. EVP-Tree services

    Note: Refer to CE-VLAN ID for Untagged and Priority Tagged Service Frames.

11. The smallest value allowed for the *EVC Maximum Service Frame Size* attribute is:

    a. 1518 bytes
    b. 64 bytes
    c. 1526 bytes
    d. 1522 bytes

    Note: Refer to Maximum Service Frame Size Service Attributes.

12. An EVP-LAN service is implemented between three UNIs. One of the UNIs is configured with *Bundling = Enabled* and *UNI Maximum Service Frame Size = 1550 bytes*. The other two UNIs are configured with *Bundling = Enabled* and *UNI Maximum Service Frame Size = 1600 bytes*. Which one of the following attribute configurations is allowed for this service?

    a. EVC Maximum Service Frame Size = 1650 bytes, CE-VLAN ID Preservation = Disabled.
    b. EVC Maximum Service Frame Size = 1600 bytes, CE-VLAN ID Preservation = Enabled.
    c. EVC Maximum Service Frame Size = 1550 bytes, CE-VLAN ID Preservation = Disabled.
    d. EVC Maximum Service Frame Size = 1500 bytes, CE-VLAN ID Preservation = Enabled.

    Note: EVC Maximum Service Frame Size must be at least 1522 bytes and no greater than 1550 bytes (the minimum value of UNI Maximum Service Frame Size across all UNIs). Refer to Maximum Service Frame Size Service Attributes. CE-LAN ID Preservation can be Disabled if the service supports only one CE-VLAN ID. Refer to CE-VLAN ID Preservation.

Answers to Review Questions
Answers: Service Connectivity Attributes

13. An EVP-LAN service is implemented between three UNIs: UNI A, UNI B, and UNI C. At UNI A four values of CE-VLAN ID map to the EVC. How many values of CE-VLAN ID map to the EVC at UNI C?

    a. Up to 4
    b. **Exactly 4**
    c. Up to 4094
    d. Up to 1522

    Note: [R81] in MEF 10.3 states: An EVC with more than one CE-VLAN ID mapping to it must have the same list of CE-VLAN IDs mapping to the EVC at each UNI in the EVC. Refer to CE-VLAN ID / EVC Map.

14. According to MEF 45, what options are available for handling an ingress L2CP service frame?

    a. Peer, Discard, Pass to EVC, Peer and Pass to EVC
    b. Peer, Discard, Tunnel
    c. **Peer, Discard, Pass**
    d. Peer, Discard, Peer and Tunnel

    Note: Refer to L2CP Behavioral Model.

15. The subscriber needs an EVP-Tree service that includes Link OAM and Link Aggregation (LACP) at all UNIs. To what value must attribute *UNI L2CP Address Set* be configured?

    a. CTA
    b. **CTB**
    c. CTA-2
    d. CTB-2

    Note: Refer to Attribute: UNI L2CP Address Set.

16. The subscriber wants an EP-LAN service that tunnels BPDUs to support spanning tree protocol (STP). How should attributes *UNI L2CP Peering* and *UNI L2CP Address Set* be configured at the UNIs?

    a. Set *UNI L2CP Address Set* = CTB and include STP in the *UNI L2CP Peering* list.
    b. **Set *UNI L2CP Address Set* = CTB and omit STP from the *UNI L2CP Peering* list.**
    c. Set *UNI L2CP Address Set* = CTA and include STP in the *UNI L2CP Peering* list.
    d. Set *UNI L2CP Address Set* = CTA and omit STP from the *UNI L2CP Peering* list.

    Note: Refer to L2CP Processing Service Attributes.

17. An E-Tree service is configured with attribute *Unicast Service Frame Delivery* set to *Deliver Unconditionally*. A unicast service frame ingresses through a Leaf UNI. That service frame...

    a. Is delivered to all other UNIs in the EVC
    b. **Is delivered to all other UNIs in the EVC, excluding other Leaf UNIs**
    c. Is delivered to all other UNIs in the EVC, excluding Root UNIs
    d. Is delivered only to the correct destination UNI (after that UNI becomes known through MAC address learning)

    Note: Refer to Data Service Frame Delivery Service Attributes.

18. An EVP-Tree service connects three UNIs (A, B and C). Three values of CE-VLAN ID map to the EVC at UNI A which is configured as a Root UNI. If UNI B is configured as a Leaf UNI, the value of *Bundling* at UNI B ...

   a. **Must be Enabled**
   b. Must be Disabled
   c. Can be Enabled or Disabled

   Note: [R81] in MEF 10.3 states: An EVC with more than one CE-VLAN ID mapping to it must have the same list of CE-VLAN IDs mapping to the EVC at each UNI in the EVC. Refer to CE-VLAN ID / EVC Map.

19. To reduce network traffic the subscriber wants an EP-LAN services that produces MAC address learning and forwarding behavior over the CEN. Attribute *Unicast Service Frame Delivery* should be set to which value?

   a. Deliver Unconditionally
   b. **Deliver Conditionally**
   c. Deliver with Bridging
   d. Deliver per IEEE 802.1Q

   Note: With conditions specified to produce MAC learning and forwarding behavior. Refer to Data Service Frame Delivery Service Attributes.

20. An E-Tree service has 3 Leaf UNIs and 2 Root UNIs. Attribute *Unicast Service Frame Delivery* is set to *Deliver Unconditionally*. A unicast service frame is sent from CE to CEN through a Leaf UNI. To how many UNIs will it be delivered?

   a. 1
   b. **2**
   c. 3
   d. 4
   e. 5
   f. 6

   Note: Refer to Data Service Frame Delivery Service Attributes.

21. EVC-1 connects UNI A, UNI B and UNI C. At UNI A, CE-VLAN IDs 101 and 102 map to EVC-1. What is the value of *Bundling* at UNI B and the value of *CE-VLAN ID Preservation* for EVC-1?

   a. Bundling = Disabled, CE-VLAN ID Preservation = Disabled
   b. Bundling = Disabled, CE-VLAN ID Preservation = Enabled
   c. Bundling = Enabled, CE-VLAN ID Preservation = Disabled
   d. **Bundling = Enabled, CE-VLAN ID Preservation = Enabled**

   Note: Refer to Data Service Frame Delivery Service Attributes.

22. An EVP-Tree service connects four leaf UNIs and one root UNI. Its EVC is configured with *CE-VLAN ID Preservation = Disabled*. The root UNI is configured with attribute *CE-VLAN ID for Untagged and Priority*

Tagged Service Frames set to 321 and that value (321) is mapped to the EVC at the root UNI. How many CE-VLAN IDs can be mapped to the EVC at the Root UNI?

> a. **1**
> b. 2
> c. 3
> d. 4
> e. 321
> f. 4094
>
> **Note:** If CE-VLAN ID Preservation is Disabled, only one CE-VLAN ID can be mapped to the EVC at each UNI. Refer to CE-VLAN ID Preservation versus Translation.

23. An E-LAN service connects three UNIs. Two of the UNIs are configured with *UNI Maximum Service Frame Size* = 1800 bytes. The EVC is configured with *EVC Maximum Service Frame Size* = 1600 bytes. From the following options, pick the <u>smallest</u> value that is acceptable for *UNI Maximum Service Frame Size* at the third UNI.

> a. 1518 bytes
> b. 1522 bytes
> c. 1526 bytes
> d. **1600 bytes**
> e. 1800 bytes
>
> **Note:** UNI Maximum Service Frame Size must be greater than or equal to the EVC Maximum Service Frame Size. Refer to Maximum Service Frame Size Service Attributes.

24. UNI-A is configured with *Bundling=Disabled, All to One Bundling = Disabled*, and *CE VLAN ID for Untagged and Priority Tagged Service Frames = 33*. CE-VLAN ID 33 maps to EVC-B at UNI-A. EVC-B is configured with *CE VLAN ID Preservation = Disabled*. At UNI-A, all service frames transmitted to the subscriber from EVC-B must be in which format(s)?

> a. **untagged**
> b. untagged or priority tagged
> c. untagged, priority tagged, or C-Tagged with VID=33
> d. untagged, priority tagged, or C-Tagged with any VID value in the range 1...4094
>
> **Note:** The question asks about the format of egress service frames (not ingress service frames). Refer to Untagged and Priority Tagged Service Frames with CE-VLAN ID Preservation Disabled.

Related Links

Review: Service Connectivity Attributes on p. 98

18.5
Answers: Traffic and Performance Management

1. At UNIs, which three of the following are MEF-permissible CoS identifiers for data service frames? (Choose three.)

   a. Ethernet DEI bit
   b. **Differentiated services code point (DSCP) in the IP header**
   c. **PCP bits in IEEE 802.1Q customer VLAN tag (CE-VLAN tag)**
   d. Ethernet CFI bit
   e. **EVC identifier**

   Note: Refer to Attribute: CoS ID for Data Service Frame.

2. A Subscriber requires an EVC that supports three Classes of Service: *Silver*, *Gold*, and *Diamond*. Which one of the following schemes is acceptable for identifying CoS at UNIs using PCP bit values (0-7)?

   a. Silver (5); Gold (6); Diamond (7)
   b. **Silver (7, 6); Gold (5, 4); Diamond (3, 2, 1, 0)**
   c. Silver (6); Gold (4); Diamond (2)
   d. Silver (0,1, 2); Gold (5); Diamond (6)
   e. Silver (4); Gold (5); Diamond (4)

   Note: Refer to CoS ID Based on CE-VLAN CoS.

3. EVC services defined by MEF 6.2 can include which two bandwidth profiles? (Choose two.)

   a. **Ingress Bandwidth Profile Per CoS ID**
   b. Ingress Bandwidth Profile Per EEC ID
   c. Ingress Bandwidth Profile Per EVC
   d. Egress Bandwidth Profile Per CoS ID
   e. **Egress Bandwidth Profile Per EEC ID**
   f. Egress Bandwidth Profile Per EVC

   Note: Refer to Bandwidth Profile Flow Granularity in About Bandwidth Profiles.

4. Which service frame field <u>cannot</u> be used to convey color information across the UNI?

   a. DEI in CE-VLAN tag
   b. DSCP in the IP header
   c. PCP in CE-VLAN tag
   d. **TPID in CE-VLAN tag**

   Note: Refer to Color ID for Service Frame Attribute.

5. A service frame colored green at ingress ...

   a. Must be delivered (must not be discarded)
   b. Must not be recolored yellow or red
   c. **Is in-profile with respect to service performance objectives**
   d. Will be delivered with the highest CoS defined for the service

   Note: Refer to Color and EVC Performance Objectives.

6. A service frame that is declared red by egress bandwidth profile processing ...

   a. Becomes eligible for discard
   b. **Must be discarded**
   c. May be delivered, but is not subject to service performance objectives
   d. May be delivered, but only after green and yellow frames are delivered

   Note: Refer to Color and EVC Performance Objectives.

7. For a particular EVC and UNI, attribute *EEC ID for Data Service Frame* is specified based on *Internet Protocol*. Which one of the following statements is NOT a requirement for this specification?

   a. It must match the specification of attribute *EEC ID for SOAM Service Frame* (for the same EVC and UNI).
   b. It must map each possible DSCP value for IPv4 to exactly one EEC.
   c. It must map each possible DSCP value for IPv6 to exactly one EEC.
   d. **It must match the specification of attribute *EEC ID for Data Service Frame* at other UNIs of the EVC.**

   Note: Refer to EEC ID Service Attributes.

Related Links

Review: Traffic and Performance Management on p. 123

18.6
Answers: Bandwidth Profiles

1. A Carrier Ethernet service for a bank needs to deliver critical data that cannot be dropped. Bandwidth profiles should be set with:

   a. CIR>0, CBS=0, EIR=0, EBS=0
   b. CIR>0, CBS>0, EIR=0, EBS=0
   c. CIR>0, CBS>0, EIR>0, EBS>0
   d. CIR=0, CBS>0, EIR=0, EBS=0
   e. CIR=0, CBS=0, EIR>0, EBS>0

   Note: Refer to Single-Rate versus Dual-Rate Bandwidth Profile Implementations.

2. Given a continuous stream of service frames with rate greater than EIR + CIR bits per second, approximately how many bytes of service frames will the single-flow bandwidth profile algorithm declare to be Yellow over a time interval of T seconds.

   a. EIR * T bytes
   b. EIR/8 * T bytes
   c. CIR/8 * T bytes
   d. (CIR+EIR) * T bytes
   e. (EIR-CIR)/8 * T bytes

   Note: Refer to Single-Flow Bandwidth Profile.

3. What happens to an Ethernet service frame that is marked Green by the bandwidth profile algorithm?

   a. It is discarded.
   b. It is placed in a higher class of service.
   c. It becomes drop-eligible.
   d. It is forwarded.
   e. It is buffered.

   Note: Refer to Single-Flow Bandwidth Profile.

4. If the ingress bandwidth profile marks a service frame Yellow, which one of the following statements is true?

   a. The subscriber is exceeding CIR/CBS, but not EIR/EBS.
   b. The subscriber is exceeding CIR/CBS and EIR/EBS.
   c. The subscriber is exceeding EIR/EBS, but not CIR/CBS.
   d. The subscriber is not exceeding EIR/EBS or CIR/CBS.

   Note: Refer to Single-Flow Bandwidth Profile.

5. Per EEC ID egress bandwidth profiles are NOT allowed for which service?

   a. **EPL**
   b. EVPL
   c. EP-LAN
   d. EVP-LAN
   e. EP-Tree
   f. EVP-Tree

   Note: Refer to Bandwidth Profile Service Attributes.

6. Three EVCs are service multiplexed at a UNI that is configured with attribute *Token Share = Enabled*. Each EVC supports two classes of service: CoS Argon and CoS Krypton. How many bandwidth profile flows can a single ingress bandwidth profile process at this UNI?

   a. Exactly 1
   b. Up to 2
   c. Up to 3
   d. **Up to 6**

   Note: At ingress, each bandwidth profile flow contains service frames for a particular CoS within a particular EVC. Refer to More Terminology.

7. A two-flow bandwidth profile is to be configured to limit egress traffic at a UNI. Color mode parameters CM^1 and CM^2 are both set to 1. Coupling flag CF^0 is set to 1. How can parameters CF^1 and CF^2 be configured?

   a. Both can be set independently, to either 0 or 1.
   b. Both must be set to the same value, either 0 or 1.
   c. **Both must be set to 0.**
   d. Both must be set to 1.

   Note: Refer to Bandwidth Profile Attribute Requirements.

8. A particular two-flow bandwidth profile includes the following settings. **For flow^2 (assigned Rank=2)**: CIR^2=10 Mb/s, CIR^2_{max}=10 Mb/s, and CF^2=1. **For flow^1 (assigned Rank=1)**: CIR^1=10 Mb/s, CIR^1_{max}=20 Mb/s, and CF^1=0. If there is no traffic in flow^2, what is the maximum continuous rate of green traffic in flow^1 (that is permitted by this bandwidth profile)?

   a. **10 Mb/s**
   b. 20 Mb/s
   c. 30 Mb/s

   Note: Because CF^2=1, the green bucket for flow^1 does not receive green-bucket overflow from flow^2 (that overflow goes the yellow token bucket). Because CIR^1_{max} > CIR^1, flow into the green bucket for flow^1 is limited by CIR^1=10 Mb/s. Refer to Explaining the Multiflow Bandwidth Profile Algorithm.

9. Which one of the following cannot impact the disposition (green, yellow, or red) of a service frame processed by a bandwidth profile?

   a. Number of tokens in the green token bucket at the time when the service frame arrives.
   b. **Destination MAC address of the service frame**
   c. Number of tokens in the yellow token bucket at the time when the service frame arrives.
   d. Size of the service frame

   Note: Refer to Single-Flow Bandwidth Profile.

10. A bandwidth profile at a UNI must be able to support which one of the following?

    a. CM=color-aware
    b. CF=Y
    c. **CM=color-blind**
    d. CF=N

    Note: Refer to Color Mode.

Related Links

Review: Bandwidth Profiles on p. 145

18.7 Answers: EVC Performance Attributes

1. Performance metrics estimate frame delivery performance for:

   a. All service frames admitted to the EVC
   b. Yellow service frames
   c. All service frames, except L2CP service frames
   d. Green service frames, per CoS
   e. Green and Yellow service frames

   Note: Refer to Performance Metric Caveats and Requirements.

2. Which three performance objectives are defined using a sliding window? (Choose three.)

   a. Availability
   b. Frame Delay (FD)
   c. Mean Frame Delay (MFD)
   d. Inter-Frame Delay Variation (IFDV)
   e. High Loss Intervals (HLI)
   f. Consecutive High Loss Intervals (CHLI)

   Note: Refer to Availability Performance and Resiliency Performance.

3. What is the maximum number of ordered UNI pairs in an EP-Tree service that has four leaf UNIs and two root UNIs?

   a. 6
   b. 8
   c. 9
   d. 10
   e. 18

   Note: 4*2*2 (root-leaf ordered UNI pairs) + 2 (root-root ordered UNI pairs) = 18. Refer to Ordered UNI Pair.

4. The Mean Frame Delay (MFD) performance objective for an EP-LAN service is specified as 80 ms. Which statement best describes the meaning of this performance objective?

   a. During an agreed time period, green service frames on average should spend no more than 80 ms in transit between CEs.
   b. For each ordered UNI pair in the pre-agreed subset of UNI pairs, the average time a green service frame spends in transit between CEs should not exceed 80 ms.
   c. No service frame should spend more than 80 ms in transit between CEs.
   d. For each ordered UNI pair in the set of all ordered UNI pairs, the average time a green service frame spends in transit between CEs should not exceed 80 ms.
   e. No green service frame should spend more than 80 ms in transit between CEs.

   Note: Refer to Frame Delay Performance.

5. FLR (Frame Loss Ratio) performance is determined by:

   a. [1 + (green service frames delivered)/(green service frames sent)] ×100
   b. [1 + (total service frames delivered)/(total service frames sent)] ×100
   c. [1 − (total service frames delivered)/(total service frames sent)] ×100
   d. [1 − (green service frames delivered)/(green service frames sent)] /100
   e. **[1 − (green service frames delivered)/(green service frames sent)] ×100**

   Note: Refer to Frame Loss Ratio Performance.

6. When a performance attribute is measured over an agreed subset of UNI pairs (more than one UNI pair), how is the final value of the performance attribute calculated?

   a. By taking the best case (highest performing) UNI pair measurement
   b. By averaging the UNI pair measurements
   c. **By taking the worst-case (lowest performing) UNI pair measurement**
   d. By determining the median value within the set of UNI pair measurements

   Note: Refer to Performance Metric Caveats and Requirements.

7. Availability for a particular one-way service between two UNIs is defined with a sliding window of $n=13$ small time intervals Δt. Which condition ensures that the first Δt in the sliding window is declared to be **available**? (No Δt is part of a maintenance interval.)

   a. The frame loss ratio (flr) for at least 7 Δt's in the sliding window is greater than threshold C.
   b. The frame loss ratio (flr) for at least 7 Δt's in the sliding window is less than threshold C.
   c. **The frame loss ratio (flr) for all Δt's in the sliding window is less than threshold C.**
   d. The frame loss ratio (flr) for all Δt's in the sliding window is greater than threshold C.

   Note: Refer to Availability Performance.

8. Which two performance metrics are defined as a percentage?

   a. **Availability and Frame Loss Ratio (FLR)**
   b. High Loss Interval (HLI) and Consecutive High Loss Interval (CHLI)
   c. Inter-Frame Delay Variation (IFDV) and Mean Frame Delay (MFD)
   d. Frame Delay (FD) and Mean Frame Delay (MFD)

   Note: Refer to Availability Performance and Frame Loss Ratio Performance.

Answers to Review Questions
Answers: EVC Performance Attributes

9. What is the maximum number of ordered UNI pairs in a EP-LAN service that includes four UNIs?

   a. 4
   b. 6
   c. 8
   d. <u>12</u>
   e. 16

   Note: *A multipoint-to-multipoint EVC with n UNIs has n*(n-1) ordered UNI pairs. Refer to* Ordered UNI Pair.

10. Which two performance objectives are defined using two or more non-empty subsets of ordered UNI pairs? (Choose two.)

    a. Availability
    b. High Loss Intervals (HLI)
    c. Consecutive High Loss Intervals (CHLI)
    d. **Group Availability**
    e. **Multiple EVC Availability**

    Note: *Refer to* Group Availability Performance *and* Multiple EVC Availability Performance.

Related Links

Review: EVC Performance Attributes on p. 166

18.8
Answers: UNI Requirements

1. A MEF Type 2.2 UNI is required to support which type of protection?

   a. Layer 2 Control Protocol (L2CP)
   b. Link OAM per clause 57 of IEEE 802.3
   c. G.8031 Ethernet Linear Protection Switching
   d. **Link aggregation per clause 43 of IEEE 802.3**
   e. G.8032 Ethernet Ring Protection Switching

   Note: (a) Not a protection mechanism. (b) Not a protection mechanism. (c) Not required. (d) Correct. (e) Not required. Refer to Link Protection Requirement for Type 2.2 UNIs.

2. Which of the following provides port protection?

   a. L2CP
   b. **Link aggregation**
   c. E-LMI
   d. Link OAM
   e. Type 1 UNI

   Note: Refer to Link Protection Requirement for Type 2.2 UNIs.

3. Which two of the following statements about the Ethernet Local Management Interface (E-LMI) are true? (Choose two.)

   a. E-LMI protects against port failure using link aggregation.
   b. E-LMI is required for Type 2.1 UNIs.
   c. **E-LMI notifies the UNI-C of changes to EVC status.**
   d. E-LMI allows the subscriber and the service provider to monitor and diagnose link-level connectivity issues between UNI-C and UNI-N.
   e. **E-LMI allows UNI-C to acquire configuration information from UNI-N so that it can automatically configure itself.**

   Note: (a) False. (b) Required for Type 2.2, but not Type 2.1. (c) True. (d) False. Describes LOAM. (e) True. Refer to E-LMI Requirement for Type 2.2 UNIs.

4. Which three of the following requirements are mandatory for Type 2.2 UNIs, but optional for Type 2.1 UNIs? (Choose three.)

   a. **Link aggregation support**
   b. Service OAM support
   c. **Link OAM support**
   d. Support of multiplexed UNI for services such as EVPL
   e. Backward compatibility with UNI Type 1
   f. **E-LMI support**

   Note: (a) Correct. (b) Mandatory for Type 2.1. (c) Correct. (d) Mandatory for Type 2.1. (e) Mandatory for Type 2.1. (f) Correct. Refer to Type 2 UNI Requirements.

Answers to Review Questions
Answers: UNI Requirements

5. Which one of the following statements about Type 2 UNIs is <u>not</u> true?

   a. Type 2 UNIs support Service OAM.
   b. MEF 20 describes two types of Type 2 UNIs.
   c. Type 2 UNI requirements apply only to the UNI-N (they are not applicable to the UNI-C).
   d. Type 2 UNIs are backward compatible with Type 1 UNIs.
   e. Type 2 UNIs support L2CP handling as defined in MEF 6.1 and MEF 10.2.

   Note: Refer to Type 2 UNI Requirements.

6. UNI Type 2.2 required protection mechanisms protect against which three types of failure? (Choose three.)

   a. Port failure on UNI-N
   b. Loss of timing
   c. Loss of "green" service frames due to bandwidth oversubscription
   d. E-LMI denial of service (DOS) attack
   e. Port failure on UNI-C
   f. Disconnection or failure of a cable connecting the CE and CEN

   Note: Refer to Link Protection Requirement for Type 2.2 UNIs.

7. Per MEF 10.3, which three values are recognized for the *UNI Resiliency* per UNI service attribute? (Choose three.)

   a. LACP
   b. None
   c. 2-Link Aggregation
   d. E-LMI
   e. Other

   Note: Refer to UNI Functionality Service Attributes.

Related Links

Review: UNI Requirements on p. 175

18.9
Answers: Extending MEF Services over Multiple Operator CENs

1. Which entity delivers Ethernet frames between ENNIs and UNIs/ENNIs?

   > a. **Operator Virtual Connection**
   > b. Ethernet Virtual Circuit
   > c. Intermediate Virtual Connection
   > d. Operator Virtual Circuit
   > e. Ethernet Virtual Connection
   >
   > *Note:* Refer to OVC.

2. Per MEF 26.1, which three values are recognized for the *Protection Mechanism* ENNI service attribute? (Choose three.)

   > a. LACP
   > b. **None**
   > c. **Link Aggregation**
   > d. E-LMI
   > e. **Other**
   >
   > *Note:* Refer to Protection at ENNI.

3. The *OVC End Points* of an operator virtual connection (OVC) must associate to:

   > a. Exactly two UNIs and any number of ENNIs
   > b. Exactly one ENNI and any number of UNIs
   > c. UNIs only
   > d. **At least one ENNI**
   > e. Only ENNIs
   >
   > *Note:* Refer to OVC and OVC End Point.

4. Two or more operators can:

   > a. connect through an ENNI
   > b. be involved in an OVC
   > c. be responsible for an EVC
   > d. **be involved in an EVC**
   > e. be responsible for an OVC
   >
   > *Note:* Refer to Extending MEF Services over Multiple Operator CENs and Terminology. Answer (a) is wrong because an ENNI connects two operators, not two *or more* operators.

Answers to Review Questions
Answers: Extending MEF Services over Multiple Operator CENs

5. Which three frame formats are permitted at an ENNI? (Choose three.)

   a. Untagged
   b. C-Tag
   c. S-Tag and no C-Tag
   d. S-Tag and C-Tag
   e. Stacked S-Tags

   Note: Refer to ENNI Tagging Requirements.

6. How many EPL services can an ENNI support?

   a. One
   b. Two
   c. Up to 4094
   d. About 16 million
   e. Unlimited

   Note: An ENNI can support up to 4094 services of any type (including EPL services). The number of services is limited by the number of unique S-VLAN ID values. Refer to Encoding Information in S-Tags.

7. Which statement about the External Network-to-Network Interface (ENNI) is true?

   a. The subscriber and service provider agree on its exact physical location so that responsibilities are clearly defined.
   b. It can only support one EPL service.
   c. Service provider is responsible for the service from the UNI to the ENNI, and then the organization in charge of the Operator CEN is responsible.
   d. It is a physical demarcation point between two Operator CENs.

   Note: Refer to ENNI and ENNI-N.

8. An OVC requires which one of the following?

   a. A UNI
   b. Two or more UNIs
   c. Two or more EVCs
   d. An ENNI
   e. Two or more ENNIs

   Note: Refer to OVC.

9. An *OVC End Point Map* has *bundling*. Which statement is true about the associated OVC?

   a. *S-VLAN ID Preservation* can be *Yes* or *No*.
   b. *CE-VLAN ID Preservation* can be *Yes* or *No*.
   c. *CE-VLAN CoS Preservation* can be *Yes* or *No*.
   d. *S-VLAN ID CoS Preservation* can be *Yes* or *No*.

   Note: S-VLAN ID Preservation, CE-VLAN ID Preservation, and CE-VLAN CoS Preservation must all be Yes. Refer to End Point Map Bundling.

10. In which category of operator service attributes is *Broadcast Service Frame Delivery*?

    a. **OVC Service Attributes**
    b. PVC End Point per ENNI Service Attributes
    c. ENNI Service Attributes
    d. Per UNI service attributes
    e. OVC per Per UNI service attributes

    Note: Refer to OVC Service Attributes.

11. An *OVC End Point Map* has *bundling*. Which statement is <u>not</u> true about the associated OVC?

    a. The OVC cannot support hairpin switching.
    b. All end points of the OVC have bundling.
    c. *S-VLAN ID Preservation* is set to *Yes*.
    d. **At least one end point of the OVC terminates at a UNI.**
    e. The OVC is point-to-point.

    Note: Refer to End Point Map Bundling.

12. Two Operator CENs connect through an ENNI. What is the advantage of using an ENNI with Link OAM?

    a. It provides link protection using two physical links, one active and one standby
    b. It allows the ENNI to support hairpin switching.
    c. **It allows both operators to monitor and diagnose ENNI connectivity issues**
    d. It allows two different types of physical layers to be connected at the ENNI
    e. It allows class of service (CoS) propagation through IEEE 802.1ad Ethernet Frames

    Note: Refer to LOAM Requirement for ENNIs.

13. Which OVC service attribute is <u>incompatible</u> with hairpin switching?

    a. CE-VLAN CoS Preservation = Yes
    b. **S-VLAN ID Preservation = Yes**
    c. S-VLAN CoS Preservation = Yes
    d. CE-VLAN ID Preservation = Yes

    Note: Refer to Hairpin Switching.

14. Which statement is <u>not</u> true about the service provider in the MEF 26.1 service model?

    a. The service provider is responsible for the service to the subscriber.
    b. The service provider is responsible for coordinating operators.
    c. The service provider may or may not be an operator.
    d. **Two or more operators can collaboratively function as the service provider.**

    Note: Refer to Service Provider and Operators.

15. The smallest maximum transmission unit (MTU) size allowed for an operator virtual connection (OVC) is:

    a. 1522 bytes
    b. **1526 bytes**
    c. 4094 bytes
    d. 4096 bytes
    e. None of the above

    Note: Refer to ENNI and OVC MTU Size.

16. How many EVCs can be supported by one OVC?

    a. Exactly one
    b. **Up to 4094 if the OVC is point-to-point between two ENNIs**
    c. Up to 4094 if UNI is configured with *Service Multiplexing* = Yes
    d. Exactly one if the UNI is configured with *All to One Bundling* = Yes

    Note: Normally an OVC represents a segment of one EVC. However, the OVC with end point map bundling is a special case. Refer to End Point Map Bundling.

17. Which three of the following statements are true? (Choose three.)

    a. **At ENNIs, drop-eligibility can be encoded in the S-Tag DEI bit or in the S-Tag PCP value.**
    b. At ENNIs, all frames require C-Tags.
    c. **At an ENNI, both Operators are responsible for setting S-Tag values appropriately before transmitting frames across the ENNI.**
    d. **Ingress ENNI frames are mapped to OVC end points based on S-VLAN ID value.**
    e. At ENNIs, CoS may be encoded in the C-Tag or in the S-Tag.

    Note: Refer to Encoding Information in S-Tags.

18. Which one of the following is <u>not</u> an ENNI requirement?

    a. **ENNIs are required to support E-LMI.**
    b. At ENNIs, all bandwidth profiles must be color-aware.
    c. ENNIs must support MTU sizes at least as large as 1526 bytes.
    d. If an ENNI includes two physical links, it must be capable of implementing link aggregation.
    e. ENNIs are required to support Link OAM.

    Note: (b) Refer to Color-Aware Bandwidth Profiles at ENNI. (c) Refer to ENNI and OVC MTU Size. (d) Refer to Protection at ENNI. (e) Refer to LOAM Requirement for ENNIs.

19. Which one of the following is an ENNI service attribute?

    a. Bundling
    b. **End Point Map**
    c. Service Multiplexing
    d. All-to-one bundling

    Note: Refer to ENNI Service Attributes.

20. The *End Point Map* attribute:

   a. is inactive if the ENNI is provisioned with all-to-one bundling
   b. **specifies how ingress ENNI frames are assigned to OVC end points based on S-VLAN ID**
   c. lists the CE-VLAN IDs that map to the EVC
   d. is an *OVC End Point per ENNI* service attribute

   Note: Refer to End Point Map.

21. A rooted-multipoint OVC has 5 OVC end points: 2 are designated Root, 2 are designated Leaf, and 1 is designated Trunk. A broadcast frame ingresses at a Leaf OVC end point. How many frames does the OVC deliver if OVC attribute *Broadcast Service Frame Delivery* is configured to *Deliver Unconditionally*?

   a. 1
   b. 2
   c. **3**
   d. 4
   e. 5

   Note: In this scenario, the broadcast frame must be delivered to both Root end points and to the Trunk end point, but not to the other Leaf end point. At the Trunk end point, the broadcast frame must be transmitted with S-VLAN ID set to the **Leaf S-VLAN ID** value, indicating that it originated from a Leaf UNI (Trunk Identifiers).

22. Why is the minimum MTU size requirement at ENNIs (1526 bytes) four bytes larger than the minimum UNI Maximum Service Frame Size (1522 bytes)?

   a. Because ENNIs do not support all-to-one bundling.
   b. To allow hairpin switching.
   c. **To account for the S-Tag.**
   d. Because color-aware bandwidth profiles are required at ENNIs.

   Note: Refer to ENNI and OVC MTU Size.

23. An EVPL service is implemented across three Operator CENs. How many UNIs, ENNIs, EVCs, and OVCs are involved?

   a. 2 UNIs, 2 ENNIs, 3 EVCs, and 1 OVC
   b. 2 UNIs, 3 ENNIs, 1 EVC, and 3 OVCs
   c. **2 UNIs, 2 ENNIs, 1 EVC, and 3 OVCs**
   d. 2 UNIs, 3 ENNIs, 1 EVC, and 2 OVCs

   Note: One point-to-point EVC: UNI–OVC–ENNI–OVC–ENNI–OVC–UNI. Refer to OVC.

24. An EPL service spans three Operator CENs and each OVC is configured with *S-VLAN ID Preservation = Yes*. Which of the following statements is true?

    a. The S-Tag VLAN identifier will match at both UNIs.
    b. The S-Tag VLAN identifier is preserved within each OVC, but can be translated at the ENNIs.
    c. The S-Tag VLAN identifier will match at both ENNIs.
    d. The S-Tag VLAN identifier will match at both UNIs and both ENNIs.

    Note: (a) S-Tags are not defined at UNIs. (b) ENNIs do not support VLAN ID translation. (c) With S-VLAN ID Preservation = Yes, the OVC that connects the two ENNIs ensures that the S-Tag VLAN ID matches at both ENNIs. (d) S-Tags are not defined at UNIs. Refer to OVC Service Attributes.

25. An EP-LAN service spans two Operator CENs that connect through one ENNI. At all UNIs, ingress bandwidth profiles are configured with CIR=0, CBS=0, EIR=20 Mb/s, and EBS=2,000 bytes. How should the service be configured to ensure that yellow frames are not "promoted" to green?

    a. At all OVC end points, configure ingress and egress bandwidth profiles with *Color Mode = Color Aware*.
    b. At those OVC end points that connect to the ENNI (not those connecting to UNIs), configure ingress and egress bandwidth profiles with *Color Mode = Color Aware*.
    c. For both OVCs, configure *Color Forwarding = Yes*.
    d. At those OVC end points that connect to UNIs (not those connecting to the ENNI), configure ingress bandwidth profiles with *Color Mode = Color Aware*. Also, do not configure any bandwidth profiles at the OVC end points that connect to the ENNI.

    Note: Refer to Color Forwarding.

26. Which statement about CoS identification at ENNIs is <u>not</u> true?

    a. CoS is determined by S-Tag PCP bit values.
    b. At a given OVC end point, an S-Tag PCP bit value can map to more than one CoS.
    c. For each OVC end point, a CoS must be associated with each S-Tag PCP value.
    d. At a given OVC end point, two different S-Tag PCP bit values can map to the same CoS.
    e. The S-Tag supports up to eight classes of service.

    Note: Refer to Encoding Information in S-Tags.

27. A service is implemented over 3 Operator CENs. Which two statements are correct? (Choose two.)

    a. All three operators are responsible to the subscriber for the service.
    b. One of the operators can be the service provider.
    c. The subscriber has a business relationship with each operator.
    d. Each Operator CEN includes at least one ENNI-N.

    Note: Refer to Service Provider and Operators and ENNI and ENNI-N.

28. An ENNI is to support many EVCs, including some EVCs configured with *EVC Maximum Service Frame Size* as large as 1800 bytes. What is the smallest value of the ENNI MTU Size that will support these EVCs?

    a. 1526 bytes
    b. 1800 bytes
    c. 1804 bytes
    d. 2000 bytes

    Note: *To support the S-Tag, the ENNI must support MTUs that are at least 4 bytes larger than the largest EVC Maximum Service Frame Size. Refer to* ENNI and OVC MTU Size.

29. For an Ethernet Virtual Private service that is implemented over multiple Operator CENs, which ENNI frame field(s) can be used to convey color across the ENNI?

    a. S-Tag DEI only
    b. C-Tag PCP or S-Tag DEI only
    c. S-Tag DEI or S-Tag PCP only
    d. C-Tag PCP or S-Tag DEI or S-Tag PCP only

    Note: *Refer to* Encoding Information in S-Tags.

Related Links

Review: Extending MEF Services over Multiple Operator CENs on p. 217

18.10
Answers: MEF-Standardized Classes of Service

1. How many classes of service does MEF 23.1 define for Performance Tier 2?

   a. 2 classes of service
   b. **3 classes of service**
   c. 4 classes of service
   d. 6 classes of service
   e. 12 classes of service

   Note: In each performance tier, MEF 23.1 defines 3 standardized classes of service denoted by CoS Labels L, M, and H *(CoS Labels and Performance Tiers)*.

2. An *Ingress Bandwidth Profile Per ENNI Class of Service Identifier* is required at an OVC end point to police ingress ENNI frames marked with *CoS Label M*. Which one of the following ingress bandwidth profiles satisfies all MEF requirements?

   a. CIR=0, CBS=0 bytes, EIR=200 Mb/s, EBS=2000 bytes, CF=Y, CM=Y
   b. CIR=200 Mb/s, CBS=2000 bytes, EIR=200 Mb/s, EBS=2000 bytes, CF=N, CM=N
   c. **CIR=200 Mb/s, CBS=2000 bytes, EIR=200 Mb/s, EBS=2000 bytes, CF=N, CM=Y**
   d. CIR=0, CBS=0 bytes, EIR=200 Mb/s, EBS=2000 bytes, CF=Y, CM=N

   Note: MEF 23.1 requires CIR>0 for bandwidth profiles associated with CoS Label M or H *(Ingress Bandwidth Profile Constraints (per CoS Label))*. At ENNIs, bandwidth profiles (if used) must be color-aware *(Color-Aware Bandwidth Profiles at ENNI)*.

3. A point-to-point service uses *CoS Label H*. Which CPO <u>must</u> be specified in the SLS?

   a. Both Frame Delay (FD) and Frame Delay Range (FDR)
   b. Both Mean Frame Delay (MFD) and Inter-Frame Delay Variation (IFDV)
   c. **Frame Loss Ratio (FLR)**
   d. High Loss Intervals (HLI)
   e. Consecutive High Loss Intervals (CHLI)

   Note: Refer to CPOs (per CoS Label and Performance Tier) and note the caveats listed under "Additionally:".

4. According to MEF 23.1, if CoS Label and Color are encoded in S-Tag PCP bits, PCP bit value 3 indicates...

   a. M, Yellow
   b. **M, Green**
   c. H, Green
   d. Nothing

   Note: Refer to CoS Label and Color Identification Using PCP Bits, DEI Bit, and/or EVC/OVC End Point.

5. Which two statements about Class of Service Performance Objectives (CPOs) are correct? (Choose two.)

   a. CPOs for *CoS Label L* are more demanding than CPOs for *CoS Label H*.
   b. CPOs for *Performance Tier 4* are more demanding than CPOs for *Performance Tier 3*.
   c. CPOs for *CoS Label M* are more demanding than CPOs for *CoS Label L*.
   d. CPOs for *Performance Tier 1* are more demanding than CPOs for *Performance Tier 3*.

   Note: Refer to CoS Labels and Performance Tiers.

6. How many performance tiers does MEF 23.1 define for CoS Label H?

   a. 3 performance tiers
   b. 4 performance tiers
   c. 6 performance tiers
   d. 12 performance tiers

   Note: For each CoS Label, MEF 23.1 defines 4 performance tiers (CoS Labels and Performance Tiers).

7. For each of the following services, all service frames map to *CoS Label L*. Which service is subject to CPO values defined in MEF 23.1?

   a. *Performance Tier 1* EP-LAN service with ingress bandwidth profile CIR > 0.
   b. *Performance Tier 4* EVPL service with ingress bandwidth profile CIR > 0.
   c. *Performance Tier 1* EPL service with ingress bandwidth profile CIR = 0.
   d. *Performance Tier 4* EVP-LAN service with ingress bandwidth profile CIR = 0.

   Note: MEF 23.1 does not define CPO values for multipoint-to-multipoint (or rooted-multipoint) EVCs and OVCs (CPOs (per CoS Label and Performance Tier)). MEF 23.1 allows CIR=0 for CoS Label L (Ingress Bandwidth Profile Constraints (per CoS Label)), but if CIR=0, all service frames are yellow (not subject to CPOs).

8. According to MEF 23.1, if CoS Label and Color is encoded in S-Tag PCP bits, PCP bit value 4 indicates...

   a. M, Yellow
   b. M, Green
   c. H, Green
   d. Nothing

   Note: Refer to CoS Label and Color Identification Using PCP Bits, DEI Bit, and/or EVC/OVC End Point.

Answers to Review Questions
Answers: MEF-Standardized Classes of Service

9. A point-to-point service uses *CoS Label H*. If Frame Delay (FD) in not specified, which frame delay CPO <u>must</u> be specified in the SLS?

    a. Frame Delay Range (FDR)
    b. **Mean Frame Delay (MFD)**
    c. Inter-Frame Delay Variation (IFDV)

    Note: Refer to CPOs (per CoS Label and Performance Tier) and note the caveats listed under "Additionally:".

10. MEF 23.1 defines CoS Performance Objectives (CPOs) for …

    a. **point-to-point services only**
    b. point-to-point and multipoint-to-multipoint services only
    c. point-to-point, multipoint-to-multipoint, and rooted-multipoint services

    Note: Refer to CPOs (per CoS Label and Performance Tier).

Related Links

Review: MEF-Standardized Classes of Service on p. 230

18.11
Answers: E-Access Services

1. Both the Access EVPL and the Access EPL... (Choose two.)

   a. Allow CE-VLAN ID translation
   b. **Associate each service instance to one S-VLAN ID value at the ENNI**
   c. Are point-to-point OVCs
   d. **Connect one ENNI and one UNI**

   Note: (a) Wrong because both require CE-VLAN ID preservation. (b) Correct. (c) Wrong because they are services involving more than just the OVC. (d) Correct.

2. Two access providers establish an ENNI connection between their networks. What types of EVC-based services can they offer subscribers using only Access EPL and Access EVPL services? Assume that one of the access providers takes the role of service provider.

   a. **E-Line only**
   b. E-Line and E-LAN only
   c. E-Line and E-Tree only
   d. E-Line, E-LAN, and E-Tree

3. Access EVPL differs from EVPL in that...

   a. Access EVPL supports multiple CoS, while EVPL supports only one CoS.
   b. Access EVPL is VLAN-based, while EVPL is port-based.
   c. **Access EVPL is OVC-based, while EVPL is EVC-based.**
   d. Access EVPL supports CE-VLAN ID Preservation, while EVPL does not.

   Note: (a) Wrong because Access EVPL supports only one CoS, while EVPL supports multiple CoS. (b) Wrong because EVPL is EVC-based, not OVC-based. (c) Correct. (d) Wrong because both support CE-VLAN ID Preservation.

4. Which service supports CE-VLAN ID translation?

   a. Access EVPL
   b. Access EPL
   c. **EVPL**
   d. EPL

   Note: EVPL supports CE-VLAN ID translation if only one CE-VLAN ID maps to the EVC at both UNIs.

5. E-Access services and E-Line services both include at least one...

   a. UNI
   b. ENNI
   c. OVC
   d. EVC

6. A service provider has been using four Access EPLs to support an EP-LAN for a subscriber. The subscriber now wants to convert the EP-LAN service to an EP-Tree service. How are the Access EPLs impacted by this change?

   a. They can no longer be used.
   b. The must be converted to Access EVPLs.
   c. They must now filter traffic.
   d. They are not impacted.

   Note: The multipoint-to-multipoint OVC in the service provider network (operator CEN) would change to a rooted-multipoint OVC. The Access EPLs remain unchanged.

7. Both Access EVPL and Access EPL...

   a. Support hairpin switching
   b. Can connect a customer site to an Internet service provider
   c. Support multiple CoS
   d. Are EVC-based services

   Note: (a)Wrong because the general OVC-based operator service can support hairpin switching, but Access EPL/EVPL cannot. (b) Correct. (c) Wrong because both support only one CoS. (d) Wrong because both are OVC-based services.

8. If an E-Access service is applied to reach an off-net customer site in an EVC-based service application, the EVC-based service...

   a. Can support only one class of service
   b. Cannot support CE-VLAN ID translation
   c. Must be point-to-point
   d. Must involve at least one ENNI

9. As a service provider you have agreed to provide an EPL service supporting IP packets up to 2000 bytes in length. However, one customer site is off-net, so you need to purchase an Access EPL service to reach that customer site. The access provider offers Access EPLs with ingress bandwidth profiles at the ENNI supporting the following values of CBS. Which value do you choose if you want to minimize CBS?

   a. CBS = 2000 bytes
   b. CBS = 2010 bytes
   c. CBS = 2020 bytes
   d. CBS = 2030 bytes

   Note: The Access EPL must support C-Tagged Ethernet frames at UNIs which have 22 bytes more than their unencapsulated payload (Size of Untagged and C-Tagged Ethernet Frames). In this case the payload is an IP packet of length 2000 bytes. So the Access EPL must support frames of length 2000+22=2022 bytes at the UNI. At the ENNI, an S-Tag is added to the frame (4 more bytes). So the Access EPL must support frames of length 2026 bytes at the ENNI. Therefore, CBS for an ingress bandwidth profile at the ENNI must be at least 2026 bytes. CBS=2030 bytes is the smallest value supported by the access provider that is greater than or equal to 2026 bytes.

10. Which of the following statements is false?

a. A UNI can support up to 4094 Access EVPLs.
b. **A UNI can support up to 4094 Access EPLs.**
c. An ENNI can support up to 4094 Access EPLs.
d. An ENNI can support up to 4094 Access EVPLs.

Note: A UNI can support up to 4094 Access EVPLs (one CE-VLAN ID per Access EVPL), but only one Access EPL (port-based at the UNI). Refer to Access EPL and Access EVPL.

11. Which two services are used to reach off-net customer sites? (Choose two.)

a. Access EVPL
b. EVPL
c. Access EPL
d. EPL

12. Access EPL is similar to EPL in that... (Choose two.)

a. **Both support untagged frames and C-Tagged frames at the UNI.**
b. Both support CE-VLAN ID translation.
c. **Both support CE-VLAN CoS ID preservation.**
d. Both are OVC-based services.

Note: (a) Wrong because Access EPL supports only one CoS. (b) Correct. (c) Wrong because neither support CE-VLAN ID translation. (d) Correct. (e) Wrong because EPL is EVC-based, not OVC-based.

Related Links

Review: E-Access Services on p. 249

18.12 Answers: Ethernet OAM

1. Which one of the following statements describes how frame loss ratio (FLR) is measured for an EPL service?

   a. For each EVC CoS, count all green and yellow frames sent and received over an agreed time interval.
   b. **For each EVC CoS, count all green frames sent and received over an agreed time interval.**
   c. For an EVC, count all frames sent and received (regardless of CoS) over an agreed time interval.
   d. For an EVC, count all green and yellow frames sent and received over an agreed time interval.

   Note: Refer to Single-Ended Service Loss and recall, from Performance Metric Caveats and Requirements, that performance objectives apply to green service frames only (they say nothing about delivery of yellow service frames). Therefore, only green frames should be used for performance measurement.

2. NE A and NE B are connected by an Ethernet link. Brian, an operator, has access only to NE B (NE B is in Brian's domain of operations, but NE A is not). Which two options below can be available (with correct provisioning) to Brian? (Choose two.)

   a. Use SOAM loopback to redirect all traffic at NE A back toward NE B.
   b. **Use SOAM loopback to verify link connectivity.**
   c. Use LOAM loopback to redirect all traffic at NE B back toward NE A.
   d. **Use LOAM loopback to redirect all traffic at NE A back toward NE B.**
   e. Use RDI to initiate LOAM link discovery.

   Note: (a) SOAM loopback does not redirect traffic. Refer to SOAM Loopback. (b) Refer to SOAM Loopback. (c) LOAM loopback creates a port-based loopback on the far side, not the near side. Refer to Link OAM. (d) Refer to Link OAM. (e) This answer is nonsense.

3. Which one of the following is <u>not</u> an SOAM frame?

   a. Connectivity Check Message (CCM)
   b. Alarm Indication Signal (AIS)
   c. **Remote defect indication (RDI)**
   d. Loss Measurement Message (LMM)

   Note: Refer to SOAM Frames. (c) RDI is not a SOAM frame. It is encoded in a SOAM frame, the CCM, but it is not itself a SOAM frame. Refer to Remote Defect Indication (RDI).

4. Which two of the following statements are correct? (Choose two.)

   a. LOAM support is required for Type 2.1 UNIs and at ENNIs.
   b. **SOAM CCMs can support 50 ms protection switching.**
   c. SOAM domains can overlap.
   d. An ME can include more than two MEPs.
   e. **An ME can include any number of MIPs.**

   Note: (a) LOAM is required for Type 2.2 UNIs and at ENNIs. Refer to Link OAM. (b) Refer to Continuity Check Message (CCM). (c) False. Refer to SOAM Domains. (d) An ME includes only two MEPs. Refer to Maintenance Entity (ME). (e) Refer to Maintenance Entity (ME).

5. If a MEP sends a Loss Measurement Message (LMM), where does it go?

   a. To all MEPs in every ME
   b. To peer MIPs in the same ME
   c. To all MIPs in every ME
   d. To all MEPs in the MEG
   e. To the peer MEP in the same ME

   Note: Refer to Single-Ended Service Loss.

6. Per MEF 30.1, to whom does the EVC MEG belong?

   a. Subscriber
   b. Service Provider
   c. Operator
   d. Subscriber and Operator
   e. Operator and Service Provider

   Note: Refer to Suggested MEs and Default MEG Levels.

7. Which PM function requires time-of-day synchronization of MEP clocks?

   a. Single-Ended Delay
   b. Dual-Ended Delay
   c. Single-Ended Service Loss
   d. Dual-Ended Service Loss

   Note: Refer to Dual-Ended Delay.

8. To isolate a fault within a point-to-point OVC, an operator can:

   a. Inspect all continuity check messages (CCMs) for the appropriate ME.
   b. Initiate SOAM Loopback over the appropriate ME.
   c. Send a frame loss measurement message (LMM) to the appropriate peer MEP.
   d. Process the most recent remote defect indicator (RDI) per IEEE 802.1Q.
   e. Initiate SOAM Link Trace over the appropriate ME.

   Note: Refer to SOAM Link Trace.

9. Which Maintenance Entity (ME) should the service provider use to monitor the performance of an Ethernet service that spans two Operator CENs?

   a. Subscriber ME
   b. EVC ME
   c. Operator ME
   d. ENNI ME
   e. UNI ME

   Note: Refer to Suggested MEs and Default MEG Levels.

Answers to Review Questions
Answers: Ethernet OAM

10. Which two SOAM frames are used for performance monitoring? (Choose two.)

    a. CCM (Continuity Check Message)
    b. **LMM (Loss Measurement Message)**
    c. LBM (Loopback Message)
    d. LTM (Link Trace Message)
    e. **DMM (Delay Measurement Message)**

    Note: Refer to SOAM Frames.

11. One-way frame delay for a service frame in an EVC-based service... (Choose two.)

    a. Measures time of travel, CE-to-CE, for the first bit in the service frame.
    b. **Includes the time of transmission between the UNI-C and the UNI-N at both UNIs.**
    c. Includes the time that the service frame waits in queue at the CE to be scheduled for transmission.
    d. **Depends on the length of the service frame.**

    Note: Refer to Frame Delay Performance.

12. Which four of the following items are connectivity fault management (CFM) functions? (Choose four.)

    a. **Remote defect indication (RDI)**
    b. **Link Trace**
    c. Frame Delay Measurement
    d. **Alarm Indication Signal (AIS)**
    e. **Loopback**
    f. Frame Loss Measurement

    Note: Refer to SOAM Connectivity Fault Management. (c) PM, not CFM. (f) PM, not CFM.

13. How many ordered UNI pairs are in a multipoint-to-multipoint EVC containing three UNIs?

    a. Two
    b. Three
    c. **Six**
    d. Nine

    Note: Refer to Ordered UNI Pair.

14. Which two statements about SOAM frames are true? (Choose two.)

    a. **AIS frames are sent away from the direction of failure.**
    b. AIS frames are sent toward the direction of failure.
    c. **CCM frames containing RDI are sent away from the direction of failure.**
    d. CCM frames containing RDI are sent toward the direction of failure.

    Note: Refer to Remote Defect Indication (RDI) and Alarm Indication Signal (ETH-AIS).

15. A PM function requires two SOAM PDUs (a message PDU and a reply PDU) to calculate a performance measurement. In MEF 35, this type of PM function is called a ...

   a. **Single-ended PM function**
   b. Dual-ended PM function
   c. Loopback PM function
   d. Reciprocal PM function

   Note: Refer to Single-Ended versus Dual-Ended PM Functions.

16. Which two PM functions can be used to measure High Loss Intervals (HLIs)? (Choose two.)

   a. Single-Ended Delay
   b. **Single-Ended Synthetic Loss**
   c. Dual-Ended Delay
   d. **Single-Ended Service Loss**

   Note: Refer to Single-Ended versus Dual-Ended PM Functions.

17. Which service attribute is important to subscribers who anticipate using Link Trace to troubleshoot connectivity issues?

   a. **Subscriber MEG MIP**
   b. Test MEG
   c. UNI MEG
   d. Link OAM

   Note: Refer to Attribute: Subscriber MEG MIP.

18. Among the following MEs, which has the highest default MEG level?

   a. Operator ME
   b. EVC ME
   c. **Test ME**
   d. ENNI ME

   Note: Refer to Suggested MEs and Default MEG Levels.

Related Links

Review: Ethernet OAM on p. 281

18.13
Answers: Access Technologies

1. What are three advantages offered by *Ethernet over Bonded Copper*? (Choose three.)

   a. Easy to deploy in rugged terrain
   b. **Low cost**
   c. No distance limitation
   d. **Supports rates up to 1 Gb/s through bonding of additional copper pairs**
   e. **Resiliency through bonding copper pairs**
   f. **Widely available copper infrastructure**

   Note: Refer to Summary: Access Technologies.

2. An office, located 3 miles (4.8 km) from the core service provider network, requires 2 Mb/s of symmetric connectivity to an EVP-LAN service. A single copper pair is available. Which of the following access technologies is most appropriate?

   a. Ethernet over DOCSIS
   b. **G.SHDSL**
   c. Ethernet over PDH
   d. 10PASS-TS

   Note: Refer to 2BASE-TL (G.SHDSL).

3. What is the advantage of having Ethernet service over WiMAX?

   a. Bandwidth split among multiple users
   b. **No cabling**
   c. Resilience
   d. No reach limitation

   Note: Refer to Ethernet over Wireless Network.

4. Which access technology can support Ethernet services in parallel with TV services as commonly deployed by MSO/Cable TV operators?

   a. Ethernet over GPON
   b. Ethernet over Bonded Copper
   c. **Ethernet over HFC**
   d. Ethernet over PDH
   e. Ethernet over Terrestrial Microwave

   Note: Refer to Ethernet over HFC.

5. A mobile backhaul operator needs to reach a cell tower located in an undeveloped rural area. Which two of the following technologies could be most quickly deployed? (Choose two.)

   a. Ethernet over PDH
   b. **Ethernet over Terrestrial Microwave**
   c. **Ethernet over Free Space Optics**
   d. Ethernet over SONET/SDH
   e. Ethernet over bonded copper pairs
   f. Ethernet over Fiber

   Note: *Refer to* Summary: Access Technologies.

6. What are two advantages of *Ethernet over SONET/SDH*? (Choose two.)

   a. Supports multiple classes of service
   b. **Highly reliable**
   c. Supports multipoint services (EP-LAN, EP-Tree)
   d. **Provides dedicated bandwidth that is not impacted by other user traffic**
   e. Supports circuit emulation

   Note: *Refer to* Ethernet over SONET/SDH.

7. An incumbent provider (ILEC/PTT) wants to provide an Ethernet service at 6 Mb/s over its existing copper network infrastructure. The UNI will be 20 km (12.4 miles) away from the nearest switching office. Which technology do you recommend for this application?

   a. Ethernet over bonded copper pairs (2BASE-TL)
   b. Ethernet over HFC/DOCSIS
   c. **Ethernet over bonded T1/E1 PDH circuits**
   d. Ethernet over bonded T3/E3 PDH circuits

   Note: *Refer to* Ethernet over PDH *(also* Summary: Access Technologies*).*

8. What is an advantage of *Ethernet over PDH* compared to *Ethernet over Copper*?

   a. Uses widely deployed infrastructure
   b. Easy, low-cost, and rapid to deploy
   c. Supports eight classes of service
   d. Supports resiliency through bonding
   e. **No distance limitation**

   Note: *Refer to* Ethernet over PDH *and* Ethernet over Copper.

9. Which two of the following access technologies support rates over 1 Gb/s? (Choose two.)

   a. **Ethernet over SONET/SDH**
   b. Ethernet over PDH
   c. Ethernet over HFC/DOCSIS
   d. **Ethernet over Active Fiber**

   Note: *Refer to* Summary: Access Technologies.

10. Which wireless access technology uses licensed frequency spectrum in high-power applications?

    a. Ethernet over DOCSIS
    b. **Ethernet over terrestrial microwave**
    c. Ethernet over free space optical
    d. Ethernet over WiFi

    Note: Refer to Ethernet over Wireless Network.

11. Which of the following access technologies has the shortest reach?

    a. Ethernet over Terrestrial Microwave
    b. **Ethernet over Bonded Copper**
    c. Ethernet over PDH
    d. Ethernet over HFC/DOCSIS
    e. Ethernet over Active Fiber

    Note: Refer to Summary: Access Technologies.

12. Which of the following is a disadvantage of *Ethernet over Active Fiber*?

    a. Distance limited to under 40 km
    b. **Lack of widespread availability for fiber infrastructure**
    c. Speed limited to 100 Mb/s
    d. Dated technology
    e. Poor bandwidth granularity

    Note: Refer to Ethernet over Active Fiber.

13. What are two advantages of using *Ethernet over GPON* versus *Ethernet over copper*? (Choose two.)

    a. The physical media is widely deployed.
    b. **Higher bandwidth**
    c. **Supports efficient multicasting**
    d. Resiliency through bonding

    Note: Refer to Ethernet over PON and Ethernet over Copper.

Related Links

Review: Access Technologies on p. 303

18.14
Answers: Transport Technologies

1. How many service instances can Multi-Protocol Label Switching (MPLS) support in one network?

   a. 16,777,216
   b. 16 million
   c. Unlimited
   d. 4094

   Note: Refer to Layer 2.5 Technologies (Multiprotocol Label Switching).

2. Which two technologies forward traffic over an explicitly provisioned traffic-engineered path (similar to Layer 1) without bridging or a control plane? (Choose two.)

   a. Ethernet over MPLS-TP
   b. Ethernet over MPLS VPWS
   c. Ethernet over MPLS VPLS
   d. Ethernet over PBB-TE
   e. Ethernet over PBB

   Note: COE technologies forward traffic over explicitly provisioned traffic-engineered paths. Refer to Summary.

3. Which two of the following statements describe an advantage of *Provider Bridging* compared to *Bridging*? (Choose two.)

   a. It allows customer VLAN Identifiers to be separated from service provider VLAN Identifiers.
   b. It can coexist in the same network with PBB-TE.
   c. It has unlimited scalability.
   d. It supports ENNIs.
   e. It can support multipoint-to-multipoint services and MAC learning.

   Note: Refer to PB (Provider Bridging).

4. Which three of the following technologies can support an EVPL service? (Choose three.)

   a. PB
   b. SONET/SDH
   c. PBB-TE
   d. WDM
   e. MPLS VPLS
   f. OTN

   Note: Refer to Summary.

5. Which two of the following protection mechanisms use CCMs? (Choose two.)

a. **ITU-T G.8031, Ethernet linear protection switching**
b. RSTP (Rapid Spanning Tree Protocol)
c. 1:1 link aggregation, per clause 43 of IEEE 802.3
d. **ITU-T G.8032, Ethernet ring protection switching**
e. FRR (MPLS Fast Reroute)
f. SONET UPSR protection

Note: *Refer to* Protection Mechanisms and Transport Technologies.

6. What is the advantage of MPLS-TP compared to MPLS VPWS?

a. It provides unlimited scalability.
b. It supports multipoint-to-multipoint services, such as EVP-LAN and EVP-Tree.
c. **It supports traffic engineered paths, resulting in a highly predictable, connection-oriented service.**
d. It supports both EPL and EVPL services.

Note: *Refer to* MPLS-TP (MPLS Transport Profile).

7. Which three of the following terms are related to a network's ability to detect and recover from faults without impacting subscribers? (Choose three.)

a. Bandwidth
b. **Resiliency**
c. **G.8031**
d. Scalability
e. **Protection**
f. VLAN awareness

Note: *Refer to* Protection Mechanisms and Transport Technologies.

8. Which three of the following technologies can support an Access EPL service? (Choose three.)

a. **PBB-TE**
b. OTN
c. Bridging
d. **PBB**
e. **PB**
f. SONET/SDH

Note: *Refer to* Summary.

9. Which two of the following technologies support MAC address learning? (Choose two.)

a. MPLS VPWS
b. PBB-TE
c. **PBB**
d. **MPLS VPLS**
e. OTN

Note: *Refer to* Summary.

10. Which technology is also known at MAC-in-MAC?

    a. Provider Bridging
    b. MPLS VPLS
    c. **Provider Backbone Bridging**
    d. PBB-TE
    e. WDM

    Note: Refer to PBB (Provider Backbone Bridging).

11. Which transport technology supports the highest bandwidth per optical fiber?

    a. OTN
    b. **WDM**
    c. SONET
    d. SDH

    Note: Refer to WDM (Wavelength Division Multiplexing).

12. Which two of the following technologies can support multipoint-to-multipoint Ethernet services? (Choose two.)

    a. MPLS VPWS
    b. **MPLS VPLS**
    c. MPLS-TP
    d. PBB-TE
    e. **PBB**
    f. SONET/SDH

    Note: Refer to Summary.

13. Which technology is also referred to as Q-in-Q?

    a. Provider Backbone Bridging
    b. OTN
    c. MPLS VPLS
    d. **Provider Bridging**
    e. PBB-TE

    Note: Refer to PB (Provider Bridging).

14. Which two of the following technologies support EP-LAN services? (Choose two.)

    a. MPLS-TP
    b. **Provider Bridging**
    c. PBB-TE
    d. SONET/SDH
    e. **MPLS VPLS**

    Note: Refer to Summary.

15. Provider Backbone Bridging allows a single Carrier Ethernet network to accommodate a total of how many subscribers?

   a. Unlimited
   b. 4094
   c. 16 million
   d. **16,777,216**

   Note: Refer to PBB (Provider Backbone Bridging).

16. Which two of the following technologies support multicasting? (Choose two.)

   a. SONET/SDH
   b. **Provider Bridging**
   c. MPLS-TP
   d. **MPLS VPLS**
   e. OTN over WDM

   Note: Multicasting requires multipoint-to-multipoint service. Refer to Summary.

17. Which two of the following technologies can support EP-LAN services? (Choose two.)

   a. **PB**
   b. PBB-TE
   c. MPLS-TP
   d. MPLS VPWS
   e. **MPLS VPLS**

   Note: Refer to Summary.

18. Which one of the following technologies cannot support an Access EVPL service?

   a. PBB-TE
   b. **Bridging**
   c. MPLS-TP
   d. MPLS VPWS

   Note: Refer to Summary.

Related Links

Review: Transport Technologies on p. 339

18.15
Answers: Applications

1. Why is CESoETH sometimes used in Carrier Ethernet mobile backhaul networks?

    a. For performance monitoring
    b. **To support voice traffic and/or to distribute timing**
    c. To multiplex traffic from multiple RAN base stations to the RAN network controller
    d. To support CoS

    Note: Refer to Mobile Backhaul Synchronization *and* Circuit Emulation Services over Ethernet.

2. A mobile operator approaches a Service Provider to provide mobile backhaul service using a hub-and-spoke topology with a single Ethernet UNI at the hub site where the RAN Network Controller is located. Which of the following is most appropriate?

    a. Use one EPL service between each RAN Base Station and the RAN Network Controller.
    b. Use one EVP-LAN service interconnecting all RAN Base Stations.
    c. **Use one EVPL service between each RAN Base Station and the RAN Network Controller.**
    d. Use one EVP-Tree service with the RAN base station designated as root and the RAN network controllers designated as leaves.

    Note: (a) Not appropriate because this solution would require multiple ports at the RAN network controller (hub). (b) Not appropriate because this solution only interconnects the RAN base stations and not the RAN network controller. (c) Most appropriate. (d) Not appropriate because the RAN base stations should be leaves and the RAN network controller should be a root.

3. A customer wants to replace a T1 private line with a Carrier Ethernet service. Which of the following bandwidth profiles is most appropriate?

    a. CIR=1.5 Mb/s, CBS=0 bytes, EIR=0, EBS=0
    b. CIR=2 Mb/s, CBS=10,000 bytes, EIR=2 Mb/s, EBS=10,000
    c. **CIR=2 Mb/s, CBS=10,000 bytes, EIR=0, EBS=0**
    d. CIR=0, CBS=0 bytes, EIR=2 Mb/s, EBS=10,000

    Note: T1 private line replacement requires CESoETH (Support for TDM Private Lines). CESoETH requires EIR=EBS=0 (CEN Requirements for CESoETH).

4. Which two of the following functions are required to support CESoETH? (Choose two.)

    a. ITU-T G.8031 Ethernet linear protection switching
    b. **Synchronization**
    c. Internet access
    d. Link OAM (LOAM)
    e. **Encapsulation and de-encapsulation**

    Note: Refer to Inter-Working Function.

Answers to Review Questions
Answers: Applications

5. Which two of the following services can be used, in conjunction with CESoETH, in the replacement of a TDM private line service? (Choose two.)

   a. EP-LAN
   b. EPL
   c. EP-Tree
   d. EVPL
   e. EVP-LAN

   Note: Refer to Support for TDM Private Lines.

6. LANs at three sites are to be interconnected. Which two of the following service scenarios can be configured to tunnel bridge protocol data units (BPDUs) so that spanning tree protocol (STP) works across the aggregation of connected LANs? (Choose two.)

   a. Each site has one UNI. All three sites are interconnected by an EP-LAN service.
   b. Each site has two UNIs. Each pair of sites is interconnected by an EVPL service.
   c. Each site has one UNI. Each pair of sites is interconnected by an EVPL service.
   d. Each site has one UNI. All three sites are interconnected by an EVP-LAN service.
   e. Each site has two UNIs. Each pair of sites is interconnected by an EPL service.

   Note: Refer to L2CP Requirements for Spanning Tree Protocols *and* Building a Layer 2 VPN with Layer 2 Service.

7. Which two of the following clock synchronization methods transmit timing packets across the Carrier Ethernet network? (Choose two.)

   a. Free run timing
   b. NTP (Network Time Protocol)
   c. SyncE (Synchronous Ethernet)
   d. TDM line timing
   e. PTP (Precision Time Protocol)
   f. External timing

   Note: Refer to Synchronization.

8. A service provider wants to offer very transparent LAN connectivity, while limiting broadcast traffic. Which service solution is best?

   a. EVP-LAN service with EVC attribute *Broadcast Service Frame Delivery* set to *Deliver Conditionally*
   b. EP-LAN service with EVC attribute *Broadcast Service Frame Delivery* set to *Deliver Conditionally*
   c. EVP-LAN service with EVC attribute *Broadcast Service Frame Delivery* set to *Deliver Unconditionally*
   d. EP-LAN service with EVC attribute *Broadcast Service Frame Delivery* set to *Deliver Unconditionally*

   Note: Refer to EP-LAN Service *and* Data Service Frame Delivery Service Attributes.

MEF-CECP Study Guide
3rd Edition - October 2015
Updated for MEF-CECP Certification Blueprint C

9. A hospital has three clinics that need to connect to it. The three clinics are independent companies that must not be allowed to share information with each other. Which two service arrangements are suitable? (Choose two.)

   a. EP-LAN service
   b. EP-Tree service
   c. An EVPL service from each clinic to a service multiplexed UNI at the hospital
   d. An EVP-LAN service

   Note: (a) No security. (b) Works if hospital is root and clinics are leaves. (c) Works. (d) Poor security.

10. Which EVC-based Ethernet services can be used for mobile backhaul?

    a. Any
    b. EVPL or EVP-Tree only
    c. EP-LAN or EP-Tree only
    d. EVP-Tree , EVP-LAN, or EVPL only

    Note: Refer to MEF Service Definitions for Mobile Backhaul.

11. A sporting goods retailer has two data centers and numerous stores throughout the country. Each store needs to regularly exchange inventory, sales, and payroll information with both data centers. Stores should not exchange data with each other. Which two service arrangements are suitable? (Choose two.)

    a. A full mesh of EVPL services interconnecting all sites
    b. A single EP-LAN service interconnecting all sites
    c. A single EP-Tree service with root UNIs at the data centers and leaf UNIs at the stores
    d. A single EVP-LAN service interconnecting all sites
    e. One EPL service connecting the two data centers and one EVPL service connecting each store to each data center

    Note: (a) Stores should not be connected. (b) Stores should not be connected. (c) Works. (d) Stores should not be connected. (e) Works.

12. An ISP wants to deliver Internet access services to up to 100 customers through a single 1 Gb/s UNI with each customer allowed up to 10 Mb/s of bandwidth. Which two the following service solutions are viable? (Choose two.)

    a. One EVPL service between each customer and the ISP
    b. One EVP-LAN service connecting all UNIs
    c. One EP-Tree service connecting all UNIs with the ISP UNI designated as a Root and all other UNIs designated as leaves
    d. One EP-LAN service between each customer and the ISP

    Note: Refer to Ethernet Access to IP Services.

13. MEF 22.1 defines four use cases for transporting mobile backhaul traffic over Carrier Ethernet services. When is CESoETH (Circuit Emulation Services over Ethernet) required?

    a. When RAN CE can connect to the Ethernet UNI through an Ethernet interface, eliminating the need for a Generic Inter-Working Function (GIWF)
    b. **When the RAN CE cannot connect to the Ethernet UNI and there is no legacy network operating in parallel to deliver timing**
    c. When timing is distributed over the Ethernet physical layer using synchronous Ethernet (SyncE)
    d. When the operator needs to support voice traffic via an existing legacy network and offload data to a Carrier Ethernet network

    Note: Refer to Mobile Backhaul Use Cases.

14. A customer wants to replace a T1 private line service between two PBXs (private branch exchanges) with a Carrier Ethernet service. Which technology is required to carry the customer's traffic over a Carrier Ethernet Network (CEN)?

    a. SONET/SDH
    b. **CESoETH**
    c. ATM
    d. Frame Relay

    Note: Refer to Circuit Emulation Services over Ethernet.

15. An enterprise has a headquarters (HQ) and four branch offices. Each branch office requires access to the Internet through a firewall at HQ, but no access to each other. In addition, HQ requires connection to the Internet service provider (ISP). Which two of the following service arrangements supports these requirements using only one physical connection at each site? (Choose two.)

    a. One EP-Tree service with HQ and ISP designated as roots and branch offices designated as leaves
    b. **Four EVPL services connecting branch offices to HQ, plus one EVPL service connecting HQ with ISP**
    c. One EVP-LAN service interconnecting the branch offices and HQ, plus one EVPL service between HQ and ISP
    d. **One EVPL service between HQ and ISP, plus one EVP-Tree service with HQ designated as the root and branch offices designated as leaves**

    Note: (a) Allows branches direct access to ISP without going through HQ firewall. (b) Works. At HQ, all four EVPLs terminate at one UNI. (c) Does not prevent communication between branches. (d) Works. At HQ, the EVPL and EVP-Tree terminate on the same UNI.

16. A subscriber needs a single EVP-LAN service to connect numerous sites to three applications. All three applications use a different VLAN. All other VLANs should be blocked. Which two attribute settings are required? (Choose two.)

    a. Service Multiplexing = Disabled
    b. **Bundling = Enabled**
    c. Service Multiplexing = Enabled
    d. **CE VLAN ID Preservation = Enabled**
    e. Bundling = Disabled

    Note: Bundling is required to support three VLANs on a single service with all other VLANs blocked. If Bundling=Enabled, CE-VLAN ID preservation must be Enabled. Service Multiplexing can be either Enabled or Disabled. Refer to Service Multiplexing and Bundling Service Attributes.

17. A subscriber requires an EP-LAN service between 6 sites: 3 in Los Angeles and 3 in Miami. The LA sites are on-net (reachable by the Service Provider's network). The Miami sites are off-net and only reachable through an Ethernet Access Provider that has no connectivity to the Service Provider. To deliver this service, the Service Provider purchases three Access EPLs from the Miami Ethernet Access Provider and one point-to-point OVC from an Interstate Operator. The Interstate Operator shares one ENNI with the LA Service Provider and one ENNI with the Miami Ethernet Access Provider. Which of the following statements is not consistent with this service scenario?

   a. The OVC in the Interstate Operator network uses end point map bundling.
   b. The OVC in the Service Provider network is multipoint-to-multipoint.
   c. The OVC in the Interstate Operator network provides hairpin switching.
   d. Three OVC end points in the Ethernet Access Provider network interconnect (through the ENNI) to a single OVC endpoint in the Interstate Operator network.
   e. Three OVC end points in the Service Provider network interconnect (through the ENNI) to a single OVC endpoint in the Interstate Operator network.

   Note: Hairpin switching occurs in the Service Provider network (not in the Interstate Operator network). Refer to following figure.

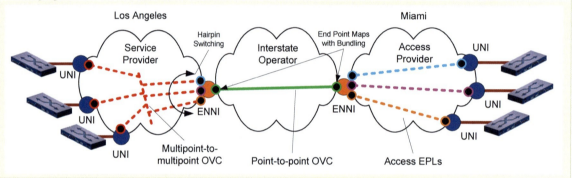

18. An Ethernet Mobile Backhaul Service provides:

   a. Radio access between cell phone users and cell tower base stations
   b. Temporary Ethernet services through a mobile WiMAX network
   c. Connectivity between two or more mobile phone users
   d. Connectivity between RAN base stations and RAN network controllers
   e. A gateway between the public mobile phone network and the Internet

   Note: Refer to Mobile Backhaul Services.

19. A service provider uses Carrier Ethernet as the access network technology to deliver an IP service. What functionality does Ethernet access provide for the service provider?

   a. A Layer 3 (IP) VPN
   b. Layer 2 connectivity to a Layer 3 service or an Internet Service Provider (ISP)
   c. Connection to the Internet through a Layer 2 (Ethernet) firewall
   d. Layer 2 emulation of a Layer 3 (IP) access service
   e. A virtual private gateway to the Internet

   Note: Refer to Ethernet Access to IP Services.

Answers to Review Questions
Answers: Applications

20. A company wants to connect two remote campuses to its corporate headquarters, extending all corporate VLANs across all three locations. Which two properties make the EP-LAN service a good choice for this application? (Choose two.)

    a. The service provider can forward frames without MAC address learning.
    b. **The company does not have to coordinate CE-VLAN IDs with the service provider.**
    c. The service can perform CE-VLAN ID translation if desired.
    d. **The company can run STP across all locations if desired.**
    e. The UNIs can support service multiplexing if desired.

    Note: Refer to EP-LAN Service *and* Building a Layer 2 VPN with Layer 2 Service.

21. Which two statements concerning Carrier Ethernet mobile backhaul are true? (Choose two.)

    a. **A mobile backhaul service must support at least 2 classes of service.**
    b. **A mobile operator using SOAM uses the Subscriber MEG level.**
    c. If LTE technology is used, the mobile backhaul service topology must be "hub and spoke."
    d. CoS Label H$^+$ must be used for packet-based synchronization traffic.

    Note: (a) Refer to Mobile Backhaul CoS and Performance Requirements. (b) Refer to MEG Levels in Mobile Backhaul. (c) Refer to Mobile Backhaul for LTE. (d) Refer to Mobile Backhaul CoS and Performance Requirements (H$^+$ can be used, but it is not required).

22. A mobile operator requests mobile backhaul services for a 4G LTE network that includes base stations (called eNodeBs) with Ethernet interfaces. Which of the following options would you recommend for interconnecting the eNodeBs to the Carrier Ethernet mobile backhaul service?

    a. Generic Inter-Working Function (GIWF)
    b. Circuit Emulation Services over Ethernet (CESoETH)
    c. GIWF in combination with CESoETH
    d. **None of the above**

    Note: If base stations have Ethernet interfaces, GIWF and CESoETH are not applicable. Refer to Mobile Backhaul Use Cases.

23. A subscriber has 10 sites with one UNI at each site. The 10 sites are interconnected by an EVP-LAN service that supports multiple VLANs between the sites. Each UNI also supports one EVPL service that connects the site to an Internet service provider (ISP). Which one of the following configuration options is <u>not</u> required?

    a. Configure all UNIs with *Bundling* set to *Enabled*.
    b. **Configure *CE-VLAN ID Preservation* for each EVPL service to *Enabled*.**
    c. Configure *CE-VLAN ID Preservation* for the EVP-LAN service to *Enabled*.
    d. Configure all UNIs with *Service Multiplexing* set to *Enabled*.

    Note: Refer to Service Multiplexing and Bundling Service Attributes *and* CE-VLAN ID Preservation

24. Which one of the following technologies interconnects a PDH interface and an Ethernet UNI?

   a. **Inter-Working Function (IWF)**
   b. Circuit Emulation Service over Ethernet (CESoETH)
   c. Long-Term Evolution (LTE)
   d. IEEE-1588 v2 Precision Time Protocol (PTP)

   Note: Refer to Inter-Working Function.

25. Time of day synchronization can be achieved using which two technologies? (Choose two.)

   a. **IEEE-1588 v2 Precision Time Protocol (PTP)**
   b. Adaptive Clock Recovery (ACR)
   c. **Network Time Protocol (NTP)**
   d. Synchronous Ethernet (SyncE)

   Note: Refer to Synchronization.

26. An enterprise needs Carrier Ethernet services that give two branch offices access to critical business applications located at corporate headquarters, but not to each other. The critical business applications use VLAN IDs 10 and 20. CE devices do not support translation of CE VLAN IDs. All other VLANs should be blocked. Both branch offices need access to both critical business applications. Which service arrangement will support this application?

   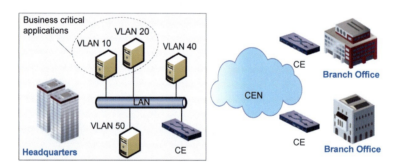

   a. One Ethernet Private Line (EPL) service between each branch and the headquarters.
   b. One Ethernet Virtual Private Line (EVPL) service between each branch and the headquarters. At the headquarters CE, both EVCs terminate on one UNI that is configured for service multiplexing.
   c. **One Ethernet Virtual Private Line (EVPL) service between each branch office and the headquarters. At the headquarters CE, the EVPLs terminate on different UNIs, which are both configured to support bundling.**
   d. One Ethernet Private Tree (EP-Tree) service with the headquarters UNI designated as the root and branch offices designated as leaves and with the root UNI configured to support bundling.

   Note: (a) Does not block VLANs. (b) Will not work because VLANs are needed to separate branch offices, but VLANs are already used to identify the critical business application. This solution might be made to work if CE devices supported CE-VLAN ID translation, but that is not allowed. (c) Works. Bundling at the headquarters UNI filters VLANs to allow access to the critical business applications but block others. (d) Bundling is not supported.

Related Links

Review: Applications on p. 378

18.16
Answers: MEF Certification

1. Which two services can include CE 2.0 certified support for CoS Label H at Performance Tier 2? (Choose two.)

   a. **EPL**
   b. EVP-LAN
   c. EP-Tree
   d. **Access EVPL**

   Note: Multipoint services cannot include CE 2.0 certified support for CoS Label H at Performance Tier 2 because MEF 23.1 does not define CoS Performance Objective (CPO) values for multipoint services. Refer to CPOs (per CoS Label and Performance Tier).

2. Which two are required for an equipment vendor to participate in MEF CE 2.0 testing? (Choose two.)

   a. **The equipment vendor must supply the equipment to Iometrix (the official MEF certification lab).**
   b. The equipment vendor must attend MEF quarterly member meetings.
   c. The equipment vendor must be ISO 9001 compliant.
   d. **The equipment vendor must be a member of the MEF.**

   Note: Refer to Equipment Certification.

3. For MEF CE 2.0 service certification, where does testing occur?

   a. At the Iometrix lab (the official MEF certification lab)
   b. **On the service provider's production network**
   c. On a representative network using MEF-certified networking equipment
   d. At an MEF testing facility

   Note: Refer to Service Certification.

4. Which one of the following is true for MEF CE 2.0 service certification?

   a. The service provider must provide on-site engineering support at the Iometrix lab during of testing.
   b. **The service provider must be a member of the MEF.**
   c. The service must terminate on MEF-certified equipment.
   d. Certification is lost if MEF membership is not renewed annually.

   Note: Refer to Service Certification.

5. Where is equipment tested for MEF CE 2.0 equipment certification?

   a. **At the Iometrix lab (the official MEF certification lab)**
   b. On the service provider's production network
   c. On the MEF service certification network
   d. At the equipment vendor's facility

   Note: Refer to Equipment Certification.

6. CE 2.0 Certification allows <u>equipment</u> to be certified with respect to:

   a. Link OAM (per clause 57 of IEEE 802.3) at the UNI
   b. **Any one or more of 8 services: EPL, EVPL, EP-LAN, EVP-LAN, EP-Tree, EVP-Tree, Access EPL, and/or Access EVPL**
   c. CESoETH (per ITU-T G.8261, G.823 and G.824)
   d. The following service only: EPL, EVPL, and/or E-LAN (EP-LAN together with EVP-LAN)

   Note: Refer to Equipment Certification.

Related Links

Review: MEF Certification on p. 391

Index

1:1 linear protection *334*
1+1 linear protection *333*
1+1 link protection *172*, *198*
10PASS-TS *296*
1DM (One-way Delay Measurement) *271*, *277*
2BASE-TL *295*

A

Access EPL (Access Ethernet Private Line) *234*, *346*
Access EVPL (Access Ethernet Virtual Private Line) *234*, *347*
access provider. *See* Ethernet Access Provider
access technology *285*
active fiber (Ethernet over Active Fiber) *289*
AIS (Alarm Indication Signal) *256*, *265*
All-to-one Bundling *31*, *70*
applications. *See* service applications
ATM (Asynchronous Transfer Mode) *327*, *362*
attributes. *See* service attributes
attributes of Carrier Ethernet *14*
Availability, Group *161*
Availability, Multiple EVC *163*
Availability performance *153*, *206*, *227*, *242*

B

bandwidth profile *107*, *126*, *133*, *139*, *200*, *242*
bandwidth profile, multiflow *133*
bandwidth profile algorithm *126*, *133*
bandwidth profile flow *138*
bandwidth profiles for E-Access service *242*
basic reference model *24*
bin. *See* PM measurement bin
BLSR protection (Bidirectional Line-Switched Ring protection) *308*
blueprint. *See* CE 2.0 Certification Blueprint, or MEF-CECP Certification Blueprint
BPDU (Bridge Protocol Data Unit) *96*
Bridge Protocol Data Unit. *See* BPDU
Bridging (802.1Q-2005) *315*
broadcast MAC address *47*
broadcast service frame *83*
bundling *31*, *70*, *205*
bundling and multiplexing for E-Access services *240*
bundling and service multiplexing *31*, *70*

byte (1 byte = 8 bits) *49*

C

Carrier Ethernet *14*
CBS (Committed Burst Size) *126*, *133*, *139*, *200*
CCM (Continuity Check Message) *256*, *264*
CE (Customer Edge equipment) *24*, *27*
CE 1.0 certification *386*
CE 2.0 certification *386*
CE 2.0 Certification Blueprint *384*
CECP. *See* MEF-CECP
CEN (Carrier Ethernet Network; equivalent to MEN) *24*
CESoETH (Circuit Emulation Service over Ethernet) *374*
CE-VLAN CoS ID preservation for E-Access *241*
CE-VLAN CoS preservation *76*, *193*
CE-VLAN ID *30*
CE-VLAN ID / EVC Map *72*
CE-VLAN ID for Untagged and Priority Tagged Service Frames *74*
CE-VLAN ID preservation *76*, *77*, *81*, *193*
CE-VLAN ID preservation for E-Access *241*
CE-VLAN ID translation *78*
CE-VLAN tag *30*
CF (Coupling Flag) *126*, *129*, *133*, *136*, *139*, *200*
CFM (Connectivity Fault Management) *264*
CHLI (Consecutive High Loss Intervals) *157*, *206*, *227*, *242*
CIR (Committed Information Rate) *126*, *133*, *139*, *200*, *224*
CIRmax (Committed Information Rate Limit) *133*
class of service. *See* CoS
clock synchronization *371*, *376*
CM (Color Mode) *126*, *129*, *133*, *139*, *200*
COE (Connection-Oriented Ethernet) *324*, *326*, *331*, *337*
color-aware *129*, *131*, *200*
color-aware bandwidth profiles at ENNI *200*
color-blind *129*, *130*
color forwarding (OVC service attribute) *201*
color identification *118*, *129*, *188*, *225*
committed burst size. *See* CBS
committed information rate. *See* CIR
connectivity fault management. *See* CFM
continuity check message. *See* CCM
CoS (Class of Service) *103*, *104*, *111*, *114*, *222*
CoS ID based on CE-VLAN CoS *116*
CoS ID based on Internet Protocol *117*
CoS identification *114*, *225*

CoS identification for E-Access services *241*
CoS ID versus EEC ID *111*
CoS Label *223*
CPO (CoS Performance Objective) *229*
CTA, CTB and CTB-2 *87*
C-tag. *See* CE-VLAN tag
C-VLAN tag. *See* CE-VLAN tag

D

data service frame *55, 83, 115, 120*
DEI (Drop Eligibility Indicator) *29, 47, 50, 118, 188, 200, 225*
demarcation *24, 25, 168, 180*
destination MAC address *46*
differentiated services code point. *See* DSCP
DMM (Delay Measurement Message) *271, 275*
DMR (Delay Measurement Reply) *271, 275*
DOCSIS (Data Over Cable Service Interface Specifications) *299*
domains. *See* SOAM domain.
Down MEP *259*
DS1 and DS3 signals *293, 352*
DSCP (Differentiated Services Code Point) *115, 117, 118, 120, 122, 226*
DSL (Digital Subscriber Line) *295*
Dual-Ended Delay (PM function) *277*
dual-rate bandwidth profile *132*

E

E1 and E3 lines *293, 352*
E-Access compared to E-Line *248*
E-Access service *232*
E-Access service applications *246, 344*
E-Access service attributes *235*
EBS (Excess Burst Size) *126, 133, 139, 200*
EEC (Egress Equivalence Class) *111, 119*
EEC ID based on CE-VLAN CoS *121*
EEC ID based on Internet Protocol *122*
EEC identification *119*
EEC ID versus CoS ID(Egress Equivalence Class) *111*
egress bandwidth profile *141, 242*
egress bandwidth profiles for E-LAN and E-Tree services *142*
egress bandwidth profiles for EPL services *141*
egress bandwidth profiles for EVPL services *141*
egress ENNI frame *183*
egress equivalence class. *See* EEC
egress service frame *52*
EI (External Interface) *180*
EIR (Excess Information Rate) *126, 133, 139, 200, 224*
EIRmax (Excess Information Rate Limit) *133*
E-LAN service type *32, 33*
E-Line service type *32, 33*
E-LMI (Ethernet Local Management Interface) *172*
E-LMI attribute *97, 174*
EMS (Element Management System) *271*
End Point Map *199*

End Point Map Bundling *205*
end point role. *See* OVC End Point Role
ENNI (External Network-to-Network Interface) *27, 180*
ENNI frame *183*
ENNI frame format *189*
ENNI MTU size *197*
ENNI protection *198*
ENNI service attributes *192, 235*
Envelope, bandwidth profile *138*
Envelopes attribute *139*
EoCu (Ethernet over Copper) *295*
EoPDH (Ethernet over PDH) *293*
EoS (Ethernet over SONET/SDH) *290, 308*
EPL (Ethernet Private Line) *32, 34*
EP-LAN (Ethernet Private LAN) *32, 36*
EPON (Ethernet Passive Optical Network) *290*
EP-Tree (Ethernet Private Tree) *32, 38*
equipment certification *387*
ETH-AIS. *See* AIS
ETH-DM. *See* PM function
Ethernet Access Provider *233*
Ethernet frame *30, 45*
Ethernet OAM (Operations, Administration, and Management) *251*
Ethernet over copper *295*
Ethernet over terrestrial microwave *297*
Ethernet packet. *See* Ethernet frame
ETH-LCK. *See* LCK
ETH-LM. *See* PM function
ETH-RDI. *See* RDI
ETH-SLM. *See* PM function
ETH-Test. *See* Test
E-Tree service type *32, 33*
ETS (Ethernet Tag Switching) *326*
EVC (Ethernet Virtual Connection) *24*
EVC maximum service frame size *69*
EVC performance service attributes *148*
EVC per UNI service attribute *59, 61*
EVC type *68*
EVPL (Ethernet Virtual Private Line) *32, 35*
EVP-LAN (Ethernet Virtual Private LAN) *32, 37*
EVP-Tree (Ethernet Virtual Private Tree) *32, 39*
excess burst size. *See* EBS
excess information rate. *See* EIR

F

fault management. *See* CFM
FD (Frame Delay) *150, 206, 227, 242*
FDR (Frame Delay Range) *150, 206, 227, 242*
FDV (Frame Delay Variation). *See* IFDV
FLR (Frame Loss Ratio) *152, 206, 227, 242*
frame delay. *See* FD
frame loss ratio. *See* FLR
Frame Relay *354*
frequency synchronization *371*

FRR. *See* MPLS FRR

G

G.SHDSL *295*
gap *See* interframe gap.
general reference model *27*
GFP frame (Generic Framing Procedure frame) *308, 310, 312*
GIFW (Generic Inter-working Function) *374*
GPON (Gigabit Passive Optical Network) *290*
green service frame *107, 126*
green token bucket *128*
Group Availability performance *161*

H

hairpin switching *185, 202*
HFC (Hybrid Fiber Coax) *299*
HLI (High Loss Intervals) *157, 206, 227, 242*

I

IEEE (Institute of Electrical and Electronics Engineers) *254, 314, 336*
IEEE 802.1ad (PB) *317*
IEEE 802.1ag-2007 (SOAM) *254*
IEEE 802.1ah (PBB) *319*
IEEE 802.1Q-2005 (Bridging) *315*
IEEE 802.1Q-2005 (frame format) *29*
IEEE 802.1Q-2011 (includes almost everything) *29*
IEEE 802.1Qay (PBB-TE) *324*
IEEE 802.1Q customer tag (C-Tag) *29*
IEEE 802.1Q service tag (S-Tag) *50*
IFDV (Inter-Frame Delay Variation) *151, 206, 227, 242*
ingress bandwidth profile *224, 242*
ingress ENNI frame *183*
ingress service frame *52*
inter-frame delay variation. *See* IFDV
interframe gap *45, 143*
Internet access *248, 358*
Iometrix (certification testing lab) *387, 388*
IP (Internet Protocol) *14*
IP network access *233, 345*
ISP (Internet Service Provider) *345*
I-Tagged Ethernet frame *51*
ITU-T (International Telecommunication Union - Telecommunication Standards) *254, 336*
ITU-T G.709 (OTN) *310, 312*
ITU-T G.8021 (SOAM) *254*
ITU-T G.8031 (Ethernet linear protection switching) *334, 336*
ITU-T G.8032 (Ethernet ring protection switching) *335, 336*
ITU-T Y.1731 (SOAM) *254*
IWF (Inter-Working Function) *374, 375*

J

jumbo frames *49*

K

known unicast *319, 330*

L

L2CP (Layer 2 Control Protocol) *87, 207*
L2CP attribute configuration *94*
L2CP behavioral model *89*
L2CP decision point *89*
L2CP processing *87*
L2CP protocol entity *89*
L2CP service frame *55, 115, 120, 227*
L2CP tunneling. *See* tunneling
L2CP Tunneling (OVC service attribute) *207*
LAG (Link Aggregation Group) *172, 198*
LAN (Local Area Network) *14*
Layer 1 Ethernet Frame *45*
Layer 2.5 technologies. *See* MPLS
Layer 2 Control Protocol. *See* L2CP
Layer 2 Ethernet Frame *45*
Layer 2 VPN (Virtual Private Network) *361*
Layer 3 VPN (Virtual Private Network) *360*
LBM (Loopback Message) *256, 268*
LBR (Loopback Reply) *256, 268*
LCK (Locked Signal) *256, 266*
leaf OVC End Point *209*
leaf UNI *33*
life cycle. *See* MEF service life cycle
linear protection, 1:1 *334*
linear protection, 1+1 *333*
line rate and CIR *143*
link aggregation *172, 198*
link aggregation group. *See* LAG
Link OAM. *See* LOAM
Link OAM attribute *97, 174*
link protection, 1+1 *172, 198*
link trace *269*
LMM (Loss Measurement Message) *271, 278*
LMR (Loss Measurement Reply) *271, 278*
LOAM (Link OAM) *170, 171, 253*
LOAM loopback *253*
LOAM requirement for ENNIs *206*
LOC (Loss of Continuity) *264, 265*
LOC condition suppression *265, 266*
loopback *253, 268*
LTE (Long Term Evolution) *366*
LTM (Link Trace Message) *256, 269*
LTR (Link Trace Reply) *256, 269*

M

MA (Maintenance Association; equivalent to MEG). *See* MEG
MAC destination address *29, 50*
MAC destination address *46*
MAC-in-MAC. *See* PBB
MAC source address *29, 46, 50*
mapping. *See* service frame mapping
maximum service frame size service attributes *69*
ME (Maintenance Entity) *258*
measurement bin. *See* PM measurement bin
measurement interval. *See* PM measurement interval
MEF-CECP (MEF Carrier Ethernet Certified Professional) *15, 390*
MEF-CECP Certification Blueprint *17*
MEF Forum *14*
MEF Reference Wiki *15*
MEF service life cycle *254*
MEF-standardized CoS *222*
MEF Web site *15*
MEG (Maintenance Entity Group) *258*
MEG Level *260*
MEN (Metro Ethernet Network; equivalent to CEN) *24*
MEP (MEG End Point) *257*
Metro Ethernet Forum *14*
MFD (Mean Frame Delay) *150, 206, 227, 242*
microwave *297*
MIP (MEG Intermediate Point) *257*
mobile backhaul *350, 362*
mobile backhaul reference model *363*
Mobile Operator *363*
MPLS (Multiprotocol Label Switching) *327*
MPLS FRR (MPLS Fast Reroute) *329, 330, 336*
MPLS-TP (MPLS Transport Profile) *331*
MPLS VPLS (MPLS Virtual Private LAN Service) *330*
MPLS VPWS (MPLS Virtual Private Wire Service) *329*
MTU (Maximum Transmission Unit) *197*
multicast MAC address *47*
multicast service frame *83*
multi CoS framework *104*
multiflow bandwidth profile *133*
Multiple EVC Availability performance *163*
multiplexing. *See* service multiplexing
multiplexing for E-access services *240*
multipoint-to-multipoint EVC *33, 68*
multipoint-to-multipoint OVC *181*

N

NE (Network Element) *271*
NMS (Network Management System) *271*

O

OAM. *See* Ethernet OAM
OAM frame. *See* SOAM frame
OCh-DPRING (Optical Channel Dedicated Protection Ring) *336*
off-net customer *233*
Operator *179*
Operator CEN (equivalent to Operator MEN) *27*
Operator MEN (equivalent to Operator CEN) *27*
Operator service attributes *192*
optical fiber *289, 308*
ordered UNI pair *149*
OTN (Optical Transport Network) *310*
out-of-franchise subscriber *233*
OVC (Operator Virtual Connection) *181*
OVC-based service *191, 233*
OVC End Point *182, 205, 209*
OVC End Point per ENNI service attributes *192, 194, 237*
OVC End Point per Per UNI service attributes *192, 196, 239*
OVC End Point Role *183, 209*
OVC MTU size *197*
OVC service attributes *192, 193, 236*
OVC type *183, 193, 236*

P

payload *49*
PB (Provider Bridging; IEEE 802.1ad) *317*
PBB (Provider Backbone Bridging; IEEE 802.1ah) *319*
PBB-TE (Provider Backbone Bridging with Traffic Engineering extensions; IEEE 802.1Qay) *324*
P-bits. *See* PCP bits
PCP bits (Priority Code Point bits) *29, 50, 115, 116, 118, 120, 121, 225*
PDH (Plesiochronous Digital Hierarchy) *293*
peer MEP *264*
Per EVC service attribute *59, 62*
performance attributes *148*
performance metrics *227*
performance objectives *229*
performance objectives for E-Access services *242*
Performance Tier *223*
Per UNI service attribute *59, 60, 192, 195, 238*
phase synchronization *371*
PM (Performance Management) *254, 270*
PM-1, PM-2, PM-3. *See* PM Solution
PM function *271*
PM measurement bin *279*
PM measurement interval *279*
PM session *279*
PM Solution *271*
PM tool *271*
point-to-point EVC *33, 68*
point-to-point OVC *181*
policing *107, 126*
PON (passive optical network) *290*
Port-based service *32, 234*
priority tagged service frame *51, 53, 71, 81*
private service. *See* Port-based service
professional certification *15, 390*

Q

Q-in-Q. *See* PB
QoS (Quality of Service) *103*, *104*
quality of service. *See* QoS

R

RAN (Radio Access Network) *363*
RAN BS (RAN Base Station) *363*
Rank, bandwidth profile *138*
RAN NC (RAN Network Controller) *363*
rate enforcement. *See* policing
RDI (Remote Defect Indication) *253*, *256*, *265*
red service frame *107*, *126*
reference model *24*, *27*, *363*
reference wiki. *See* MEF Reference Wiki
Resiliency performance *157*
ring protection *335*
rooted-multipoint EVC *33*, *68*
rooted-multipoint OVC *181*, *209*
root OVC End Point *209*
root UNI *33*

S

scalability *14*, *306*
SDH (Synchronous Digital Hierarchy) *290*, *308*
service applications *343*
service attributes *58*, *192*, *235*
service certification *388*
service connectivity attributes *67*
service definitions *58*
service frame *29*, *52*
service frame delivery *83*
service frame tag recognition *53*
service frame transparency requirements *83*
service frame versus synthetic frame *273*
service level agreement. *See* SLA
service level specification. *See* SLS
Service Level Specification (OVC service attribute) *206*, *242*
service multiplexing *28*, *31*
Service OAM. *See* SOAM
Service Provider *24*, *179*
service transparency *34*, *36*, *38*, *83*
service type *32*, *33*
SHDSL *295*
Single-Ended Delay (PM function) *275*
Single-Ended Service Loss (PM function) *278*
Single-Ended Synthetic Loss (PM function) *276*
single-rate bandwidth profile *132*
SLA (Service Level Agreement) *65*
SLM (Synthetic Loss Message) *271*, *276*
SLR (Synthetic Loss Reply) *271*, *276*
SLS (Service Level Specification) *65*
SOAM (Service OAM) *254*

SOAM component *256*
SOAM domain *255*
SOAM frame *256*
SOAM link trace *269*
SOAM loopback *268*
SOAM PDU. *See* SOAM frame
SOAM PM (SOAM Performance Management) *270*
SOAM PM framework *271*
SOAM related service attribute *262*
SOAM service frame *55*, *116*, *121*
SONET (Synchronous Optical Network) *290*, *308*
source MAC address *46*
Source MAC Address Limit *85*
Spanning Tree Protocol. *See* STP
S-Tag (IEEE 802.1ad outer VLAN tag) *188*
S-Tagged service frame *53*
STP (Spanning Tree Protocol) *96*, *334*
STP-based protection *334*
Subscriber *24*
Subscriber MEG MIP attribute *262*
S-VLAN CoS *188*
S-VLAN CoS preservation *193*, *236*
S-VLAN ID preservation *193*, *236*
synchronization. *See* clock synchronization
Synchronous Mode attribute *97*, *174*
synthetic frame *273*

T

T1 and T3 lines *293*, *352*
target applications *344*
Taxonomy of EVC-based services *32*
TDM (Time-Division Multiplexing) *14*, *352*, *362*
TDM private line *352*
Test (Test Signal) *256*, *268*
Test MEG attribute *262*
time-of-day synchronization *371*
token bucket *128*
Token Share attribute *139*
TPID (Tag Protocol Identifier) *29*, *50*, *53*
traffic management *103*, *104*
translation of CE-VLAN ID *78*
transport technology *306*
Trunk Identifiers *213*
trunk OVC End Point *209*, *213*
tunneling *36*, *87*, *89*, *93*, *96*, *207*
Type 1 UNI *168*
Type 2.1 UNI *168*
Type 2.2 UNI *168*
Type 2 UNI *168*
Type 2 UNI requirements *170*

U

UNI (User-to-Network Interface) *24*, *168*
UNI-C (UNI Client) *25*, *168*

unicast MAC address *47*
unicast service frame *83*
UNI functionality *25*, *168*
UNI L2CP Address Set attribute *92*
UNI L2CP Peering attribute *92*
UNI maximum service frame size *69*
UNI MEG attribute *262*
UNI-N (UNI Network) *25*, *168*
UNI Resiliency attribute *97*, *174*
unknown unicast *319*, *330*
untagged service frame *29*, *49*, *53*, *71*, *81*
Up MEP *259*
user priority bits. *See* PCP bits

V

VCAT (virtual concatenation) *308*, *310*
VDSL *296*
VID (VLAN identifier) *29*, *50*
virtual private service. *See* VLAN-based service

VLAN (Virtual LAN) *32*
VLAN-based service *32*, *234*
VLAN Tagged service frame *53*
VPN (Virtual Private Network) *359*

W

WAN (Wide Area Network) *14*, *354*
WDM (Wavelength Division Multiplexing) *312*
WiFi *297*
wiki. *See* MEF Reference Wiki
WiMAX *297*
wireless access technology *297*

Y

yellow service frame *107*, *126*
yellow token bucket *128*

Printed in Poland
by Amazon Fulfillment
Poland Sp. z o.o., Wrocław